250 HTML and Web Design Secrets

250 HTML and Web Design Secrets

Molly E. Holzschlag

WILEY

Wiley Publishing, Inc.

Published by
Wiley Publishing, Inc.,
10475 Crosspoint Boulevard,
Indianapolis, IN 46256,
www.wiley.com

Copyright © 2004 by Wiley Publishing, Inc., Indianapolis, Indiana

Published simultaneously in Canada

ISBN: 0-7645-6845-0

Manufactured in the United States of America

10 9 8 7 6 5 4 3 2

For general information on our other products and services or to obtain technical support, please contact our Customer Care Department within the U.S. at (800) 762-2974, outside the U.S. at (317) 572-3993 or fax (317) 572-4002.

Wiley also publishes its books in a variety of electronic formats. Some content that appears in print may not be available in electronic books.

Library of Congress Cataloging-in-Publication Data

About the Author

In the world of Web design and development, Molly E. Holzschlag is one of the most vibrant and influential people around. With over 30 Web development book titles to her credit, Molly is also a noted columnist, speaker, and educator.

As a Steering Committee Member of the Web Standards Project (WaSP), Molly works along with a group of other dedicated Web developers and designers to promote open standards for the Web. She serves as an advisor and spokeswoman for the World Organization of Webmasters. Molly speaks regularly at conferences in addition to teaching and developing curriculum for a number of colleges and universities, including the University of Arizona, University of Phoenix, New School University, and Pima Community College.

Many recognize Molly from her column, "Integrated Design," which appeared in the much-missed *Web Techniques Magazine* for three years, and from sister publication *Webreview.com*, where Molly served as Executive Editor for a year during the best of the San Francisco dot.com era. Molly has been honored as one of the Top 25 Most Influential Women on the Web. For more information about Molly, drop by at www.molly.com/.

Credits

Acquisitions Editor
Katie Mohr

Development Editor
Marcia Ellett

Technical Editor
Ethan Marcotte

Production Editor
Pamela Hanley

Copy Editor
TechBooks

Editorial Manager
Mary Beth Wakefield

Vice President and Executive Group Publisher
Richard Swadley

Vice President and Executive Publisher
Robert Ipsen

Vice President and Publisher
Joseph B. Wikert

Executive Editorial Director
Mary Bednarek

Project Coordinator
TechBooks

Proofreading and Indexing
TechBooks Production Services

To Bill Cullifer for his unflagging enthusiasm for the Internet, desire to uplift and educate, and for his friendship

Contents

Part II: HTML, XHTML, CSS, and Accessibility 113

Chapter 6: Crafting Pages with HTML 115

Chapter 7: Moving Ahead with XHTML 143

Acknowledgments

This was my first book with Wiley Publishing, and I'm happy to say it was a delightful experience. Katie Mohr is a most awesome acquisitions editor. Marcia Ellett always had a steady, calm eye as my development editor. My thanks also to the entire editorial team who helped make this book possible.

It's a fairly regular convention that computer book authors get to pick their technical editors. It's also a fairly regular convention that there's limited budget for TEs, but Ethan Marcotte (www.sidesh0w.com/) kept me on the straight and narrow with his technical edits and endless good cheer.

From Waterside Productions, my agent David Fugate is always my shimmering knight in armor.

For providing technical support, research, comments, and resources directly affecting this book, my thanks go in no specific order to Stephanie Troeth, Dunstan Orchard, Matthew Mullenweg, Eric A. Meyer, Tantek Çelik, Porter Glendinning, Dori Smith. At large: AdaptivePath, Boxes and Arrows, Digital Web Magazine, the entire blogging community, and, of course, to all my readers who keep me inspired and happy as a computer book author—no easy task.

Introduction

Web design has come a long way in just over a decade. The concerns facing anyone working on Web sites are so complex and changing so rapidly that it's downright overwhelming. From a consumer perspective, Web designs and redesigns can be very expensive. The goal of this book is to provide you with all the top-flight information you need to know to get up to speed with the best practices and standards being used by today's practical but progressive Web sites such as ESPN and Wired News. We all need help to improve workflow, develop rich designs that can be accessed by numerous browsers and alternative devices such as cell phones and PDAs, create sites that meet legal concerns regarding content and accessibility, managing sites for the long term, and improve the financial bottom line by significantly reducing bandwidth and increasing revenue.

Most likely you are a person who is working on public or private Web sites and is somewhat experienced with HTML and Web graphic design and are interested in ramping up to the next level of expertise. If you're like me, you want to make your life easier by streamlining the design process and management, and increasing awareness and promotion of the sites you design and develop. Your primary job might not even be that of a Web designer—perhaps you are a scientist, librarian, documentation specialist, promotions specialist, educator, or serving in the armed forces. The people working on Web sites at this point in history come from a very wide range of backgrounds and professions, and we come from all parts of the globe. Some readers will be avid hobbyists, too, using the Web as a means for self-expression via Weblogs, social networks, and special interest groups.

250 HTML and Web Design Secrets looks into the detailed work required to create successful Web sites and provides extremely up-to-date approaches to dealing with an array of challenges that the creation of Web sites presents. Technologies and topics covered include tools, project management, information architecture, usability, content development and management, HTML, XHTML, and CSS, graphics and multimedia for the Web, accessibility, best uses of dynamic content and rich media, keeping content fresh, improving site ranking and promotions, and managing redesigns.

Using This Book

Focusing on theory, standards, and rigid practices is, in a word, dry. *250 HTML and Web Design Secrets* takes a fresh and fun approach, providing insider techniques that will help designers get the information they need.

Instead of teaching individual languages or technologies, the lessons here are broken down into specific "secrets" that will help you immediately improve your current sites; help you build new sites that are visually exciting, extremely portable, and cross-platform compatible; help you manage redesigns; and take your sites from the past into a successful future. Another unique quality of the "Secrets" format of this book is that while it's written to be read from start to finish, it can also be used as a quick reference when you're facing a specific problem.

The book consists of 15 chapters broken into three parts: "Tools, Planning, and Content;" "HTML, XHTML, CSS and Accessibility;" and "Designing Sites for Long-Term Success." There are also three appendices to help you get more resources for Web site service provision, application, and database technologies, and references of a wide range of helpful Web sites, articles, books, and organizations that can help you constantly challenge and improve your skills beyond the scope of this book.

Part I

Tools, Planning, and Content

Setting up a
Master Toolbox

◆ ◆

Secrets in This Chapter

◆ ◆

W hy start a book on Web design secrets with tools? Shouldn't that be something left for an appendix, perhaps? After all, you want to get right down to the nitty-gritty, and I appreciate that.

As any working Web designer knows, the master designer really needs very few tools at hand to create the ultimate Web design toolbox. A great designer can make do with a text editor, a Web browser, an imaging software program, and an FTP client.

So why all the fuss?

Well, for one thing, in today's busy, mobile world, most Web designers' work requires a range of specialty tools to help make life easier.

This chapter comes first because I have an agenda. My goal is to celebrate the ideologies of the Web itself: open standards, cross-platform interoperability, accessibility, and portability.

So while you'll find plenty of familiar commercial tools in this chapter, what you'll also find is a range of alternatives that are designed under open source licenses and that are available across platforms.

In today's economic environment, many professional programs can cost significant money, making a comprehensive toolbox seem at first glance to be cost-prohibitive. Yet the Web is filled with alternative software that is either distributed under GNU open source licensing, as freeware, or as low-cost shareware. While typically the open source tools were in use on UNIX and related open source platforms such as the many variants of Linux, there have been many recent ports to Windows and Mac OS X. As a result, a world of free or very low-cost tools has opened up to the Web designer. This chapter points you to those resources wherever available.

> **note** GNU licensing refers to licenses distributed under the GNU project, which first emerged as an alternative to UNIX systems, resulting in the now very popular Linux program, and related operating systems. The GNU project is part of the Free Software Foundation, whose mission is to preserve and promote free software. More information on this important alternative form of software distribution can be found at **www.gnu.org/**.

The tools in this chapter help you to do the following:

- Author markup and CSS with ease
- Create great Web graphics
- Validate pages
- Test sites in a range of Web browsers
- Draw in vector-based environments
- Use bitmap imaging tools for Web graphic production
- Design animations
- Use plug-ins for video and audio
- Convert and clean up documents
- Compress documents

While this chapter won't tell you how to use these tools, it will tell you which utilities you might want to consider adding to your toolbox; give guidance as to which tools are considered most useful and sophisticated, and provide resources as to where you can find the tools in question. You're sure to find something new and helpful to add to your kit.

Secret #1: Web Browsers

AOL has closed Netscape's doors, and Microsoft has announced that no more standalone Internet Explorer (IE) versions will be produced and is waiting instead for the Longhorn Operating System, which includes an integrated browser. New browsers have been entering the market with somewhat daunting regularity— Apple Safari has fast become popular among many Mac users, and Mozilla Firefox is attracting users who want a lean but sophisticated Web browser. Opera continues to improve quietly, and Mozilla continues to develop its capabilities, now under the auspices of a nonprofit agency, The Mozilla Foundation, whose goal is to "preserve choice and innovation" on the Internet.

Browsers are clearly political. It's very difficult to write about Web browsers at this time because they are in such a state of flux, and historically have been in a state of flux.

Web browsers have been a number one concern for designers. The Web browser is the primary piece of software used by the designer and the site visitor to access Web pages. As a result, the ways in which browsers interpret (or don't interpret) the languages and techniques we use to design our pages can cause significant frustration for both the designers and site visitors.

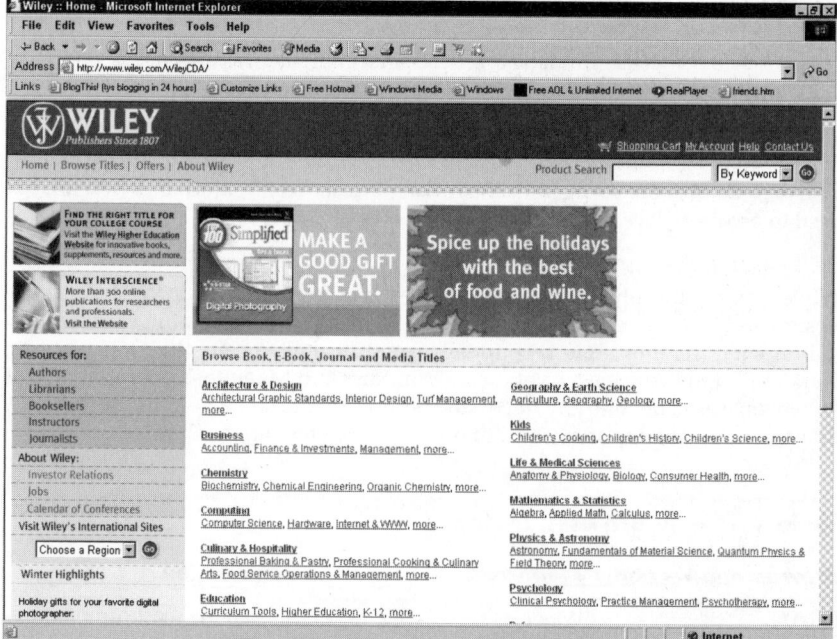

Figure 1-1: As of this writing, Internet Explorer 6.0 for Windows is felt to be the most used browser.

What can you do to navigate these difficult waters? The secret boils down to having a twofold approach.

* Select the browser you want to use for development
* Have a range of browsers to emulate your client's needs

Fortunately, there are ways of determining which browsers you'll want to have for testing. One way is from general statistics, which show you that at this time, IE 6.0 is considered to be the most used browser on earth (see Figure 1-1).

You can also look at your own server logs, which tell you the browsers visiting the sites in question (see Figure 1-2).

|	Top 15 of 1601 Total User Agents	
#	**Hits**	**User Agent**
1	16977 12.96%	Mozilla/4.0 (compatible; MSIE 6.0; Windows NT 5.1)
2	14331 10.94%	Mozilla/4.0 (compatible; MSIE 6.0; Windows NT 5.1; .NET CLR 1
3	7067 5.39%	Mozilla/4.0 (compatible; MSIE 6.0; Windows NT 5.0)
4	5685 4.34%	Mozilla/5.0 (Windows; U; Windows NT 5.0; en-US; rv:1.4) Gecko
5	5213 3.98%	Mozilla/4.0 (compatible; MSIE 6.0; Windows 98)
6	4466 3.41%	Mozilla/5.0 (Windows; U; Windows NT 5.1; en-US; rv:1.5) Gecko
7	3695 2.82%	Mozilla/4.0 (compatible; MSIE 6.0; Windows NT 5.0; .NET CLR 1
8	2864 2.19%	Googlebot/2.1 (+http://www.googlebot.com/bot.html)
9	2068 1.58%	Mozilla/4.0 (compatible; MSIE 5.01; Windows NT 5.0)
10	2015 1.54%	Mozilla/5.0 (Macintosh; U; PPC Mac OS X; en-us) AppleWebKit/1
11	1972 1.51%	Mozilla/4.0 (compatible; MSIE 6.0; Windows NT 5.1; FunWebProd
12	1887 1.44%	Mozilla/5.0 (Windows; U; Windows NT 5.0; en-US; rv:1.5) Gecko
13	1672 1.28%	Mozilla/5.0 (Macintosh; U; PPC Mac OS X; en-us) AppleWebKit/8
14	1617 1.23%	Mozilla/4.0 (compatible; MSIE 5.0; Windows 98; DigExt)
15	1390 1.06%	NetNewsWire/1.0.6 (Mac OS X; http://ranchero.com/netnewswire/

Figure 1-2: Browser usage from Molly.Com, Inc. shows me which browsers are being used to access my Web pages.

While you should always use statistics as a determining factor in how you will design and test a given site, you will want some specific browser in your toolbox no matter what (refer to Table 1-1). Ideally, you'll also have more than one platform to work on—at the very least a version of Windows and Macintosh operating systems. However, this is not entirely necessary, and I provide some helpful tips here if you don't have the luxury of more than one available testing machine.

Table 1-1: Web Browser Toolbox

Browser and Version	Platform	Reason Needed
IE 6.0	Windows	Considered the most commonly used browser
IE 5.5	Windows	Common browser, specific bugs in CSS support that require testing

Browser and Version	Platform	Reason Needed
IE 5.01	Windows	Still in widespread use; has bugs, and should be used in testing
Netscape 4.7	Windows	Problematic browser because of partial CSS support. Despite the fact that it's over four years old, this browser remains on many institutional systems due to security and application concerns
Mozilla	Windows, Macintosh, Linux, and others	Sophisticated browser with excellent standards support, cross-platform consistency, and an excellent browser for development
Opera	Windows, Macintosh, Linux, and others	Good browser for CSS testing; OperaShow is an excellent CSS-projection feature not found in other browsers. The Macintosh version has not been advanced as far as other versions
IE 5.0	Macintosh	Popular browser used by many Macintosh users, especially those on operating systems earlier than OSX
Safari	Macintosh	Sophisticated browser from Apple, of growing interest within the Macintosh community, but only available for OSX and above. Is the default browser on all new Apple computers
Lynx	Windows, Macintosh, VMS, UNIX	Text-only browser helpful in testing for accessibility purposes

note

You can now run more than one version of IE on a given machine. This was only recently made public when a bug was found in the developer upgrade to IE 6.0. See www.skyzyx.com/archives/000094.php for more information.

For a pay-per-view testing service, see www.browsercam.com/, which allows you to see your work on a variety of browsers and platforms you might not have for a reasonable fee. You can see how your site looks in the current version of Safari at www.danvine.com/icapture/, and to see how your site will look in the Konqueror browser, visit http://kcapture .eadz.co.nz/.

My personal favorite browser in which to develop sites is Mozilla (see Figure 1-3). The reason is because there are a number of tools both within it and available for it so it becomes an ideal working environment (you can get similar functionality

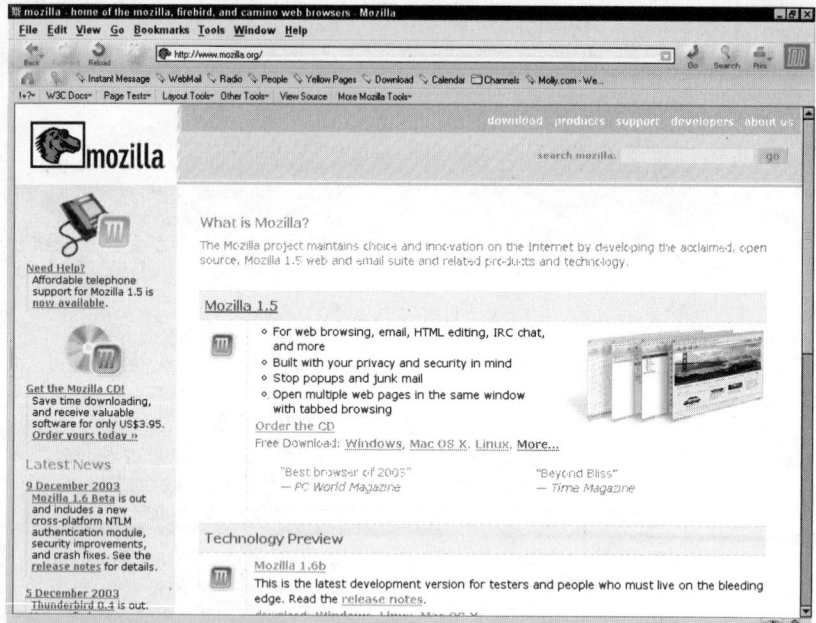

Figure 1-3: The Mozilla Web browser is an extremely flexible, useful browser with special features for designers and developers.

with Netscape 7.0 and Mozilla Firefox). What's more, it's available for every conceivable platform, is open source, and constantly improving.

Secret #2: Choosing a Code Editor

There are three primary categories of editors you can use to write HTML, XHTML, XML, CSS, and JavaScript (as well as any other ASCII-based languages).

- **ASCII text editors.** These editors have very few features beyond word-wrap and save, but if you know your code, they can be excellent for quick fixes or even full jobs.

- **Commercial code editors.** These editors are ASCII editors with power tools, such as wizards, to help you add images. They are my personal favorite for most of the work I do with HTML, XHTML, and CSS.

- **Commercial visual editing packages.** These are full-service Web design software applications that include some means for the designer to work visually without worrying about the code being generated.

Table 1-2 shows some of the primary products within each category type along with platform and features.

So how do you make the best choice? The secret is to have at least one of each type available. You'll find yourself using a combination of tools for most jobs.

My dream team editing toolboxes are as follows.

Table 1-2: Popular Code Editor Features

Editor	Editor Type and Platform	Features/Availability
vi	ASCII text editor for UNIX, OS X, Linux, VMS	Native to most UNIX systems; free
Emacs	ASCII text editor for UNIX, Linux, OS X, VMS and even Windows	Open-source, `www.gnu.org/software/emacs/emacs.html`.
Notepad	ASCII text editor for Windows	Native to Windows systems; free
SimpleText	ASCII text editor for Macintosh (pre OS X)	Native to Macintosh prior to OS X; free
TextEdit	ASCII text editor for OS X	Native to OS X; free
Homesite	Windows-based HTML editor with support for a number of ASCII-based languages	Very popular with many professional designers on the Windows platform. Fee-based, but there's a 30-day full trial version to try before you buy, `www.macromedia.com/software/homesite/`
BBEdit	Macintosh-based HTML editor with support for numerous ASCII-based languages	Very popular with many professionals on the Mac platform. Fee-based, but with a try-before-you-buy demo, `www.barebones.com/products/bbedit/index.shtml`
Adobe GoLive CS	Visual editor for Macintosh and Windows	Popular with some professionals; has improved greatly but still generates some problematic and proprietary markup. Fee-based, free demo
Macromedia Dreamweaver MX 2004	Visual editor for Macintosh and Windows	Popular with many Web design professionals, has very good standards support and integrates well with application technologies such as ColdFusion, JSP, and so forth. Fee-based, free demo
Microsoft FrontPage 2003	Visual editor for Windows	In widespread use due to the proliferation of Office in many organizations. Biggest appeal is its ease of use for nondesigners. Has some nice features including good support for CSS, but is typically not recommended for the Web design professional unless he or she is also educated in markup and CSS

For Windows:

◆ Notepad (see Figure 1-4)
◆ Homesite (see Figure 1-5)
◆ Macromedia Dreamweaver MX 2004 (see Figure 1-6)

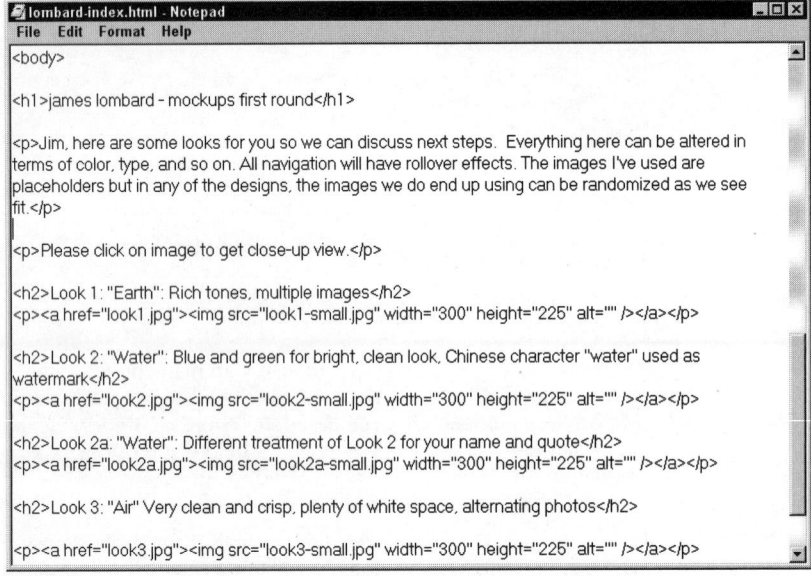

Figure 1-4: Editing a page in notepad.

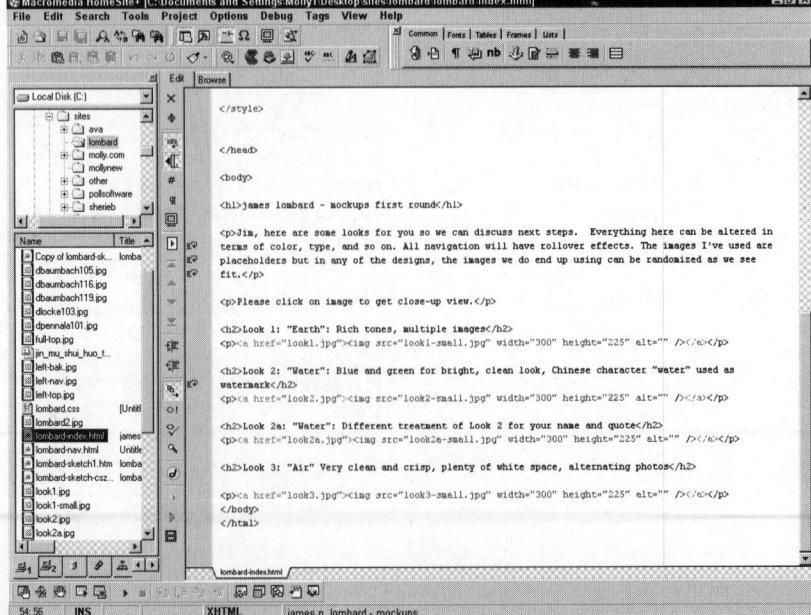

Figure 1-5: Using Homesite, a more robust editor.

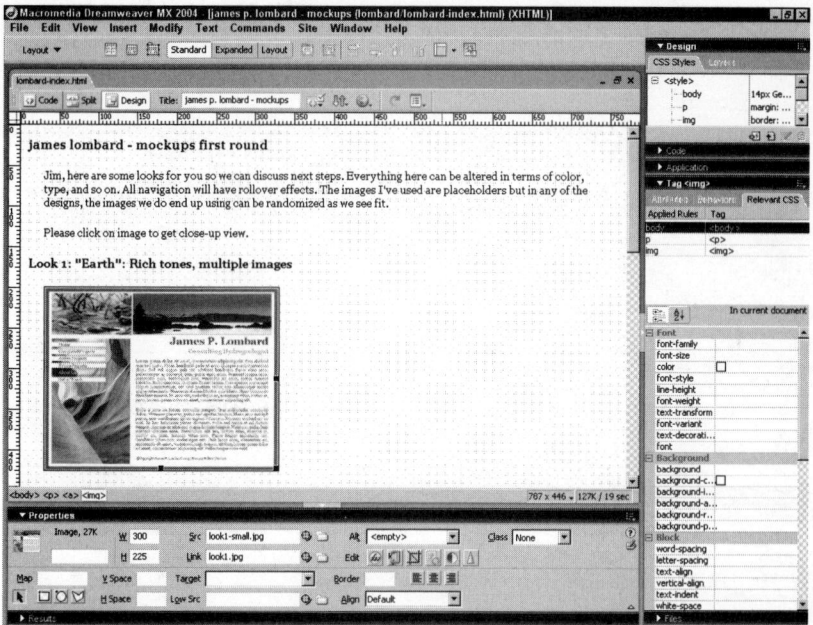

Figure 1-6: Working on the same document in design mode of Dreamweaver MX 2004.

For Macintosh:

♦ SimpleText (or TextEdit on OS X)
♦ BBEdit
♦ Macromedia Dreamweaver MX 2004

However, just because these are my favorite combinations doesn't mean they'll be yours. The best thing you can do is download the free trials and work with a range of tools before making any decisions.

tip **There are many more editors than I've named here. You can do broader-range searches at your favorite search engine to ensure that you'll find those editors most appropriate to your needs.**

Secret #3: File Management with FTP

File Transfer Protocol (FTP) is one of a variety of protocols that run on the Internet. An FTP client allows you to transfer any kind of file from a local computer to a remote server, and depending upon the capabilities of the client you're using, perform important functions such as changing file permissions.

There are many FTP clients—even Web browsers and mechanisms within OS can act as FTP clients. But for full features, most folks turn to a handful of respected and flexible FTP software. Table 1-3 provides details.

Table 1-3: Popular FTP Clients and Features

Client	Platform	Features/Availability
WS_FTP	Windows	Full-featured file transfer program, customizable, inexpensive
CuteFTP	Windows	Popular, full-featured FTP, inexpensive
FTPClient	Macintosh	
Transmit	Macintosh	
Fetch	Macintosh	

Unlike browsers or code editors, you only need one FTP client on hand (see Figure 1-7).

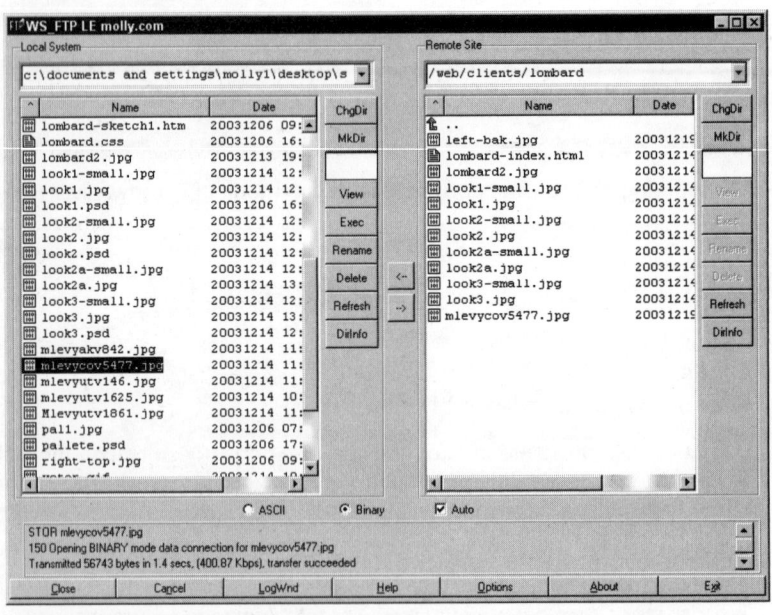

Figure 1-7: Use WS_FTP (classic view) for a wide range of transfer and file management needs.

Many HTML and visual editors have FTP features built right in. However, even with those features, because most Web designers work using a variety of tools, having a standalone FTP client in your toolbox is a definite plus.

Secret #4:   Telnet and SSH

Like FTP, Telnet is an Internet protocol. Its function is to allow you to have line-based entry to a remote server so that you can perform remote functions from your local machine with ease. Telnet is available natively on most operating systems. For example, if you select Start ➪ Run and type *telnet* into the textbox in Windows, you'll get a Telnet console. Telnet clients provide additional features that can be very useful too, so it's often good to have at least one on hand.

Secure Shell (SSH) is a form of Telnet that includes increased security features. Nowadays, most well-run Web servers will prefer you to use Telnet with SSH enabled. Many standalone Telnet clients now integrate SSH into their feature lists, and many operating systems, including Mac OS X and Windows 95, 98, 2000, and XP, have some form of Telnet built into the system.

Table 1-4 describes the top three Telnet/SSH clients and related features.

Table 1-4: Telnet and SSH Clients

Telnet/SSH Client	Platform	Features/Availability
PuTTY	Windows, all versions	Free and downloadable from www.chiark.greenend.org.uk/ ~sgtatham/putty/
NiftyTelnet	Macintosh, pre OS X	Freeware, available at http://asg.web.cmu.edu/andrew2/ dist/niftytelnet.html
OpenSSH	Linux and related platforms	Freeware, www.openssh.com/. OpenSSH is also the SSH technology built into Mac OS X

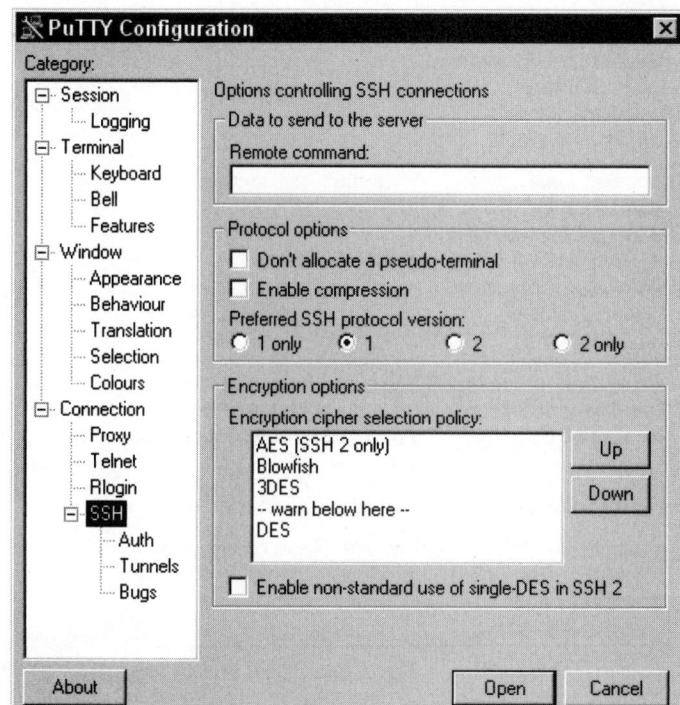

Figure 1-8: Configuring PuTTY on Windows 2000 to perform an SSH login to a remote Web server.

You'll only need one Telnet/SSH client in your toolbox, so take advantage of what's either built in to your operating system or to one of these excellent freeware utilities. Figure 1-8 shows me using PuTTy to log in to a remote Web server and perform tasks.

Secret #5: Validation Tools

Validating markup, CSS, and accessibility is becoming more and more important for professional Web designers. A variety of online validators can be helpful, but there are also standalone and add-in products for existing programs. Table 1-5 describes some of the popular validation tools available to you.

Figure 1-9 shows a page being validated by the CSE HTML Pro standalone validator.

Table 1-5: Validation Tools for Markup, CSS, and Accessibility

Validation Tool	Platform and Usage	Availability
W3C HTML and XHTML Validation	Online service. You can add by URL or by upload	http://validator.w3.org/
W3C CSS Validation	Online service. Validate by URI, paste into text area or upload. A standalone version is available	http://jigsaw.w3.org/css-validator/
CSE HTML Validator Pro	A professional standalone for Windows that validates XHTML, HTML, CSS, and Accessibility. Very powerful, highly recommended	www.htmlvalidator.com/
Bobby	Offers both online and standalone validation for accessibility	Standalone:www.watchfire.com/products/ desktop/bobby/default.aspx Online: http://bobby.watchfire.com/bobby/html/ en/index.jsp
Cynthia Says	Online validator	www.cynthiasays.com/
Lift	Multiple plug-in, standalone, and online accessibility and usability validation	www.usablenet.com/products_services/ products_services.html
Macromedia Dreamweaver MX, MX 2004	Built-in HTML, XHTML validation	Good validation if preferences are set up properly. Can be integrated with the Lift validation tool for Macromedia for accessibility and usability

Validation Tool	Platform and Usage	Availability
Adobe GoLive	Built-in validation for HTML and XHTML	Good validation, but nothing for CSS or accessibility
FrontPage 2003	No internal validation	Can be used with the Lift validation tool for Microsoft FrontPage for accessibility and usability

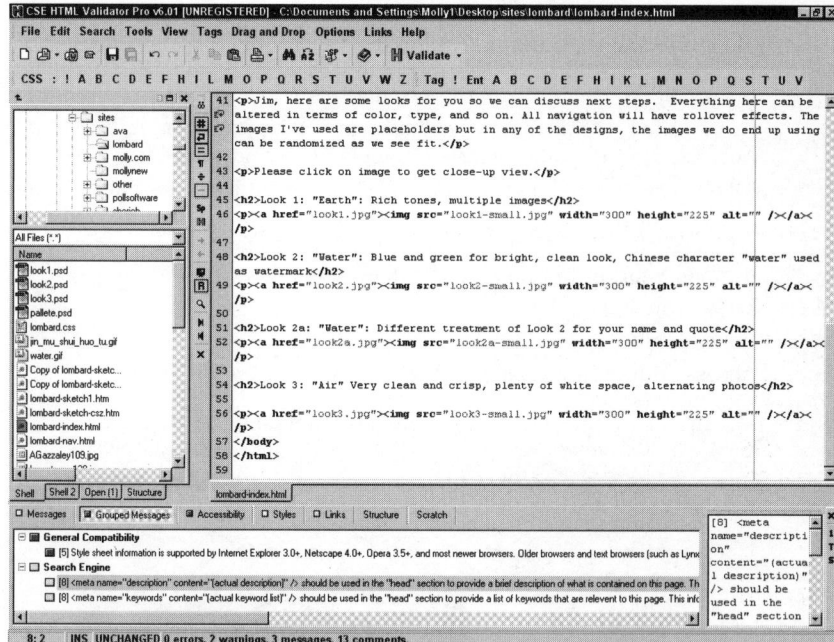

Figure 1-9: Validating a page with CSE HTML Pro.

Of course, as with other tools mentioned in this chapter, these are popular and comprehensive tools. A range of additional tools perform these or similar processes; they are available for multiple platforms and offered as freeware, shareware, and commercial licensing. Again, the secret is to find the best validation services for your needs and stick to them.

caution

Accessibility validation is an especially difficult issue because it's recommended that you use multiple validators. In addition, accessibility validators don't measure visual issues, so you have to use them just as you would a grammar checking utility—rely on a balance of the validator feedback and your own knowledge. Markup and CSS validators are more specific because they test against the specifications for the defined languages in question.

Secret #6: PNH Toolbar

Till this point, you've read about tools that are broad in scope. The PNH toolbar is a very specific utility that I've found absolutely invaluable as part of my Web design toolbox.

The PNH toolbar is completely free, available across platforms, and can be installed in Netscape 7.0+, Mozilla 1.0+, and Mozilla Firefox Web browsers instantly. Once installed, you can use its reference links and fantastic utilities while you're developing pages.

Some of the PNH toolbar features include the following:

- Instant access to W3C reference materials
- Page testing where any open document can be run through HTML, CSS, Accessibility, and other validation tools in a background tab
- Allows you to disable styles on a given page, add an external style sheet to any page open within the browser, outline block elements, outline replaced elements, outline table cells, turn off images, and resize your browser window to custom as well as conventional sizes
- View form and cookie details
- View source
- Access additional Mozilla and related tools instantly

Figure 1-10 shows me turning on the table cells of a table-based page.

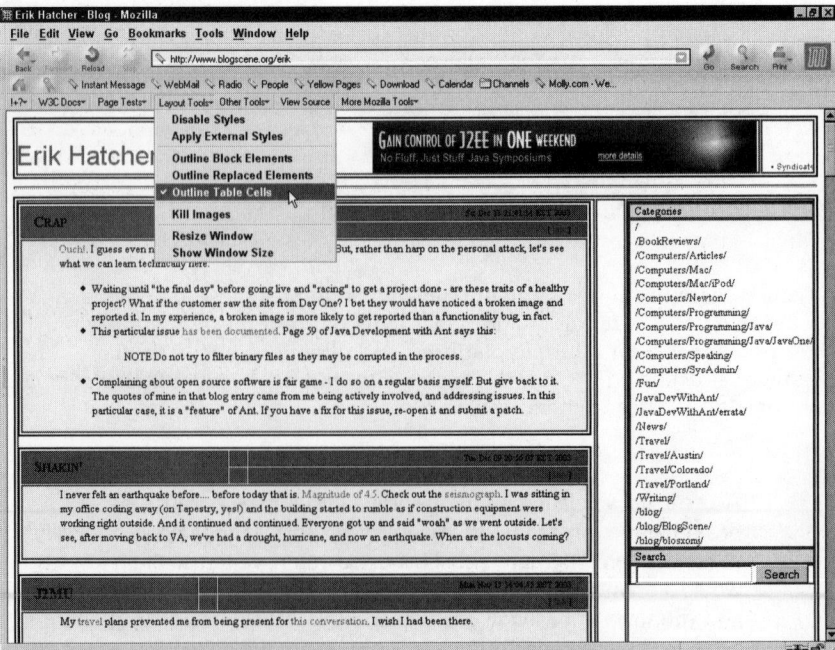

Figure 1-10: Using the PNH toolbar to view the table structure of an HTML page.

note
> Download the PNH toolbar from **http://placenamehere.com/ pnhtoolbar/**.

Secret #7:   Sidebar Reference Panels

Netscape 7 and Mozilla contain a sidebar panel (F9). This panel has a range of utilities, such as search, with which the browsers ship, but there are also additional sidebar panels that individuals have created. Some of these panels are extremely valuable for Web designers to have as they offer immediate, in-browser access to aspects of design.

Sidebar panels of immediate relevance to Web designers include the following:

◆ CSS 2 and CSS 2.1 sidebar reference panels (available in French, too)

◆ HTML 4.01 sidebar reference panel

◆ Document Object Model 2 (DOM 2) sidebar reference panel (also available in French)

◆ JavaScript sidebar reference panels and guides (multiple versions)

◆ XSLT 1.0 (Extensible Style Language with Transformations) sidebar reference panel

Each of these panels is available completely free and install instantly. Once in place, the panels act as references by both the information they contain within them and the fact that references are linked to the specifications they represent. If I'm working on a site using CSS 2, and I want to know how to use a certain property, I simply open the CSS 2 side panel (shown in Figure 1-11), find the property in question, and click the reference. My browser then takes me directly to the topic within the specification (see Figure 1-12).

Currently, sidebar panels can be downloaded from the Netscape DevEdge site, http://devedge.netscape.com/toolbox/sidebars/. It's unknown at this time whether AOL will continue to host that site indefinitely. If you cannot resolve the site, visit the Web Standards Project, www.webstandards.org/, which has committed to ensuring the location of these panels will always be made available.

tip
> Side panels are quite easy to make for anyone with HTML skills, so if you are interested in creating helpful tools and utilities, you might want to read more about how to make side panels at **http://devedge.netscape.com/ viewsource/2002/sidebar/**.

Secret #8:   Bitmap Image Programs

Bitmap graphics are the primary form of graphics on the Web, and having a program that creates and optimizes them is essential. Bitmap graphics, also referred to as *raster* graphics, are graphics where the image is made up of tiny boxes of color, known as pixels. Pixel-based graphics typically can be compressed very well, but

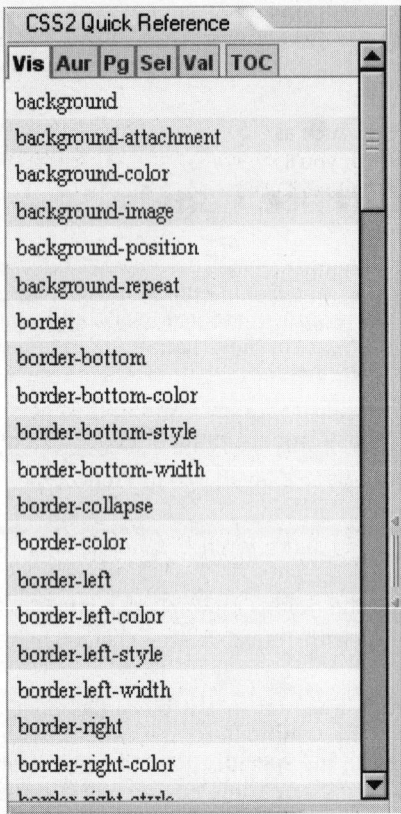

Figure 1-11: The CSS 2 side panel, close-view.

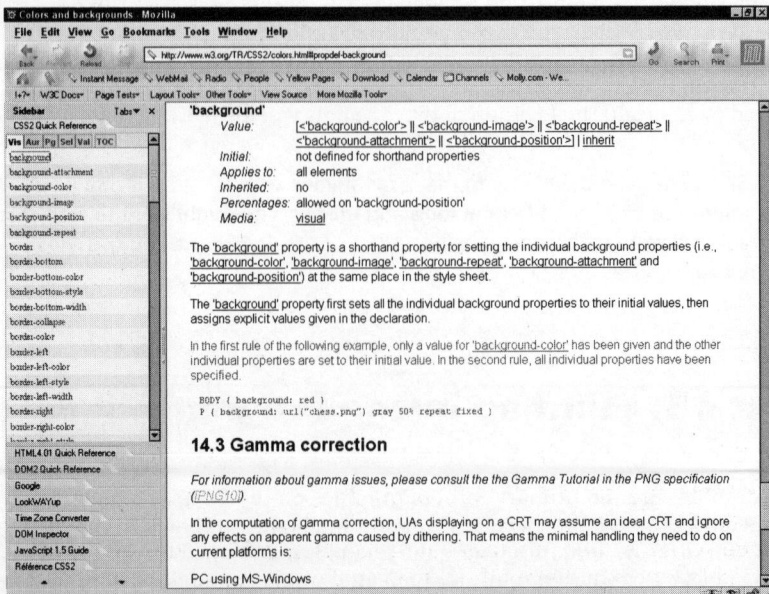

Figure 1-12: The CSS panel with the specification open in the browser window.

do not scale well because data becomes lost as you attempt to enlarge a pixel-based image.

note

Many bitmap-based imaging programs, such as Photoshop, do contain some support for vector-based graphics, which you'll read about in the next secret. Still, they are primarily used for the creation of raster graphics.

One thing that's no secret is how ubiquitous Photoshop is for Windows and Macintosh users. And while every professional Web designer should really be familiar with and use Photoshop (shown in Figure 1-13), some other bitmap imaging programs also enjoy fairly widespread use.

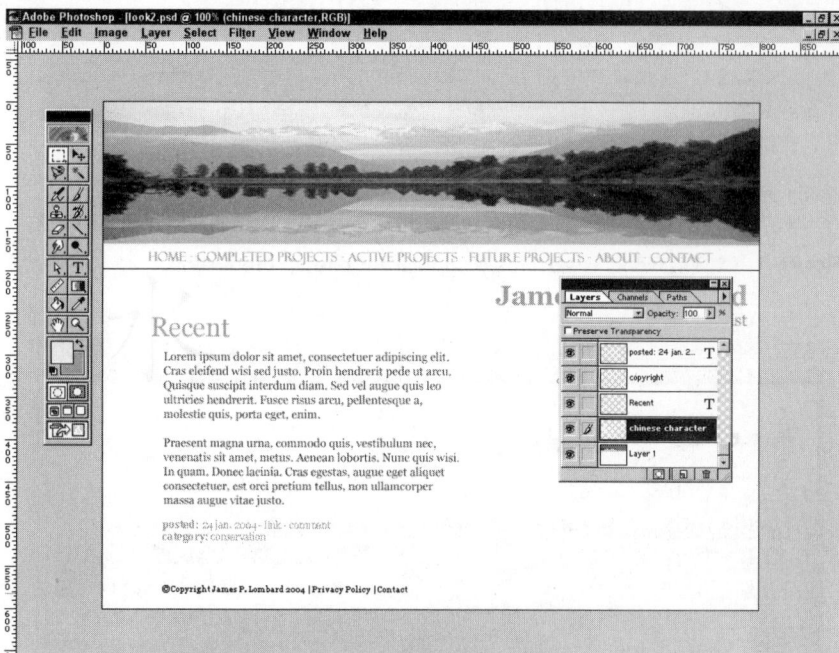

Figure 1-13: Working on a client site in Photoshop.

For Macintosh and Windows, Macromedia Fireworks (shown in Figure 1-14) is a very popular bitmap imaging program, and JASC's Paint Shop Pro has a certain cult-like following among Windows-based Web design enthusiasts. Corel offers a complete drawing program with its Draw suite, but its use seems very limited among people working on the Web.

A surprise for bitmap imaging needs is The Gimp. The Gimp stands for "GNU Image Manipulation Program" and is an open source bitmap drawing software program that works on UNIX and related systems, as well as having versions for the Macintosh and Windows (see Figure 1-15).

The Linux and Windows versions of Gimp are freely distributed. You can also run Gimp under OSX for free, although the MacGimp version runs around $20 to download (a far cry from the hundreds to even thousands of dollars other bitmapping programs will cost you).

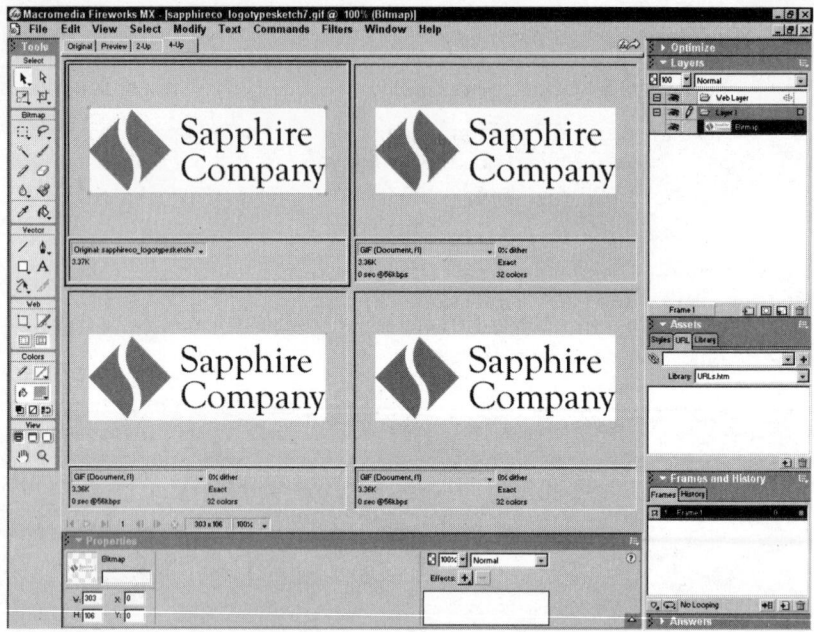

Figure 1-14: Fireworks is extremely popular for bitmap production.

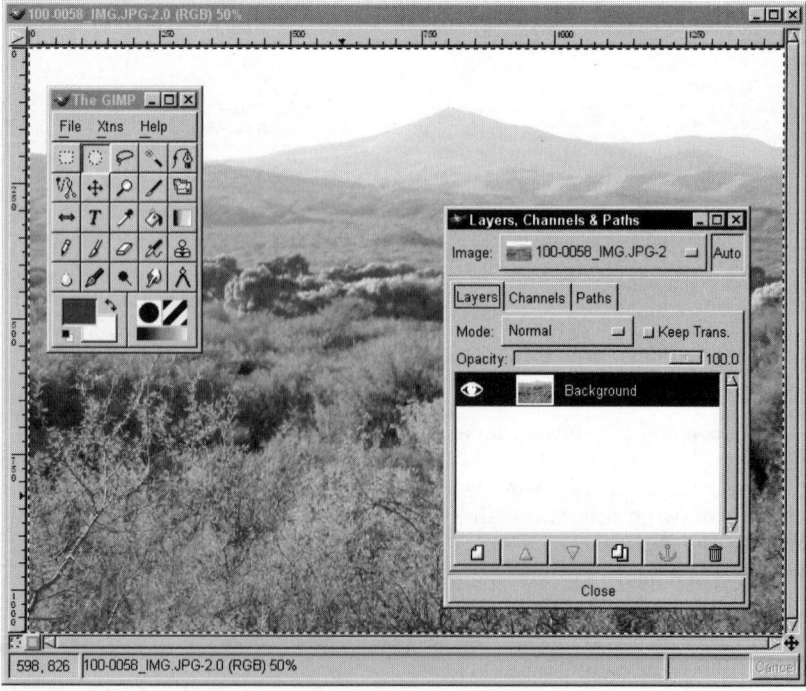

Figure 1-15: Designing graphics using The Gimp, a freely distributed open-source imaging program.

note For information on Adobe Photoshop, please visitwww.adobe.com/. Macromedia Fireworks can be found at **www.macromedia.com/**. Corel products are showcased at **www.corel.com/**, and JASC's Paint Shop Pro is available at **www.jasc.com/**. The Gimp for UNIX and Windows can be found at **www.gimp.org/**, and The Gimp for Mac OS X is at **www.macgimp.org/**.

Secret #9: Vector Image Programs

For those of you who create logos, refine type, and enjoy drawing, the two most common drawing programs are Adobe Illustrator and Macromedia Free-hand (shown in Figure 1-16). Vector-based images differ from bitmap graphics in that they contain the mathematical information necessary to allow them to be scaled without loss of quality. They are extremely useful for creating curves and shapes. Of course, you will need to rasterize your final work by converting it to bitmap formats, such as GIF or JPEG, if you're going to use your illustration on the Web, but you can achieve far more complex drawing tasks in a vector-based program.

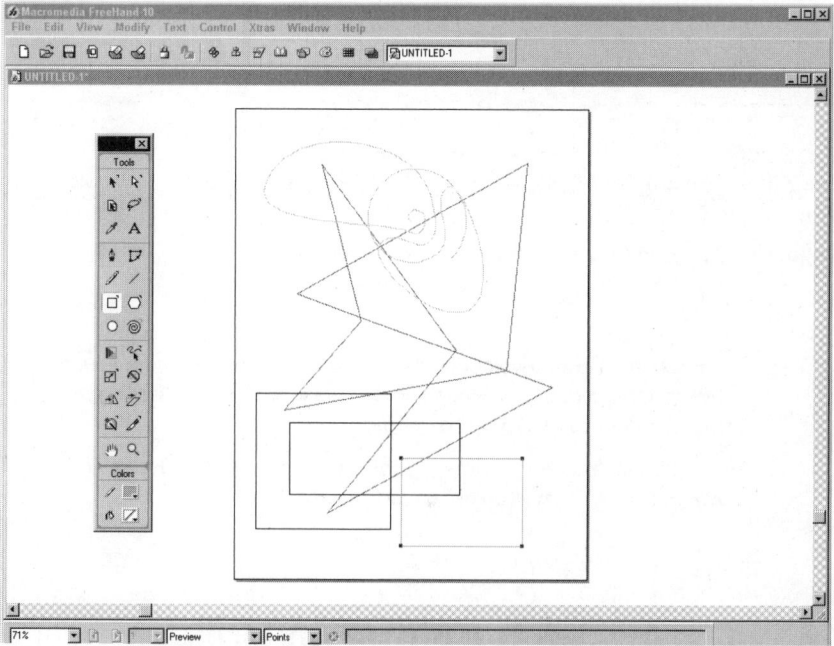

Figure 1-16: Drawing geometric shapes in Macromedia Freehand.

As with bitmap programs, there are a few shareware and open source gems that shouldn'tbe overlooked, especially for those on a limited budget, who have lighter-weight needs for vector drawing.

Two such bitmap programs are:

♦ **Mayura Draw** is a shareware vector drawing program for Windows, at $39.00 per license. Used mostly by scientists and engineers for technical illustrations, Mayura Draw can be an invaluable and inexpensive tool in your design toolbox (see Figure 1-17).

♦ **Sketch** is a freely distributed open source drawing program for Linux, with a Windows port version called "Skencil."

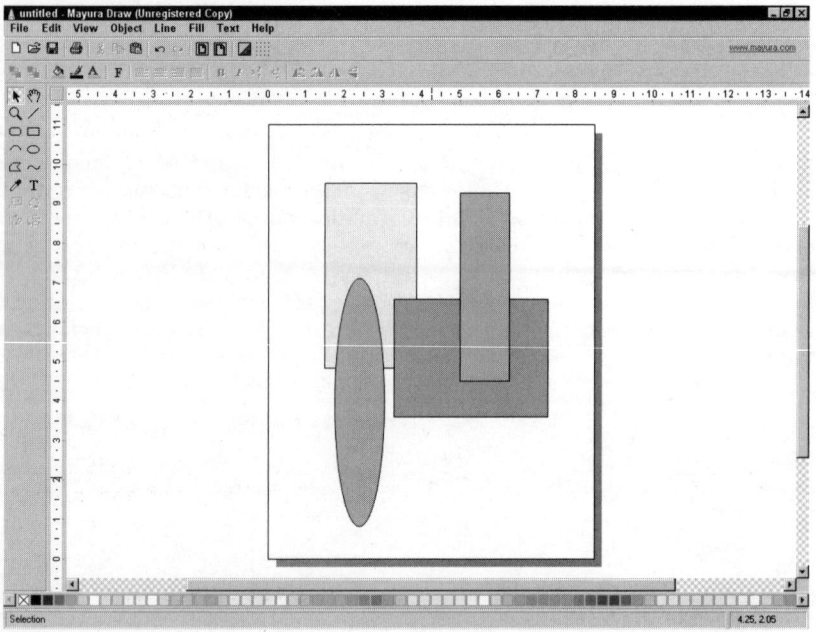

Figure 1-17: Using Mayura Draw for vector-based design.

> **tip** Web designers and developers using Linux platform and open source software for designing graphics should check out LinuxArtist.Org, at `www.linuxartist.org/2d.php`.
>
> For additional free vector drawing software resources, see `http://bourbon.usc.edu:8001/tgif/vector.html`.

Secret #10:   Web Animation Utilities

Outside of animation for advertising, GIF animations have somewhat fallen out of favor for use on professional Web sites—except for those instances where very subtle effects are desired. Of course, much of this has to do with the proliferation of Macromedia Flash (which has also influenced Web advertising). Nevertheless, GIF animations are sill desired in some cases, so make sure you have one on hand.

As with all software and utilities, some of the available Web animation utilities are commercial, and some are completely free. Table 1-6 provides a variety of popular options from which to choose.

Table 1-6: Popular Web Animation Utilities

Software	Platform and Usage	Availability
Ulead Gif Animator	Windows; very popular with many designers	Commercial, low-cost product with 30-day demo, www.ulead.com/ga/runme.htm
GIF Construction Set	One of the oldest GIF animators around for Windows	Low-cost shareware, www.mindworkshop.com/alchemy/gifcon.html
GIF Builder	Very popular for Mac OS 9 and earlier	Low-cost shareware, www.mac.org/graphics/gifbuilder/
GIF Builder for OS X	Mac OS X (will run on Mac OS 8 and above)	Freeware, www.macupdate.com/info.php/id/235
GIF Merge	Linux and related platforms	http://the-labs.com/GIFMerge/

The majority of Web designers, however, tend to use Adobe ImageReady for animations. ImageReady (shown in Figure 1-18) ships with Photoshop and is available for Windows and Macintosh.

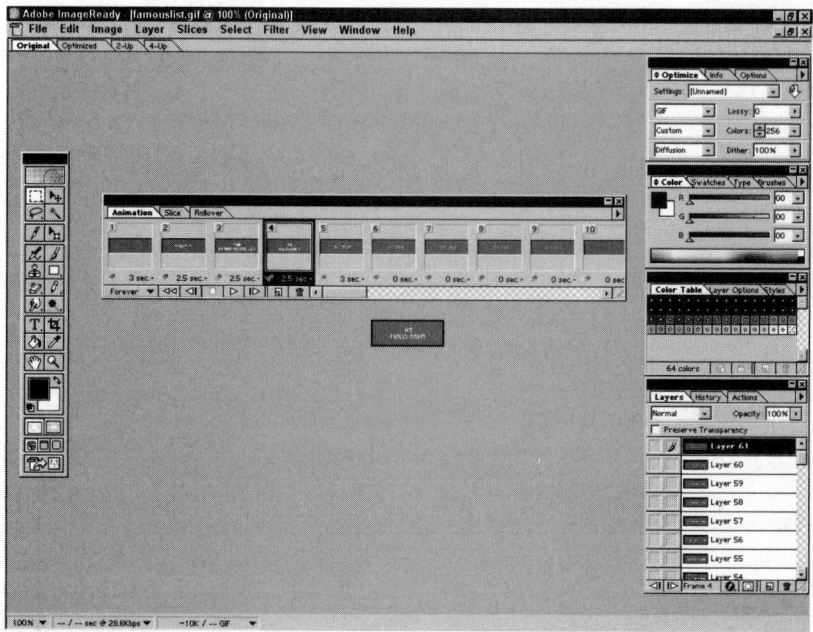

Figure 1-18: Creating a GIF animation in Adobe ImageReady.

Secret #11:   Screen Capture Utilities

By far, some of the most helpful utilities I've ever used are those that assist with screen capturing. Such utilities are invaluable when creating Web site portfolios, sharing mockups with co-workers and colleagues, and so on.

While screen captures can be done with almost any imaging program, such as Photoshop, screen capture utilities let you hone in on specific portions of the screen and capture menus, dialogs, and toolbars with ease. This can be very helpful and save a lot of time—instead of cropping full-screen images, you can instantly get what you need and, in most cases, output it to numerous useful file formats.

Many excellent screen-capture utilities are available for all platforms, but the three most reportedly beloved are as follows:

- For Windows, SnagIt by TechSmith is an amazing utility that I find myself using almost daily. You can find this low-cost shareware at www.techsmith.com/products/snagit/.

- Find low-cost shareware ScreenShot Pro, for Mac and Mac OS X at www.code-line.com/software/screenshotpro.html. OSX is packaged with two screen-capture utilities, one within the operating system itself, and the other a feature called Grab.

- For Linux, the KDE desktop environment has screen shot utilities built in (www.kde.org/), and The Gimp, discussed in the bitmap imaging section earlier, does a great job with screen captures.

Figure 1-19 shows me preparing to capture a screen using SnagIt.

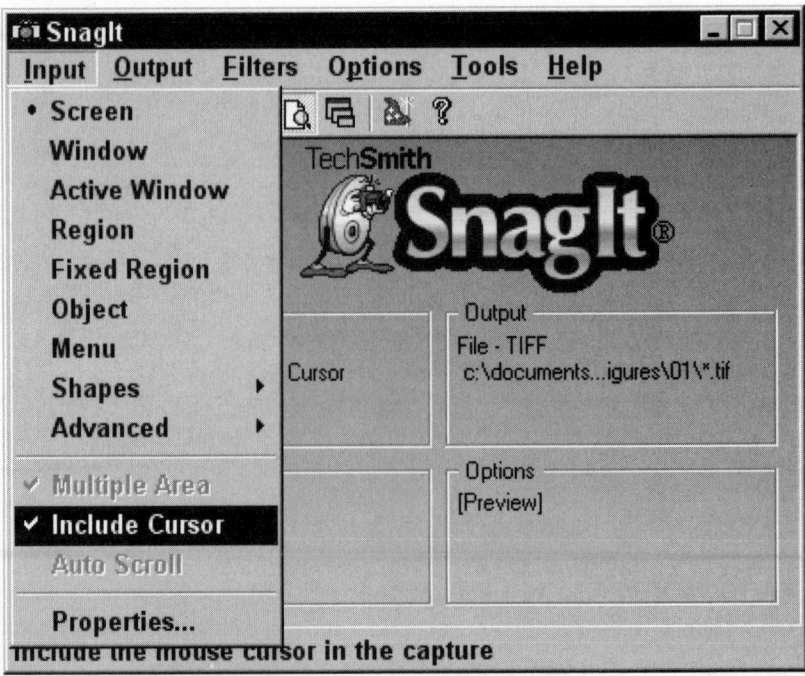

Figure 1-19: Working with SnagIt to create screen shots.

Secret #12:   Rename Utilities

For the many Web designers working on a Windows platform, easy ways to rename numerous files locally can be problematic. Let's say you want to take a directory full of files with the suffix .html, retain the files' unique prefixes, and change the suffix globally to .php. To do this directly on an open-source operating system from the command line is very simple, but for Windows and Macintosh (except if you use the command line in OS X) you need a rename utility to perform the task effectively.

For Windows and Mac OS X, a low-cost, shareware program that'll help you perform rename tasks on your local machine is "A Better File Rename." Not only does it do the job, but the company that makes the product, PublicSpace, also has a special Web master program allowing you to link to the company and get the software free. Or, if you run a site where you can place their ad banner, you can get more than one product free.

Figure 1-20 shows a rename process using A Better File Rename.

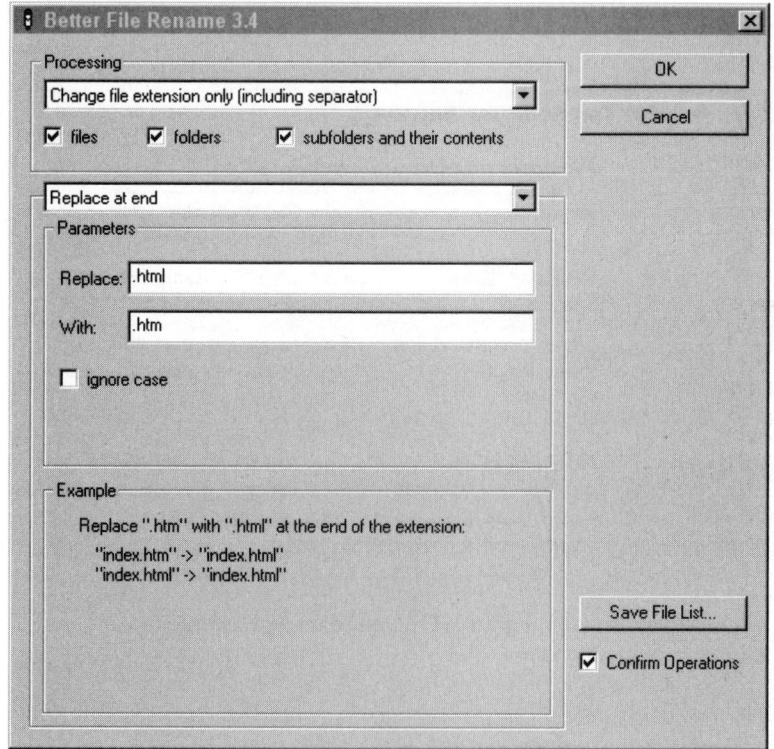

Figure 1-20: Working with A Better File Rename to batch rename files locally.

note   To download A Better File Rename, see www.publicspace.net/ABetterFinderRename/.

For the Web master program, visit www.publicspace.net/webmasters/index.html.

Secret #13:   Tag Strippers

Another important utility that you'll want to have is an HTML *tag stripper*. Utilities of this type let you take an HTML or related Web document and strip all the code out of it, leaving you with just the text.

In some cases, commercial Web design software contains such utilities. Examples include Macintosh BBEdit (mentioned in the previous "Code Editor" section), Homesite, and ColdFusion Studio. In the case of Dreamweaver for both Macintosh and Windows, you can add an extension such as Tag Stripper, (www.massimocorner.com/dw/commands/tag_stripper.mxp), which will do the trick for you. Check your favorite editor for this feature.

Even if you have features of this nature within your main software, you still might want to have a lightweight, fast, standalone stripper available. What's more, tag strippers tend to offer more advanced features anyway, such as maintaining logical formatting of text, converting tables into tab-delimited format, and changing HTML entities to proper text characters. Table 1-7 shows a variety of helpful, low-cost tag strippers.

Table 1-7: Helpful Tag Stripper Software

Software	Platform and Usage	Availability
Detagger	Windows	Low-cost shareware, www.jafsoft .com/detagger/
HTTC – HTML to Text Converter	Windows, Linux	Free under GNU license, www. franksworld.net/httc/
Html2text	Linux; command line in English and German	Open source freeware, http:// userpage.fu-berlin.de/ ~mbayer/tools/ html2text.html
HTML Markdown	Macintosh Classic	Low-cost shareware, www. printerport.com/klephacks/ markdowndocs.html

Figure 1-21 shows me stripping an HTML page using Detagger.

Secret #14:   HTML Tidy

Just as a handy tag stripper gets rid of tags, conversion software such as HTML Tidy can be really useful. Not only does Tidy convert text to HTML, but it also converts HTML to XHTML or to XML. It also validates your markup and fixes additional markup problems. A very sophisticated tool, it's available for every platform and is freely distributed via http://tidy.sourceforge.net/.

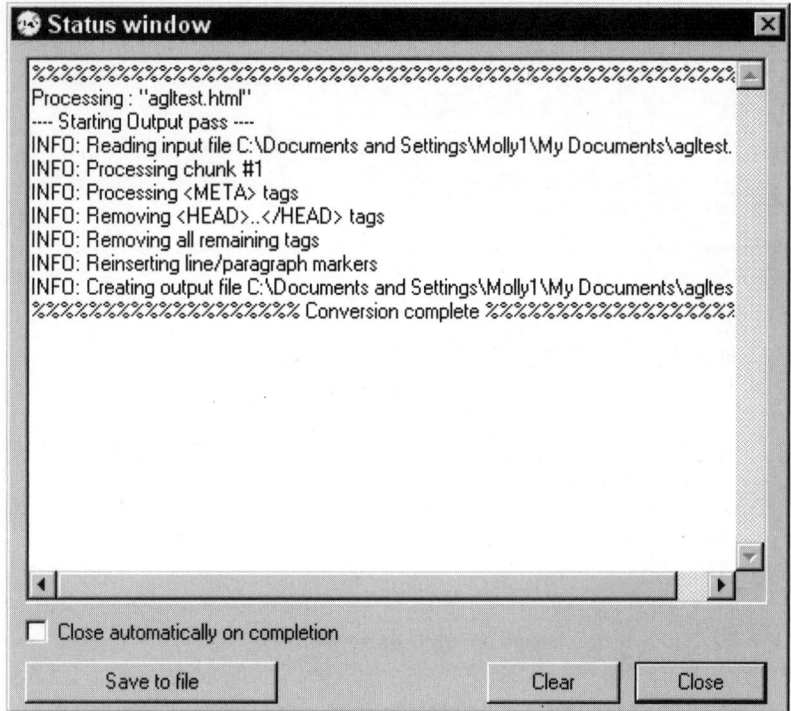

Figure 1-21: Using Detagger to remove HTML tags.

---

tip ❖ **HTML Tidy is built into a wide range of shareware code editors and utilities. Be sure to check the sourceforge Web site for additional resources.**

In Figure 1-22, I'm using TidyGUI, a simple GUI interface to Tidy, to clean a document.

Secret #15:   Compression Utilities

Compression utilities are one of the most critical tools you'll need. And, with to-day's more efficient compression, not only are you able to compress files for more efficient e-mail, FTP, Web site downloads and storage, but you can extract them easily, too.

One of the biggest issues in compression is cross-platform compatibility. In the past, most UNIX and related operating systems used certain compression formats, Macintosh used others, and Windows still others. Sending files back and forth or making them available in compressed formats on Web sites always means making sure you've got software capable of cross-platform compression and extraction.

For Windows, the most widely used package for this is WinZip (www.winzip .com/), a low-cost shareware utility that creates and extracts a wide number of compression formats that are used across platforms (see Figure 1-23).

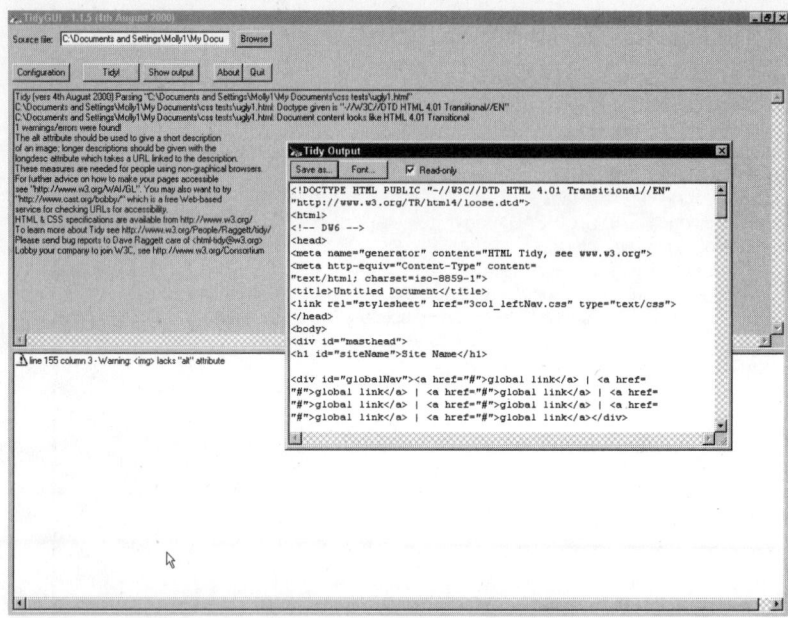

Figure 1-22: Tidy literally "tidies up" your documents.

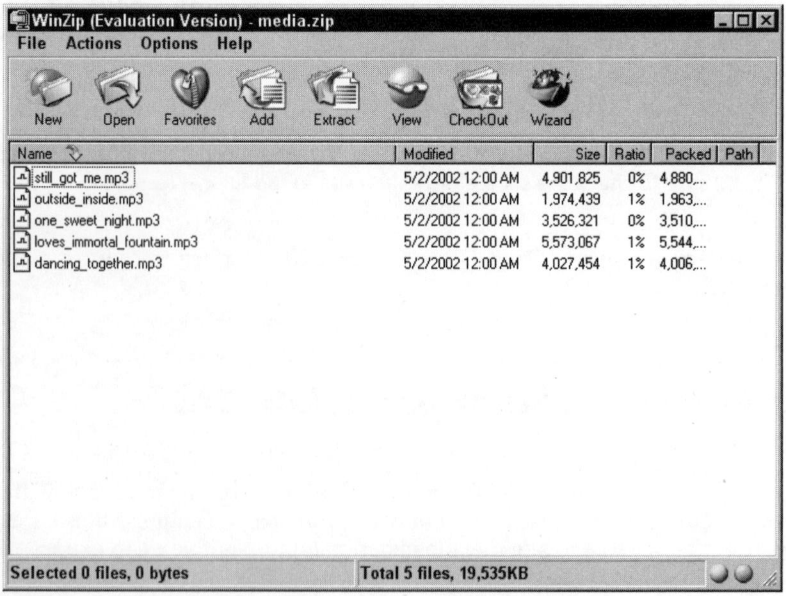

Figure 1-23: Creating a zip format for downloadable media files.

For Macintosh, a commonly used package is StuffIt, which is also available for Windows and Linux. It's an excellent commercial choice—it's low-cost, cross-platform compatible, and easy to use. You can find it at www.stuffit.com/.

For a good graphical interface that provides multicompression, multiextraction on Linux, gnochive is available for free at http://gnochive.sourceforge.net/.

Secret #16:   Audio and Video Players

Audio players are necessary for Web designers who are both working with audio and video as well as visiting Web sites where forms of audio and video are in use. At this point, many audio players are also video players, as you'll see.

Many players are available these days. Table 1-8 provides a best-of-breed and most popular list.

Table 1-8: Popular Audio Players

Software	Platform and Features	Availability
RealPlayer	Windows, Mac, Plug-in for Linux. Support for all common audio and video formats with emphasis on Real streaming media and SMIL formats	Free and pay versions available at www.real.com/
Apple QuickTime	Windows, Mac. Support for all common audio and video formats with an emphasis on the QuickTime format	Free and pay versions available at http://quicktime.apple.com/
Microsoft Windows Media Player	Windows, Mac. Popular media player capable of supporting almost all audio and video formats, emphasis on Windows Media file format	Available with Windows Operating Systems and the IE Web browser and for download, at www .microsoft.com/ windows/windowsmedia/
WinAmp	Windows. Very popular media player with support for most media types	Free and pay versions available at www.winamp.com/

> **note** An emerging alternative for multimedia is Ogg Vorbis, a project that is fully open, nonproprietary, patent and royalty free, available at **www.xiph.org/ ogg/vorbis/**.

Secret #17:   Plug-Ins

For a number of technologies, it's helpful to have plug-ins already installed in your browsers. This helps you avoid having to download plug-ins for commonly used tasks.

note   For Real and QuickTime plug-ins, see the player pages available in the preceding Audio and Video Player section.

The most ubiquitous plug-in is for Flash. You can download the Flash plug-in at www.macromedia.com/software/flashplayer/. You'll also want the Shockwave plug-in, found at www.macromedia.com/software/shockwaveplayer/.

Another very important plug-in is Java. This product establishes a connection between your Web browser and Java platform products. It's available at http://java.sun.com/products/plugin/.

The Acrobat plug-in is invaluable for Web designers. It allows you to download Portable Document Format (PDF) files directly to your Web browser; find it at www.adobe.com/products/acrobat/readstep2.html.

Secret #18: SVG and SMIL Support

While not prevalent, Scalable Vector Graphics (SVG) and Synchronized Multimedia Integration Language (SMIL) are two open-standards technologies geared at aspects of imaging and multimedia.

Because of growing interest in these technologies, you will want to have some resources at hand should you decide to work with either.

To study and work with SVG and SMIL, you need the following (free) support items:

   ◆ Adobe offers an SVG viewer for Windows and Macintosh at www.adobe .com/svg/viewer/install/main.html.
   ◆ Corel has an SVG viewer for Windows at www.smartgraphics.com/ Viewer_prod_info.shtml.
   ◆ RealPlayer offers the best support for SMIL at www.real.com/ realoneplayer.htm.

Secret #19: Software for Security and Safety

While the majority of security concerns in Web design and development lie on the server side of things, protecting your local computer(s) is an essential aspect of being a professional Web master. The reasons are many and include the protection of your intellectual property (IP) to limit or eliminate the possibility of spreading viruses or worms in networks, software, Word documents, and e-mail; and to prevent the proliferation of spyware, adware, and other malicious browser-oriented concerns that can be spread via browsers and peer-to-peer communication systems.

To do a good job of protecting any local machine, you'll want:

   ◆ Up-to-date antivirus software

- Firewall software (many firewall features are being built into operating systems, but they aren't always considered as safe as additional products)
- Adware protection

You should also always make sure to perform routine upgrades to your operating system and add patches when they are available.

Table 1-9 lists helpful security and safety software.

Table 1-9: Helpful Security and Safety Software

Software	Platform and Features	Availability
McAfee Software	Variety of commercial packages for antivirus, firewall, and additional protection for Windows	Commercial standalone and subscription products available at www.mcafee.com/
Norton Software	Variety of commercial packages for antivirus, firewall, and additional protection for Windows and Macintosh	Commercial standalone and subscription products available at www.norton.com/
Sophos	Antivirus software for multiple platforms	Commercial standalone software, available at www.sophos.com/
Vexira Anti Virus	Antivirus software for Windows and Linux	Commercial software, available at www.centralcommand.com/
Zone Alarm Firewall	Firewall software for Windows	Free and fee-based options, available at www.zonelabs.com/
Brick House	Firewall software for Macintosh OS X	Low-cost shareware, available at http://personalpages.tds.net/~brian_hill/brickhouse.html
Firestarter	Firewall software for Linux and related systems	Freeware, available at http://firestarter.sourceforge.net/index.php
Spybot	Windows removal system for spyware and related problems	Free (donations at your discretion), available at www.safer-networking.org/
AdAware	Windows removal system for spyware and related concerns	Highly recommended, free and pro versions available at www.lavasoftusa.com/
Internet Cleanup	Macintosh removal system for spyware and related issues	Commercial product, low-cost, available at www.aladdinsys.com/mac/cleanup/index.html
Mac Scan	Macintosh removal system for spyware and related issues	Free, and available at http://macscan.securemac.com/

Windows platforms are the most vulnerable to viruses and spyware. Macintosh is less so, especially OS X, but there are still some concerns with the Macintosh platform. Linux platforms suffer very few problems, if any, with viruses, spyware, and adware, because experienced users spot malicious code, and Linux and related platforms are very, very security-conscious to begin with.

Figure 1-24 shows me using AdAware to scan my local drives for adware, spyware, and other malicious software.

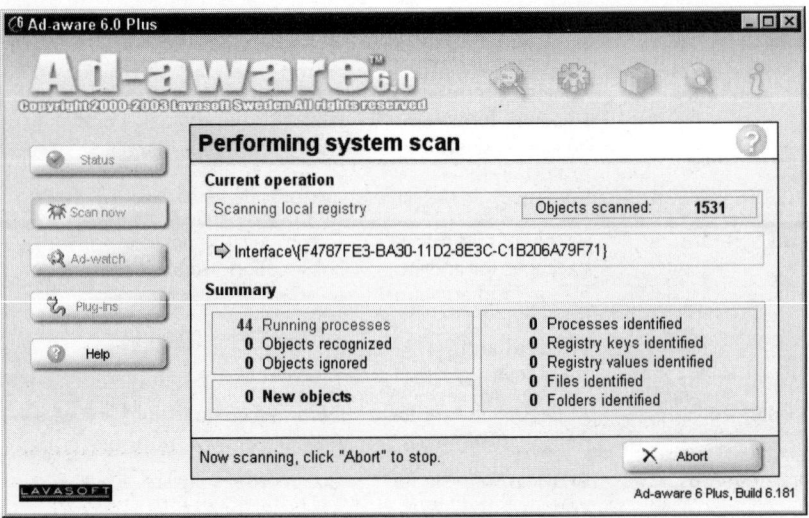

Figure 1-24: Creating a zip format for downloadable media files.

Secret #20: Collaborative Communication Software

You *know* that instant messaging (IM) can be totally counterproductive to workflow. On the other hand, for those Web designers and developers working collaboratively from different locales—possibly even around the world—there's nothing like IM to make life easy.

There are four primary IM clients:

◆ AOL Instant messenger (AIM) can be downloaded at www.aim.com/ (for Windows, Mac, or Linux).

◆ MSN Messenger is downloadable from http://messenger.msn.com/ (for Windows and Mac).

◆ Yahoo! Messenger can be downloaded from http://messenger.yahoo .com/ (for Windows, Mac, UNIX and UNIX-related systems).

◆ ICQ is available from www.icq.com/ (for Windows and Mac).

All of them are free, and all entertain some level of popularity. The problem is that they are all proprietary and don't work with each other (with the exception of AIM and ICQ, as both are owned by AOL)—meaning that if your collaborator pal in

Moscow uses AIM and you use MSN, you're not going to be able to chat if you're using the proprietary clients.

Fortunately, there are alternative clients available that transcend the proprietary silliness and do so in impressive ways, as shown in Table 1-10.

Table 1-10: Cross-Service Collaboration Software

Software	Platform and Features	Availability
Trillian	Windows. Supports AIM, MSN, Yahoo!, ICQ, IRC, has e-mail support, chat, plug-ins can extend the software to incorporate Winamp audio, RSS newsfeeds. Very popular and very useful software	Free, pro version available for a donation at `www.trillian.cc/`
Fire	Mac OS X. Supports all of the primary popular protocols	Free, at `http://fire .sourceforge.net/.`
Jabber	All platforms. Suite of open-protocol services and applications for nonproprietary messaging	Free, at `www.jabber.org/`
Gaim	Linux and Windows. Supports AIM, MSN, Yahoo!, ICQ, and other protocols	Free, at `http://gaim .sourceforge.net/`

I use Trillian for all my IM contacts, additional e-mail accounts, and RSS news-feeds.

Summary

The master Web designer must have a range of helpful tools on hand, and doing a complete audit of your software will help you figure out what you need. Of course, depending upon your work environment, there are tools here that you might never use, but being aware of them is empowering.

And, while the cost of tools can really add up, once you've got the perfect toolbox in place, maintenance and upgrades are going to be less problematic and costly. The biggest secret when it comes to tools is finding a balance between what's out there and what you like to work with. After all, it's you, not the tool, that's responsible for creating awesome Web sites.

Managing Your Web Project

◆ ◆

Secrets in This Chapter

◆ ◆

With an expert toolbox in place, the next step is to define the scope of the project and put a process in place to manage it effectively. This is a step that many Web designers miss or don't put a lot of emphasis on.

However, it is critical not only for a client or company's Return On Investment (ROI) to have sites developed and managed in a timely, accurate fashion, but proper planning and management is also essential for the long-term vision and desired outcome of the project.

The secrets in this section help you organize and manage your projects with greater efficiency.

You'll learn to do the following:

- Define your team.
- Identify the best project manager.
- Work to improve collaboration between team members.
- Learn as much about the client, project stakeholders, and audience as possible.
- Work within a budget.
- Create a project workflow.
- Manage time and quality assurance of your project.

The Challenge of Web Project Management

Project management is an art and soft science that has had hundreds—if not thousands—of years to emerge. The process—whether it be for huge industrial construction projects, humanitarian endeavors, or even the day-to-day management and workflow of a fast-food restaurant—of managing a given task from fruition through to completion has been undertaken hundreds of millions of times.

So why does managing Web projects seem to be particularly challenging? There are unique difficulties in terms of how various personalities interact within Web teams.

Some of the problems can be narrowed down into three main issues:

- There is no specific structure when it comes to Web teams.
- There is no industry-wide standard for Web project management.
- There are disparities in the way various members of a given team think.

Toward Consistent Organizational Structure

In the early days of the Web, it appeared that the individual Web designer could address most site needs. There was no call at that time for complex database integration or e-commerce. In fact, most of the technologies now used to manage those complicated tasks didn't even begin to emerge until 1995.

Prior to 1995, most Web sites were small and relatively easy to maintain by one person. But once the Web hit the desktops of consumers, a dramatic shift occurred. Sites needed a lot more to run securely, effectively, and required updating and managing more frequently. This took more hands, and it's where the concept of Web teams really emerged.

The economic shakeups in recent years forced a lot of design firms to close completely, or to reduce staff significantly. This has resulted in great differences in how Web projects are dealt with in various companies, government agencies, and education environments. As with many issues in Web design, there is no real "one-size-fits-all" model, and the likelihood is that there won't ever be, at least not in our lifetimes.

So how do you manage? The secret is to find the sweet spot in the individual project circumstances.

Creating Industry-Wide Standards for Web Project Management

Another challenge is that currently no industry-wide standards exist for Web project management. While some techniques have emerged over the years, such as Rapid Application Development (RAD), Rational Unified Process (RUP), and the concept of Extreme Programming—a means of fast-cycling software projects—the fact is these techniques exist in the programming sector, and while they may be used for Web-related applications development or database integration, they are rarely applied to the overall Web development and design processes themselves. In fact, there are very few standards for the business side of Web design, and it's only been through convention, past experience, and drawing from other models that any form of consistent management practices have emerged.

This is not to say that there aren't emerging books and resources available to help those who are given the job of managing a Web project. This chapter provides as many resources for you as possible, but the reality is that as a Web project manager, you must be a very resourceful individual capable of setting project standards and guidelines appropriate for the team and/or project at hand.

Fixing Disparities in Problem-solving Approaches

A widely discussed topic in managing Web projects is the disparity in personality and subject matter expertise. All of us have, at one time or another, been party to such personality differences within our fields.

The programmer often thinks in abstract but linear chunks of information, whereas a designer might only focus on the visual and creative feel of a project. Marketing departments have their own lingo, as do the financial folks. In Web teams, you end up with not only disparate points of view, but also differences in language use and expression.

While ideally all people working on the Web would at some point be exposed to effective communication skills (often referred to as *soft skills* in the corporate world), the reality is that most people focus their energies on what pays the bills and what interests them specifically, without a lot of encouragement to be more integrated in their thinking and language. This is not a fault, but it does point to the fact that no educational or professional standards have emerged just yet for those of us in the field. As a result, most of what you pick up you learn by the bootstrap method, from colleagues and friends, and on your own via books and Web sites.

As a result, effectively communicating across the subfields within the industry becomes a significant challenge. When working on team-driven projects, this challenge can surface into real problems.

A great project manager can solve this by effectively identifying roles, responsibilities, and goals, and organizing the project in such a way that respects the diverse nature of individuals within a team, while also getting that team to work in tandem toward a common, clear goal.

Secret #21:   Selecting the Project Manager

The job of the project manager is a tough one. He or she has to perform such complex tasks as the following.

♦ Organizing and defining roles of team members

♦ Defining audience, company, and client needs

♦ Finding symbiosis between those often divergent needs

♦ Creating the overall project workflow plan

♦ Ensuring the workflow is followed and any problems are dealt with efficiently

♦ Determining and staying within the project budget

♦ Coordinating communications between all parties involved with the project

♦ Keeping the peace

From a knowledge standpoint, project managers should have a *minimum* of some knowledge regarding every topic that the project will touch. Does this mean that the project manager has to know how to set up and maintain a Web server? Not necessarily, but understanding the broad issues and jargon involved should be part of his or her knowledge base.

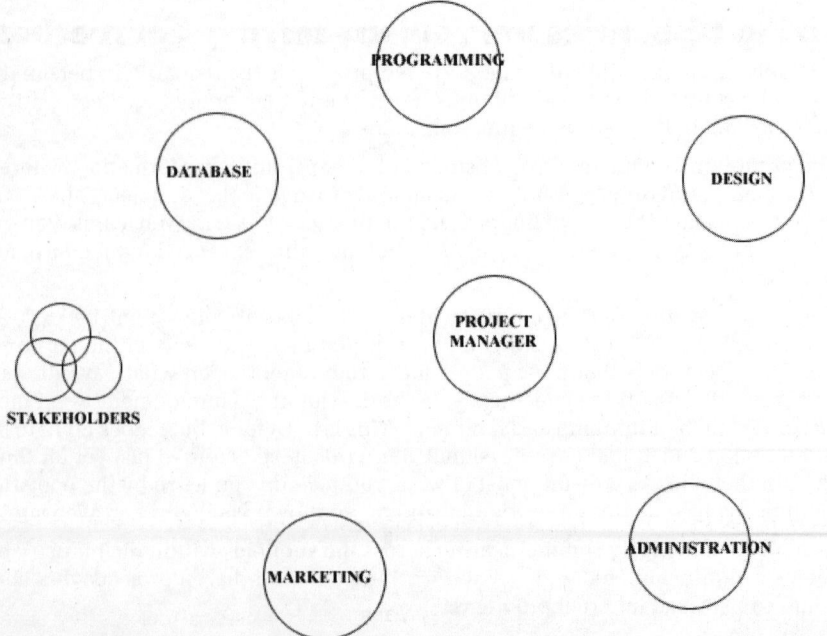

Figure 2-1: The project manager is the hub of any project.

In terms of skills, the most important one a project manager can have is the skill of effective communication. The project manager is the hub in the wheel—all spokes are joined at the hub. It is the project manager's job to keep the wheel rolling along (see Figure 2-1).

> tip
>
> For a wide range of information about project management, check out The Project Management Institute, a nonprofit member organization serving project managers, at `www.pmi.org/`.
>
> The United Kingdom has a range of active resources for project managers, including the Association for Project Management (APM), `www.apm.org.uk/`.
>
> Additional international associations can be found at the International Project Management Association (IPMA), `www.ipma.ch/`.

Secret #22: Defining the Budget

No matter what a project's scope is or the number of individuals involved with its life cycle, budget is going to play an enormous role in how the project is run. Effective budgetary administration of a project means the following:

- ♦ Gaining a full understanding of the project's scope
- ♦ Budgeting for human resources according to real cost
- ♦ Purchasing hardware, software, or related items falls within the project budget
- ♦ Restricting spending on unnecessary steps

Of course, "time is money" so a critical aspect of effective budget management is effective use of time.

> note
>
> A wide range of tools is available to help project managers manage time, delegate responsibilities, and otherwise take care of the business of management.
>
> Visit `www.business.com/directory/management/operations_management/project_management/software/` for more information about helpful budget and project management-related software.

Secret #23: Identifying Goals

If the topic of this secret seems rather basic, let me assure you that while not difficult, it is the most often overlooked or rushed-through part of the planning process. It's also the primary reason that projects wind up with problems.

Specific goals must be defined prior to any project. They include the following:

◆ **Client goals.** These goals are those that the client hopes to achieve.

◆ **Audience needs.** Perhaps the most overlooked issue within an overlooked issue, the audience *must be* taken into consideration at all steps of the project.

◆ **Site intent.** This is the reason the site is being developed in the first place. Interestingly, many people don't really realize why they're creating Web sites, and many failures come about from having an unclear idea of what the site is intended for.

While many planning software packages can help you identify some of these critical issues, nothing beats a pen and paper. Sit down and make lists, as detailed as possible, of each of these goal areas.

Secret #24: Determining the Stakeholders

In the corporate world, the term *stakeholder* has taken on some interesting connotations. Originally a term used to describe the individual who would hold the prize during betting, the word now tends to refer to anyone within an organization who holds power. In terms of a Web project, a stakeholder would be anyone who makes final decisions.

One of the greatest challenges in today's Web design is to sort out who really has power in any given situation. A major secret to successful Web project management means figuring out *exactly* who is holding the power within the organization in terms of final decision making. Typically, this is a job the project manager should undertake, although anyone providing administrative assistance can help work it out.

In analyzing the circumstances, you might very well find that there are numerous stakeholders.

Some general guidelines for clarifying stakeholders follow:

◆ Always determine who has the last word. This person should go on top of your hierarchy and should always be the final go-to person if problems arise.

◆ Determine secondary stakeholders. These are the individuals who will make decisions for specific portions of a project, such as the Marketing Manager, IT Manager, or Art Director. It's helpful if you can make notes about the type of relationship they have with the primary stakeholder—good relationships between a secondary and primary stakeholder can in fact be used to the project manager's advantage should disputes arise during the project.

◆ Try to get agreement ahead of a project that the primary stakeholder (or someone he or she designates) will have the final word in any dispute.

◆ Consider drawing up a hierarchy so the chain of command is clearly understood.

> **tip** While identifying the key decision makers is a very important step toward success, how you interact with them is just as important. Clarifying roles makes this process somewhat easier, but certainly in many cases relationships are challenged.

Consider appointing a moderator at the early stage of any project whose role is solely to help moderate disputes should they arise. This person would be someone other than the project manager who can moderate disputes between the project manager and stakeholders.

If significant problems exist within your organization, some kind of external moderation via a third party might be necessary if disputes cannot be settled.

Secret #25:   Determining Market Needs

Once you've got an idea of the project, the basic needs of the client, site intent, and audience, it's time to determine whether the market will bear out a site of the nature you're trying to develop. This is specific to public Web sites, but even private intranets may be improved by asking similar questions.

The goals of determining market needs include the following:

- Understanding the market size for the product or service, which you'll be representing
- Preparing to manage any economic or other challenging factors within the market in question
- Knowing the market players and examining their methods for success or stumbling blocks
- Identifying potential *competitors* for long-range tracking
- Identifying potential *collaborators* for long-term, mutually beneficial relationships

At this stage of the game, it's very helpful for the project manager to sit down and do serious research to answer the following questions:

- Who are the existing market players?
- How are they using their sites effectively (or not)?
- Who is their targeted demographic and is it different from the one defined by this project?
- Is there any current measure of customer satisfaction?

Of course, the real work comes in once you've got this information. By studying market players, economics, demographics, and current satisfaction levels, you will be best able to position your project effectively in the current market.

Secret #26:   Identifying Roles and Responsibilities

The next step is to identify your team. Have a decent idea of who you have and what they are capable of doing. Even if you are working solo, identifying your role and what aspects of the project you are fully confident that you can be responsible for, helps you determine aspects of the projects for which you'll require outsourcing.

Getting this information organized early on in the game is essential to a project's success.

For both group and individual projects, use the checklist sample shown in Table 2-1 as a guideline for auditing and organizing your role and responsibilities for a project.

Table 2-1: Sample Chart for Web Team Roles and Responsibilities

Individual	Skills	Project Role
Jackie	HTML, CSS, scripting, document management, information architecture, some project management	Markup and CSS coordinator
Lee	Visual design, Web graphic production	Visual rendering of site design, graphic design and production for site
Jerry	Application developer	Provide solutions for server-side interactivity
Kelly	Database developer	Develop necessary database and integrate with site
Max	IT systems administration, security	Set up, run, and maintain Web servers and other technical components
Nicky	Information architect	Design site infrastructure and long-term growth management plan
Sal	Usability and Accessibility specialist	Ensure site is usable and accessible
Terry	Marketing, brand specialist	Oversee the way the site is integrated into the company's larger-scale marketing scheme
Tony	Administrative, organizational, workflow management	Administrator

After the team players are identified, a better idea of who is responsible for what emerges. During your evaluation exercise, you might wish to include any secondary interests of individuals. For example, the IT guy might be a fantastic artist and capable of offering some ideas to the benefit of the team. Ideally, teams work in an integrated fashion, although some experts feel that individuals should only be responsible for their particular depth field.

> **note**   At this point, many experts recommend profiling personalities within the team and associating individuals with such profiles as:
>
> ♦ Ego-oriented
> ♦ Results-oriented
> ♦ Relationship-oriented
> ♦ Detail-oriented

Profiling is said to help categorize personalities within a group and therefore facilitate managing disparate points of view and language use. However, profiling of this nature can also pigeonhole people and limit them to their primary skills without acknowledging that they might have multiple talents to bring to the table.

Secret #27:   Creating a Project Workflow

Okay, your team is in place, you know who the stakeholders are, and you understand the general goals of your project and the constraints of your budget. It's time to put a workflow in place.

Even though project management is as old as the hills, that doesn't mean anyone has come up with the perfect workflow recipe. A lot of information has to be gathered first, including defining specific tasks. However, for this secret the emphasis is on understanding the overarching event cycle.

While there are many models for project workflow, the general flow may be helpful for you to get an overview of how all of the secrets in this chapter can aid you in achieving your goals.

Table 2-2 shows a general project life cycle and which tasks are associated with each aspect of the project.

Table 2-2: Project Workflow Example

Workflow Phase	Associated Tasks
Pre-production	Company and client agree to project, project manager is appointed, management team is appointed, stakeholders are identified, budget and market needs are understood
Task Identification	Tasks are exhaustively examined by the project team, and team members are associated with the tasks
Production	Content is gathered. The project manager oversees team members in all the aspects of the project: Web graphic design, HTML, and other coding, Web programming, content management, and editoria.
Quality Assurance	This important phase places the project under scrutiny. Testing of Web pages, usability, accessibility, multibrowser and platform tests, and other assurances of quality are challenged and, where necessary, repaired
Launch	During launch, the project goes live and marketing and related maintenance tasks ensue
Post-production	Any upgrades, maintenance, and marketing tasks are performed. Many project managers recommend a post mortem of sorts at this phase of the project, inviting all project members to get together and review the project: what worked, what failed, and how can we learn from our experiences?

Secret #28:   Listing Creative Tasks

In order to flesh out the workflow plan, separating out tasks by type will enable assignments to be made in an organized fashion. Clarifying the creative tasks for a given project includes identifying all the design and brand-related tasks.

Examples of creative tasks include:

 ◆ **Content.** What is the voice of the site? How will content be arranged, written, and presented?
 ◆ **Design.** How will the site look and feel? Which company colors, logos, and other identifiers need to be collected and produced?
 ◆ **Multimedia.** Will the site require multimedia? If so, which technologies will be used?

Project managers can work with their design team member(s) to come up with a comprehensive list of creative tasks appropriate to your project's needs.

Secret #29:   Clarifying Technical Tasks

Along with creative tasks, technical tasks must be defined and slotted into the scope of the project.

Technical tasks include the following:

 ◆ Identification of any client-side markup and scripting needs (HTML, XHTML, CSS, and JavaScript)
 ◆ Determination of whether application languages will be required, and if so, which language and platform
 ◆ Discovery of whether database functionality is required for this project, and if so, what kind of database is optimal
 ◆ Server administration (will the server be purchased, co-located, or hosted with an ISP?)

note   **Sometimes client-side markup is managed by the design department or by another team member entirely. Paying special attention to intra-team politics is especially important here, because this is where clashes between designers and technologists most commonly occur.**

Secret #30:   Defining Administrative Tasks

There are numerous administrative tasks, mostly overseen by the project manager, although he or she should feel free to delegate where sensible.

Administrative tasks include the following:

 ◆ Researching and defining the project in clear terms

- Budgeting the project
- Defining team members and tasks
- Overseeing completion of tasks within the context of the project workflow
- Managing client concerns and needs
- Ensuring resources are available
- Managing project timeframes and dealing with potential slip-ups

Secret #31:   Listing Marketing Tasks

Another area where potential issues arise in team dynamics is in marketing. The goals of marketing and the goals of creating an excellent product are sometimes at odds with one another. Defining the tasks before setting project milestones can help shake these issues loose early on in the project process and may well assist the project manager in preventing delays due to warring factions of the team.

Marketing tasks can consist of the following:

- Analysis of demographic
- Research of best marketing options for product or service (ad-based marketing, ranking on search engines, cross-promotional events, and reciprocal links on collaborative sites)
- Organization of press events, including writing and delivery of press releases, and preparation and scheduling of any special events for launch
- Long-term evaluation of market needs, including scheduling of follow-ups past the site's launch and post production, as needed

Secret #32:   Addressing Quality Assurance Concerns

Once a site enters the production phase and everyone is happily at work, attention shifts to managing your project effectively by putting quality assurance (QA) and testing phases in place. If a project manager fails to identify quality assurance issues early in the project and is unable to schedule them accordingly, significant workflow issues can ensue.

Some of the issues examined during the QA phase include the following:

- Validation of markup and CSS
- Testing of all programming features
- Load-bearing tests (especially if the site is expected to be very heavily trafficked)
- Multibrowser and platform testing
- Accessibility testing
- Usability testing
- Editorial review of all content

You measure QA differently depending upon the project, its scope, and its contents. For example, if the site is required to be Section 508-compliant, you must be prepared to test for that compliancy, or time can be lost. Similarly, testing for usability must be assessed, and the methods by which you're going to test will make a huge difference in how the project proceeds. If you're outsourcing to a usability lab, for example, preparing for possible delays within the initial workflow milestones is a helpful way to avoid project slippage.

> **tip**
>
> Many project managers are suggesting that QA be comprised of a separate team that works along with the primary team throughout the project's production phase. This is thought to reduce errors during the production process and shave time off of the QA process itself as a result. I've definitely seen this work in very collaborative environments, but with those teams that might be less comfortable with the idea that someone is constantly looking over their shoulder during production, the idea should be introduced diplomatically, if at all.

Secret #33: Setting Milestones

Once you've got all your research in order, your tasks defined, and your team is chomping at the bit to go, it's time to make the schedule and set specific by-date and project-percentage milestones. Remember the following three points:

- **You have to set milestones!** Not doing so at the outset could cause catastrophic problems that become unmanageable later on.
- **Pad the time.** Figure out a probability for the length of each phase and add at least one-fifth of that time to the schedule.
- **Always be willing to change them.** If you see a slip coming, try to readjust the schedule *without having to affect the bottom line.*

> **tip**
>
> Many experts say that the key to effective scope management is keeping extremely detailed and accurate records of *time*. Every team must do this independently, and the project manager will gather that information and input it into the workflow management software, constantly analyzing where the project is, how far it needs to go, and whether that precious 100 percent date will be met. For more information on productivity software for project managers, see www.project-management-software.org/.

Secret #34: Getting Signoff Throughout the Process

Signoff in this case can refer to any number of steps within the project, but usually has to do with administrative (budget, team structure), technical (use of a specific technology), or creative (approval of design).

The effective project manager will, at this point, have added very specific milestones according to the needs of the project to the master schedule that include getting stakeholder signoff more than once throughout a project process.

In a hierarchical stakeholder model such as that described earlier, this likely means getting secondary stakeholder signoff for part of the project, and primary stakeholder signoff at least a few times during the process.

> tip
>
> **If you're having difficulty getting signoff from a stakeholder, remember that time and money are always deal makers or breakers. Show the stakeholder how you are saving time or money, or the worst case scenario: let them know that without signoff, the project could be delayed or cause budget problems.**

Secret #35: Encouraging Collaboration

As mentioned earlier, some experts believe that encouraging collaboration isn't a very good idea. The argument is this: If disparate personalities are allowed to collaborate, it will take far more time to reach the goal.

While this is often true, and your unique project situations will dictate how much or how little collaborative efforts can be built-in to the project, the highly effective project manager should easily be able to include brainstorming sessions in the project timeline.

Without collaboration, a wide range of problems can occur. It's essential to figure out a good strategy for encouraging effective, collaborative meetings.

Some tips for running effective collaborative meetings include the following:

+ Set a specific goal for the meeting, such as "By the end of this meeting, we'll determine which browsers the Web site must support."
+ Make sure everyone gets an agenda prior to the meeting, outlining the topics, goals, and start and end times.
+ Ask attendees to prepare for the meeting in advance. The designer could be asked to provide mockups of how the site will look in a variety of Web browsers; the server administrator could be asked to collect log data showing browsers using a current (or similar) project site; and the marketing person could bring in demographic information of the current and projected site visitor base.
+ Allot time for each individual to discuss his or her materials, for open discussion, and for closing the meeting.
+ Always walk away from a meeting with a specific action/results item, such as "Team determined that backward compatibility with Netscape 4.x browsers is not relevant to our audience. However, since it is simple enough to at least provide readable content to these users, we will incorporate those practices into the project."

> tip
>
> **Perhaps the wisest advice I've ever heard regarding meetings is this: If you don't need a meeting, don't have one. This means that project managers need to not only write effective schedules, but also be flexible enough to decide when a meeting is needed—or not needed as the case may be.**

To manage a team efficiently (even if you're a "solo" Web designer using outside resources), helping everyone on your team get involved with a given project and to feel a personal relationship with the success of a project helps the individual to be at his or her best, which in turn results in a better project.

If you do decide to encourage collaboration, it's essential to work those brainstorming meetings into the project workflow, and for the project manager to take a strong but diplomatic approach.

You can find some very helpful resources online to aid you in organizing and running meetings more effectively (see Figure 2-2 for one example).

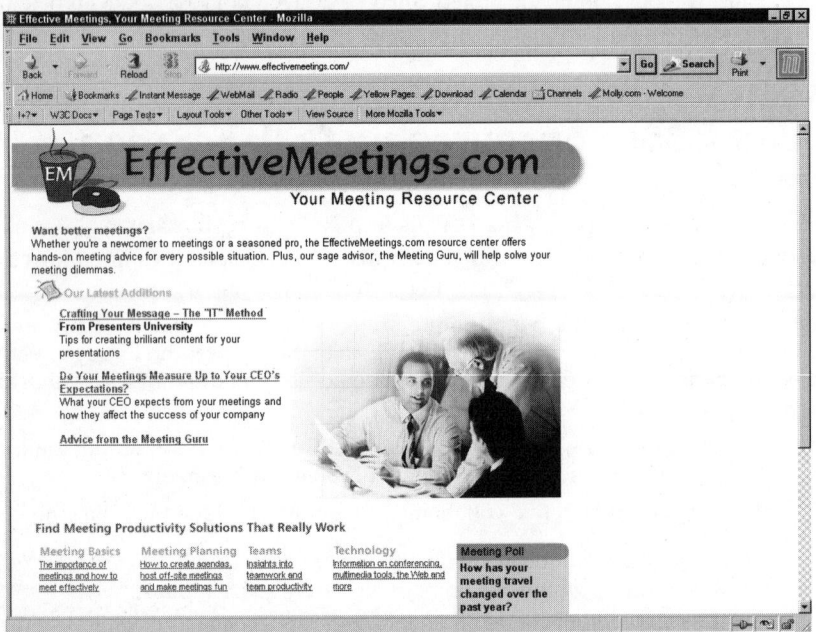

Figure 2-2: Want some help managing meetings effectively? See EffectiveMeetings.com.

Secret #36:   Managing Scope Creep

Scope creep is the slipping of your project from the schedule that you built. If you have to, you'll add to the project, but this is always, always a last resort.

Of course, scope creep occurs frequently, even with very good managers and teams at the helm.

> **note**   Extreme Programming, also known as XP, is a project management process in the programming world that has been especially created for risk-oriented projects. For more information on XP, see **www.extremeprogramming.org/**.

So what do you do if you see dates slipping away? Sit down and reevaluate.

♦ Isolate the problem(s).

- ◆ Work with relevant team members to get a hold of the problem in a timely and sensible fashion without sacrificing important tasks.
- ◆ Consider adding resources (human or technical) if you believe doing so will assist the scope creep rather than adding concerns.
- ◆ If a situation becomes seemingly unmanageable, consider bringing in an external manager or moderator to help solve problems.

There are still so many emerging factors in Web design and development that it's hard to identify risks within Web projects. The best project managers do everything within their knowledge and skill base to prevent scope creep, but the cost of quality must always be measured against the time and money factors, too.

tip

Care for your team members! One of the best ways to avoid scope creep is to avoid burning out your teams. Taking everyone out of the office and doing fun activities can lighten up the emotional load and actually assist in more productive team members, and in turn, result in a better quality project.

Summary

Project management has been around since the beginning of human time. How we found food, learned to cook it, preserve it, and eventually farm, sell, and broker it provides a perfect metaphor: People naturally figure out needs and create organizational structures to go with those needs.

Web project management is still in a nascent form, largely due to the issues raised at the beginning of this chapter. However, with a little of that natural instinct and a lot of looking at other projects—both Web and otherwise—the savvy project manager or project team member will be able to find helpful and even innovative ways to deal with the unique management concerns today's Web professional must face.

Architecting Your Information

◆ ◆

Secrets in This Chapter

◆ ◆

H ow information is designed both from a conceptual and technical standpoint immediately impacts the short- and long-term evolution of a site. Understanding what information is available, how to structure it in such a way that makes sense both to the end-user and the behind-the-scenes interrelationship of other documents within the Web site, and managing growth effectively can be extremely helpful in avoiding problems down the road.

What Is Information Architecture?

Long before the Web, the act of organizing and architecting information was in place. Richard Saul Wurman, author of over 80 books including the acclaimed *Information Anxiety* about making information understandable, coined the term "unformation architecture" in 1976, even though the profession really emerged and matured after people began to struggle with managing information on the Web.

While the exact definition of the term is still being debated, most will agree that *information architecture* is the process of identifying, organizing, and structuring site content. By my way of thinking, this has to extend to the technical implementation of site infrastructure needs. A strong infrastructure means a stable, clean-running, underlying technology, which enables designers to create navigation and interface designs that are useful and relevant to both the information and the needs of the user. People working in this field, which is called "IA" by inside professionals, are referred to as Information Architects.

note

As with many individual topics within Web design and development, IA concepts overlap with other topics. So, some of the topics in this chapter are relevant within all three practices. A good example of this is wireframing and prototyping—both techniques are part of designing for usability as well as appearing within the IA umbrella. Another example would be that the creation of persuasive navigation could fit under either heading. Finally, the creation of style guides may fall to the information designer, the visual designer, the project manager, or the usability specialist.

Sites Big and Small, New and Old

Because the architecture of a Web site so critically influences its interface, IA has taken a very important place in the Web site design process. Web designers working alone are becoming aware of how important organization is to a smooth process.

Designers often come face-to-face with the difficult considerations that must be made during the architecting of a site as the technical and design issues are worked out. IA is not just for large-scale sites or sites that are being redesigned, either—the principles within the field apply equally as much to the small business Web site as they do a major bookseller.

Organic Growth and the Web

Currently, many Web sites are suffering from *organic growth syndrome*—an outgrowth of the innovative yet often haphazard way by which Web sites have been built over the past years.

IA for the Web has emerged as a powerful approach to these concerns, and within this special study area are tremendously helpful secrets to empower Web designers as they develop the information and infrastructure on their sites.

Secret #37: Performing a Content Audit

All of us have gone to the grocery store and come out having spent more time and money than we originally intended. If I'm preparing to cook a big meal or stocking the house with needed items, it's infinitely more practical to audit those items I have and make a list of what I actually need. Then, I know precisely which items I'll want at the grocery and be able to navigate its aisles and lines in less time, stick to a predefined budget, and forget fewer—if any—items than had I not taken the time to audit and plan my errand.

Before any actual architecting of information can begin, a complete audit of content must be performed. This is true of brand new as well as established Web sites. In either case, an audit provides the architects with a real view of what elements they work with.

Goals of a content audit include the following:

+ Identify the strengths and weaknesses within the content and infrastructure of the existing or planned site
+ Discover problems with current architecture and site performance
+ Organize content into logical groups
+ Prepare content for examination and implementation of content hierarchies and management
+ Gain real information regarding the scope of the project at hand

As you read in Chapter 2, the project manager is often responsible for organizing his or her team and coordinating site production-related activities, including content audits. If you are working alone, the content audit should be performed at some point immediately after the information-gathering period.

note
Content audits are important not only to the large-scale project, but smaller sites, too. Both team and solo designers and developers need to know what information is being managed.

Activities typical to the content audit process include the following:

+ **Thorough review of all existing content.** In this step, all content for the Web site is organized and charted in preparation of evaluation.
+ **Evaluation of all content.** During the evaluation step, the gathered content is evaluated for its integrity. Unnecessary or duplicate content is often removed after an evaluation, helping to streamline the process of the site's architecture.
+ **Sorting of content by relevancy.** An excellent way of improving the organization of content is to group like items, just as you'll find in a well-organized grocery. All the soups are arranged together, as are the juices, and cleaning supplies. Certainly, this sorting of like items in real-world situations is not accidental—it is, in fact, a form of IA applied to the real, rather than virtual world.

tip If you are working in a team environment, it can be very helpful to delegate the evaluation and sorting of content as it relates to a given department. For example, the Web graphics on an existing site are likely to be managed by the team's designers or document authors, and they may well have a better idea of what they have and what they need. Then, the designated IA project manager or design team member can review and audit the information more readily.

Table 3-1 shows a simple example of a content audit in the relevancy phase for a fictitious shoe company, "Meyer Shoes." In this case, the audit is looking at graphics and Web-related documents for its current catalog offering.

Table 3-1: Content Audit (By Relevancy) for Fictitious Project "Meyer Shoes"

Men's Shoes	Women's Shoes	Children's Shoes
20 thumbnail graphics of all men's styles for 2004	45 thumbnail graphics for all women's shoe styles for 2004	12 thumbnail graphics for children's styles for 2004. Missing 3 thumbnail images
20 full-size graphics for catalog detail pages	40 full-size graphics. Missing several styles	15 full-size graphics covering all children styles for 2004
20 HTML documents with complete descriptions of all 2004 styles	No HTML documents for the catalog available at this time	5 of 15 children's shoe styles are ready; project manager expects the remainder to be completed within one week

The relevancy, or categorization, of the information into three separate categories, Men's, Women's, and Children's shoes, helps streamline the audit process. By breaking it down into categories of relevance, you can quickly see what's complete and where missing items appear.

The breakdown of content into categories becomes a critical part of the information's technical structure. Instead of having a single image section for all shoes, for example, the infrastructure of the site can now be managed by category, making it easier from a maintenance and upgrade perspective as well as forming the basis for a much more reasonable, usable front end.

Content audits are extremely beneficial for a number of reasons. The two most immediate are that audits result in identifying problem areas and a roadmap emerges as a guide to moving ahead with content repair, replacement, and management.

Secret #38: Determining Hierarchies of Content

Hierarchies are the basis of much of our world—from governments and organizations, to the structure within computer programming—hierarchies are frameworks for organization.

> **note** When dealing with information for the Web and how it will be architected, understanding hierarchies is a basic requirement. Understanding that hierarchies should be crafted and built as specifically to the categorization of content as possible is critical, too.

A hierarchy has a root, and the root appears at the top of the hierarchy. It is from there, not from the farthest leaf, that you measure the system. Each branch is specialized, and becomes increasingly more specialized as you follow the branch system.

In Secret #1, you reviewed a simple relevancy example, which, if mapped out, displays a very clear hierarchy, such as that shown in Figure 3-1.

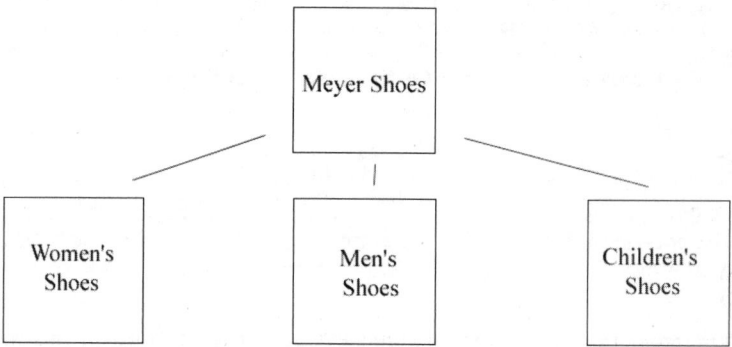

Figure 3-1: A simple hierarchy built from category relevance.

In this case, Meyer Shoes is the root of the hierarchy, with the branches consisting of the three categories defined earlier, Women's shoes, Men's shoes, and Children's shoes, comprising the top level of the hierarchy. To make a simple site structure from this hierarchy, you'd end up with a Home Page and three main sections for the site.

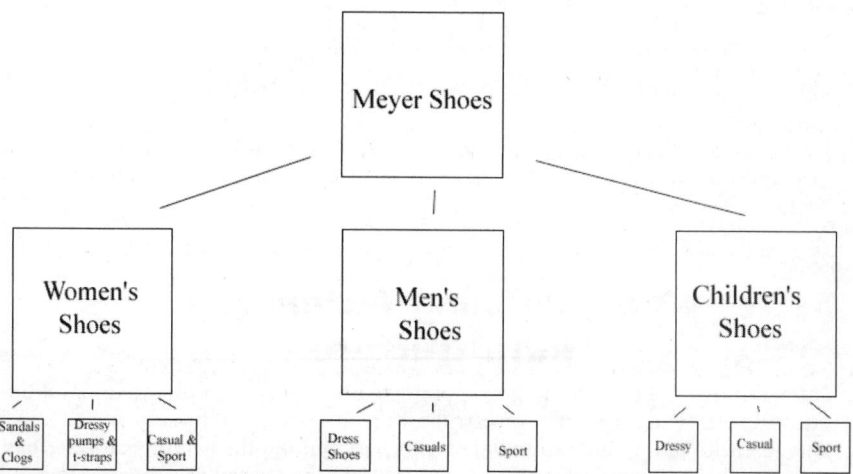

Figure 3-2: A more explicit hierarchy based on further breakdown of content.

Realistically, as you study your audited content and accurately categorize it, you will get more and more explicit with your hierarchy determination. Depending on the size of your site, you will determine hierarchies within hierarchies, as shown in Figure 3-2.

> **tip** How explicit your hierarchies become should relate directly to the amount of content you have. The smaller the Web site, the easier it is to manage by keeping it simple. If you are working with a very large amount of content, the content hierarchy is going to be far more explicit.

Web sites that have a hierarchy with many top-level categories but not a lot of explicit hierarchy structure beneath those categories are referred to as *shallow*. Those with fewer top-level categories but deeper content are referred to as *deep*. Table 3-2 provides a comparison of the two.

Table 3-2: Comparing Hierarchy Options for Web Sites

Shallow Hierarchy	Deep Hierarchy
2–5 tiers	Up to 9 tiers
Contains root (home page) and top-tier categories, few or no lower tiers	Contains root, top-tier, and at least one or more additional tiers within the structure

Experts recommend that sites with a smaller content base, such as a small business Web site or personal site (see Figure 3-3), use shallow hierarchies.

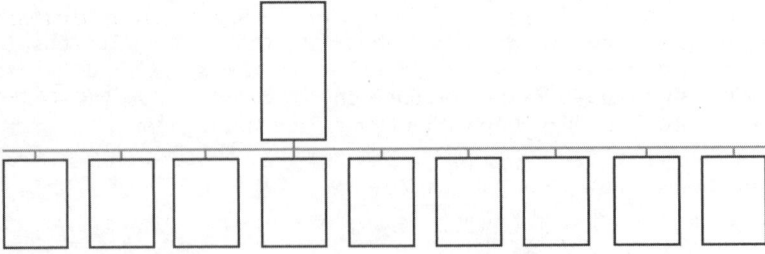

Figure 3-3: Smaller sites work well with a shallow hierarchy.

Deep hierarchies are applicable to those sites where large amounts of content are being managed and archived, such as news, portal, and commerce sites (see Figure 3-4).

Secret #39: Defining Technical Infrastructure

Interestingly, not all information architects are involved in the creation of the technical infrastructure. This infrastructure is the system of folders and files on the server. Quite often, the individual or group managing the server puts together the infrastructure. Divorcing the site structure from the overall IA process can result in many problems, the "organic growth syndrome" issue being an excellent example.

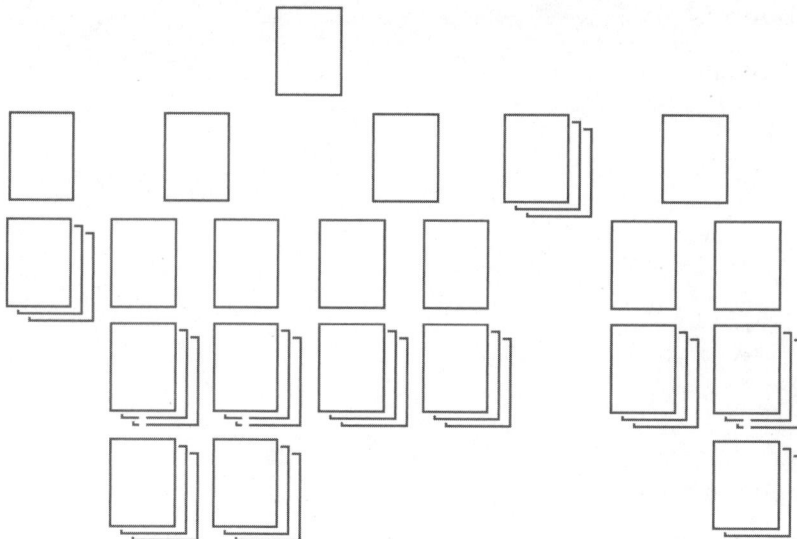

Figure 3-4: A deep hierarchy is effective for larger Web sites.

While it is impossible to envision what a successful Web site will look like in one year, or ten years, it is possible to build a technical infrastructure that reflects the content while leaving room for growth. That's why I think ensuring that the content hierarchy process and the technical infrastructure process are closely integrated—with the designer or team members working on infrastructure *only after a complete audit and content hierarchy* has been designed.

Some of the compelling reasons an effective architecture based on content is necessary include the following:

- Information on the server will be organized in direct response to the real, existing data about content categories.
- Images and other media can be organized by category and type.
- It provides better control over URL length.
- It brings far more awareness of exactly where specific types of data should be stored on the server.
- Better organization provides more flexibility in making the content hierarchy wider and deeper should the need arise, preventing or minimizing out-of-control growth.

If you take the simple Meyer's Shoes content hierarchy and work on a directory structure based on the three categories defined earlier, you'd end up with a technical structure somewhat like that found in Figure 3-5.

Secret #40: Determining Naming Conventions

I've read a lot of material geared toward educating Web designers and developers about naming conventions and, unfortunately, this topic is often glossed over. "Create file and directory names that make sense to you" is written more times in

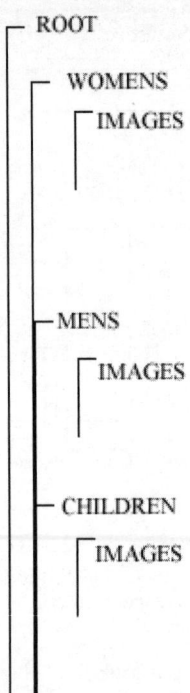

Figure 3-5: Technical architecture model for sample Web site.

the literature than I can count, and while the thought is fundamentally correct, it's incomplete.

Yes, your directory and filenames should make sense to you, but they should also make sense to your users as well as any other developers and designers working on the site. The reasons for this have mostly to do with usability and how users experience and interact with Web sites. There are also practical considerations such as case, use of characters, and length of resulting URLs.

Here's a list of guidelines to help you determine good naming conventions for your technical architecture:

- ◆ **Use short, clear terms.** Naming the Meyer Shoe site directory structure with men, women, and children, respectively, keeps things very clear, and helps your visitors to orient themselves within a site. This is also true of document and image filenames. A good rule of thumb is to ensure that all names should be ten characters or less (preferably less).
- ◆ **Use lower case.** Some Web servers are case-sensitive. As a result, you need to be sure your paths are consistent. I recommend choosing lower case for directory and filenames in all instances.
- ◆ **Avoid reserved (also known as "special") characters.** A number of characters are reserved for specialty use when configuring servers and their behavior and working with protocols specific to the Web. While you can conceivably use any character in a filename that you want, to avoid problems, it's best to steer clear of any of these characters in your filenames (see Table 3-3 for more detail).

Table 3-3: Characters and their Use in Naming Conventions

Character	Use
Space	Never
|	Avoid
&	Avoid
*	Avoid
%	Avoid
~	Can be used for directory naming on properly configured servers
_	Freely
-	Freely

note   You will see some of these characters, especially the ampersand and percent sign, appear in URLs generated by server-side applications. This is acceptable. The point here is to have you avoid using these symbols in your actual directory and filenames.

Another interesting point is that while you can use the dash (-) and underscore (_) freely within directory and filenames, a lot of controversy has been generated over this seemingly innocuous issue. The tendency is for most technical people to prefer an underscore, but in this case, it really is a personal choice. My recommendation is to choose one or the other and stick with it consistently.

If you imagine the resulting URL for the Children's running shoe page, it's www.sitename.com/childrens/running/. Not too long, yet very intuitive.

Secret #41:   Site Mapping

Creating site maps is the physical mapping of your site's contents. Site maps may be generated throughout a project's life cycle. They provide a powerful tool for all team members to gain an aerial view of the Web site.

note   A site map is also referred to as the *blueprint* of a Web site.

Site maps can contain a variety of information, including the following:

+ Visual representation of site pages
+ Hierarchical representation of the site in a flow-chart style
+ Notations regarding links between pages
+ Notations regarding external links

warning   The larger a site, the more complicated its map. Therefore, it's extremely important that it be mapped correctly and updated frequently during the project life cycle.

Typically, mapping the site is done using mapping tools. Many commercial Web projects help keep track of your content and generate a subsequent site map. Figure 3-6 shows a map of my Web site as displayed in Dreamweaver MX 2004.

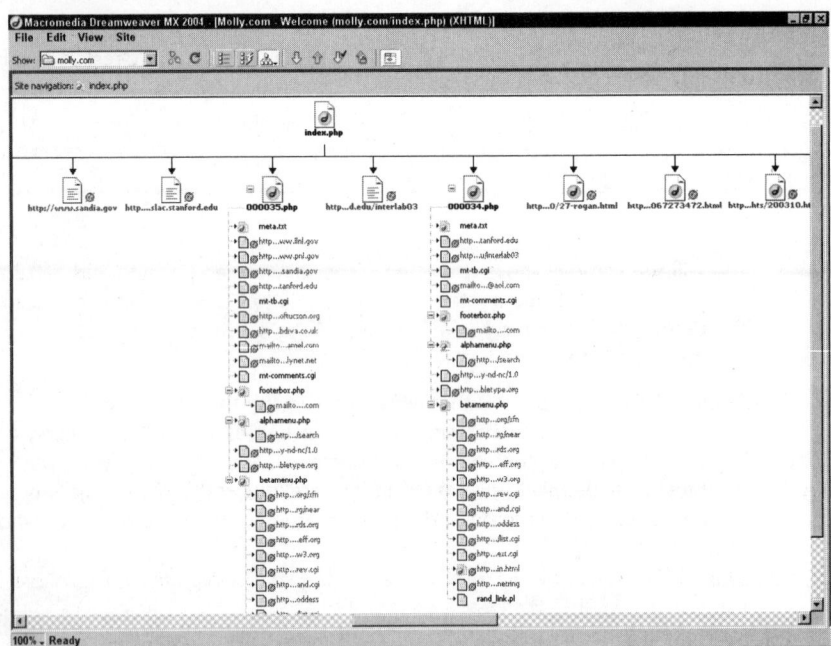

Figure 3-6: Site mapping in Macromedia Dreamweaver.

Secret #42:   Understanding Wireframing

In his book *Information Anxiety2*, Richard Saul Wurman (mentioned earlier as the man who coined the term IA and is considered its "father" by many) claims that there are two parts to a given problem. He defines these as being the "what" and the "how."

Wireframing addresses the *what* portion rather than the *how*. In the process of wireframing, the site's content and hierarchies are "framed" in a series of documents (the wireframes) that actually reflect the physical makeup of your documents. Bear in mind that these documents are far more focused on the structural than the visual, and for good reason. This is the step that comes *before* prototyping the site. You're not looking for information such as which colors will be used for the navigation links (that's considered a "how"). You're looking for what the navigation consists of (that's a "what").

Information typically dealt with in the wireframing process includes the following:

- Clarifying section names and how they'll be represented on the site
- Detailing primary navigation
- Defining secondary navigation where needed
- Providing a basic layout sketch for known content

note   **Wireframe documents can be created in a number of ways. Some designers sketch their wireframes, and others use HTML and related tools, such as Dreamweaver. Many designers who wireframe their sites use charting or drawing programs such as Visio, Photoshop, or Illustrator.**

In the case of Meyer Shoes, the wireframe pages would reflect the general layout scheme, navigation schemes, and planned content areas.

tip   **You'll find an excellent article, "HTML Wireframes and Prototypes: All Gain and No Pain" by Julie Stanford at www.boxesandarrows.com/ archives/html_wireframes_and_prototypes_all_gain_ and_no_pain.php.**

Secret #43:   Developing Prototypes

While similar to wireframing, the prototype portion of an architectural process is applying the "how" to the "what" of a wireframe. In the wireframe process, your goal is to find the somewhat intangible place between concept and fruition—the piece that fits between the actual structure and the visual representation.

A prototype, unlike the wireframe, seeks to define aspects of the site such as its visual appearance. Prototypes are flat, noninteractive graphical mockups of a page's layout.

Prototyping is important because of the following:

- Prototypes can be shared with the full team and the client for input and modification prior to production.
- Prototyping allows you to see the visual counterparts of the structural relationships you've created.
- A prototype can prepare your site for early usability testing (see Chapter 4, "Making Sites Usable and Persuasive").

Most experienced designers understand that in order to make prototyping cost-effective, not all pages of a site are prototyped. If I were prototyping the Meyer Shoes site, I would prototype the following documents only:

- Home page
- Top-tier page
- Product page

This way, changes can be implemented promptly prior to actually producing all pages of the site. The only exception to this streamlined approach would be if the actual top-tier pages were significantly different than each other in some way.

> **tip**
> Getting sign-off from stakeholders on a completed prototype is not only wise, but should be considered imperative. It is from this point forward that heavy production on the site ensues. Be sure you are designing to an approved prototype.

Secret #44:   Creating User Pathways

Take a close look at this book. Look at the front cover. Find any teasers that get you to open the book? Look at the back cover—any information there to help you as a reader to get to the information you actually want? Flip through the book; what catches your eye? Now examine the Table of Contents, and check out the Index.

All of these aspects of a technically-oriented book are what's referred to as the *flip factor*. Books are architected in very specific way to provide you, the reader, with various paths you can take to get to information.

In terms of a Web site's "flip factor," auditing, wireframing, and prototyping all lead us to the shaping of our site's architecture and, ultimately, the site's usability and content design. We're creating the interface between a site's technical back-end and its welcoming front-end. If a book, which is a mostly linear medium, can benefit from user pathways, so can a Web site. What's more, because different types of people use navigation schemes and site entry points in different ways, creating a variety of pathways to information is a necessity.

> **note**
> Not all Web site visitors will enter your site via the home page. Depending upon your visitor's personality, he or she might use different or even unusual steps to get from one place to another within the site.

The experienced Web designer and developer will right away notice the crossover between IA and usability at this point in the process. *How* users will navigate your site is a major part of usability and user interface design (see Chapter 4). Despite the crossover in application, putting the implementation of user pathways into the IA process lays down the opportunity for usability testing to begin very early in the process.

To figure out how a user might trailblaze his or her way through your site, you must figure out the scenario: Which user is attempting to achieve what? For example, a buyer goes to the Meyer Shoe site with the goal of buying a pair of women's shoes. How the buyer gets to the right place to take that action is another matter. She may go to the site via its home page and follow the options from that point. Or, as a returning customer, she may have the women's shoes main page bookmarked. Another scenario could be that she originally bought a pair of running shoes for her ten-year-old nephew, and has the children's section bookmarked. If she starts on the main children's shoe page, how does she get to women's shoes? It's your job to help the buyer by first figuring out who is visiting your site and under what range of potential circumstances.

Begin by listing all the various tasks an individual might perform at your site, such as the following:

♦ Sign up for a new diet plan
♦ Research new minivans
♦ Go shopping for home electronics
♦ Check bank account balances

Study potential user scenarios in relation to these tasks, and then list the potential pathways that can be used to complete those tasks.

note   In their excellent book, *Web ReDesign: Workflow that Works,* workflow experts Kelly Goto and Emily Cotler say that there are two predominant types of user pathways.

A *functional* pathway is a pathway that results in having to use functional and programmatic aspects of the site, such as shopping carts, logins, and complex searches.

A *nonfunctional pathway* is one that is not dependent upon technical requirements, rather its goals are related to information such as looking at the company's principals, looking up phone numbers, and so on.

In all cases, knowing the goal of the individual is imperative to making sure they get to the function or feature they require.

With many small Web sites, the user pathway process shouldn't take very long. However, if you are working on a very large Web site, the process can be time consuming. Project managers should keep a close eye on this part of the project—it's a very necessary step and, as mentioned, helps get usability testing started far earlier in the process. If it's taking too long, focus more on functional pathways first, because nonfunctional pathways are usually easier to construct.

Secret #45:   Creating Archive Systems

A commonly overlooked area of architecture is how to design archive systems. The challenge with archives comes about when you're creating date-related content that you want to keep available for site visitors, but will roll off of the top-level hierarchy at some point. Managing the means by which this content is published means a world of difference when it comes to the site visitor being able to find that content.

While not a specific step within the IA process, the need to create effective archives is becoming increasingly clear as Web sites grow in scope. Archive systems are most relevant to the following:

♦ Large-scale public Web sites
♦ Intranet sites for industry, government, research, and education
♦ News sites
♦ Personal Weblog sites (some of these sites are becoming enormous!)

The main issues in creating archive systems are as follows:

♦ Understanding your content
♦ Categorizing content accordingly
♦ Structuring the directories and documents in such a way that they can be permanently stored and retrieved

If you're thinking "Hey! I did all this when auditing my content," you're correct. The big difference is figuring out how to make a given document *permanent*. Changing a URL or filename is a major issue, so you don't want to do that if you can avoid it. The best way to do this is to know while going in, which documents will require archiving and permanently house them by date, category, and topic.

> tip
>
> **The best thing you can do to ensure long-term structure for archives is to determine which documents will be archived, and leave them in that location forever.**

These days, archives are managed by a content management system (CMS). CMSs are an extremely hot topic these days, mostly due to the fact that they are very often extremely expensive and difficult to implement. What's more, any good CMS will allow you to import existing information into its format, so if you aren't using a CMS with archiving for a given project, consider building your own archiving structure and then worrying about the technology later.

> note
>
> **Having a search feature on all pages is a tip you're going to read quite often in this book. If you have a very large site, you can provide additional user pathways to detailed content such as archives via advanced searches that allow the site visitor to search using date, keyword, content, and topic filters.**

Secret #46: Considering Frequency of Updates and Redesigns

Another issue that sneaks into the long-term concerns of a site's architecture is how frequently the information is going to be updated and the site freshened up. This relates to IA because it is during the IA process that you can determine areas of potential technical growth of the site for the long term, allowing designers to tap into technologies such as server-side includes, application and database technologies, and other document and function-related processes *without having to redesign the infrastructure*.

> note
>
> **Always anticipate that a Web site will grow or be redesigned. If you don't build your architecture without some organized awareness of what might *potentially* emerge, you are at a serious disadvantage later on, when growth does occur and redesign is imminent.**

Along with helping to create a scalable architecture, ensuring that you make plans to update and redesign the site early on allows you to anticipate with improved accuracy what kind of growth your document base is going to expect. This means you'll be able to architect your site to allow for scalability.

Secret #47: Setting Site-Wide Standards

As I mentioned earlier, it may be up to someone other than the IA to set and document the standards being used. However, it can also fall into their jurisdiction because the IA should at this point have a deep understanding of how the site and its interface work.

Whether managed by your IA team, design team, or content team, it is always helpful to set site-wide standards. These are the various production guidelines that the entire team will follow as it works through the production concerns of the site. Setting these standards can be the job of the lead designer, the project manager, or can be done by a full team.

> tip   If you are working in a team environment, getting feedback from all team members for site standards will help you avoid leaving important information out.

Some of the concerns for which you should study your site and create a standard include the following:

- Code
- Code commenting
- Colors
- Directory structures
- File naming conventions
- Graphic formats
- Maintenance list
- Accessibility guidelines
- Content guidelines
- Team members and roles
- Policies

> tip   Project managers should encourage site-wide standards early on, and check on all relevant site standards during the Quality Assurance (QA) phase.

Secret #48: Developing a Site-Wide Style Guide

The style guide gathers up all the various standards you've created for your site and places them in a single guide so that all members of a team can access the information and ensure that all the guidelines are followed. Whenever a team member has a concern, he or she can check the guide before asking questions, saving everyone time.

Style guides typically reflect all the information found after the development of site-wide standards. During their redesign of the New York Public Library, Jeffrey Zeldman and Carrie Bickner co-created an excellent style guide for coding standards (see Figure 3-7).

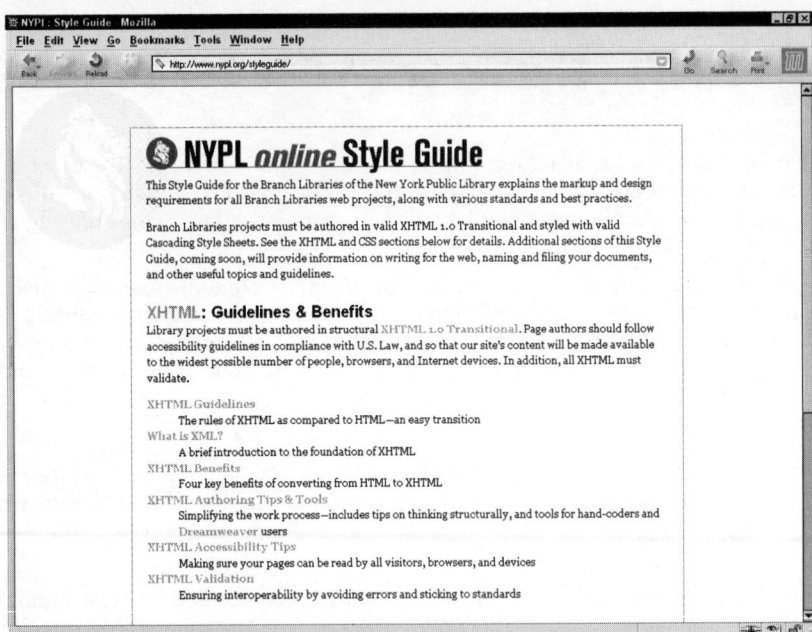

Figure 3-7: The online style guide for the New York public library.

The NYPL Style Guide, at www.nypl.org/styleguide/, is extremely straightforward and provides a starting-point guideline for those interested in developing a practical style guide.

> **tip**
>
> I've found it especially helpful to publish the guides in multiple formats: PDF, Web, and print. This makes the guide widely available to everyone no matter where they are.

Summary

How information is managed can be a very challenging process. There is no doubt that the redesigns and upgrades for many Web sites have proven the need for intelligent IA going into a project. In deconstructing these sites, many of which suffer from organic growth problems—inconsistent naming, poorly organized archives, navigation systems that are limited because they were designed to reflect a more simple architecture—we become very aware that IA is as essential to the site development process as graphic design or HTML.

As we begin applying IA methods, we also begin to grasp the way the various fields within the Web profession are layered and interwoven. Good project management and planning are integral to a smooth project, good IA is essential to bridge the technical and presentational aspects of a Web site, and IA inevitably is a portion of usability and content design—two of the topics you'll be delving into more deeply in the following chapters.

Chapter

4

Making Sites Usable and Persuasive

◆ ◆

Secrets in This Chapter

◆ ◆

S triking a balance between usability recommendations, practical experience, and usability testing is an accurate factor in making choices when it comes to usability practices and user experience.

This chapter offers some tried-and-true wisdom of usability as it applies to common Web site features to help you find that middle ground. Although this chapter is not a comprehensive usability tutorial, it can provide you some of the best secrets to ensuring your site is both usable and persuasive for its intended audience.

Secret #49:   Create Consistent Branding

When you think of branding, you might think of logos, colors, taglines, and names relating to a given product, company, or service. Although branding encompasses those elements, *true* branding is a far more powerful and subtle issue than you might expect.

Successful branding is about creating an emotional relationship between an individual and the representative company or product. This means that good branding creates a response in people—whether a tagline makes us feel comfortable, or a logo makes us feel energetic, or a color scheme makes us calm—these responses are the desired results of effective branding.

Branding can be achieved using a variety of techniques. Contemporary marketing theory breaks down branding into two types:

◆ **Direct Experience.** In direct experience branding, the emotional relationship is one-to-one. If you have a great burger at Ye Olde Burger Shoppe, the satisfying results of that meal relate emotionally to the product and brand.

◆ **Indirect Messaging.** The indirect method uses slogans, sponsored events, and promotions to connect people to product brands. The key to successful indirect messaging is repetition, usually in the form of TV and magazine ads, and billboards.

Web sites can benefit from both forms of marketing (Figure 4-1), although Web sites themselves are almost always going to be a direct experience for people these days. You go to a site for a reason—to read a Weblog, purchase copies of a favorite author's books, and so forth. You interact with the site, and your experience there creates the emotional one-to-one feeling found within direct experience marketing.

When creating a lasting relationship between an end user and a product, company, organization, or service, Web designers need to plan the direct experience to have a specific emotional result.

For example, my bank's Web site provides excellent service, useful management tools, and provides me with an emotional sense of security. This kind of bonding between a site's visitor and a product can be accomplished using a range of specific usability techniques—many described throughout this chapter.

But we can also draw from indirect messaging techniques to enhance our goals. All of the following things can work on the indirect level by providing repetitive images:

◆ Using consistent placement for logos from page to page

◆ Using consistent color and graphic styles

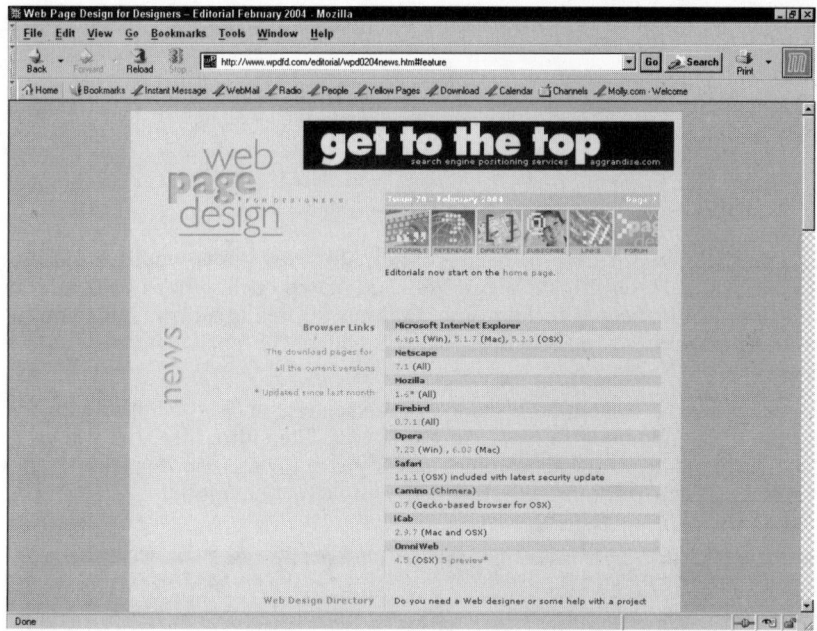

Figure 4-1: Ads on Web sites are considered indirect messaging, but the actual Web site itself is a direct experience.

◆ Typography
◆ Iconography

Combining an effective direct experience and consistent statement of brand will help you to bond your site visitors to your site, creating lasting, rewarding relationships.

Secret #50: Determining Primary Navigation

A primary navigation scheme is the main navigation for your site. It may be the only navigation you have, or you could combine it with other navigation, depending upon the scope and requirements of the site.

At the heart of any Web site's usability lies its navigation. How you evolve your navigation schemes will depend upon a lot of the work you've done in planning and architecting the site. But it is vitally important to make sure you really hone in on the primary features and functions of your site, reducing the number of options and placing them in an order that is logical.

An example of logical ordering might be as follows:

1. Home
2. Books
3. Video
4. Audio
5. Contact

Whereas illogical ordering might be the following:

1. Video
2. Contact
3. Audio
4. Home
5. Books

Looks pretty simple, right? Well, that's the point. You know what it's like to do certain tasks, such as driving a car. We've repeated such actions over and over in our lives, so the acts of accelerating, braking, signaling a turn, and so on have become a part of us. We're not actively thinking out each step; it's become automatic and easy.

Navigation should be that for a visitor. Some readers may be familiar with Steve Krug's aptly named book *Don't Make Me Think!*. The entire idea that site visitors should not have to work out complex tasks just makes sense. Figure 4-2 shows Designtopia, a site with a common-sense approach to navigation.

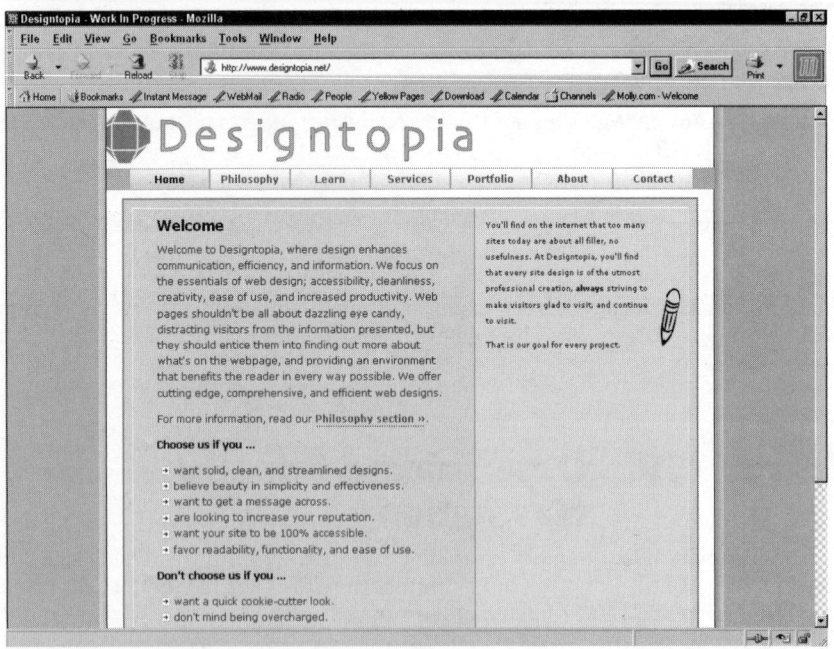

Figure 4-2: Designtopia offers extremely simple, persistent, and obvious navigation on all of its pages, making the experience of navigating the site a no-brainer.

Using the information you gather when wireframing, prototyping, and mapping your site, primary navigation schemes emerge quite readily. And when it comes to any navigation scheme, one thing is certain: Simple is always better.

> tip
>
> You can also think of navigation as a form of indirect messaging. Always keep primary navigation in the same location, using the same visual styles, throughout your site.

Secret #51:   Secondary Navigation

Secondary navigation assists users in drilling down further into the hierarchical structure of your site. Secondary navigation should be reserved for detail—the primary navigation remains dominant and consistent in its placement throughout a site.

Forms of secondary navigation include the following:

◆ **Alternative text links.** This technique is a very common practice of including text links on those pages where image-based navigation is in use. This helps with the accessibility of the site (see Figure 4-3).

Figure 4-3: Alternative text links provided on Lynda.com. This technique is in widespread use as optional navigation.

◆ **Drop-down menus.** These are menus for quick access to specific areas of a site (see Figure 4-4).

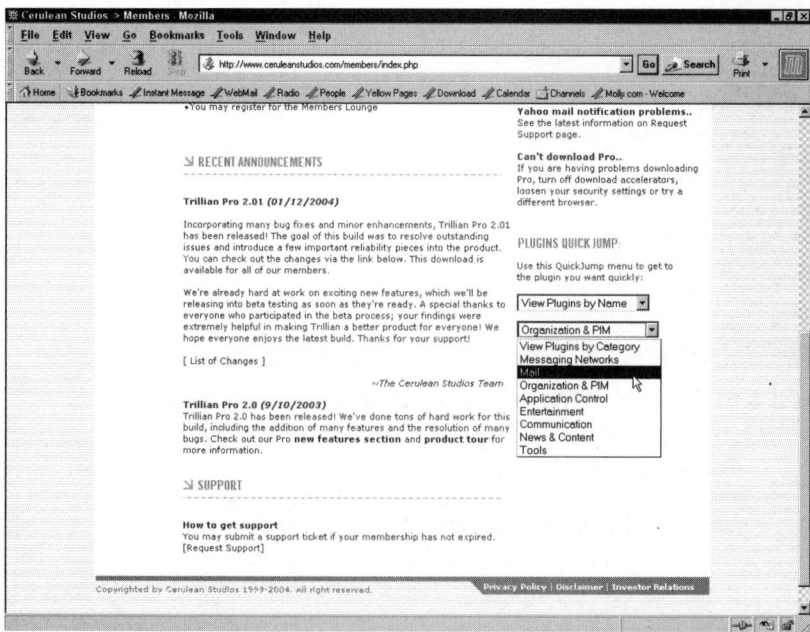

Figure 4-4: Drop-down menus are a popular means of adding quick access to site sections.

◆ **Section submenus.** Larger sites often have submenus for individual sections (see Figure 4-5).

Adaptive Path Reports

Figure 4-5: Primary navigation with a section submenu on the Adaptive Path Web site provides a classic example of secondary navigation.

The most important secret when designing secondary navigation is to *make sure it doesn't conflict* with the primary scheme. It should appear in a different location, whether below or to the side of the primary navigation, and it should appear only when necessary.

Figure 4-6 shows a prototype page with "zones." Notice how primary and secondary navigation are in distinctly different zones.

Figure 4-6: Mapping potential navigation zones on a prototype page.

> note
>
> Secondary navigation should be distinctive in its visual design, yet not so much so as to call more attention to it than the primary.

Secret #52: Grouping Navigation by Like Items

While working with your information architecture, you'll find that as you begin to develop navigation schemes, you'll be listing out specific areas of a site. It's very helpful to take such a list and then group like items, combining them to reduce the number of options and the need for the site visitor to think much about where things might be located.

Here's a list of potential Web site navigation items for a portal site:

- Quote
- Horoscope
- Technology
- Sports
- Fortune
- Weather
- World
- Nutrition
- Business
- Poll
- Fitness
- TV listings
- Movie listings
- Lottery
- Travel

When you have the list of items complete, sit down and try to identify like groups. Right off the bat here, I see two primary groups. The first is News:

- World
- Sports
- Weather
- World
- Business
- Technology

The other group could be Activities:

- Quote
- Horoscope
- Fortune
- Poll
- Fitness
- Nutrition
- TV listings
- Movie listings
- Lottery
- Travel

Upon closer examination, activities can be broken up into activities and entertainment. Activities would be related to the site itself:

- Quote
- Horoscope
- Fortune
- Lottery
- Poll

The entertainment category would include the following:

- TV listings
- Moving listings
- Fitness
- Nutrition
- Travel

At this point, we have three top navigation areas: News, Activities, and Entertainment. Depending upon the site's needs and structure, you can break things down even further. The point is for you to organize, merge, and combine topics in effective logical groups so the site visitor doesn't have to.

Secret #53:   Iconography and Language Use

The use of icons (iconography) in navigation was a popular technique long before we began studying navigation for the Web. Navigation is, of course, a part of any user interface—whether it be software programs such as Word, kiosks, CD-ROMs, or Web sites.

Iconography typically relies on metaphor. Metaphor is the symbolic representation of an object or idea. That representation defines some likeness between the symbol and its related object or idea. Familiar uses of metaphor in iconography include the following:

- An envelope to represent e-mail
- A shopping bag or stack of wrapped boxes to represent shopping
- A stock ticker to represent finances
- A pencil to represent articles
- A briefcase to represent job and work

If you think about these examples carefully, you'll see that they are very clear in their relationship. This is referred to as a *concrete* metaphor. The symbol is very literal (see Figure 4-7). These icons were designed specifically to assist foreign students whose first language might not be English in finding services online such as e-mail, weather information, medical information, prescription refills, and assistance.

> note The icons in Figure 4-7 and the Web site screen shot in 4-9 are © Chris Silverman, and used here with permission. Please see Chris's site, www.csideaworks.com/, for some great iconographic design and inspiration.

Another type of metaphor in iconography is referred to as *abstract*. An abstract metaphor can be a literal image that is abstractly related to the corresponding object or idea. More commonly, abstract metaphors are created symbols that have no specific meaning until related to the object or idea in question. The designer makes the suggestion between the icon's design and the related idea—with abstract metaphors, the meaning is not literal (see an example in Figure 4-8).

Figure 4-7: Concrete iconography from designer Christopher Silverman.

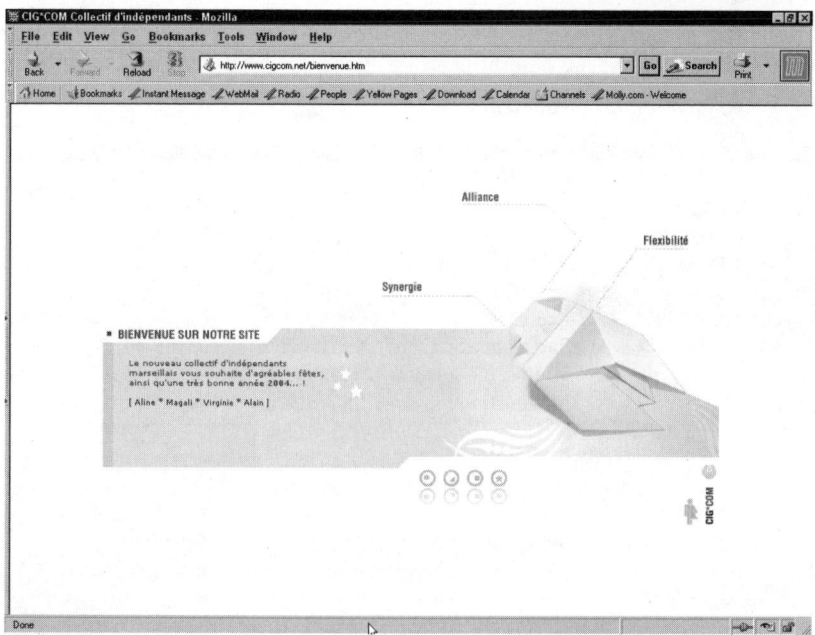

Figure 4-8: Can you find the navigation? It's the circles with shapes along the bottom of this design. Abstract iconography is based on the designer's conceptual response to the ideas being expressed.

Generally, if you're trying to make your site very usable, very concise, and are encouraging the "Don't Make Me Think" ideology, the designer should stick to concrete metaphor in iconography. Of course, your content and audience will shape your design decisions. For example, abstract iconography might work well on a Web site featuring the works of abstract artists. Only your research and planning will help you determine if abstract metaphor is a reasonable choice for your navigation icons.

Of course, many designers never choose to use iconography because language is sufficient. Simply styling the text or creating images using words to suggest navigation options is a completely legitimate way to go. And now, with the many ways we can use CSS for style navigation, we don't even need to use JavaScript to toggle images for creative effects.

cross ref   For more information on using CSS for style navigation, refer to Chapter 8.

Consider the following guidelines when using text for navigation:

◆ **Keep text options short and concise.** Instead of "Visit Other Weblogs," you would use "Other Weblogs," or even just "Weblogs."

◆ **Avoid jargon or location-related terminology where possible.** This is especially true in those situations where you are trying to reach a broad audience that might not always speak the language in which your site is authored.

◆ **Stick to convention.** Everyone knows what "Contact" and "About" means, but they might have to think twice about the words "Where" and "What" being used to represent the same thing.

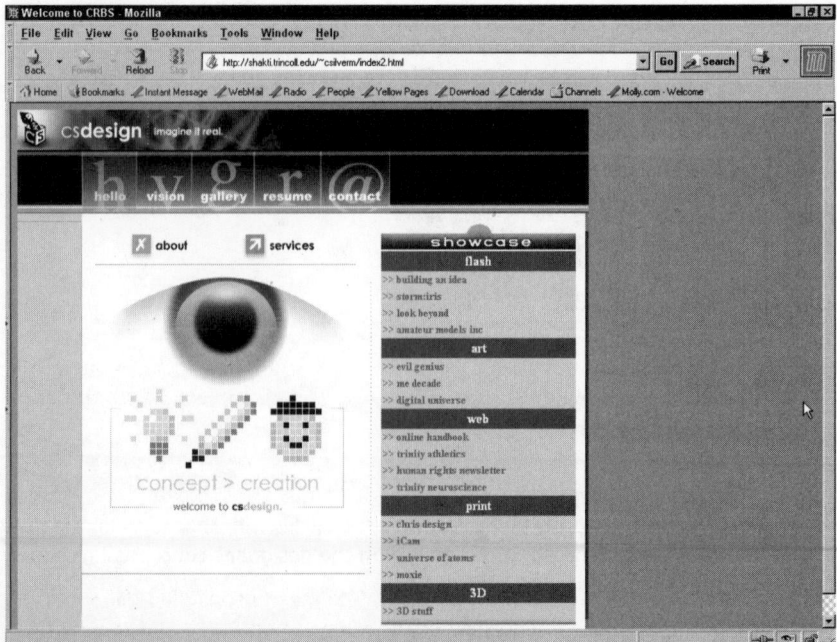

Figure 4-9: Combining iconography with text for clarity in the primary navigation.

Of course, there's a happy medium here. Many designers combine iconography with text. If you're after clear communication, combining the word "e-mail" with your envelope icon does the trick (see Figure 4-9).

If you want to create a more abstract design but still assist with clear navigation, you can use the abstract icons along with the literal text.

note | For more information about clarifying language usage for better comprehension and accessibility, please see Chapter 10.

Secret #54: Managing External Links

It's no secret that the longer you keep a person on your site, the more of an emotional relationship you can develop between what your site represents and that individual.

This is true of all types of Web sites, including Weblogs, commerce sites, and portals. Commerce sites are especially concerned with this issue, because while you'll visit your favorite Weblog to enjoy the content, you might never be back to the "Baby Stuff" Web site again, yet you can be sure they hope you'll be buying your friend's baby shower gifts there.

So, managing external links becomes very important in those situations where keeping a person on the site up through the desired outcome of their visit is mission-critical.

Typically, this means avoiding any external links in content close to the top of the page. Keep links short and relevant. You can even write the surrounding content of links in such a way to make them more—or less—attractive for your visitors to follow. Here's an example of a link (see Figure 4-10) I'd probably follow:

```
Finding the popular and controversial ``Heya Charlie Brown'' movie
hasn't been easy. But I've found the <a
href=''http://thatsite.com/heyacb.mov''>last link on earth</a> for
the upbeat little flick. Get it now!
```

And here's a link (see Figure 4-11) I might skip:

```
That Heya Charlie Brown thing really got <a
href=''http://thatsite.com/heyacb.mov''>out of hand</a>.
```

In the preceding figure, it's not only the lack of enthusiasm in the voice of the content, but also the placement of the link. Had it been placed around "Heya Charlie Brown," it would likely be more noticeable.

There are more problems than just these concerning links and Web site usability. Table 4-1 describes some of those problems and provides suggestions for managing links more efficiently.

note | You can find more information on link validators and link validation services at www.business.com/directory/internet_and_online/site_management/link_monitors/.

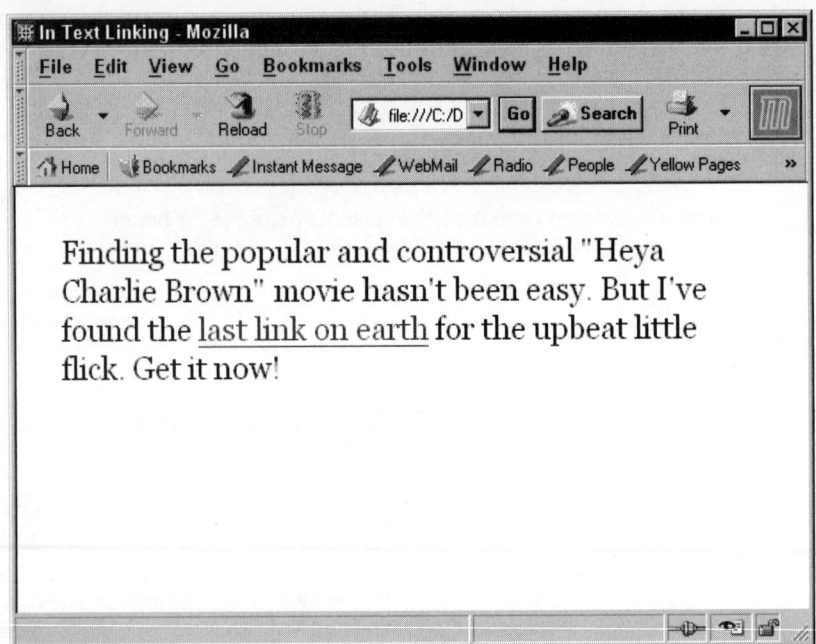

Figure 4-10: A persuasive link.

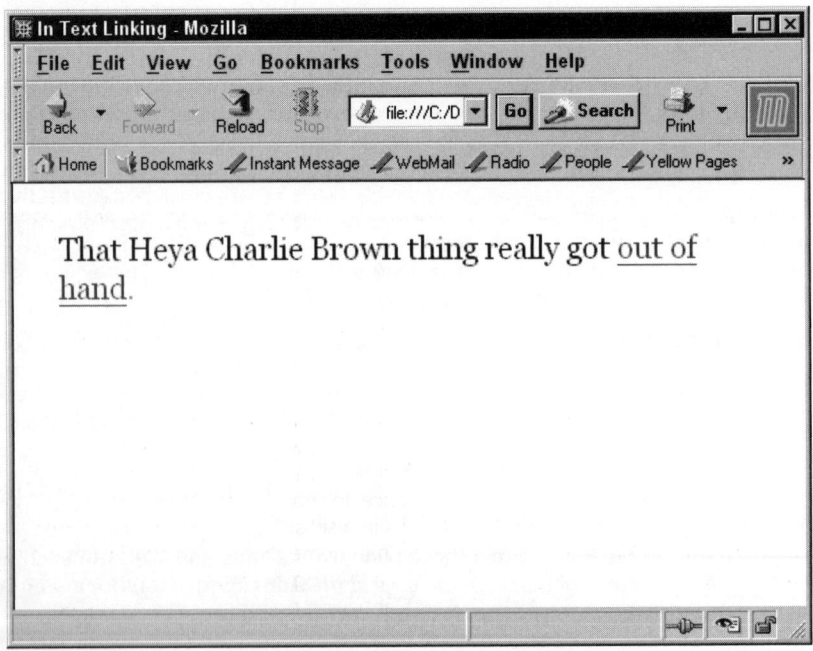

Figure 4-11: The content isn't enthusiastic, and the link falls in an odd spot. I probably would not follow this link.

Table 4-1: Link-Related Problems in Usability

Problem	Suggestions and Solutions
Link has incorrect URI	This common problem may not have anything to do with the way you originally managed your external links. Sites go away, or move files, and servers go down. Or, you might have simply mistyped the URL. The best way to find these problems is to run your site through link-checking software. You can do this with many products, including Web development products such as Dreamweaver. A number of online services also provide regular link checking and reports (see resources note following this table)
Link has no URI	This happens to me quite often as a result of adding link markup with no URI because I'm using it as a placeholder. It can also happen for the same reasons mentioned for incorrect URI listings. If you are creating placeholder links, use some kind of consistent dummy text, and then use your editor to find those dummy links when you're ready to add the URLs. You may also use any of the link-checker products as a means of finding missing links
Link text not visible inline	Links in text are often difficult for readers to discern, particularly if the link colors are close to the text colors. The proper technique for colorizing text is a much-debated issue. Some purists, such as Jakob Nielsen, who authored the seminal book *Designing Web Usability* and is one of the leading pundits in the field, believe that link colors should remain the conventional browser default colors, but most designers don't agree. No matter which track you decide to take, it's important that there is some discerning feature about your inline text links, such as ensuring the link colors contrast effectively with the text, making them easier to identify
Too many links in a page	When the rise of the portal site came about some years back, I was pretty flummoxed about what to tell Web designers about how to manage links for portal sites. Portal sites tend to be all about linking elsewhere, but with so many links on a page, how do we know where to go first? There's no guidance. In recent years, Weblogs are becoming portals in a sense, offering far more links on a page than home pages of the past (Figure 4-12 shows a Weblog example). The best solution to the issue of having many links is to first assess what really needs to be there and remove what doesn't. Then, organize your links into effective groups. This will help your users a great deal

continued

Table 4-1: *(continued)*

Problem	*Suggestions and Solutions*
Link is to a non-HTML document	You will often have cause to offer users download links to non-HTML document formats such as PDF files, Word documents, Excel spreadsheets, audio and video files, and so on. Because not all browsers support non-HTML document formats either with or without plug-ins, if you are offering the file specifically for download, be sure to note what type of file it is and how large it is (as shown in Figure 4-13). You may also want to offer any plug-ins on your site so your audiences are prepared
Link text is very long	I'm sure you've seen link text that is a paragraph long. When I see long passages that are linked, I assume the person doing the markup made a mistake! Typically, links should be at least one word and up to as many as six or seven, but not more. Usually three to five words, clearly written, are sufficient

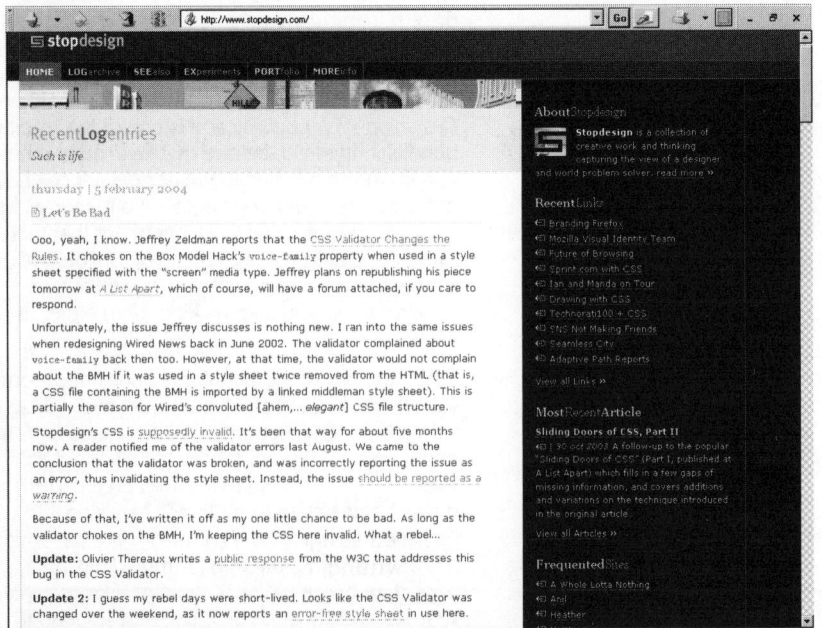

Figure 4-12: Weblogs are becoming link farms. The best solution is proper organization, as seen here on the right-side link options of designer Doug Bowman's Stopdesign Web site.

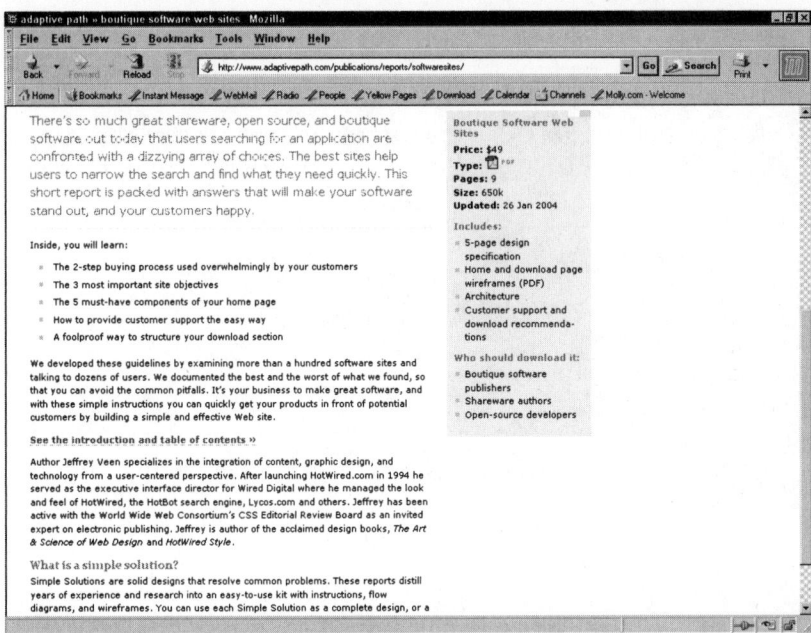

Figure 4-13: If you're offering downloads to non-HTML file formats, describe to your audience what they're downloading, which format it's in, and how large the file size is.

Secret #55:   Direct Access to Site Features

What's the most important reason people come to your site? If you don't know, you need to find out—because making sure you get your visitors from their point of entry to the feature they want is a prime directive.

Notice that I wrote "from their point of entry." That's because not everyone will come to your site via the home page. So even if your home page has immediate access to the fabulous online game you're famous for, what happens if someone comes in via your discussion board page?

You've not only got to have direct access to the critical features on your site, but you've got to make that access consistent (it looks and behaves the same way) and persistent (it exists in the same location on each page) throughout the site, as well.

The Web Standards Project (WaSP) has been struggling with an issue that exemplifies this problem quite well. As of this writing, one of WaSP's primary goals is to offer designers and developers standards-related references and resources. We call this the LEARN group, which has access from the top level of our navigation (see Figure 4-14).

Yet, when you click on the learn link, you get an expanded menu with a variety of options (as shown in Figure 4-15). I personally feel this menu is extremely confusing, because the options do not guide me to any specific place. I have to really think to figure out where the information I want might be. And what's the difference between "reference" and "resources" anyway? A visitor could easily

Figure 4-14: The learn section is clearly demarcated at the top level, fourth option down from the top.

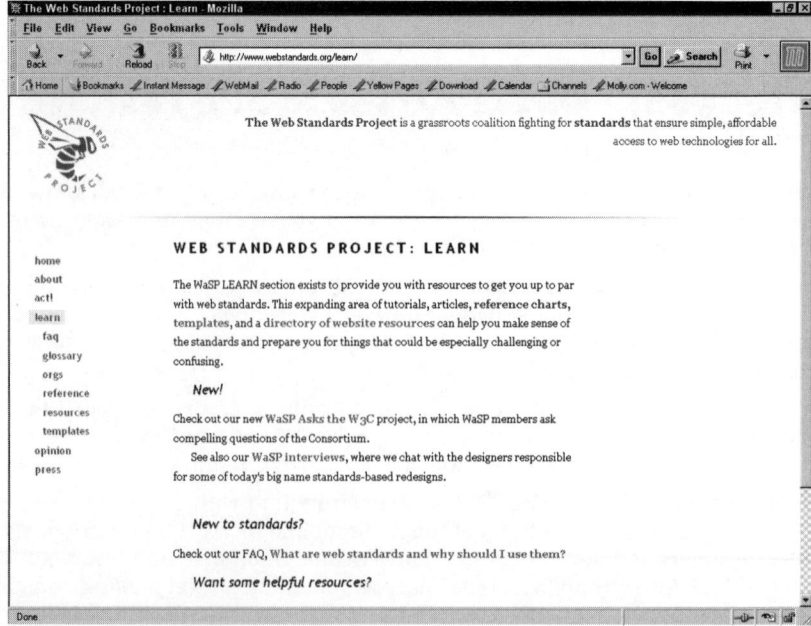

Figure 4-15: The "learn" submenu is unclear and, as a result, places site features too far from the individual.

click one and end up in the wrong place. In addition, if a visitor came in at one of these lower pages, he or she might be even more confused.

Back up for a second and think about all the logical things we've been discussing—the need for planning, understanding audience, keeping things orderly and clear—they do help. And it's not that the WaSP design team didn't do those things. But you can see that, at this time, the WaSP Web site does not provide true direct access to one of the most important features it wants to make available to site visitors.

I'm not exactly sure if it brings comfort or concern to you to know that some of the most respected Web designers and developers couldn't quite nail the information architecture and usability of a Web site—especially one in a state of transition—but it does exemplify that these techniques are still being worked out and that these challenges are keeping all of us on our toes. Fortunately, WaSP is re-examining its goals and design, which often is the best any of us can do—create, study the problems, and improve.

Secret #56: Placement of Critical Information

In the newspaper industry, headlines are said to run "above the fold." This means that the critical news is placed above the fold of the paper, so that it's the first thing people see.

While the concept of "fold" is really nonexistent in Web design, the idea that critical information needs to be placed at or toward the top of a page remains a good thought (see Figure 4-16).

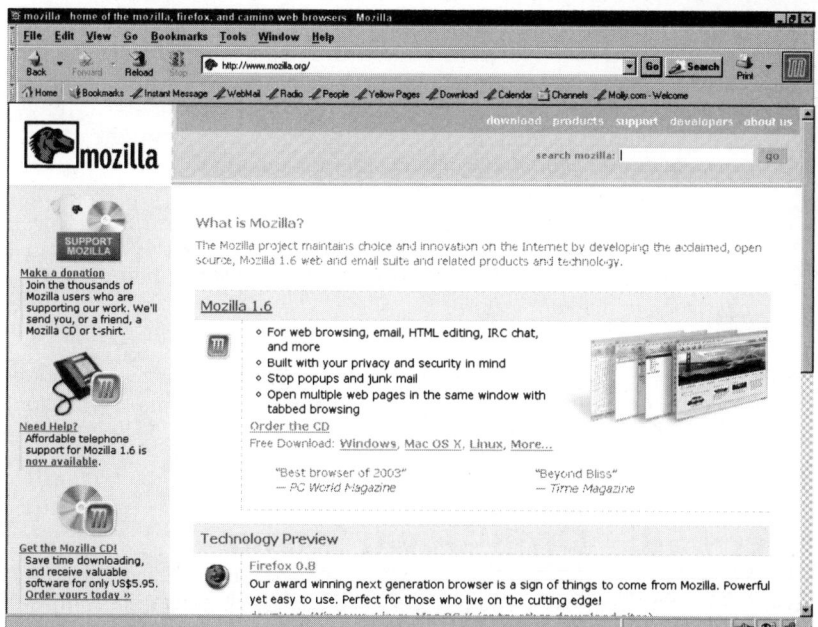

Figure 4-16: Critical elements should be placed high up on a page.

Despite the fact that a new Mozilla project had just been released, the primary information on this page is about Mozilla's hallmark product, the Mozilla Web browser. Therefore, it holds first position on the page.

Secret #57:   Consistent Placement of Elements

Another very significant issue in terms of successful user interface design is the consistency of page elements, both in terms of visual placement of logos and navigation, and of their style.

More than likely, you've visited a Web site where you started to dig in, and ended up on a page within that site that had no consistency in the placement of elements or the design as you moved from page to page. The problem is less pervasive than it used to be—particularly as awareness of usability concerns in design grows.

When working on the placement of elements, include the following:

♦ **Logos.** Typically, a logo will be persistently placed in one spot throughout the site. A common technique is to make the logo larger on the home page and somewhat smaller on subsequent pages, but in all cases the location should be the same.

♦ **Navigation.** As already discussed, the consistent placement of navigation is a critical aspect of successful, usable design.

♦ **Link to Home.** All pages of your site should have a persistent link (or links) to the home page. It's conventional to link the logo graphic to the home page, use a persistent option on the navigation bar, or both. Most usability experts recommend that if an option exists for the home page link on the home page, it should not be live.

♦ **Search.** While not all sites offer search capabilities, it's becoming more common for medium-to-large-scale sites to implement them. Effective search can make a site visitor's experience easier, so all Web designers and developers should consider search features for their sites. Many experts recommend that the search feature be very prominent, often appearing as a first option on the primary navigation bar.

> note   Many usability advocates feel that there are at least two exceptions to consistent placement of elements, search pages and forms, because they often require different features.

Figure 4-17 shows a screenshot of the Wiley Web site. The logo, primary navigation, search, contact, help, account, and shopping cart information remain persistent as well as consistent throughout all levels of the site.

Secret #58:   Drop-Down Menus

Drop-down menus are a very popular means of offering navigation options and options within forms. Drop-down menus can be especially effective because they are familiar to Web audiences, are easy to use, help reduce errors, and take up a lot less screen space than long menu systems.

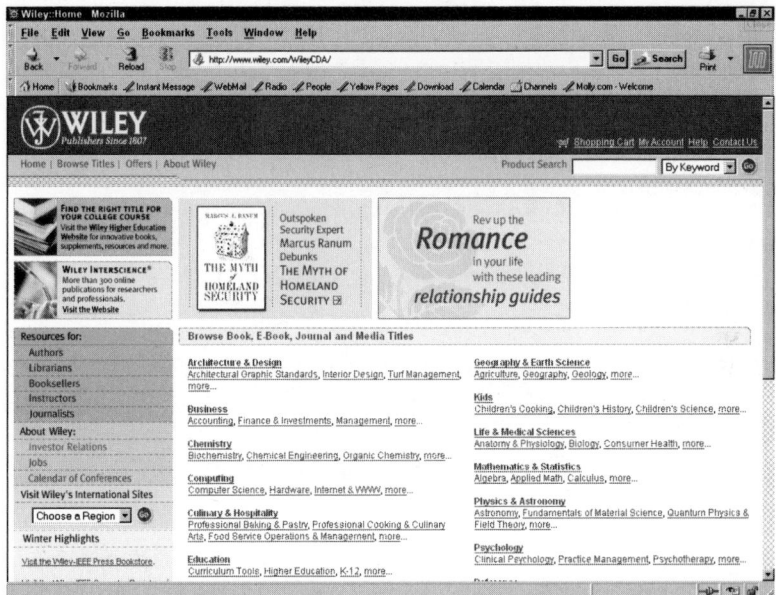

Figure 4-17: Consistent placement of elements assists users in navigating and orienting within a site.

However, using drop-down menus shouldn't be something done just for these reasons. Offering a menu like this has to make sense. What's more, usability experts such as Jakob Nielsen make some excellent recommendations when it comes to using drop-downs, such as the following:

◆ **Avoid very long menus.** Too many options in a drop-down menu become problematic because they require the site visitor to scroll uncomfortably. This can also cause problems for the mobility impaired, limiting the site's accessibility.

◆ **Avoid menus with short entries.** Any menus offering options with very short entries, such as state abbreviations, also become problematic for visitors. Typing the abbreviation into a text box is easier.

◆ **Avoid menus of known information.** Nielsen points out that information we type frequently, such as our birth dates, are better collected via text boxes than drop-down menus. His claim is that this kind of information is "hardwired" to people's fingers, and that it's easier on them to type it than go through the trouble of selecting a drop-down menu.

Despite these warnings, I've often favored drop-down menus for quick links to site locations, or for enhancing search (see Figure 4-18).

Secret #59: Pop-Up Windows

The trouble with popups is easily illustrated by the proliferation of pop-up blocking software and implementation of pop-up blocking in Web browsers such as Mozilla. But most of this has been as a result of the proliferation of interstitial advertising. Various, reasonable uses of popups have been around for a while.

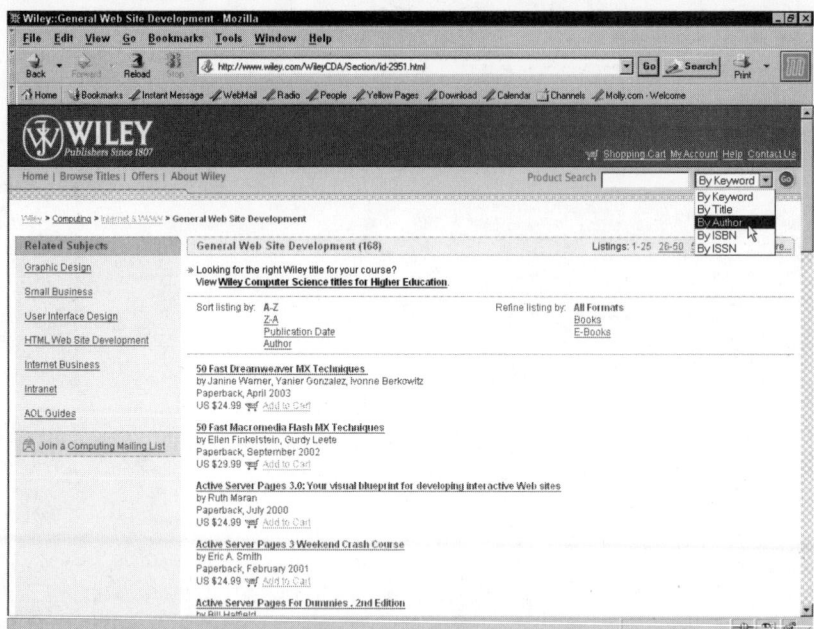

Figure 4-18: The search drop-down menu in use here is very effective due to its familiarity and short list of options.

When working with popups, first and foremost, be aware that many people will have popups blocked in the public sector, so they simply may not be the best choice.

Some applications that are considered reasonable for popups include the following:

- **Product details.** If you are offering a product on a page with other products and would like to provide specific details for each, the use of a pop-up window is credible.
- **Visual details.** Details of graphics can be extremely helpful. Consider sites displaying mechanical and scientific information and commerce sites. Details of devices and products can be provided in popups.
- **Code samples.** One of my favorite uses for popups is for code samples in tutorial and script reservoir sites.
- **Weblog comments.** A current common use for pop-ups is for comment systems in Weblog software (see Figure 4-19).

note   In Weblog comments, URLs are often shared. While linking within popups isn't considered the best practice, many Weblog users are adept at managing links within popups. For more general audiences, you may wish to avoid links within your popups.

If you do choose to use popups, consider the following guidelines as a way of reducing problems related to accessibility and usability:

- Let your visitors know that the link leads to a pop-up.
- Avoid links within the windows (see preceding note for exception).
- Ensure windows are available even if JavaScript is disabled.

Figure 4-19: Pop-up commenting system on my Weblog.

> **note**
>
> Accessibility specialists suggest that you should not remove any of the browser's components from your pop up, including browser frame, menus, and scroll bar, and that you should be sure that your users can resize the window.
>
> For more information about making sites more accessible, see Chapter 10, "Adding Accessibility Features."

Secret #60:   Consider Tabbed Navigation

Any lover of Amazon.com knows that they were one of the first sites to implement what eventually became a practically ubiquitous means of managing navigation—tabbed navigation.

Tabbed navigation is an attractive option for numerous reasons, including the following:

- ♦ **Tabs are familiar.** Tabbed navigation is so common both online and offline (the familiar tabs within a file folder) that even the most inexperienced of site visitors can use it with ease.

- ♦ **Tabs are persistent.** Tabs are by nature persistent from page to page. The only thing that should change is that the tab related to the current page should appear as the dominant tab (see Figure 4-20).

- ♦ **Tabs are consistent.** Along with persistence, tabbed navigation is consistent in its general visual features.

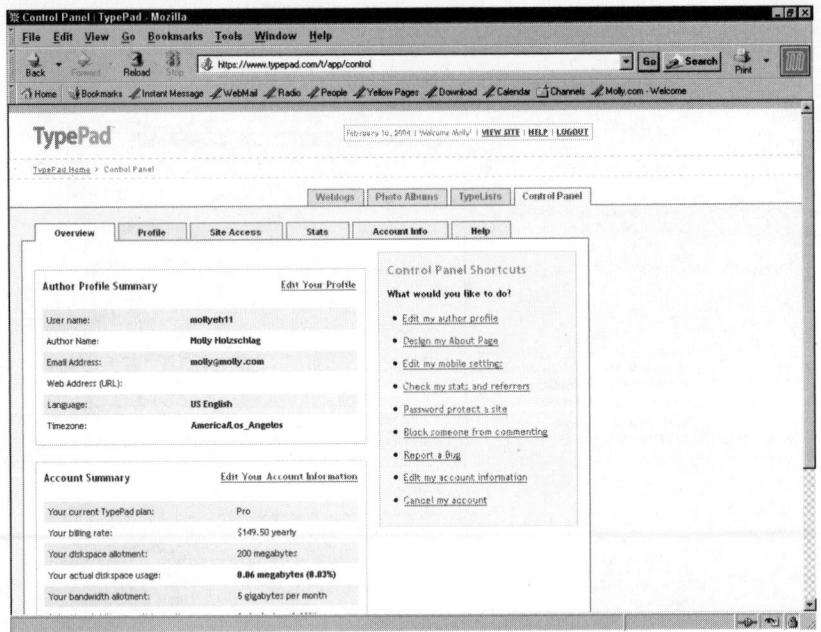

Figure 4-20: Dominant tabs should contrast well with other aspects of the tab. You can see this in two instances on my TypePad control panel page.

> **tip**
> If you're using tabs, the current tab and the related space below it should contrast well with tabs in the background.

Secret #61: Provide Orientation

The concept of *orientation* is another major aspect of user interface design. At any point while visiting a Web site, the user relies on subtle (and sometimes not-so-subtle) cues to keep a sense of where they are within the site.

> **note**
> As mentioned earlier in this chapter, not every site visitor enters your site from the home page. Therefore, it's very important to offer orientation aids on all pages.

You can assist your site visitors with orientation in a number of ways, including the following:

- ♦ **Show site name and location in title bar.** By showing the site name and specific location in the title, you can improve orientation. If you have a very large site, just having the site name and subsection of the site, such as "All News: Technology Headlines Today" will be a helpful aid to your visitors, even if there's no easy way to create individual titles for all the specific topic pages.

◆ **Use some change in navigation to reflect location.** A very familiar technique is having the color or style of a navigation link or image change to indicate that you're on a specific page (see Figure 4-21). Using arrows or other symbols is also common.

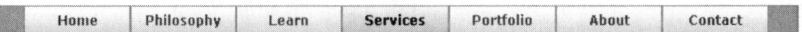

Home	Philosophy	Learn	**Services**	Portfolio	About	Contact

Figure 4-21: Changing a link style in some way can assist with orientation.

◆ **Make sure sections are clearly demarcated.** Each section within a site should be identified. Whether you use iconography, text, photos, color-coding, or other visual design techniques to achieve this, make it clear to visitors when they're in the "Books"section of your site rather than the "DVD"section.

◆ **Use breadcrumb navigation.** Breadcrumb navigation is an excellent way to keep visitors oriented, as well as to provide them with ways to link back to other sections within the site (see Figure 4-22).

Wiley > Computing > Internet & WWW > **General Web Site Development**

Figure 4-22: Breadcrumb navigation remains one of the most helpful ways to keep a site user oriented, as well as provide additional navigation features.

◆ **Provide a site map.** Especially important for very large sites, a site map denoting locations with links to individual areas can be extremely helpful for people trying to orient themselves to your site.

Secret #62:   Date and Time Formats

The web is a worldwide phenomenon, and there are numerous ways across the world to denote time and date. Sometimes these formats can conflict depending upon the format used in a given country.

Consider the following date:

    09/02/04

If you're a reader in Europe, you'll likely interpret this to mean that it's the ninth day of February of the year 2004 (dd/mm/yy). U.S. readers understand this time format to mean the second day of September of the year 2004 (mm/dd/yy). And you'll find still other date formats in use around the world.

The secret when it comes to date formats is to use the *International Date Format*. This is an International Organization for Standardization (ISO) standard, which makes it truly international. It places the century and year first, then the month, then the day. So for the ninth day of February 2004, you'd write the following:

    2004/02/09

Or, effectively, ccyy/mm/dd.

Another way you can assist users with date formatting is to write the date out in some way, such as in the following examples:

```
9th of February, 2004
February 9, 2004
9 FEB 2004
9 February 2004
```

If you choose to do this, it's recommend that you do so in *addition* to including the international format.

> note   **You can learn more about international standard formats at the ISO Web site, www.iso.ch/. The date and time standard is ISO–8601.**

A related issue is the way we describe time in documents. Most of the world uses the 24-hour time format—something that people in the United States typically refer to as "military time" and only use in formal settings. Otherwise, we use an A.M./P.M. format to denote time.

Most of the world: 13:00

U.S.: 1 P.M.

Fortunately, most people in the United States are familiar with the 24-hour time format, so use it to reach the broadest audience possible.

The ISO 8601 standard echoes this logic: it says to use 24-hour time in all cases.

However, while this is a reasonable solution, there are going to be cases where using international formatting isn't the best choice, such as with U.S.-based intranets or U.S.-centric sites. In those cases, using U.S. formats may be the better choice.

> tip   **If you're going to use U.S. time formats, include the "A.M." or "P.M." for greater clarity.**

Secret #63:   Cost-Controlled Usability Testing

Perhaps one of the greatest controversies in Web design is how to perform usability tests that provide results without incurring significant cost to the client.

There are two primary types of usability testing: Lab-based and remote.

In the lab-based version, testers observe site visitors as they manually go through a set of tasks. Testers will interview the participants and write up an overview of their research. The research results can then be applied to the site to improve its usability. The advantage of lab-based testing is that the process can be tightly controlled and cleanly observed. The major disadvantage of lab-based testing is that it can be extremely costly.

In remote testing, the people to be tested are using the Web site in question, online. The key component of remote testing is finding good online meeting tools and online applications so testers can observe remote site visitors. The advantages of remote testing include being able to reach a wider audience and keeping costs down. Usability studies can be offered throughout the life cycle of a site's development, something that many usability specialists recommend. The drawbacks to remote testing are that it can be technically problematic (connectivity problems, slow applications), and those who are administering the test have limited or no visual feedback from the individual's face or physical demeanor.

Usability testing is important for any major site. However, the way in which you achieve your test and apply results is going to vary greatly based on budget, project life cycle, and human resources.

note

For more information on the pros and cons of remote usability testing, see "Experience remote usability testing, Part 1" at IBM developerWorks, www-106.ibm.com/developerworks/library/wa-rmusts1/.

Another excellent article on the topic is "Remote Online Usability Testing: Why, How, and When to Use It" at Boxes and Arrows, a rich resource for those interested in real-world applications of usability techniques.

Finally, to learn about usability-related Web sites, additional articles, and books, see Appendix C, "Helpful Reading, Web Sites, and Resources."

Summary

The study of usability and user experience on the Web is so active an area that it's producing massive quantities of documentation, methodology, and testing techniques. The Web design field grows deeper by the day, partly due to the attention being paid to how users use the Web, why they use it, and how we can help them use it more effectively.

Of course, a site can be extremely usable, but what good is usability without real content? Chapter 5 gives you a look at how to create and manage content, increasing your ability to persuade audiences and making their experience easy as well as rewarding.

Creating and Managing Fantastic Content

Chapter
5

♦ ♦

Secrets in This Chapter

♦ ♦

A Web site's content is the most persuasive aspect of a site. But creating content for the Web is a totally different activity than creating content for other media such as books and white papers.

Along with creation of Web content comes protecting and managing Web content. After you've prepared it appropriately, legally protecting your (or your client's) property and strategically managing it can be a huge issue.

This chapter shares secrets that will help you create and manage content in effective ways, including how to write more effectively for the Web, understand intellectual property (IP) issues and how they influence the work of Web designers, and what is required to make strategic decisions about long-term management of content.

note

This chapter is very U.S.-centric because it deals with language and law, and these issues vary greatly from country to country. I've included some international resources here and there, but depending upon the languages you work with, some of the material here may not apply. The (IP) information centers on U.S. law. You will have to check with your country's approach to rights management to see if similar laws and methods are in place. In all cases involving legal concerns or questions, a visit to an attorney is advised.

Secret #64:   Finding Your Voice

The human voice can express a wide range of sound: It can be loud or soft, silky or gravelly, or suave or gruff. The variety of sound has significance—how you use a given sound can help you in your conversations with others—to persuade them, calm them, express concern, and so forth.

Voice in writing is the personality and character of the language used. You find it in literature, of course—where the author or characters in a given story have their individual style of language. You also see many examples of voice in the advertising world—think about the last commercial you saw on TV. Well-written advertising uses language that will influence and persuade the audience highly.

Using these techniques on the Web is as important to the effective communication of your site's intent as it is in more traditional forms of media. Consider how different one site is from another—each has its own personality. Some examples of how voice can be helpful for a type of site include the following:

+ **Popular clothing catalogue.** If you're selling the latest style of jeans, your site might benefit from the use of hip, trendy language. The target audience, feeling comfortable and enjoying the fun and familiarity of the jargon, will be more likely to buy from a site that quite literally "speaks to them" than a similar site that uses bland language. Check out Girlshop at www.girlshop.com/ for a great example of a site that uses voice to communicate effectively with its young clientele (see Figure 5-1).

+ **Family car dealership.** For a local car dealership aimed at selling mid-size cars and SUVs, language that expresses comfort and confidence can persuade by instilling a sense of security in its site visitors. For example, the Ford Motor Company Web site, www.ford .com/, has a section called "Heritage" in which Ford's commitment to

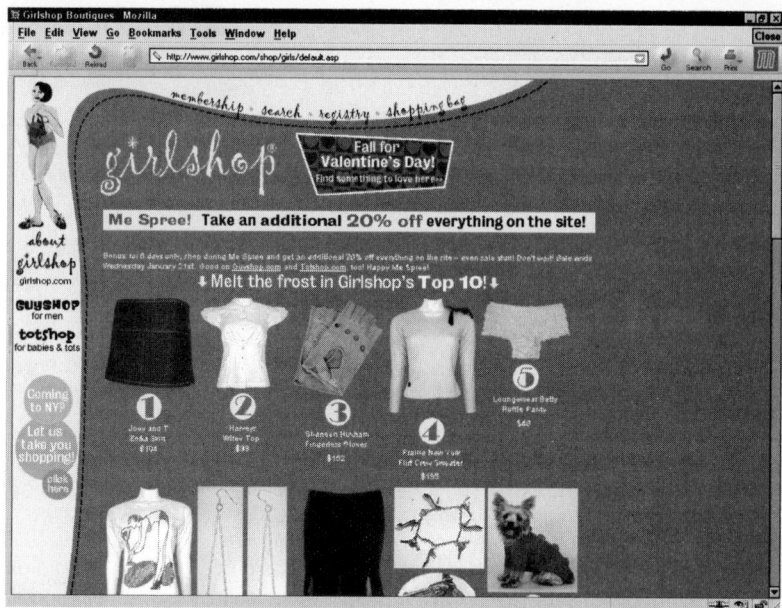

Figure 5-1: Girlshop uses fun, light language to sell to its young audience.

quality is expressed through its company history and profiles of Henry Ford and his family. In this case, more conservative language is being used as a means of conveying stability and quality.

♦ **Anti-drug public service site.** In this case, a more somber use of language is in order. The nature of the message may even benefit from a stern voice, compelling site visitors to take the message very seriously. For example, read the Bryan Lee Curtis story at whyquit.com (http://whyquit.com/whyquit/BryanLeeCurtis.html), a Web site dedicated to helping people quit smoking.

Whether you are creating a site for a clothing manufacturer, a car dealer, or a drug education Web site for a nonprofit organization, voice is going to matter. Take some time to review your site's intent, your target audience, and develop a voice that is appropriate to your site goals.

Secret #65: Clarifying Site Purpose

An issue that drives me completely mad (and will turn your visitors away faster than you can say "boo!"), is a site that fails to immediately identify its reason for being.

You're certain to be familiar with this scenario. You get to a Web site, maybe you followed a link from another site or from Google, and the site has no clear purpose. The content doesn't reflect in any easily discernable way what the site is about.

On my personal Web site, I stuck my tongue in my cheek in an effort to make fun of this problem (see Figure 5-2).

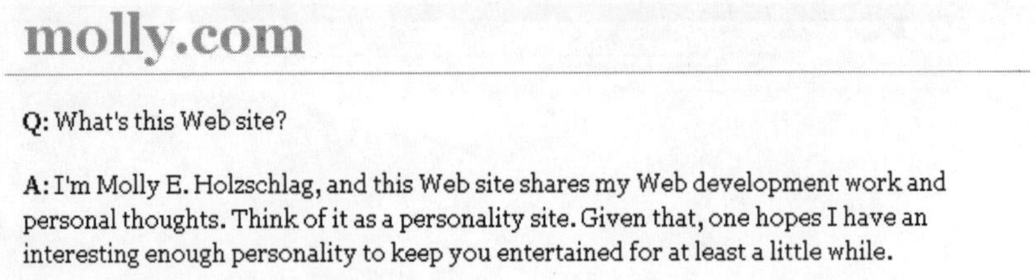

molly.com

Q: What's this Web site?

A: I'm Molly E. Holzschlag, and this Web site shares my Web development work and personal thoughts. Think of it as a personality site. Given that, one hopes I have an interesting enough personality to keep you entertained for at least a little while.

Figure 5-2: Screenshot of Molly.Com clarifying the site's purpose.

But just because I have the liberty to play doesn't mean you will when it comes to a professional circumstance. Clarifying site purpose is achieved using a number of techniques, as follows:

- Ensure that you have some language on your home page that clearly defines the purpose of the site.
- Ideally, make your site name clear and self-evident, such as "The Anti-Smoking Site." If you're working with a company that's more ambiguous, such as "Rad Industries," consider including a descriptive tagline. I might not know what the company name refers to if I see it alone, but if you include the tagline "electric power for the future," I'm going to more readily understand the significance of the name, and therefore, the site itself.
- Your headings and navigational elements should be written to reflect the topics within your site. If you're working on the content of an anti-smoking site, using words such as "smoking," "quitting," and other language related to smoking helps to further express the primary topic of the site.
- Title your pages effectively. This is something a lot of Web designers (including myself, I'm ashamed to admit) often overlook. Using effective titling within the HTML <title> ... </title> tags on pages helps orient the site visitor as well as reinforce the site's purpose. Always begin with the site's name, followed by the location within the site. A simple example that reflects this idea would be using "The Anti-Smoking Site: Welcome!" for the home page. By consistently using the term "The Anti-Smoking Site" in titles, it becomes far easier for site visitors to remain oriented.

Not identifying your site and its purpose is a dreadful mistake and should be avoided at all costs. Every site must have some mechanism by which the intent of that site is clearly expressed.

Secret #66: Text and the Computer Screen

One of the difficulties in preparing text content for Web sites is that computer screens vary greatly in their technical complexity and the way they are affected by the operating system software the computer is running. So, much of effective text rendering depends upon the configuration of the site visitor's computer, including the following:

♦ **Screen resolution.** Screen resolutions vary greatly, and it will influence the size and appearance of text. In Figure 5-3, you can see text at the resolution of 640 × 480, and in Figure 5-4, you'll see text at a resolution of 1024 × 768. Of course, many people are viewing the Web at other resolutions, including the very popular 800 × 600 and 1280 × 1024 and higher. The variations are indeed significant, so always keep this in mind when working with copy.

Figure 5-3: Text as seen at a resolution of 640 × 480.

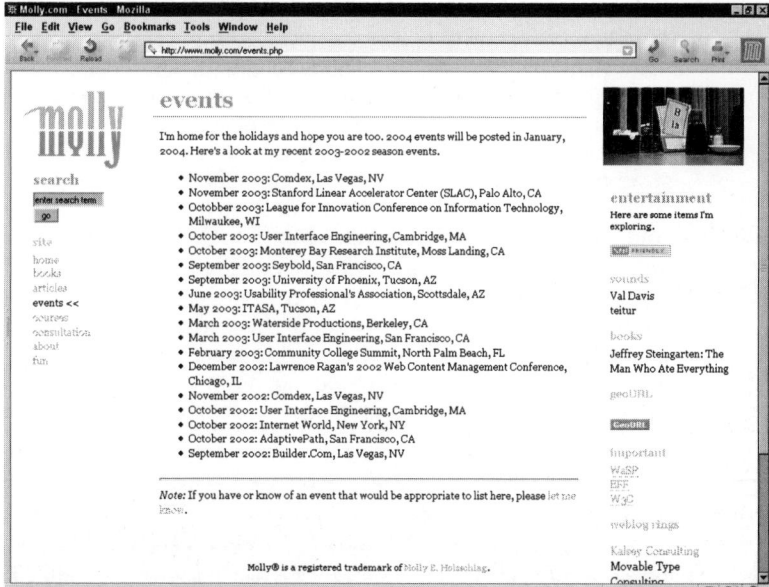

Figure 5-4: The same text viewed at a resolution of 1024 × 768.

♦ **Color management.** The way color is interpreted on screen varies greatly, too. Color is managed in part by the video card, in part by the monitor, and in part by the operating system in use. The variations are so great from set-up to set-up that it's impossible to be sure how a person reading a Web site will perceive a given color. What's more, some monitors run "hot," meaning they exude a lot of brightness. While this is usually adjustable, many nontechnical people don't realize they can make that adjustment. Hot monitors can cause headaches and fatigue, making people less likely to read long passages of text on screen.

♦ **Font smoothing.** Without smoothing, which is usually controlled by the operating system, fonts can appear very jagged and difficult to read (refer to Figure 5-5), adding yet another challenge for the Web designer to manage. Choosing appropriate fonts for text can help address this issue.

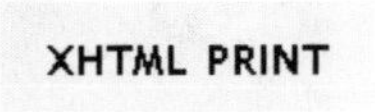

XHTML PRINT

Figure 5-5: Without font smoothing, this title text appears jagged.

cross
ref   For more information on choosing appropriate fonts, refer to Chapter 8.

Because of these influences, the on-screen experience varies greatly from person to person. To the technological issues, add those physical issues affecting an individual and the problem becomes even more complex. Such physical factors include the following:

♦ **Color blindness.** Some form of color blindness affects about one in 20 people. That's a significant number of people, so when you're designing text for the computer screen, it's incredibly important to be sure you make color choices for your text that address this issue.

♦ **Low vision.** People over the age of 55 are one of the fastest growing demographics on the Web. While problem vision is common in all age groups, for this particular group, poor vision is abundant. Knowing that audiences comprise numerous individuals who have vision problems can help you ensure that there's ample contrast between your foreground and background text colors, that you offer sizing options (See Chapter 8), and that you have ample white space to help balance things out.

♦ **Blindness.** Many Web users are completely blind. This causes concerns related to accessibility, about which you'll read more in Chapter 10, "Adding Accessibility Features." For the purposes of this discussion, keep in mind that you're writing in some cases for people who will be hearing (or in the case of Braille printers, touching) your words. Write as clearly as possible at all times.

note   There's a great Web tool called "Color Vision" at www.iamcal.com/toys/colors/index.php that emulates all forms of color blindness. You simply choose the type of color deficiency, then select your actual colors, and the tool displays them the way the person who has that deficiency will see them.

Secret #67:   Writing Effective Paragraphs

My mother is a noted author and scholar of multicultural literature. She has a Ph.D. in English, when she sits down to write e-mails, they're written in very long paragraphs with few breaks, as though they were in essay form. Beautiful letters, but because of the limitations of the on-screen medium, difficult to read unless printed out, which sort of defeats the purpose.

I remember learning in school that a paragraph must contain at least four complete sentences. Of course, formal writing has changed significantly over the past 30 years, but I believe the point of having at least four sentences has more to do with the ability to write effectively and clearly than encouraging wordiness where it isn't necessary. As is exemplified by my mother's writing style, what works on the printed page may not translate well at all to the electronic environment.

Because of the physical constraints of the computer screen, writing for the Web has become a study of its own, and while the rules I learned in school all those years ago may no longer apply specifically, the goals of writing effectively and clearly do.

The popular term for dealing with text on the Web is called "chunking." This is the act of breaking up your information into digestible bits, aiding in the goal of clarity. Depending upon the voice you're using, and the type of site you have, the length of your sentences, type of vocabulary you employ, and the length of your paragraphs are going to vary.

Consider this text example I received from a client.

Here's a view of the cottonwood trees along the San Pedro River at the Three Links Farm, north of Benson, Arizona. This place is important to me because it is the first river I have had a hand in resuscitating. The Nature Conservancy bought this farm partly because of computer modeling work that I did for them starting in 1996, in order to retire the irrigation pumping and let the river flow again without interference from heavy irrigation pumping.

The river flows year round now that the pumps are out of the ground, and we hope that the flow will continue to increase and benefit several miles of the river downstream as well. I am planning a drive out there this weekend, to take some pictures of the rusty old irrigation pumps stacked up in the shed, and give the kids a chance to mess around with driving a stick shift—super farm roads to drive on.

As you can see, it reads pretty well but it's a lot of text without any line breaks. My "chunking" broke up the paragraphs and ultimately created a more visually pleasing affect because of the added white space, too (see Figure 5-6).

Here's a view of the cottonwood trees along the San Pedro River at the Three Links Farm, north of Benson, Arizona. This place is important to me because it is the first river I have had a hand in resuscitating.

The Nature Conservancy bought this farm partly because of computer modeling work that I did for them starting in 1996, in order to retire the irrigation pumping and let the river flow again without interference from heavy irrigation pumping.

The river flows year round now that the pumps are out of the ground, and we hope that the flow will continue to increase and benefit several miles of the river downstream as well.

Figure 5-6: Chunking text adds white space and makes it easier to read on screen.

I am planning a drive out there this weekend, to take some pictures of the rusty old irrigation pumps stacked up in the shed, and give the kids a chance to mess around with driving a stick shift—super farm roads to drive on.

The rule of thumb with paragraph writing on the Web is to chunk all text to its most essential ideas. Sometimes this means a paragraph is going to contain fragments, or have less than the recommended four sentences. It doesn't matter how short the paragraph gets—it matters that its content remains meaningful and clear.

Secret #68: Varying Pace

If you're going to have a lot of information on your site, keep in mind that along with voice and chunking, the pace of your language is going to influence your visitors.

A catalog description can read at a slow pace.

The "Leatherman" style of shoes is made of high quality leather for maximum comfort, fit, and style. These shoes are perfect for the casual gentleman and wear well from a day at the office to an evening on the town.

To pick up the pace, simply shorten the sentences, use fragments, and add some energy.

You're a guy on the go. From the office to a night out, choose Leatherman! It's the perfect style.

Nick Usborne is a copywriting and content expert whose Web site, Weblog newsletters, books, and presentations have helped Web designers create convincing copy (see Figure 5-7).

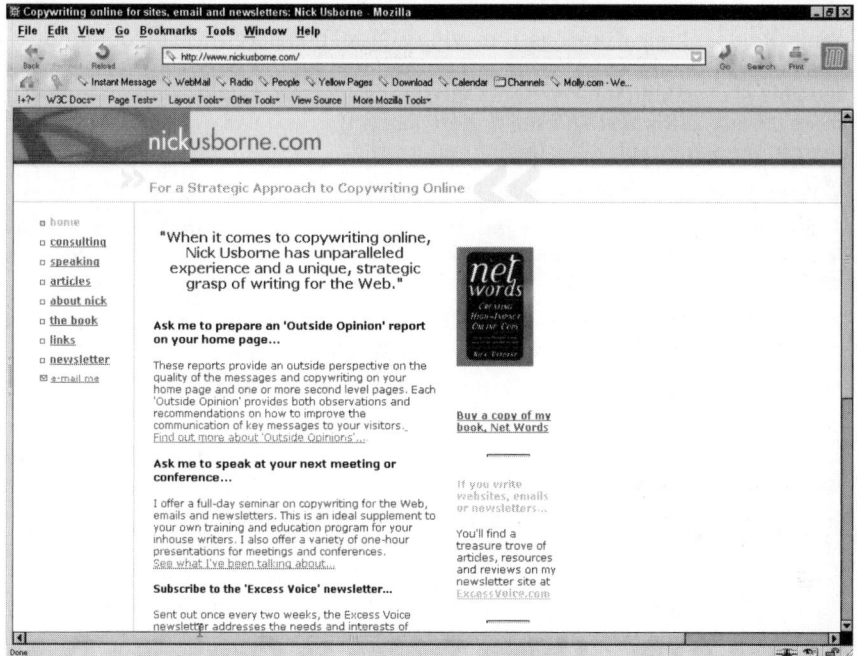

Figure 5-7: Nick Usborne's Web site provides excellent resources for individuals preparing content for the Web.

Usborne suggests three steps to help improve the pace of your text:

♦ **Be sure the language fits the voice appropriate to your site.** If the pace is too quick on a serious site, it can come across as insincere. Conversely, if you have a site that requires an active, spirited voice, pacing the voice too slowly can be detrimental.

♦ **Fit the pace to the purpose.** A privacy policy shouldn't be written in a short, sharp, hip fashion just as a commerce-oriented site should avoid long descriptions on any pages where a buying decision could be made. You can always have additional information on a product located elsewhere on the site, or downloadable in PDF format. This way, site visitors can get complete specifications for a product, which is important, but they do it at their discretion instead of becoming impatient reading through information just to get to the purchase process.

♦ **Vary the pace.** No matter your audience or your goal, keeping a fast pace or slow pace throughout the language of an entire site is going to cause fatigue and boredom for many of your visitors. You can vary pace by following the simple technique shown in the preceding example.

note   You can visit Nick Usborne at **www.nickusborne.com/**.

Secret #69:   Removing Extraneous Information

While it seems kind of obvious, removing information not critical to communication can come in handy when writing or editing text for the Web. This relates back to the idea of chunking information. Once you've got the chunks, you can look a little more closely at the text and see if there's anything you can get rid of, or if you can rewrite the paragraph to be leaner and meaner.

Consider the following "chunked" paragraph from the earlier example.

The river flows year round now that the pumps are out of the ground, and we hope that the flow will continue to increase and benefit several miles of the river downstream as well.

Any language that doesn't relate to the heart of the discussion, is in a somewhat confusing order, or adds extraneous detail can be removed.

Now that the pumps have been removed, the river flows year round. Hopefully, the flow will continue to increase as it benefits several miles of the river.

I reduced the paragraph by seven words, improved its pace, and made its main idea more prominent.

In the case of writing for the Web, less is almost always more.

Secret #70:   Using Tables to Organize Data

Along with chunking, it's important to take advantage of the various means of formatting available with HTML. HTML tables offer some rich features for organizing data. Add Cascading Style Sheets (CSS) to the mix for style and you can come up with terrific tables for your information that also break up the monotony of too much text by adding color and space.

Tables have a stormy history on the Web. They were introduced to HTML as a means for scientists and researchers to adequately manage tabular data. Prior to tables, the only way to accomplish columnar layouts was to use preformatted text and painstakingly figure out how many spaces belonged between each entry.

Later, tables became the grid system upon which most Web sites through the 1990s and into the early part of this century were built. However, using tables for layout has many significant problems, so a move to CSS for layout has become the popular cry. Despite the unpopularity of tables, they are still wonderful and necessary to do exactly what they were developed to do: organize content.

Some of the content you can successfully input into well-designed tables includes the following:

- ◆ **Financial information.** Many companies and organizations (especially banks) use tables to display financial data (refer to Figure 5-8).
- ◆ **Calendar-based information.** Tables are a natural choice to design a calendar layout for the Web (see Figure 5-9).

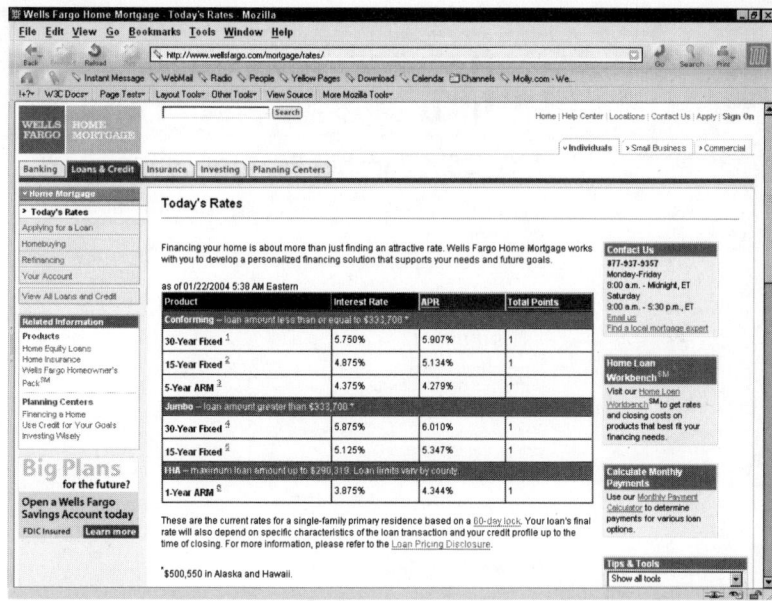

Figure 5-8: Tables are an excellent way to format financial content.

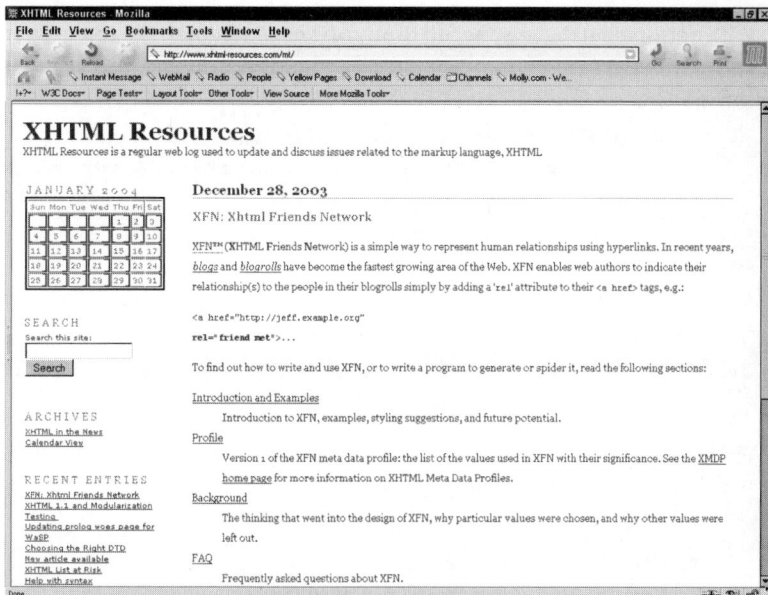

Figure 5-9: Calendars are familiar constructs and useful in the display of date-related content. I've turned the borders on so you can see the table structure of the calendar itself.

◆ **Product tracking or feature comparisons.** Many commerce companies use tables to reflect product status, availability, pricing, tracking, and comparison (as shown in Figure 5-10).

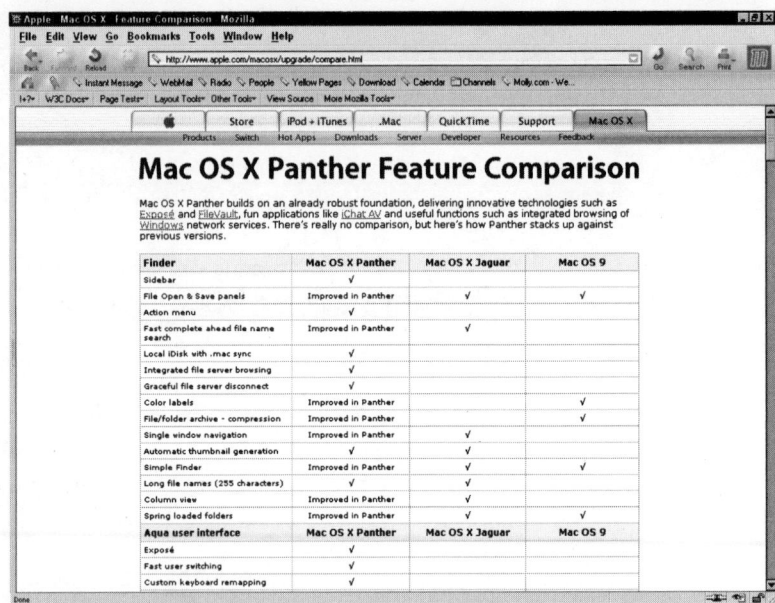

Figure 5-10: Displaying product features is an excellent use of tables.

With a strong database attached to any of these examples, the integration of content and technology becomes clear.

> **note** A good introduction to using tables for data can be found at
> `http://mark1.f2o.org/tutorial/tables/Advanced_Tables`
> `.html`.

Secret #71: Using Lists to Simplify Ideas

From a content standpoint, lists are extremely useful—especially unordered lists, which achieve the following:

- Assist the content writer in his or her goals to improve pace
- Keep information chunked
- Ensure clear communication of ideas
- Break up the visual space for improved readability

Ordered lists are very helpful in certain cases, especially if you're giving directions, as in the following example:

1. Take this book.
2. Close it.
3. Go have a coffee and/or take a walk.

You can see why we use lists so much in technical book writing.

cross
ref

You'll be working with lists a great deal in this book. Here are some cross-references for your list-learning pleasure.

Learn about using lists for structure in Chapter 6, "Crafting Pages with HTML" and the correct process for nesting lists in XHTML in Chapter 7, "Moving Ahead with XHTML."

Lists are an extremely popular way of creating visually rich yet accessible and interoperable navigation. See Chapter 8, "Style Tips for Type and Design."

Secret #72:   Using Headers Meaningfully

Headers have been used as a means of hierarchically organizing written ideas for centuries. However, the way headers are supposed to be used—both in writing and structurally within markup—is only recently coming into widespread understanding for those people working with markup.

As any reader even somewhat familiar with HTML knows, header markup consists of an "h" followed by a numeric value, and there are six values, h1–h6. These headers have a conventional visual representation in Web browsers, with h1 being bold and large and h6 being bold but quite small; this visual representation is up to the browser manufacturer to implement.

HTML specifications are not concerned with visual presentation per se. HTML and especially XHTML are concerned with structure and semantics. Instead of presentation, markup is concerned with the *meaning* of the elements. A header level 1, h1, isn't about being bold and large. It's about being the most significant heading on the page.

Structurally speaking, think about the text in this chapter. There's a chapter header—that would be a header level 1. Then, you have subheads, which would be header level 2, and so on. Because this book has style applied, there are specialty headers, such as the header style used for each secret. Using CSS, you can take the standard HTML h1–h6 level headers and style them with the same finesse.

Follow these tips when using headers:

*   **Reserve h1 headers for the most significant header on the page.** It's also recommended by many developers that you don't use more than one h1 header. Some who argue the issue claim that it's simply more semantically correct to only have one instance of an h1. There are also concerns that because many search engines look at h1s for cataloguing purposes, intentional misuse of h1s has become popular.
*   **Avoid "widowed" headers.** With the exception of h1, you should have at least two subheads for each section. This is a classic concern in making information balanced and readable and has become conventional in print. While you can deviate from the norm, typically your content will be more understandable when broken up into sensible sections.

◆ **Avoid stacking headers.** Always have text between headers. The purpose of headers is to separate text into discernable sections.

◆ **Use clear language.** Writers are always wondering why their editors are changing the titles the writer has so painstakingly crafted. I've come to learn that the reason is while I'm trying to be witty or clever with my titles, I'm not telling the reader what the content is about. Clear use of language within headers is, as with any other text, imperative.

---

cross ref | To learn how to structure headers using HTML, see Chapter 6, "Crafting Pages with HTML."

Secret #73:   Applying Style Standards

In Chapter 3 you read about the defining of style standards and creation of a style guide for a given site. You learned that style guides help with the site development process in a wide range of applications: code, visual design, and, of course, content.

Many issues must be confronted when determining style guidelines for your text on the Web. Using a traditional style guide such as Strunk & White is helpful, but some issues seem to pop up on the Web a great deal more frequently than other print-related issues, such as the following:

◆ **Case and titling.** Traditional "title" case has been modified style-wise in print and on the Web. Pick a case convention and stick to it.

◆ **Punctuation.** Determine a punctuation style, particularly in terms of hyperlinks and list items. Typically, placing punctuation after hyperlinks is advisable. Using periods after list items is a debated topic, but again, choose what works in your best judgment, and then stick with it.

◆ **Avoid additional spaces in hyperlinks.** This will help keep links contained to the text that's supposed to be linked, rather than additional space.

◆ **Determine which special characters are to be used.** Certain grammatical elements, such as quotes, symbols, hyphens, em dashes, and so forth require special characters. Also referred to as *character entities*, these characters sometimes have browser support problems. Figuring out what you're going to use and not use ahead of time will help anyone working with copy be more efficient in applying the site's style standards.

---

note | The US Department of Housing and Urban Development (HUD), at `www.hud.gov/library/bookshelf15/policies/standard.cfm`, has published an interesting style guide that can both serve as a model and provide additional information on content-related standards.

To read more about traditional grammar style, see The Elements of Style at `www.bartleby.com/141/`.

Secret #74:   Avoiding Problem Grammar

While defining a style guide and sticking to it can cut down on grammar-related problems, some very common grammar problems are unavoidable. At some point, you've probably typed "your" when you've meant "you're" or "affect" when you meant "effect."

Having a few good grammar books for your language on hand can be helpful. There are excellent resources online for style and grammar. Check those mentioned in this chapter and in Appendix C, "Helpful Reading, Web Sites, and Resources."

> **note**   For common grammar annoyances in English, see "Common Errors in English" at **www.wsu.edu/~brians/errors/index.html**.

Another interesting topic is how to write without bias toward gender, race, or physical ability. The American Psychological Association (APA) has published some excellent style guidelines in this area. I highly recommend reading these guidelines and making them available to anyone with whom you will be developing site content.

- Removing Bias in Language: Disabilities,
  www.apastyle.org/disabilities.html.
- Removing Bias in Language: Sexuality,
  www.apastyle.org/sexuality.html.
- Removing Bias in Language: Race and Ethnicity,
  www.apastyle.org/race.html.

Secret #75:   Understand Copyright!

There are three main branches in traditional IP law: copyright, trademark, and patent. Web designers and developers would do well to have a practical understanding of these issues, and copyright is the most important with which to begin.

> **note**   The spirit of U.S. Copyright—and all IP law for that matter—exists for an intriguing reason. It is meant to place balance between the artist and the public value of a work. The founding fathers suggested that neither the creator nor the public should gain all the benefits of any piece of IP. So, while you as an artist can and should reap all the rewards due to you for your contributions, the original copyright laws were designed to protect you for only 14 years, with the option to renew for an additional 14. After that time, your work is entered into the public domain, allowing the public to build upon and innovate on it. Times have changed, of course, and at the time of this writing, a copyright can last up to 70 years after the death of the creator.

Copyright in the United States covers any original work of an author. Examples include the following:

+ Literature, including fiction, nonfiction, stage plays, screenplays, poetry, Weblog entries, and original copy for Web sites
+ Music, including compositions, song lyrics, and recordings
+ Art and craft works such as pottery, painting, and sculpture

Works are considered copyrighted the moment they are created—you do *not* have to register a copyright to own the rights and display the copyright symbol. Of course, registering the copyright provides you with more formal and explicit protection, so it's a good idea.

You need to do a few things as a Web professional when it comes to copyright:

+ Determine the copyright holder. Is the content already copyrighted by the client? Typically, clients do retain the rights to their work and it is questionable ethics to try and own their property. If your client hasn't copyrighted their Web site content, encourage them and assist them in doing so.
+ If you created the work for yourself, be sure to register the copyright to protect the work.
+ Display the copyright symbol appropriately. Most Web sites carry the copyright at the very bottom, often linked to more detailed information about the content rights for the site.

note

The U.S. Copyright office has great resources, including links to registration forms for formal copyright registration, at `www.copyright.gov/`.

Copyright information for the United Kingdom is available through The UK Patent Office, at `www.patent.gov.uk/copy/`.

The Canadian IP Office can be found at `http://strategis.ic.gc.ca/sc_mrksv/cipo/welcome/welcom-e.html`.

What about using others' materials? If a work is copyrighted, using any significant amount of the work is illegal without permission. You should always try to obtain permission for the reuse of copyrighted materials.

Most readers will have heard the term "fair use". This is a narrow window into the use of copyrighted materials. Fair use examples include the following:

+ Quotations (length is limited, and the quote must be fully attributed)
+ Parodies
+ Photocopies for nonprofit and educational use only
+ Home copying of television programs

Getting permission to use other people's materials is still the best safety net. If you have detailed questions, please see an attorney who specializes in IP.

Secret #76: Extending Copyright with Creative Commons

Creative Commons is a group of attorneys and interested parties who are interested in re-examining the original vision of IP that the founding fathers had with the hope of offering extensions to allow easier sharing of property without violation (refer to Figure 5-11).

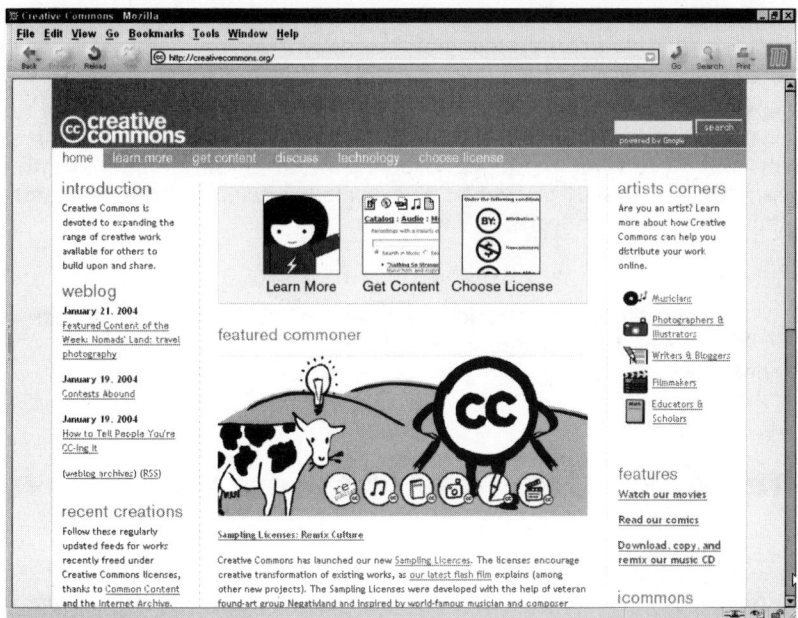

Figure 5-11: The Creative Commons Web site is a great place to learn more about IP in the digital age.

Their efforts have thus far resulted in the creation of three licensing options under the Creative Commons that extend copyright. The licenses clarify to anyone interested in your materials how you'd like your content treated.

The three licenses allow you to extend a copyright to someone else with the following extensions:

+ Available for all use, including commercial use
+ Available for noncommercial use, provided that attribution is made
+ Not available for use

Licenses from Creative Commons are growing in popularity largely because of Weblogs and the desire of Weblog authors to aggregate their content effectively. An extension of copyright to others via Creative Commons makes it very clear how a work can be disseminated—or not—as the author sees fit.

> **note**   The Creative Commons Web site, at `www.creativecommons.org/`, is a very informative site for those interested in pursuing more knowledge about IP and the Web.

Secret #77:   Protecting Intellectual Property with Trademarks

Trademarks are any word, name, symbol, or device used in the trade of goods. To that end, Web designers and developers need to pursue trademarks of their logos and company names, and encourage their clients to do so as well.

Trademarks protect only the symbol or the name, not the services that you are offering. So while you can protect your company logo, you can't prevent other people from providing the same kind of service you're providing.

Getting something trademarked can be a long process—it took me nearly three years to trademark the name "Molly" (names are notoriously difficult to trademark as well)—but if you want to protect symbols relevant to your trade, it's worth the process. This is especially true when it comes to hanging on to domain names—something that directly affects the Web designer.

note   For more information on trademarks, see the U.S. Patent and Trademark office Web site, www.uspto.gov/index.html.

Secret #78:   The Role of Patents on the Web

Along with copyrights and trademarks, patents make up the third area of U.S. IP law. Patents exist to cover inventions, and to protect inventors in the same way that copyright protects the creator of a work of art.

Unless your company or a client invents a new technology, Web designers usually do not run into the need to obtain or advise someone to pursue a patent. However, patents do affect Web designers in peripheral ways via hardware and software inventions.

Patent policies are also a concern of anyone wishing to ensure that Web technologies remain open standards. Patents can directly affect the tools and technologies of the Web, as evidenced, for example, in the recent Eolas versus Microsoft lawsuit. Eolas successfully sued Microsoft regarding technology related to the plug-in engine used by the Internet Explorer (IE) Web browser. Eolas claimed it owned the patent on the technology. The case continues unfolding at this time, with appeals in the works. The impact of this sort of dispute can radically affect the way Web designers work—they would have to redo any pages using embedded objects, such as Flash, Java Applets, movies, and audio—and also the way future policy will be created.

note   The World Wide Web Consortium (W3C) has a working group dedicated to patent policy and the Web. You'll find the Patent Policy Working Group home page at www.w3.org/2001/ppwg/.

To learn more about the Eolas patent suit and how it has affected Web designers, see "What does Eolas v. Microsoft mean to you?" at http://builder.com.com/5100-6373-5083455.html.

Secret #79:   What Is Digital Rights Management?

Another area where IP is affecting the work of anyone creating content for the Web is Digital Rights Management (DRM). DRM is the attempt to provide social, legal, and technical solutions for protecting IP in the digital age.

Many major software companies are adopting DRM in some fashion. Office 2003, for example, has all kinds of digital signatures and security-related features to allow authors to protect their documents.

But DRM is extremely controversial, largely due to the fact that many people feel restricting rights goes directly against the greater spirit of innovation and the sharing of the resources of common goods.

DRM gained momentum via the Digital Millennium Copyright Act (DMCA). This act, which was signed into law by President Clinton, is considered to be the most significant reform in U.S. IP history. DMCA outlines, in great detail, how digital rights should be managed. DMCA is as controversial as DRM, because many advocates for a free and open exchange of ideas see the DMCA as favoring big business, restricting innovation, and ultimately limiting the ability of technologists to move technology forward without constantly having to face lawsuits or limitations due to rights restrictions.

note
You can read the actual DMCA at `http://thomas.loc.gov/cgi-bin/query/z?c105:H.R.2281.ENR:`.

Follow the anti-DMCA controversy at `http://anti-dmca.org/`.

Learn about Digital Rights Management and its related controversy at `www.epic.org/privacy/drm/`.

Secret #80:   Exploring Content Management Systems

Content management systems (CMS) are a hot topic these days as a means to wrangle all the content created for a site and manage it more efficiently. CMS also attempts to eliminate the need for content-related workers to have to be markup specialists. The goal is to allow anyone to create new files and copy and paste data from other applications into Web-based documents for publication on public or internal sites.

Sounds pretty reasonable, right? Well, one of the more sobering issues related to CMS is cost. When the early systems emerged, such as Vignette Storyserver, the price tag caused many a weak heart to wane. Investments for CMS ran into the multi-million-dollar range, and the frustration level of getting the CMS to work properly was extremely high, causing grave concern about the high maintenance cost of managing content.

Fortunately, the concerns of cost and functionality helped focus attention on the improvement of the CMS situation. It is still very far from the day where CMS solutions are easily chosen, but more information exists to help designers and developers recommend, install, and design sites using CMS.

A variety of CMS types include the following:

♦ **Commercially packaged CMS software.** These are systems that you purchased and installed for your company or client. They are typically very costly and often difficult to install, configure, and maintain. However, they can also be excellent for certain situations, especially when there are many people working on content, the site is very large, and the site is continuing to grow.

◆ **Open-source based CMS software.** The open-source community has a number of CMS solutions that are very good and far less costly than proprietary packages. However, as with almost all open-source software requiring server-side attention, the installation and implementation is best left to those experienced with open-source languages and methods.

◆ **CMS application service provider.** In this case, instead of installing the CMS on your server, a provider offers the technology for you. Your job is to configure templates and permissions, allowing various individuals access to those content areas they will be managing. CMS provision of this nature can be a reasonable choice for many situations because of the low overhead, lower cost, and usually excellent support that goes with the service.

◆ **Custom CMS development.** A good programmer can create a CMS from scratch or customize one from any number of open-source options for less money. The disadvantage of rolling your own CMS is that it takes a lot of time, and you will need to take into account that ongoing support will likely be required.

Along with major CMS applications and services are smaller content-related tools that have emerged for the purposes of Weblogging. In the case of smaller sites, some of these tools—such as Movable Type—are excellent choices for content management. Tools of this nature are highly customizable (they are often open-source) and tend to be very affordable.

Before jumping into a CMS, make sure you have a detailed process to evaluate the short- and long-term content requirements of a given project, submit a reasonable budget, and study the available options and how they might best serve you or your client needs.

---

note   To learn about open-source CMS, see `www.cmsinfo.org`. The site keeps details about a wide range of open-source CMS projects.

For a complete guide to CMS news, analyses, reports, and other helpful information to assist you in making choices regarding content management, see CMS Watch at `www.cmswatch.com/`.

Summary

You should now have a very good idea of what challenges working with content on the Web can bring. Be confident that with good resources and a sensible approach to the creation and management of content, you won't have much trouble improving and streamlining the content aspect of your work.

At this point in the book, you've come through the organization and strategy aspects of site development and design. Now it's on to markup and style! The upcoming part contains chapters covering HTML, XHTML, CSS, and accessibility.

Part II

HTML, XHTML, CSS, and Accessibility

Crafting Pages with HTML

Chapter
6

♦ ♦

Secrets in This Chapter

♦ ♦

J ust the other day I was reading someone's Weblog and he was thanking a pal for helping him unravel the "tangle" of the Hypertext Markup Language (HTML) tags that he'd gotten wrapped up in. He'd been using a visual editor to build his site. Not being very familiar with markup, he had the good sense to get someone to help him who was, or he wouldn't have reached his goal of having a working Weblog for himself.

What interested me about this fellow's comment was how he viewed HTML—a tangle. HTML is a primary slice in the Web site creation pie.

Is HTML Easy?

The fact is that HTML is pretty easy to play around with and get some results from without having much experience with it. That's not so much due to HTML itself. Rather, Web browsers are incredibly forgiving when it comes to errors in HTML. If they weren't, the Web would never have become so thriving and multifaceted. As a result, people tend to think HTML is easy and don't dig deeper into its features, nuances, rules, and limitations.

HTML is a Markup Language

HTML is not programming per se; some will argue it isn't even code. What HTML is at core is a system of tags that are interpreted by a user agent such as a Web browser, a browser in a hand-held device such as a PDA, or an assistive device. A user agent's job is to interpret and then render the language of the document being requested.

> note   User agents can be as complex as the most contemporary Web browser created for today's commercial computers, or as simple as required by wireless, Web-enabled devices such as mobile phones and pagers.

As with any language, HTML has grammar. There are rules of structure and semantics. HTML has a distinct vocabulary, and complicated specifications define the many aspects of HTML as a formal language.

But browser competition has often led to the emergence of elements and features related to a given browser. Some of these elements have in fact been introduced into the specifications (which are the documents that define "Web Standards") and have been integrated into the language, but some have not been adopted.

All working Web professionals should have some awareness of HTML as it is specified rather than as most of us learned it—by viewing source, asking a colleague, and employing hacks and workarounds to get the various desired results.

Face the Changes

The by-our-bootstraps days of learning markup are gone. Awareness among the professional community has grown strong, in no small part due to the work of The Web Standards Project (WaSP), a grass-roots organization dedicated to promoting Web standards and resources for Web professionals. Figure 6-1 shows the WaSP site.

> note   For news, resources, and reference materials about Web standards, visit the WaSP Web site at www.webstandards.org/.

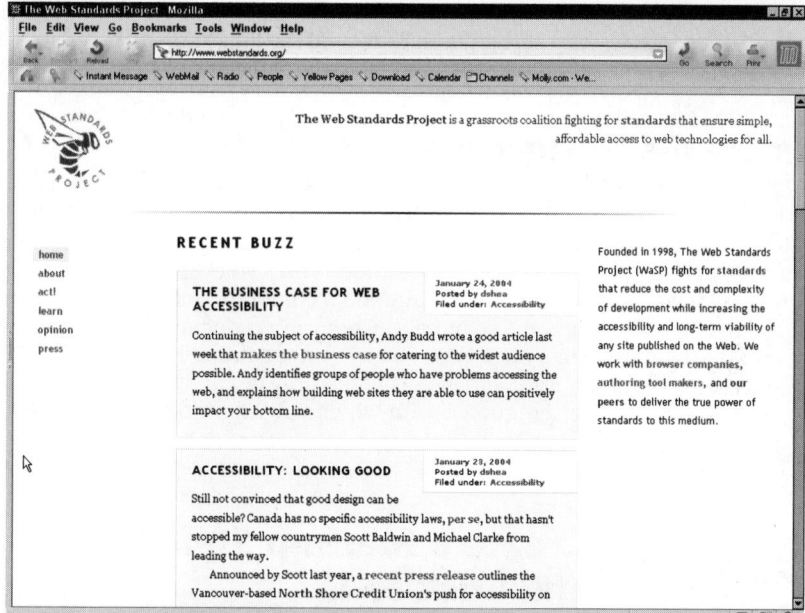

Figure 6-1: WaSP is a grass-roots volunteer organization advocating the use of Web standards.

In addition, we now have very good CSS support in all modern browsers. This means we can clean up the hacks we used to lay out pages visually, remove extraneous tags from our HTML, and write cleaner, clearer, more structured and less confusing documents, making HTML a lot easier to use—even for complex needs. What's more, many product vendors, especially Macromedia, are becoming more interested in making sure their products allow users to create and maintain valid pages, which helps us all in the long run.

So, if you're still building your sites with nested tables, graphic shims, and sliced graphics, the time has definitely come to begin exploring the more sophisticated options available to you. Even if you are unable to drop those conventional practices for contemporary, specification-driven ones, you can become more aware of the language requirements of an HTML document, how to keep it as structured as possible to assist with accessibility and portability across browsers and platforms, and how to write a conforming document even if you're using practices that are being shelved in favor of more effective options.

Document Conformance

Document conformance in Web markup means that each page of HTML (or XHTML) you author conforms to the official W3C specification to which it is written.

Author to the Specification

This means each of your HTML pages will have markup within them that is part of this conformance. In the case of HTML, the language type you use is found within a DOCTYPE, a declaration at the top of the HTML document that declares what kind of document it is and which version of HTML the DOCTYPE in question is referring to. You'll learn about language versions shortly, but keep in mind that along with a DOCTYPE, you must make sure that all the tags and attributes you use are allowed within the language version that you are declaring.

Validate the Document

Conformance is checked by the process of *validation*, which is covered later in this chapter. Validation is the comparison of your document with the language you declared in your DOCTYPE, just to see if you've made any errors. Validators return a list of errors, which you can then correct. Once you validate the document without any errors whatsoever, it is considered a *conforming* document, which is also referred to as a *compliant* document. Conforming documents are easier to work with, particularly when more than one document author is involved, and the process of validation is an excellent means of not only eliminating errors, but also of learning more about the languages with which you are working as a result.

Secret #81: Create a Markup Style and Stick to It

One of the biggest headaches in managing the code side of Web design is the variations that exist in how markup is formatted. I don't mean how it will look on display, but how the code itself is formatted behind the scenes. Readers authoring their documents by hand have often developed their own formatting practices (see Figure 6-2 for an example), such as indenting tables and lists, by placing elements in uppercase and attributes in lowercase, and not quoting attributes. Add to this

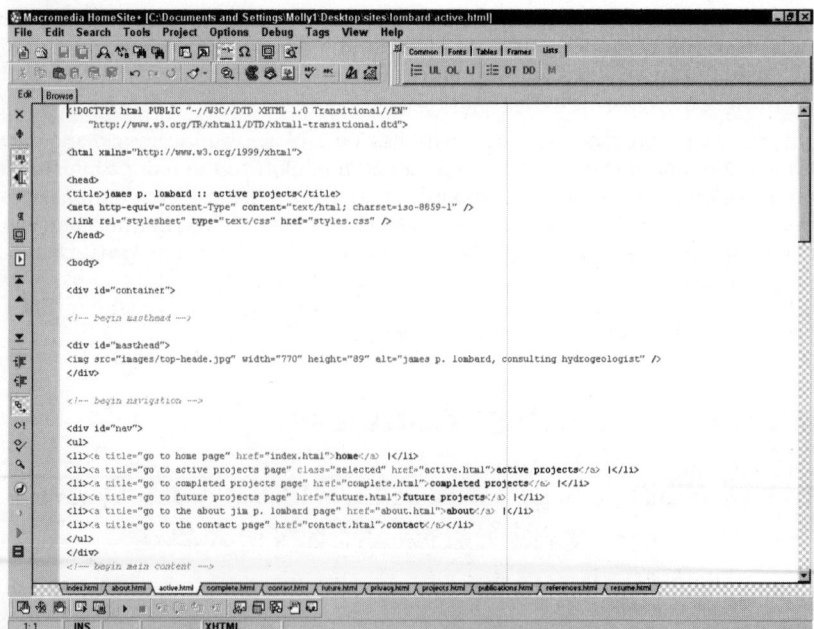

Figure 6-2: A look at my personal formatting habits within my favorite editor, Homesite.

the discrepancies in Web publishing software (refer to Figure 6-3), and what you have is a big mess.

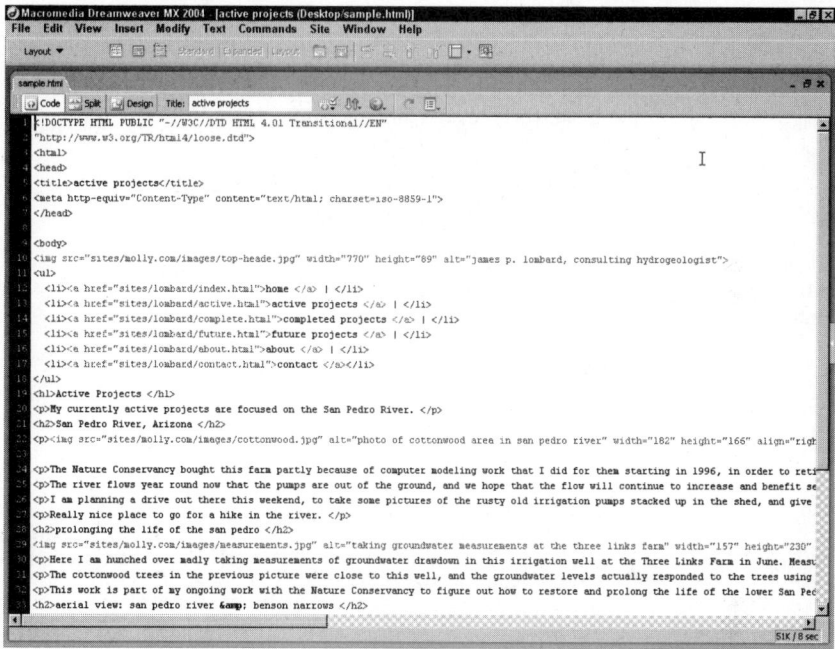

Figure 6-3: Here's an example of formatting in Dreamweaver MX 2004.

Imagine working in a group environment where files are modified and updated by numerous content and document authors. If there is no consistency in the style of markup, chaos not only can, but most likely will, ensue.

Even if you're working on your own, disparities in how you format your HTML within the page can affect you. For example, perhaps you'd like to perform a search and replace on a large number of documents, but the formatting is vastly different from one document to the other. Most software won't recognize something that is formatted dramatically differently than the piece of markup you might be searching for, making the time required to fix or update those 100 pages far greater.

So whether you're working on a team or by yourself, making some decisions about how to properly format your markup can help save hours of frustration for all.

Table 6-1 offers some ideas for better success with formatting HTML.

Secret #82: Understand Document Types and Language Versions

Not all markup was created equally. When Tim Berners-Lee and his colleagues were cooking up the Web in their particle physics lab at The European Organization for Nuclear Research (CERN) in Switzerland, the need for a very simple markup language for formatting text on-screen with the ability to have hyperlinks became obvious.

Table 6-1: HTML Formatting Strategies

Action	Benefit	Example

Indenting Table Cells	For streamlined tables, some indentation is helpful when working with nested portions of the table. This provides white space and allows the person working on the markup to quickly find specific data or problems within the code itself	`<table>`
		`<tr>`
		`<td>content here</td>`
		`<tr>`
		`</table>`

Indenting List Items and Nested Lists	As with nested table cells, indenting nested lists can be very helpful in troubleshooting and more effectively finding content that requires repair	`<ul>`
		`<li></li>`
		`<ul>`
		`<li></li>`
		`</ul>`
		`<li></li>`
		`<li></li>`
		`</ul>`

Managing Case	HTML is not case sensitive. Prior to XHTML (See Chapter 7, "Moving Ahead with XHTML"), case in HTML was irrelevant, so you'd often get a total mishmash of case styles—even within the same document. XHTML is case sensitive, and I recommend all authors use lowercase at this time, even if they're working in HTML. If an upgrade to XHTML is ever in the future of those documents, the process will be far easier and less time-consuming as a result	In HTML you can have a variety of cases:
		`<HTML LANG="EN">`
		`<html lang="en">`
		`<HTML lang="EN">`
		`<HtMl LaNg="eN">`
		`<htML laNG="eN">`
		All of these mean the same thing. When you advance to XHTML it changes. As a result, contemporary authoring is best kept to lowercase:
		`<html lang="en">`
		For more information on case in XHTML, see Chapter 7

Managing Quotes	The concerns regarding quotes around attribute values in HTML are similar to those for case. HTML is far less strict than XHTML in terms of quoting rules. While you can never go wrong in HTML quoting an attribute value, you can go wrong not quoting it. So, quote all attributes, even in HTML where the rules about quotes are fairly arbitrary	In HTML, you could correctly write the following: `<body bgcolor=black background="blackdot.gif">` It will likely work in the vast majority of browsers. However, think about the error margin that emerges here. You could add a start quote but forget the ending quote. A mistake of that nature can leave you in troubleshooting hell for hours. By quoting all attribute values, you reduce or even eliminate this kind of problem

Action	Benefit	Example
Using Comments	Comments are a gift from the programming forefathers and we should take care to use them effectively. Properly commenting particular areas within a document means you, or your colleagues, can find that area more quickly. You can also provide information about the content, directions to other authors or content specialists, and hide information from a browser that might be needed sometime in the future	Add comments to the beginning of a section: `<! -- begin meta data -->` As directions: `<! -- content authors begin adding content here -- >` To hide information for later use: `<! -- <h2>Holiday Specials!</h2> -->` One important note here is to use comments but to do so where most needed. Over-commenting a site can be just as troublesome as having no comments available at all

HTML in its infancy included very simple markup—at the time Berners-Lee was adding the spices to his stew, the Web did not serve up a graphical user interface (GUI). Therefore, the primary markings needed were related to simple structural elements such as headings, paragraphs, line breaks, lists, and horizontal rules.

Of course, the Web shot out of the hands of CERN researchers faster than you could say "it's soup!" and suddenly the Web was everywhere. GUI interfaces began to emerge (Mosaic being the first in widespread use), and with a graphical means of displaying pages, new features were desired. Over the next few years, chaos ensued, and HTML became so mixed up that sites using no formal HTML are referred to as being written in "tag soup." This became extremely problematic, as there was no consistency in workflow, browser support, and developer tools support.

note
: **The W3C creates specifications for three primary audiences: browser developers, Web developers, and software developers creating programs for Web design and development.**

To address the changing needs, the W3C broke HTML 4.0 up into three distinct types. Each of these varieties is governed by a separate Document Type Definition (DTD). A DTD is the list of elements, attributes, characters, colors, and related requirements for a given language, or in this case, language variety.

The three DTDs for HTML 4 are as follows:

- **Strict.** Strict versions of HTML call for a separation of structure and presentation. Few presentational attributes or elements are available in this version, such as font tags, alignment attributes, and so on. The idea is that strict versions are to be used with CSS. Strict DTDs do not allow for anything that is considered obsolete (no longer in use) or deprecated (still in use but moved aside to make way for a better method) in the language to be used.

◆ **Transitional.** A lot more leniency exists with presentational attributes. You can freely use font elements in a transitional document, although it's not recommended nor is it considered necessary because of the widespread support of most font-related features in CSS. Transitional DTDs allow deprecated elements and attributes with the understanding that people using these techniques are transitional—not quite ready to commit to a strict DTD.

◆ **Frameset.** The frameset DTD defines the allowed elements and attributes within the frameset document. This document controls frame-based sites. Documents within a framed site should be written according to either strict or transitional DTDs.

note   HTML 4.01 is a minor editorial update to HTML 4.0. Most people who work with HTML now use HTML 4.01 as their language, with the DTD varying depending on their site needs.

Secret #83:   Use DOCTYPEs

DTDs are declared in the document using a DOCTYPE declaration, which, as mentioned earlier, describes the language, version, and language type. Using a DOCTYPE is *required* to have a document that conforms. DOCTYPEs are placed at the very top of a document, above the opening <html> tag.

Consider the following snippet, which is a DOCTYPE declaration for HTML 4.01 Strict:

```
<!DOCTYPE HTML PUBLIC "-//W3C//DTD HTML 4.01 Transitional//EN"
        "http://www.w3.org/TR/html4/loose.dtd">
```

For those familiar with HTML, you'll recognize some of what's here, but some of the syntax is different. That's because DOCTYPEs aren't HTML; they are SGML constructs.

To translate this DOCTYPE declaration, one could say this:

The document type in question is an HTML document. It is PUBLIC, which means that the DTD it refers to is publicly available for use. It was authored and is housed at the W3C, and it refers to the HTML 4.01 Transitional DTD, in English, and is located at the URL typically found indented on the second line of the declaration. (This placement is convention—you can place all the information on a single line or break it up differently, as long as those items that require a space between them get the space, and those items that have no spaces are kept intact.)

Table 6-2 shows the appropriate DOCTYPEs for HTML 4.01.

DOCTYPEs used to be passive code until validation, when the validator used the code to determine which DTD to compare your document to. In today's browsers, however, a new technology called "DOCTYPE switching" exists, making the use of proper DOCTYPEs not only required, but critical to the stability of your designs.

Either way, the professional designer or developer uses correct DOCTYPEs.

Table 6-2: DOCTYPEs in HTML 4.01

DTD	DOCTYPE
Strict	<!DOCTYPE HTML PUBLIC "-//W3C//DTD HTML 4.01//EN" "www.w3.org/TR/html4/strict.dtd">
Transitional	<!DOCTYPE HTML PUBLIC "-//W3C//DTD HTML 4.01 Transitional//EN" "www.w3.org/TR/html4/loose.dtd">
Frameset	<!DOCTYPE HTML PUBLIC "-//W3C//DTD HTML 4.01 Frameset//EN" "www.w3.org/TR/html4/frameset.dtd">

cross ref

For more information about **DOCTYPE** switching, see Chapter 7.

Secret #84:   HTML is Root

Now that you have an idea of what DOCTYPEs and DTDs are, you can begin authoring your documents. Oddly enough, in early versions of HTML the <html> tags *were not required*. In fact, if you create a document and leave the <html> tags out of it, it will surely display, even though it won't be a conforming document.

However, the <html> tagset does form an important piece of the structure of a document—one that you will later want to have available for use with style and scripting, and for global application of the lang attribute, discussed later this chapter. It's also important to move forward with XHTML, as you'll see in Chapter 7.

The html element is what's referred to as the "root" of the document. It is from this root that the document tree grows. Document trees are a means of showing the schematic relationships of elements within the document. Being able to identify trees within documents will help you immeasurably as you work with style and scripts.

Check out Listing 6-1. In it, I've begun to build a document using HTML 4.01 Transitional. While incomplete, it includes the proper DOCTYPE declaration and the root element with its opening and closing tags.

Listing 6-1: Building a document tree with a DOCTYPE and html as root

```
<!DOCTYPE HTML PUBLIC "-//W3C//DTD HTML 4.01 Transitional//EN"
    "http://www.w3.org/TR/html4/loose.dtd">

<html>

</html>
```

tip

Think of elements that have an open and closing tag (also referred to as a "tagset") as containers. As you add a tag, always add its companion at the same time. This helps to avoid missing a necessary closing tag.

Secret #85: Use <head> and <body> Appropriately

Once your root elements are in place, you can add the head and body portions of your document. Addressing the idea of not using these very basic HTML elements might seem silly, but I have seen countless pages where these critical tags either don't exist, are improperly nested, or appear more than once—or have the wrong type of information within them.

The head portion of a document comes after the root and before the body elements. The head of a document is like the head of a human—it contains all the stuff that's used to keep things working, such as the following:

+ **Title.** This is the title that will appear in the browser's title bar.
+ **Metadata.** All forms of meta information, including description, keywords, and character set definitions.
+ **Scripts.** Document-related scripts can appear in the head within or linked to the document via the script element.
+ **CSS.** Embedded CSS can appear in the head between the style element, external CSS can be imported using the style element, and external CSS can be linked using the link element.
+ **Aggregation.** XML-based aggregation such as Rich Site Summary (RSS), Resource Description Framework (RDF), and related formats can be linked from the head using the link element.
+ **Favicons.** You know them as the little icons that appear in the address bar of certain browsers. You can add them using the link element with the head portion of a document.

cross
ref
You can find more information about aggregation technologies in Chapter 13, "Keeping Content Fresh and Engaging."

HTML markup that is not allowed in the head portion of a document is any html element or attribute not related to metadata, scripting, style, and other information *about* rather than *on* the page. The only exception to these items is that special characters *can* be used in the text content of titles:

```
<title>Sugar &amp; Spice</title>
```

Directly below the head and its contents is the body. Almost every element and attribute used within the body relates either to the structuring of content, or to its formatting (although again, CSS is encouraged for all presentation). Sometimes scripting is included.

Listing 6-2 adds the head and body elements to our growing document.

Listing 6-2: Adding the head and body elements

```
<!DOCTYPE HTML PUBLIC "-//W3C//DTD HTML 4.01 Transitional//EN"
    "http://www.w3.org/TR/html4/loose.dtd">

<html>
<head>
```

```
</head>
<body>

</body>
</html>
```

Secret #86:   Always Use <title>

While style, scripting, aggregation, and metadata are all optional elements within the head element based on what's required by a specific site, a title with a good description *is never optional*.

You must always have a title element for your page, or the page will not validate. Keep titles clear, and use them to orient your site visitors.

> **cross ref**   **Read more about writing titles in Chapter 5, "Creating and Managing Fantastic Content."**

Listing 6-3 shows the growing document including a title.

Listing 6-3: Adding the title element

```
<!DOCTYPE HTML PUBLIC "-//W3C//DTD HTML 4.01 Transitional//EN"
      "http://www.w3.org/TR/html4/loose.dtd">

<html>
<head>
<title>Creating a Conforming HTML Document</title>
</head>
<body>

</body>
</html>
```

Secret #87:   Manage Character Sets

Languages use characters, and different languages have different characters. Character sets in HTML define the character set used in the document and inform the user agent which character set is in use.

Character sets can be defined in one of three places:

♦ **An XML declaration.** This declaration can be used in XML documents, including XHTML. See Chapter 7 for specifics about the XML declaration. If you are using an XML declaration (and there are certain reasons you probably should not), it is an acceptable place to add character set information.

- **A `meta` element.** This is a common way to include character set information in a document. I think it's a good idea to use it, even if you are using other forms. It's simply a preference—it's easier to validate a document locally if the character set is defined within a `meta` element.
- **On the server.** Server administrators can define the character set in the server's HTTP headers. This is actually the most recommended method, but it's out of the hands of most Web designers and developers, who can easily implement character sets using the `meta` element.

Many character sets are available for use. For documents in most Latin-based languages including English, Spanish, French, Italian and so on, the Latin set is often used. The following HTML snippet shows the `charset` attribute with a value for the Latin set:

```
<meta http-equiv="Content-Type" content="text/html;
charset=iso-8859-1">
```

UTF-8, a more universal character set, is also growing in use:

```
<meta http-equiv="Content-Type" content="text/html; charset=UTF-8">
```

> **note**
>
> Values for other languages include shift_js for Japanese, EUC-JP, which is another Japanese encoding, and ISO-8859-5, which supports Cyrillic.
>
> For a complete discussion and linked references regarding character sets in Web documents, see "HTML Document Representation" for HTML at the W3C, www.w3.org/TR/REC-html40/charset.html.

Listing 6-4 shows the document with the meta element for a Latin character set (suitable for English) in place. While it's not necessary to have this for a valid document (due to the fact that character sets can also be denoted elsewhere), it is necessary to validate the document via upload using the W3C's validator, discussed later this chapter.

Listing 6-4: Adding the meta element

```
<!DOCTYPE HTML PUBLIC "-//W3C//DTD HTML 4.01 Transitional//EN"
    "http://www.w3.org/TR/html4/loose.dtd">

<html>
<head>
<title>Creating a Conforming HTML Document</title>
<meta http-equiv="Content-Type" content="text/html;
charset=iso-8859-1">

</head>
<body>

</body>
</html>
```

Save this listing to your local computer for use as a basic template for almost all HTML authoring needs.

Secret #88:   Author Documents Structurally

With everything in place, DOCTYPE and structural components of the document such as head and body intact, you're ready to add content to your document.

In Chapter 5 you read about the fact that Web authors and authoring tools don't always use headers properly—instead of a hierarchical implementation, they are used because of how they display. This, while not a conformance problem, is a problem that will cause you countless hours of frustration later on as you attempt to style your document effectively. So, keeping documents very cleanly structured is important. This means using headers, paragraphs, even horizontal rules with sensitivity toward the semantic meaning of the tag.

Listing 6-5 shows an example of structural markup with content.

Listing 6-5: Adding structural markup

```
<!DOCTYPE HTML PUBLIC "-//W3C//DTD HTML 4.01 Transitional//EN"
     "http://www.w3.org/TR/html4/loose.dtd">

<html>
<head>
<title>Creating a Conforming HTML Document</title>
<meta http-equiv="Content-Type" content="text/html;
charset=iso-8859-1">

</head>
<body>
<h1>Welcome to Meyer Shoes</h1>
<p>Welcome to the Meyer Shoes web site. Here, you'll find a
complete catalog of our styles for men, women, and children as
well as information about our company and fast, responsive
customer service.</p>

<h2>Meyer Style</h2>
<p>If you hunger for style, crave quality, and desire comfort,
look no further! Meyer Shoes is a specialty shoe company that uses
only the highest quality leathers and fabrics to handcraft each of
its unique styles.</p>

<h2>Custom Style</h2>
<p>Whether you are looking for men's, women's or chidren's styles,
we're sure we can help you find a shoe that meets all your wishes.
And if we somehow don't offer a style that yells "Me!" we'll
custom design a pair that is distinctly yours.</p>
<hr>

<p>Copyright 2004 <a href="mailto:meyer@meyershoes.biz">Meyer
Shoes</a>, Inc.</p>

</body>
</html>
```

This simple document shows appropriately structured headers, paragraphs and rules within the body element.

Secret #89: Use Lists to Enhance Structure and Readability

A structured document is one that is portable across user agents and platforms and far easier to style and manage for the long term.

Lists, as I mentioned from a content perspective in Chapter 5, are a very good way to enhance readability on a page, and they are an equally good way to structure information.

In the past few years, it's become extremely popular to use lists for navigation. As the awareness of structure becomes more widespread, and the use of CSS becomes

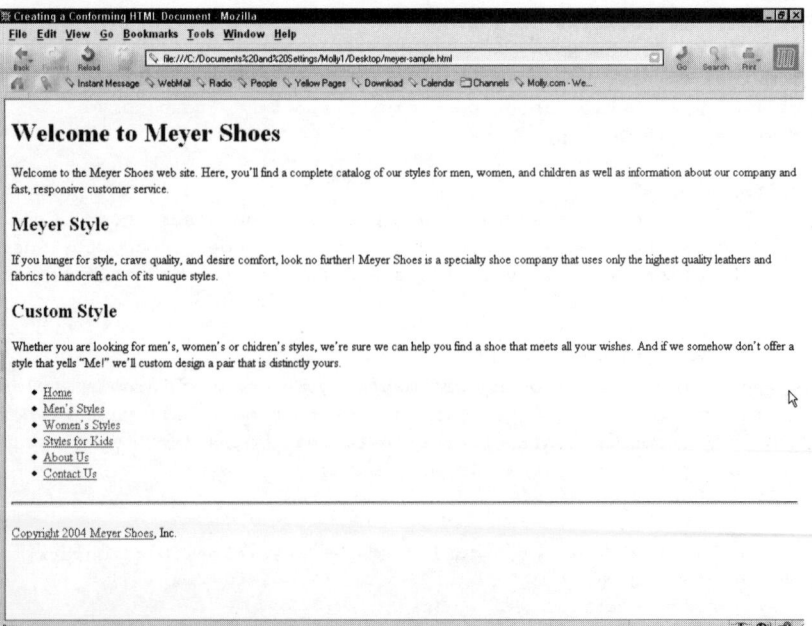

Figure 6-4: The unstyled but very structured results.

more readily available for most Web designers, lists—especially of the unordered variety—have begun to form the markup side of very impressive navigation design that doesn't rely on any scripting for visual enhancements.

> **note** You'll learn to create navigation—both vertical and horizontal designs—all using lists in Chapter 8, "Style Tips for Type and Design."

It makes a great deal of sense to use lists for navigation. Even if you style the list to appear on a Web page horizontally, it's still a list of like items—all links to other locations on the site. The logic pans out, too. If we add a list of navigation links to our current document, while it won't look very pretty for now (Figure 6-4), it surely makes logical sense.

Listing 6-5: Adding a list

```
<!DOCTYPE HTML PUBLIC "-//W3C//DTD HTML 4.01 Transitional//EN"
    "http://www.w3.org/TR/html4/loose.dtd">

<html>
<head>
<title>Creating a Conforming HTML Document</title>
<meta http-equiv="Content-Type" content="text/html;
charset=iso-8859-1">
</head>
<body>
<h1>Welcome to Meyer Shoes</h1>
<p>Welcome to the Meyer Shoes Web site. Here, you'll find a
complete catalog of our styles for men, women, and children as
well as information about our company and fast, responsive
customer service.</p>

<h2>Meyer Style</h2>
<p>If you hunger for style, crave quality, and desire comfort,
look no further! Meyer Shoes is a specialty shoe company that uses
only the highest quality leathers and fabrics to handcraft each of
its unique styles.</p>

<h2>Custom Style</h2>
<p>Whether you are looking for men's, women's or chidren's styles,
we're sure we can help you find a shoe that meets all your wishes.
And if we somehow don't offer a style that yells "Me!" we'll
custom design a pair that is distinctly yours.</p>

<ul>
<li><a href="index.html">Home</a></li>
<li><a href="mens.html">Men's Styles</a></li>
<li><a href="womens.html">Women's Styles</a></li>
<li><a href="childrens.html">Styles for Kids</a></li>
<li><a href="about.html">About Us</a></li>
<li><a href="contact.html">Contact Us</li>
</ul>
```

(continued)

Listing 6-5: *(continued)*

```
<hr>

<p>Copyright 2004 <a href="mailto:meyer@meyershoes.biz">Meyer
Shoes</a>, Inc.</p>

</body>
</html>
```

> **note** If you think this looks like a document you might have written in 1994, good. The point is to get back to the simplicity of markup and content. We have CSS to perform all the presentation now. If you open this document up in browser it's going to look boring as heck, but that's because it's an unstyled document. What's more, you can look at it in any kind of browser conceivable, even Mosaic 1.0, and the document contents will display. And while it's still without style, it's formatted in a logical way, since it's structured logically.

Secret #90: `<em>` and `<strong>` versus `<i>` and `<b>`

Many people wonder what the difference is between these text formatting options: em, strong, i, and b. The em and strong are structural, semantic elements, whereas i and b are considered presentational.

The fact that any content marked with an em element will display as italic and strong as bold is convention. It is not required that these elements appear specifically as italics and bold. If a blind person reading a Web page using screen reader technology comes across text markup with emphasis, the reader voice modulates to emphasize the words in question. Similarly, the strong element will be read in a more full voice.

The i and b elements are meant for presentation: italics and bold. There is a difference between structure and presentation, and it matters big-time in today's contemporary design practices. I recommend using em and strong in all cases where you might have thought to use i and b.

> **note** Another element to add to your avoid list is the u element, used to make an underline. Critics of this element say that underlining text confuses users because underlines typically signify links on the Web.

In Listing 6-6, I've added instances of emphasis and strong to our current document to show how they might be used.

Listing 6-6: Adding emphasis and strong

```
<!DOCTYPE HTML PUBLIC "-//W3C//DTD HTML 4.01 Transitional//EN"
      "http://www.w3.org/TR/html4/loose.dtd">

<html>
```

```
<head>
<title>Creating a Conforming HTML Document</title>
<meta http-equiv="Content-Type" content="text/html;
charset=iso-8859-1">

</head>
<body>
<h1>Welcome to Meyer Shoes</h1>
<p>Welcome to the Meyer Shoes Web site. Here, you'll find a
complete catalog of our styles for men, women, and children as
well as information about our company and fast, responsive
customer service.</p>

<h2>Meyer Style</h2>
<p>If you hunger for style, crave quality, and desire comfort,
look no further! Meyer Shoes is a specialty shoe company that uses
<em>only</em> the highest quality leathers and fabrics to
handcraft each of its unique styles.</p>

<h2>Custom Style</h2>
<p>Whether you are looking for men's, women's or chidren's styles,
we're sure we can help you find a shoe that meets
<strong>all</strong> your wishes. And if we somehow don't offer a
style that yells "Me!" we'll custom design a pair that is
<em>distinctly</em> yours.</p>

<ul>
<li><a href="index.html">Home</a></li>
<li><a href="mens.html">Men's Styles</a></li>
<li><a href="womens.html">Women's Styles</a></li>
<li><a href="childrens.html">Styles for Kids</a></li>
<li><a href="about.html">About Us</a></li>
<li><a href="contact.html">Contact Us</li>
</ul>

<hr>

<p>Copyright 2004 <a href="mailto:meyer@meyershoes.biz">Meyer
Shoes</a>, Inc.</p>

</body>
</html>
```

Figure 6-5 shows the modified markup as rendered in Mozilla Firebird.

Secret #91:   Know your Document Tree

Now that we have an entire document, we can map out the tree.

In the document we just created, we began with the DOCTYPE declaration, which isn't considered part of the tree. Think of it as the tree's label. It denotes what kind of a tree it is. But if we begin with the html element and chart the hierarchical

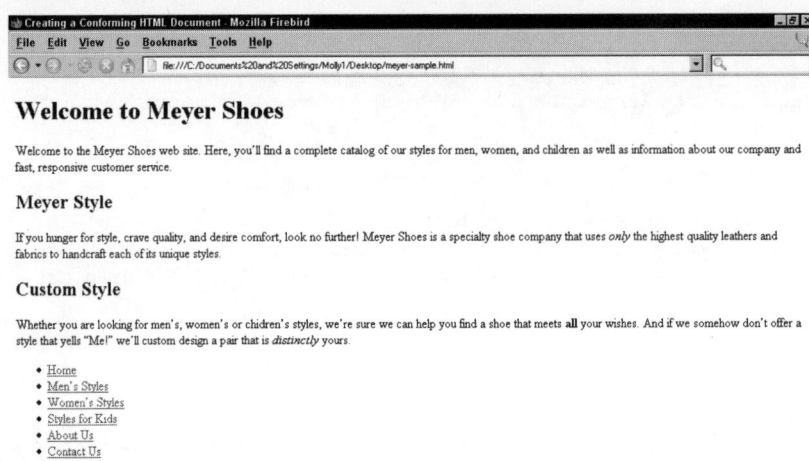

Figure 6-5: Viewing the document in Mozilla Firebird.

relationships between elements, we end up with a graphical representation very similar to a family tree (see Figure 6-6).

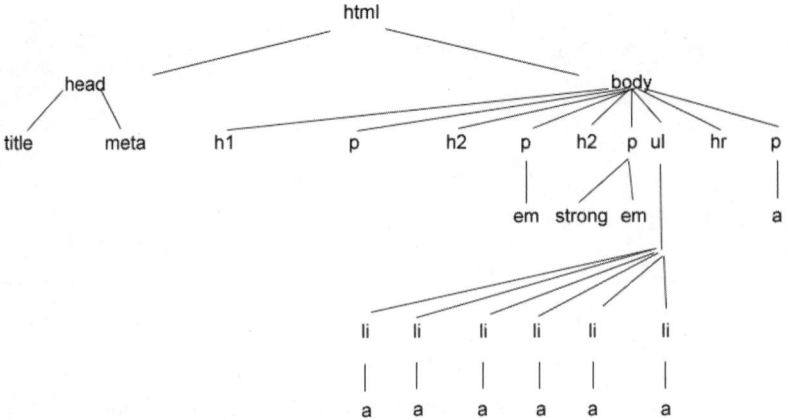

Figure 6-6: Map of the document tree.

The terminology used to describe relationships with elements is very familial. The html element is a parent element to its children, the head and body elements.

Because the head and body elements sit on the same level of the hierarchy, they are considered siblings. This language becomes important in CSS, when you examine the concept of *inheritance*. This is the idea that properties (which you can think of as traits) are passed down from one element to another. So, if I were to give a style rule to html that contained inheritable traits, those traits would be inherited right on through the tree.

> **tip**   Choose a document you're working on and sketch out its tree. This is a good
> way to become comfortable with the way elements relate to one another.

Secret #92:   Elements, Tags, and Attributes

One thing that drives me to distraction is the way terminology is constantly misused
in HTML. Very few of today's working Web designers have had formal training in
the language, so misuse of nomenclature is understandable. However, the trouble
it causes is twofold:

- ◆ Vague use of language makes it difficult for team members, including
  project managers, to make clear, understandable statements.
- ◆ An individual with an improper understanding of terminology may
  influence or incorrectly instruct co-workers, causing confusion.

An *element* is a tagset, or a tag and any content it relates to. An element can be made
up of an opening and closing tag or a single tag. Any element that contains text
content (such as headers, paragraphs, and list items) is considered a *nonempty*
element and usually requires an opening and closing tag in HTML (although
as previously mentioned, HTML versions don't require a closing tag for certain
elements, such as paragraphs and list items).

Any element that does not contain content is considered an *empty* element. Examples include line breaks, horizontal rules, and images.

Elements are also considered to be either *block* or *inline*. A block element is one
that is self-contained. Block elements generate a carriage return. Examples include
headers, paragraphs, and list items. Inline elements are those used within a block
but without generating any breaks, such as links, images, emphasis, strong, and
so on.

Tags are the literal markup tags that are used to express the element, such as
`<h1>...</h1>`, `<hr>`, `<meta>`, and so on.

Attributes allow certain traits to be applied to an element. Attributes are made up
of two components, the attribute *name* and the attribute *value*. The name defines
what the attribute is, and the value (which can vary in value types) describes how
the attribute is to be applied, such as in the following example:

```
align="right"
```

Figure 6-7 shows the anatomy of an element, including its attributes.

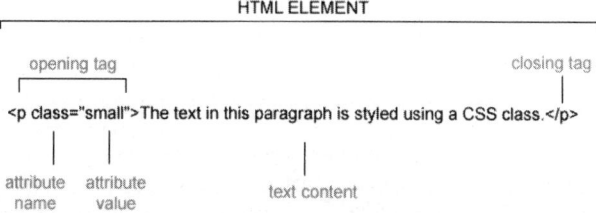

Figure 6-7: Anatomy of an element.

Secret #93: Intrinsic Events

Intrinsic event handlers are a type of attribute reserved as a way to handle events within the browser, and to attach scripts to elements via the Document Object Model (DOM). The DOM is the interface within a browser that enables scripting to actively influence elements and their behavior. The attribute value will be related to the script in question.

Table 6-3 shows event handlers in HTML and what they do.

Table 6-3: Intrinsic Events in HTML 4.01

Intrinsic Event	Description	Allowed Elements
onload	This event occurs when the browser finishes loading a document into a window, or all documents are loaded within a frameset	body frameset
onunload	This event occurs when the document is removed from the browser	body frameset
onclick	This event occurs when a user clicks on an element	Almost all elements
ondblclick	This event occurs when a user double-clicks on an element	Almost all elements
onmousedown	This event is triggered when the mouse button is in the down state over an element	Almost all elements
onmouseup	This event occurs when the mouse button is released from the element	Almost all elements
onmouseover	This event occurs when the mouse passes over the element	Almost all elements
onmousemove	This event happens when the mouse is moved over an element	Almost all elements
onmouseout	This event occurs when the mouse is moved away from the elements	Almost all elements
onfocus	When an element receives focus either via a pointing device or tabbed navigation, this event occurs	a area label input select textarea button
onblur	When an element that had focus loses focus due to the pointing device or tabbing moving away from the element	Same as for onfocus

Intrinsic Event	Description	Allowed Elements
onkeypress	This event occurs when a key is pressed and released over an element	Almost all elements
onkeydown	This event occurs when a key is pressed and held down over an element	Almost all elements
onkeyup	This event is triggered when a key in a pressed position is released	Almost all elements
onsubmit	This event occurs when a form is submitted	This applies to the form element *only*
onreset	This event occurs when a form is reset	Also applies to the form element only
onselect	This occurs when text in a text field is selected	input textarea
onchange	This occurs when a form control loses input focus and the value has already been modified	input select textarea

> **tip**
>
> Many people use camel case for their intrinsic events, such as **onMouseOver**. This is a popular convention, but wise to avoid if you're using or ever plan on upgrading your HTML documents to XHTML. In XHTML, you can't have any uppercase characters in your attribute names (See Chapter 7).

Secret #94:   Special Characters

Another area where you, as the designer, should take care to conform to specifications is in working with special characters. Special characters, or *character entities*, are a series of codes that control symbols, letters, and math-related characters. You've probably come across some of these entities in your work. Common examples include the entity for the copyright symbol, © and the entity for a nonbreaking space, .

> **note**
>
> There are numerous entities, but not all of them are considered standard. Unfortunately, some Web design software packages include entities that aren't standardized, which makes working with them even more difficult, although validating a document with nonstandard entities will return a helpful error. For a complete set of conforming character entities, see "Character Entities in HTML and XHTML" at the Web Standards Project (www.webstandards.org/learn/reference/entities.html).

There are three types of character entities within HTML (and XHTML):

- **ISO 8859-1 characters.** This set includes the Latin set of character entities.
- **Symbols, mathematical characters, Greek, and Latin letters.** This set includes entities for various symbols (such as copyright symbols and so on), math characters, and Greek and Latin letters.
- **Markup-significant characters.** This set includes internationalization characters such as those required for bi-directional text.

All characters are represented by both a named and numeric value. You can use either value as long as you find the character among those considered valid, and test the character in the target browsers for your project.

tip	If you've chosen a named or numeric value that doesn't display consistently in your target browsers, consider using the other value type.

Secret #95: Limit Color Names to Standard Colors

As with special characters, numerous color names in HTML are not standardized. In fact, the list of standard names for use with HTML is so short that it's included in this section in its entirety.

You should remember a few things about color names:

- You can use any standard color name in place of a hexadecimal value in an HTML document.
- Because there are only 16 standard names, you might prefer to use hexadecimal values instead.
- Not all standard color names are part of the Web-safe palette, if that's a concern to you.
- You can use these color names with CSS, too. CSS offers more color value options than HTML, and it's no problem to combine names and other available values, but if you're going to use a color name, it has to be one of the following in order to be valid.

Table 6-4 shows standard color names. The corresponding hexadecimal values are included so you can see what's Web-safe and what's not.

note	Want the truth about Web-safe colors? See Chapter 11, "Sophisticated Visual Design in a Global Market."

Secret #96: Avoid the font Element

The font element was a problem element from its inception. It's not that it isn't well supported because, ironically, it happens to be very well supported. And it's not that more font faces are available in CSS—the same issues concerning font

Table 6-4: Standard Color Names for Use in HTML, XHTML, and CSS

Color Name	Corresponding Hex Value
Black	#000000
Silver	#C0C0C0
Gray	#808080
White	#FFFFFF
Maroon	#800000
Red	#FF0000
Purple	#800080
Fuchsia	#FF00FF
Green	#008000
Lime	#00FF00
Olive	#808000
Yellow	#FFFF00
Navy	#000080
Blue	#0000FF
Teal	#008080
Aqua	#00FFFF

support occur in CSS and in HTML, although CSS offers more sizing and display options.

Problems arise for two main reasons. The first is that using the font element goes against the premise that ideally we separate our structured document (which you've learned to do in this chapter) from anything that is presentational. Historically, presentation via CSS wasn't very well supported. However, at this time, almost all font features in CSS are supported across every conceivable contemporary browser, as well as having some support in older browsers such as Netscape 4.x versions and Internet Explorer (IE) as early as 3.0, which incidentally was the first commercial browser to include any CSS support.

The second concern is that using the font element clutters up documents greatly. This is especially true in table-based layouts, where a font has to be redefined in every single table cell. Using the font element within tables accounts for the majority of unneeded page weight out there on the Web.

What's the bottom line when it comes to the font element? *Don't use it.* It's unnecessary at this point in history, and CSS is much more practical.

> **note** Warren Steel's "What's Wrong with the Font Element" is still one of the most requested Web documents around. The article gives a detailed look at problems related to the font element; find it at www.mcsr.olemiss.edu /~mudws/font.html.
>
> Another interesting article is "<FONT FACE> Considered Harmful," in which the specifics of the face attribute are criticized. Read it at http://alis.isoc.org/ web_ml/html/fontface.en.html.

Secret #97: Avoid the center Element

What's wrong with the center element? It's valid in transitional documents, it works, and we've used it for years.

Introduced by Netscape back in the day, center was very valuable in terms of helping us center text or tables on a page. We now know that this was a kludge to begin with.

Here is what's wrong with the center element:

* The syntax of center is ambiguous. It is semantically more suited to be an attribute, not an element.
* It is a deprecated element in HTML 4.01, and as with all deprecated elements, it should be avoided (as addressed in the next secret).
* The concept of center is presentational, so its use has fallen out of favor. Use CSS instead.

> **note** Centering in CSS is its own challenge. See "CSS Centering" in Chapter 9, "Laying Out Pages with CSS."

Secret #98: Avoid All Deprecated, Obsolete, and Proprietary Elements and Attributes

If an element or attribute is deprecated, obsolete, or proprietary, avoid it.

A deprecated element or attribute is one that is allowed for use in some DTDs, but a preferred method exists. I always imagine a deprecated element or attribute as being the kid in the dunce cap—he's still in the room, but he's almost on his way out.

Deprecated elements that should be avoided include the following:

* applet
* basefont
* center
* dir
* font
* isindex
* menu
* s
* strike
* u

Obsolete elements are those that have been removed from a specification, but had been there at some point in the past. Typically, you won't have likely ever even seen obsolete elements, which include such elements as listing, plaintext, and xmp.

Proprietary elements and attributes are those that are browser-specific and have never been entered into any specification. One such proprietary element that causes challenges to designers seeking to work within the specs is the embed element, used to embed Flash and other media into Web pages. The standard alternative is to use object, but there are browser compatibility issues with that.

---

cross ref   For more information on how to add media to a page using standards-compliant workarounds, see Chapter 12, "Spicing it Up with Dynamic Content and Rich Media."

Some common proprietary attributes include leftmargin and rightmargin. These attributes are often used to set page margins (but we have CSS for that now).

---

tip   Validating documents will find any instances of obsolete or proprietary elements and attributes. Deprecated elements and attributes will not cause errors in validation if you are using a DTD that supports them, which will typically be a transitional rather than strict DTD. Note that you can even use deprecated elements in Transitional XHTML (see Chapter 7), but again, if you can use CSS for the job, do so.

Secret #99:   Use Elements as They Were Intended

Another issue with HTML elements is that people use them to achieve visual results—something for which HTML was never intended. Using elements in an inappropriate way is also referred to as a hack, and you want to avoid hacks in most instances.

Whether it's to add space by stacking break tags on top of each other:

```
<br>
<br>
<br>
```

Or using a space within a nonempty element to create space:

```
<p> </p>
```

Or adding space at the end of a line of list items:

```
<ul>
<li>Here's my item<br><br></li>
</ul>
```

The point is that while usage of this nature might not be invalid, it's not recommended. Space can be controlled using style, and that control is far more effective and less problematic than using hacks of this nature. Always try to use elements as they were intended to be used.

Secret #100:   Restrict Use of Tables

Using tables for layout is the biggest HTML hack around.

Table elements and attributes were developed for one reason: to display tabular data. Using them for any other reason is inappropriate.

That someone got the bright idea to turn off borders and create a grid system upon which we could lay out our Web documents so they were attractive on screen was truly revolutionary.

Despite the standards movement and a growing understanding of why using tables for layout has so many disadvantages, the vast majority of Web sites use tables as their means of page layout.

But we're now moving into a more sophisticated realm of understanding. It's becoming clear that restricting the use of tables brings many advantages, including the following:

- ♦ Cleaner, more streamlined pages, which are easier to manage
- ♦ Improvement of support for multiple user agents and device types including mobile phones, pagers, and PDAs.
- ♦ Improved accessibility for those with physical impairments
- ♦ Reduction of page weight by an average of 50 percent, resulting in faster download times and economic savings in bandwidth and storage.

These are all very attractive advantages, but if you're not using tables, how do you lay out your Web sites? If you can use all CSS-based layouts, you should. If you have to support browsers that have partial, imperfect, or nonexistent CSS support, use tables if you have to. Then, supplement with CSS where you can.

The use of tables with some CSS for layout purposes is referred to as *transitional design* and is a very good option for those designers who have to support diverse browsers. If you do choose this option, follow these guidelines for best results:

- ♦ Reduce the number of nested tables as much as possible.
- ♦ Reduce the number of table rows.
- ♦ Reduce the number of table cells.

In other words, use as simple a table as possible to achieve your layout, and fill in with CSS where you can.

note   **For an interesting perspective on the transition from tables to CSS for layouts, see "From Table Hacks to CSS Layout: A Web Designer's Journey" by Jeffrey Zeldman, at www.alistapart.com/articles/journey/.**

Secret #101:   Restrict Use of Frames

Just as with tables, restricting use of frames makes for a more manageable, accessible, and usable Web site.

Frames can serve a few important purposes. They are excellent if you're creating some kind of a Web-based application where static content is desirable. IFrames are popular for managing advertising, and frames can be written to be completely valid. But they are known to have all kinds of problems associated with them, such as the following:

♦ The focus of frames is layout, which goes against HTML as a structural language.

♦ Because of their presentational nature, frames are limited to Web browsers and are not supported at this time by those user agents on mobile devices, limiting your site's portability and interoperability.

♦ Frames require multiple documents to create a single visual output. This means more documents to manage and store.

♦ Frames are difficult or downright impossible to manage by screen readers and other assistive devices used by those with physical disabilities.

♦ If a user agent doesn't support frames, there is no way to degrade the documents; the agent simply can't display the results unless you provide script-based workarounds, meaning extra work for you and all kinds of support problems for your users.

Deciding to use frames for any reason should be a decision that comes about after researching other alternatives for achieving the same goals.

Secret #102:   Validate, Validate, Validate!

Find out if your document conforms by validating it. Validation is the process of comparing your completed document to the DTD defined in the DOCTYPE. Your document is compared and any errors will be displayed.

Typically, begin troubleshooting invalid documents by fixing the first error along with any errors related specifically to proprietary or problem elements and then revalidate. Fixing the first reported error and then revalidating will often reveal that numerous other reported errors were a result of that first, incorrect error.

> tip   You can validate documents using any number of validation tools. See
> Chapter 1, "Setting up a Master Toolbox" for more details.

I ran the document we created in this chapter through the validator at the W3C. You can see the favorable results in Figure 6-8. Also, because we have no presentational elements or attributes in our document at all, we can now rest comfortably

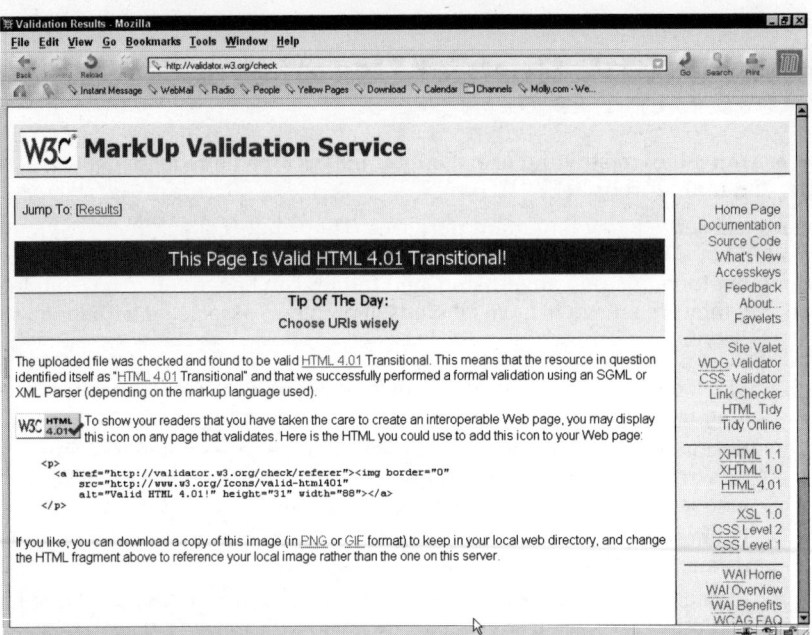

Figure 6-8: Validation success.

knowing that the document is a conforming, compliant, standards-based structural document ready for styling.

Summary

Everything in this chapter was geared to help those who have been working with visual editors or marking up documents according to conventions rather than standards, move toward a more sophisticated understanding of the languages with which you work.

Next, we take a look at XHTML. While it is perfectly acceptable to use HTML for your Web documents, XHTML offers more insight into structure and semantics, greater flexibility, and a more forward-thinking methodology with which to author our documents.

Moving Ahead with XHTML

Chapter
7

◆ ◆

Secrets in This Chapter

◆ ◆

This chapter debunks myths, explains what XHTML is and why it's so very important, and provides all the scoop on how to author XHTML documents that you can use in every browser known to humankind—even those for alternative devices such as PDAs and cell phones.

About XHTML

If you're wondering why we need another language when HTML seemed to work just fine, you're not alone. Many people in the Web industry—including some markup experts—aren't necessarily convinced that XHTML offers any of the advantages for most Web designers that HTML does.

You might be surprised to read that I agree. For the most part, if you're designing Web sites, you can use HTML or XHTML. My major concern is that you use one or the other according to the standard and according to the rules and practices described here and in Chapter 6, "Crafting Pages with HTML."

Aside from that, I do believe that XHTML is a better choice for a few significant reasons, and this introduction and the subsequent secrets here reveal the advantages that XHTML does offer.

History

As you are aware, SGML is the meta-language from which Tim Berners-Lee created HTML. As the Web progressed both as a social and technical phenomenon, working groups at the W3C began to study long-term ideas for the languages and methods used on the Web. Many technologies have since emerged, including the Extensible Markup Language (XML).

XML, like SGML, is a meta-language that consists of specifications and guidelines for creating applications and other language subsets. XML, like HTML, also emerged from SGML, although not as a subset language itself. Think of XML as SGML "lite" for the Web—it is more streamlined than SGML, yet retains SGML's strict rules while simultaneously offering its authors flexible customization options.

With XML in hand, HTML 4.0 in place with its three DTDs, and CSS available, the W3C began re-examining HTML and determined that it had limitations in the way it is specified and would not extend beyond those limitations after a certain point in time. Seeking stricter practices but wanting to offer extensibility, the W3C looked to XML as a means to influence HTML.

So HTML was *reformulated* as an application of XML (rather than its original SGML) and the Extensible Hypertext Markup Language (XHTML) was born.

Goals of XHTML

The limitations of HTML largely emerge from its very specific vocabulary, which carries over into XHTML. XML itself is very semantic—remember in Chapter 6 the discussion of semantic meaning and tags? In HTML, we use specific tags to achieve a given goal. In XML, tags are more specific to the topic at hand and are entirely generated by the author. XHTML attempts to provide some bridge from the limitations of a specific vocabulary to a more open specification where the author can create his or her own DTDs and modify the language as required.

Following are some of the specific goals of XHTML:

- ◆ To bring more *rigor* (rigid rules) to the authoring of Web documents

- ◆ To provide extensibility to Web authors
- ◆ To support a growing number of alternative devices such as set-top boxes, PDAs, pagers, and other mobile or unique devices tapping into Web-based information

Newcomers sometimes ask if XHTML is backward compatible and supported in older browsers. Yes, XHTML is supported by any browser that can interpret HTML (see Figure 7-1), because XHTML uses HTML's vocabulary. The main difference is in the rigor, how the language is written, and how strictly its rules are adhered to.

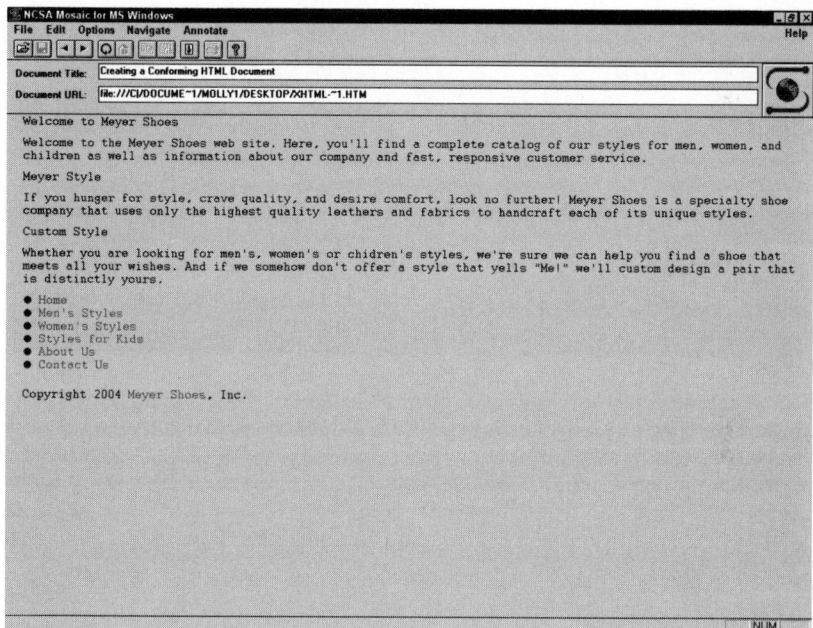

Figure 7-1: I took the valid HTML document created in Chapter 6, upgraded it to XHTML 1.1, and viewed it in Mosaic, the Web's first widely used graphical Web browser. It works!

> **note** An excellent repository of Web browsers is available at http://browsers .evolt.org/.

XHTML Versions and DTDs

Like HTML, XHTML comes in versions and offers a range of DTDs from which to choose. Table 7-1 describes the language versions, DTDs, and uses for XHTML.

You can see that a major change occurred with XHTML 1.1. This is because by this point in the language, there is no longer any need for Transitional DTDs—CSS can handle presentation, and all that's really required in the document itself is the structural markup and content.

Another important point about XHTML 1.1 is that it's *modularized*. It's broken down into individual modules such as text, tables, forms, and so on. This gives authors the flexibility to write their own DTD, pull in only those modules they

Table 7-1: XHTML Versions and Document Types

XHTML Version	Document Type	Usage
XHTML 1.0	Transitional DTD	In widespread use insofar as XHTML goes—it's the version generated by most contemporary Web editors with XHTML support, such as Dreamweaver MX and MX 2004
XHTML 1.0	Strict DTD	In use by most Web designers working with CSS and Web standards
XHTML 1.0	Frameset DTD	For use in XHTML framesets only
XHTML 1.1	XHTML 1.1	XHTML 1.1 is the currently recommended specification. It has only one DTD, based on XHTML 1.0 Strict. It is not in widespread use due to concerns related to the way it's served (discussed in detail later this chapter)

want, and leave others out. This is especially important for browser and user agent developers designing for multiple devices—think about it, you can't run a complex Java application on a smart pager or mobile phone just yet due to technological limitations, but you can access basic Web content. There isn't the same need on smaller devices to support the kinds of features and functions necessary on desktop and notebook computers.

> **note** Read more about the modularization of XHTML at the W3C site, www.w3.org/TR/xhtml-modularization/.

The ability to write one's own DTD is part of the essence of XHTML because it is there that we find the extensibility and customization features that HTML cannot offer. Writing your own DTD can also enable you to include elements and attributes in the language that don't exist in the public DTDs at the W3C. This is more trouble than it's worth for smaller Web sites, but for very large sites using custom features, it can be extremely useful to have that flexibility available.

> **note** To see a custom DTD in action, visit www.ibm.com/ and take a look at the DOCTYPE in use. IBM, being one of the earliest adopters of SGML applications for document management, authors and adheres to its own DTDs.

At the time of this writing, XHTML 2.0 is being worked on and has caused some controversy as the working group studying it has decided to add some elements and take away others—some that are popular and widely used. As a result, new features will have to be supported by browsers without any chance for backward compatibility, and features that are removed can no longer be used.

note As I've already suggested, just because a language type or version exists or is a current recommendation doesn't mean you have to use it. You can choose to use any language you want. Remember, most of the Web isn't even using valid markup. For the best results, choose a language and DTD that is appropriate for the work you do and for your target browsers.

So Is XHTML Better?

Back to the question at hand: If we have HTML and it serves its purpose on the Web, is XHTML better?

I believe it is, and here are my reasons:

- You get greater rigor in authoring results in more consistently authored documents.
- Grammar rules are far less arbitrary in XHTML than they are in HTML. As a result, authors with good knowledge of markup will make fewer errors and waste less time debugging and troubleshooting.
- XHTML is suitable for a wide range of needs (not just Web), making it a good choice for those designers and document authors looking to extend their content beyond the Web.
- XHTML is easier to learn and teach because the rules are stricter.
- Greater rigor in the language means greater consistency in documents from author to author.
- Extensibility features, even if never tapped into, provide long-term flexibility should the need arise.

tip If you'd like to upgrade to XHTML but have a limited budget, begin using XHTML on new projects or new portions of your Web site. This way, you begin tapping into the advantages of XHTML without spending money and time redoing older HTML pages.

Secret #103:   Choose a DTD

Since you already know that you must have a DOCTYPE that declares a proper DTD, the first step when working with XHTML is to choose the DTD with which you're going to work.

You have the following choices:

- **XHTML 1.0 Transitional.** Choose XHTML 1.0 Transitional when you want any kind of presentational elements or attributes in your documents.
- **XHTML 1.0 Strict.** XHTML 1.0 Strict is great when you are relying on CSS for all presentation.
- **XHTML 1.0 Frameset.** Use this DTD for frameset documents. Individual framed pages can be in any valid format.

♦ **XHTML 1.1.** The XHTML 1.1 DTD is based on XHTML 1.0 Strict, but it must be served as application/XML, a media type used to define applications using XML.

> **tip**
>
> Choose XHTML 1.0 Strict in place of using XHTML 1.1 to avoid media type problems.

XHTML 1.1 is *supposed* to be served using the media type application/xhtml+xml, not as text, even though you can serve it as text and have it work properly—there's a bit of dissent about this in the technical community (see the note that follows for more details). The problem with serving XHTML as XML is that the Web server in use must be configured properly or use content negotiation—concepts outside the realm of this book, and the browser must be able to properly display the results. At this time, it's a hit-or-miss issue, so most people either write in XHTML 1.1 and just serve it as text or avoid it altogether.

> **note**
>
> To understand the media type issues in more detail, see `www.w3.org/TR/xhtml-media-types/`.

At this time, unless I'm expressly asked to author something in HTML, I use XHTML 1.0 Strict along with CSS for almost all my Web documents.

Secret #104:   Avoid the XML Declaration

The XML declaration (also referred to as an *XML prologue* or *XML prolog*) is a bit of XML markup that you can place in XHTML documents *above* the DOCTYPE declaration, as follows:

```
<?xml version="1.0" encoding="UTF-8" ?>
<!DOCTYPE html PUBLIC "-//W3C//DTD XHTML 1.0 Strict//EN"
     "http://www.w3.org/TR/xhtml1/DTD/xhtml1-strict.dtd">
```

The purpose of the XML declaration is to identify the document as being an XML document, and you can denote the version of XML as well as the character encoding (see Chapter 6, "Crafting Pages with HTML").

Unfortunately, the XML declaration causes a lot more trouble than it's worth for Web designers at this time. There are several reasons for this, all of them due to browsers not properly knowing what to do with the XML syntax used by the declaration. Known problems with the XML declaration include the following:

♦ Browsers not interpreting or rendering the markup, but displaying the source instead

♦ Browsers rendering the XML tree (see Figure 7-2) instead of the document

♦ Browsers with DOCTYPE switching support (discussed later this chapter) not performing the switch

According to the XHTML specifications, the W3C says that the XML declaration is recommended, but it is *not* required for an XHTML document to be valid. Because

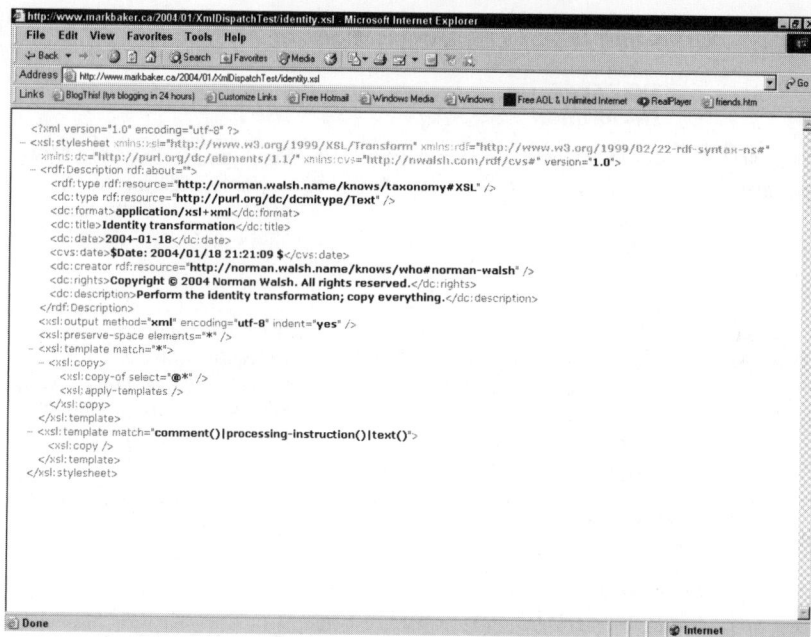

Figure 7-2: The XML declaration can cause some browsers to render the XML tree rather than the document. Here's a sample of how that might look.

of these rendering problems, my suggestion is to leave it out. However, if you have a specific target browser that has no problem interpreting documents properly with the XML declaration in place and you do not have to support any that do, you can consider using it.

note   For a helpful chart displaying those browsers with and without issues related to the XML declaration, see www.webstandards.org/learn/reference/prolog_problems.html.

Secret #105:   Use Correct XHTML DOCTYPEs

As with HTML, the DOCTYPE declaration must appear at the top of your document for a document to be validated—and to validate. DOCTYPEs are required in both HTML and XHTML.

Once you've chosen the appropriate DTD and begin to construct a document template, you'll want to include the correct DOCTYPE.

Table 7-2 shows the available DOCTYPEs in XHTML.

As you surf around and view source, you'll notice that not all DOCTYPEs look like the ones you've seen in this book. Some of them are shorter, without the URL. Some have relative URLs. These DOCTYPEs aren't necessarily incorrect, but they may not be functional both in validation and in DOCTYPE switching if they are not among those listed here (and in Chapter 6, for HTML DOCTYPEs).

Table 7-2: DTDs and DOCTYPE Declarations in XHTML

DTD	DOCTYPE Declaration	Use
XHTML 1.0 Transitional	`<!DOCTYPE html PUBLIC "-//W3C//DTD XHTML 1.0 Transitional//EN" "www.w3.org/TR/ xhtml1/DTD/ xhtml1-transitional .dtd"`	Very good for broad use; use any time you'll be including presentational elements and attributes in your document
XHTML 1.0 Strict	`<!DOCTYPE html PUBLIC "-//W3C//DTD XHTML 1.0 Strict//EN" "www.w3 .org/TR/xhtml1/DTD/ xhtml1-strict.dtd">`	Excellent choice for contemporary Web sites using CSS and no presentational elements or attributes within the document
XHTML 1.0 Frameset	`<!DOCTYPE html PUBLIC "-//W3C//DTD XHTML 1.0 Frameset//EN" "www.w3 .org/TR/xhtml1/DTD/ xhtml1-frameset.dtd">`	Use is restricted to frameset documents
XHTML 1.1	`<!DOCTYPE html PUBLIC "-//W3C//DTD XHTML 1.1//EN" "www.w3.org/TR/ xhtml11/DTD/ xhtml11.dtd">`	Use is limited to strict documents served as XML, which has limited support, unless you serve it as text, which is a controversial issue discussed earlier in this chapter

warning Flip back a few pages and compare the HTML DOCTYPEs to the XHTML DOCTYPEs here. You'll notice that the "html" in HTML DOCTYPEs is in uppercase, whereas the XHTML DOCTYPEs show "html" in lower case. This case difference will influence the validity of your documents. HTML can be upper or lowercase, whereas XHTML DOCTYPEs will *only* validate with the "html" in lowercase.

Secret #106: Add the Namespace to Root

With your DOCTYPE in its spot above all else, it's time to add the html element to the page. Recall the discussion in Chapter 6 about html being the root element—the element from which all other elements extend. XHTML is exactly the same semantically, but different in terms of syntax.

In XHTML, the namespace is defined. Namespaces help differentiate elements in XML, which allows you to include different DTDs in documents. By identifying the namespace, elements won't conflict. Because the idea of XHTML is to be extensible, and you can mix other DTDs (such as MathML) with XHTML, defining the namespace in XHTML is required.

Namespaces are typically identified with an attribute. In XHTML, you'll add the `xmlns` (XML namespace) attribute name along with a URL value to the opening tag in the root element, as follows:

```
<html xmlns="http://www.w3.org/1999/xhtml">
```

Close out the element with its closing tag, add a `head` and `body` element, and a `meta` element for encoding purposes. You'll notice the slash at the end of the `meta` element—this is one of the influences of XML, and you'll learn about its significance later in this chapter.

There you have it—everything you need for a basic XHTML document (see Listing 7-1) all ready for your content.

Listing 7-1: Conforming strict XHTML document

```
<!DOCTYPE html PUBLIC "-//W3C//DTD XHTML 1.0 Strict//EN"
"http://www.w3.org/TR/xhtml1/DTD/xhtml1-strict.dtd">

<html xmlns="http://www.w3.org/1999/xhtml">
<head>
<meta http-equiv="content-Type" content="text/html;
charset=iso-8859-1" />

</head>

<body>

</body>
</html>
```

> **note**
> To read more about the meaning of namespaces, see the Dublin Core Metadata Glossary entry, which provides a detailed definition, at http://library.csun.edu/mwoodley/dublincoreglossary.html#N.

Secret #107:   Implementing Style in XHTML

XHTML has some specific issues related to style that should be addressed.

The main issue is that the W3C specifications recommend (but do not require) that all style in XHTML be *external* to the document. So, while you can use embedded (and as a result, imported) and inline styles in XHTML, it's not recommended. After all, keeping the main document free of anything that can be moved elsewhere means faster loading times for that document, and more interoperability.

Ideally, your style sheets will be linked. Style is attached using the `link` element within the head portion of the document. You can link to as many style sheets as you desire.

Listing 7-2 shows an XHTML document along with a properly marked up link to style.

Listing 7-2: Linking to an external style sheet in XHTML

```
<!DOCTYPE html PUBLIC "-//W3C//DTD XHTML 1.0 Strict//EN"
"http://www.w3.org/TR/xhtml1/DTD/xhtml1-strict.dtd">

<html xmlns="http://www.w3.org/1999/xhtml">

<head>

<meta http-equiv="content-Type" content="text/html;
charset=iso-8859-1" />

<link rel="stylesheet" type="text/css" href="styles.css" />

</head>

<body>

</body>
</html>
```

The rel attribute should always be in place with a value of stylesheet except under those circumstances where you are using that attribute for other purposes (see Chapter 8 "Style Tips for Type and Design").

If you're going to embed style in XHTML, be sure that you use the proper syntax, including the type attribute in the style element:

```
<style type="text/css">

</style>
```

Without the type attribute in place, XHTML documents will not validate.

Secret #108: Adding Scripts in XHTML

Similarly, scripts should also be external to XHTML documents. Again, while you *can* use scripts inline and you almost are sure to do so at some point while working with XHTML, ideally the script is external.

Linking to scripts works differently than linking to a style sheet. Instead of using the link element, you use the script element, placed in the head of the document (see Listing 7-3).

Listing 7-3: Linking to an external script in XHTML

```
<!DOCTYPE html PUBLIC "-//W3C//DTD XHTML 1.0 Strict//EN"
"http://www.w3.org/TR/xhtml1/DTD/xhtml1-strict.dtd">

<html xmlns="http://www.w3.org/1999/xhtml">
```

```
<head>

<meta http-equiv="content-Type" content="text/html;
charset= iso-8859-1" />

<script type="text/javascript" src="funscript.js"></script>

</head>

<body>

</body>
</html>
```

Please be sure to include the closing `</script>` tag, as it is required. You must also include the `type` attribute with a value of `text/javascript`. Then, add the location to the opening script tag using the `src` attribute with the path to the script as the value.

---

note At one time, the language attribute was in wide use. It was deprecated in HTML 4.01, so don't use it.

Secret #109:   XHTML and Case Sensitivity

HTML is not case sensitive, XML is. XHTML is case-specific, meaning you must use lowercase for all elements and attribute names, with no exceptions allowed.

In HTML, you could have the following markup:

```
<P ALIGN="right">This text would align to the right</p>
```

It would be perfectly valid. In XHTML, any capitalization of elements or attribute names will throw validation errors. The correct markup would be as follows:

```
<p align="right">This text would align to the right</p>
```

---

note This markup example could only occur in a Transitional document, because it contains presentational attributes.

You might have noticed that I specifically wrote that elements or attribute *names* are affected, not attribute *values*. The reason for this is practical—without having the flexibility to have uppercase characters in values, there's no means of inputting information that in and of itself might be case sensitive.

A good example of a need for mixed case in values would be in a URL, where the server can be case sensitive and the URL has to be written in mixed case:

```
<a href="http://www.molly.com/MOLLY/FILES/Sample.html">Download a
sample file</a>.
```

Here, the uppercase /MOLLY/FILES/ and the first letter of the file, Sample.html, must be preserved. You can now see why attribute values in XHTML are not case-sensitive. However, if you have no specific reason to use uppercase in your attribute values, stick to lowercase in all instances.

Secret #110: Quotation of Attribute Values in XHTML

If it seems that XHTML is full of rules, you're right. As mentioned in the introduction to this chapter, XML's influence has brought a great deal of rigor to the language.

I personally see this as a good thing, because if you know the rules, you're less likely to make errors. One of the most common errors in markup is forgetting a quotation mark somewhere. As a result, your page won't display, or it'll display in a bizarre way, or the document won't validate.

In HTML, you don't have to quote all attribute values. It's perfectly valid to write the following markup:

```
<img src="images/me.jpg" width=200 height=200 alt="picture of me">
```

The lax quotation rules in HTML clearly create inconsistencies within a document. It becomes too easy to type in a quotation mark and then miss its pair:

```
<img src="images/me.jpg" width="200 height=200 alt="picture of me">
```

This will definitely throw a validation error or, in many Web browsers, not display at all.

In XHTML, you quote all attribute values, *no exceptions*. Here's the corrected markup:

```
<img src="images/me.jpg" width="200" height="200" alt="picture
of me" />
```

A question that is often asked regarding quoting is whether single quotes are allowed in XHTML. Indeed, they are. So, if you prefer using single quotes, the following markup is perfectly valid:

```
<img src='images/me.jpg' width='200' height='200' alt='picture of
me' />
```

Secret #111: Managing Nonempty Elements

In XHTML, empty and nonempty elements are carried over from HTML. The difference is that they're treated in a more disciplined way.

Nonempty elements, as you'll recall from the discussion in Chapter 6, are those elements that contain text content. These include such elements as headers, paragraphs, and list items. You'll also remember that some nonempty elements aren't required to have a closing tag in HTML. For example, list items can be written as follows:

```
<li>List item one.
<li>List item two.
<li>List item three.
```

Paragraphs are another prime example of a nonempty element for which, in HTML, the closing tag is considered optional. This is a perfectly valid practice in HTML.

In XHTML, all nonempty elements *must be closed*. The corrected markup sample would then be as follows:

```
<li>List item one.</li>
<li>List item two.</li>
<li>List item three.</li>
```

tip
I recommend making it a practice of closing nonempty elements in HTML too, even though it's not a requirement. If you ever choose to upgrade those files to XHTML, it'll be much easier. Also, it can improve CSS rendering in some browsers.

Secret #112: Terminating Empty Elements

All empty elements must be terminated. Empty elements are those elements without text content, and they are always represented by a single tag.

In XML, empty elements are terminated with a trailing slash:

```
<para/>
```

XHTML adopts this practice so empty elements can terminate the same way, as in the following:

```
<br/>
<hr/>
<meta/>
```

You might have noticed that a space appears before the trailing slash in most XHTML documents. This really emerged as a browser hack for older browsers that couldn't properly interpret the slash if it came immediately after a character.

Since the specifications allow the white space, most XHTML authors and authoring tools use the space to avoid browsers misinterpreting empty elements:

```
<br />
<hr />
<meta />
```

Secret #113:   Managing Minimized Attributes

A minimized attribute is one that is represented only by the attribute name. There's no associated value. In HTML, familiar examples would include attributes such as the following:

+ noresize
+ noshade
+ nohref
+ nowrap
+ multiple
+ checked
+ ismap
+ compact

Here's a sample:

```
<hr noshade>
```

In XHTML, the minimization of attributes is disallowed. The attribute name is given a value of itself:

```
<input type="checkbox" checked="checked" />
```

So, in all cases where you find a single-word attribute, you must give it a value of itself for the attribute to be valid in XHTML.

note

During classes I often ask students to guess what the attribute value of a minimized attribute becomes in XHTML. Many guess that the value is "true", which makes absolute sense. The selected attribute is considered a Boolean attribute, and you can read more about their unique history and use at www.w3.org/TR/REC-html40/intro/sgmltut.html.

Secret #114:   Entities and XHTML

Chapter 6 examined character entities and their role in HTML. Used for the display of special characters in both HTML and XHTML, entities are also used in XHTML to escape certain characters in scripts and URLs.

The best example of this is the ampersand (&), which appears in JavaScript and also in some URLs.

Because the ampersand is considered reserved for use, the more rigid rules of XHTML expect you to escape all inline instances of ampersands not related to a special character.

Take the following URL, for example:

```
http://www.molly.com/books/250.cgi?chapter=1&section=2
```

The ampersand must be escaped using the character entity:

```
http://www.molly.com/books/250.cgi?chapter=1&amp;section=2
```

The same is true in any inline or embedded JavaScript. Consider the following snippet from a routing script:

```
if (browser == "Microsoft Internet Explorer" &&
navigator.appVersion==version)
```

If this JavaScript appears as an embedded script, the ampersands must be escaped:

```
if (browser == "Microsoft Internet Explorer" &amp;&amp;
navigator.appVersion==version)
```

> **note**
>
> Escaping characters in URLs or scripts will not affect the functions related to either. You do *not* need to do this for any external script.
>
> For more information on entities in XHTML and other helpful XHTML workarounds, see www.simonstl.com/tips/archive/workarounds.html.

Secret #115: alt Attribute Required

Unlike HTML, where the `alt` attribute is a recommended inclusion for accessibility purposes, you can't leave it out in XHTML.

Incorrect:

```
<img src="molly.jpg" width="100" height="200" />
```

Correct:

```
<img src="molly.jpg" width="100" height="200" alt="photograph of
molly" />
```

There are no exceptions to this rule, even if you leave the value empty:

```
<img src="spacer.gif" width="25" height="1" alt="" />
```

However, since you can use CSS for effective spacing, spacer graphics are unnecessary anyway.

> **note**
>
> Interestingly, while width and height might seem presentational, they are available for use in strict DTDs and XHTML 1.1, because having width and height attributes present will assist with better graphic rendering in most browsers.

Secret #116: Understand Well-Formedness

Well-formedness is simply the proper nesting of elements. It is important in HTML, although it's not brought up too often as a discussion point until you begin to study XHTML in earnest.

What happens if you want to have something being both emphasized and strong at the same time? Well, you can apply both elements to text. The important issue is that the elements nest properly.

Correct:

```
<p>Welcome to <em><strong>my super duper</strong></em> web
site!</p>
```

Also correct:

```
<p>Welcome to <strong><em>my super duper</em></strong> web
site!</p>
```

Incorrect:

```
<p>Welcome to <strong><em>my super duper</strong></em> web
site!</p>
```

Also incorrect:

```
<p>Welcome to <em><strong>my super duper</em></strong> web
site!</p>
```

A great way to help visualize this is to draw an arc from an opening tag to its companion closing tag. If the arcs intersect, your elements are improperly nested (refer to Figure 7-3). The same is true for the vertical, too (see Figure 7-4).

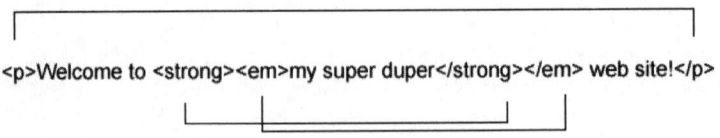

Figure 7-3: Improper nesting of elements along the horizontal axis.

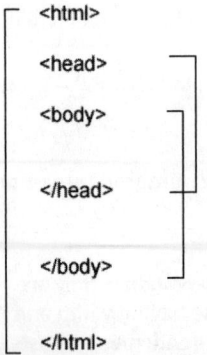

Figure 7-4: Improper nesting of elements along the vertical axis.

Secret #117:   Proper Nesting of Lists

One thing that markup authors moving to XHTML stumble over early on is how to nest lists properly in XHTML.

In HTML, you could leave off the closing </li> tag, and nest lists like this:

```
<ul>
<li>Pens

    <ul>
    <li>Felt tip
    <li>Highlighter
    <li>Fountain
    </ul>

<li>Envelope
<li>Stamp
</ul>
```

The results (shown in Figure 7-5) are a nested, unordered list.

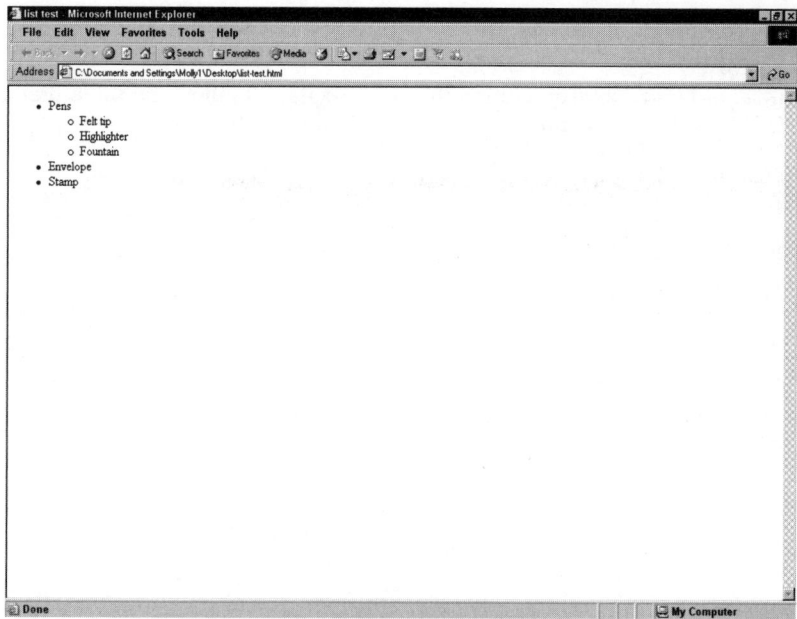

Figure 7-5: A nested unordered list created using HTML.

Logic says if you're closing all your nonempty elements in XHTML, you'd do this:

```
<ul>
<li>Pens</li>

    <ul>
    <li>Felt tip</li>
```

```
<li>Highlighter</li>
<li>Fountain</li>
</ul>

<li>Envelope</li>
<li>Stamp</li>
</ul>
```

But proper nesting rules in XHTML place the nested list *inside* a list item as *part* of that item, not as a separate part of that list. As a result, the correct listing procedure in XHTML looks like this:

```
<ul>
<li>Pens

    <ul>
    <li>Felt tip</li>
    <li>Highlighter</li>
    <li>Fountain</li>
    </ul>

</li>

<li>Envelope</li>
<li>Stamp</li>
</ul>
```

Of course, ordered lists (see Figure 7-6 for an example) follow the same practice in XHTML, with nested ordering placed within the list item:

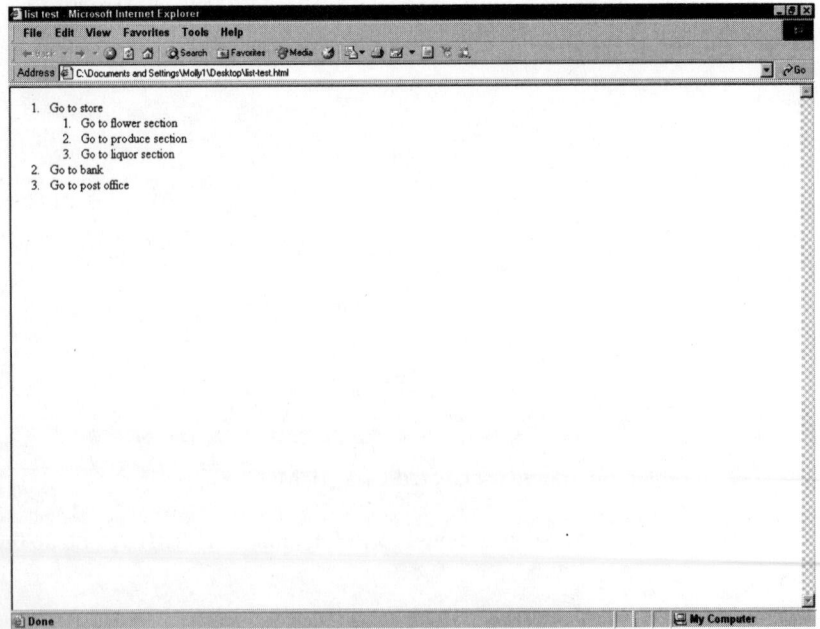

Figure 7-6: A nested ordered list created using XHTML.

```
<ol>
<li>Go to store
   <ol>
   <li>Go to flower section</li>
   <li>Go to produce section</li>
   <li>Go to liquor section</li>
   </ol>
</li>

<li>Go to bank</li>
<li>Go to post office</li>
</ol>
```

You can also mix and match lists, as long as they are properly nested:

```
<ol>
<li>Go to store
   <ul>
   <li>flowers</li>
   <li>salad fixings</li>
   <li>white wine</li>
   </ul>
</li>

<li>Go to bank</li>
<li>Go to post office</li>
</ol>
```

Figure 7-7 shows the results.

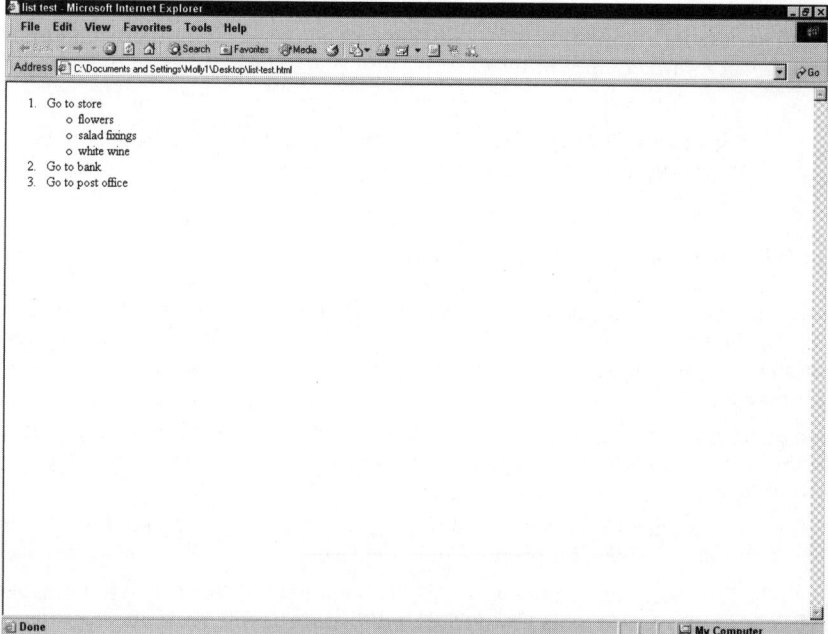

Figure 7-7: A nested unordered list within a numbered list created using XHTML.

note   CSS provides some terrific ways to style list bullets and numeric values. See Chapter 8, "Style Tips for Type and Design" to learn more.

Secret #118:   DOCTYPE Switching

As you've come to learn in these markup chapters, DOCTYPEs are required components of a valid HTML or XHTML document. The DOCTYPE declaration has historically been passive, with no actual function until the document is passed through a validator and uses the declaration to determine which DTD to validate the document against.

Historically, many Web authors have not validated their documents, much less authored to standards, although, fortunately, that is a changing trend. Understanding the way the languages with which we work and how the browsers respond to them is surely the road to long-term success and survival as a Web designer. So knowing this stuff is really important.

Another equally important but lesser known reason that the DOCTYPE declaration is so significant has to do with a switching mechanism that's been added to all contemporary browsers to allow those browsers to identify documents that appear to be standardized. This allows them to render the documents more quickly and accurately. This becomes very important when you begin using CSS, especially for layout.

Studying the problem of CSS implementation in browsers, Tantek Çelik, a programmer for Microsoft who has been involved with browser development and standards for some years now, recognized that no browser could afford to move ahead with more compliant and consistent technologies without allowing for reasonable backward compatibility.

cross ref   See Chapter 9, "Laying Out Pages with CSS" for more details about how DOCTYPE switching influences display.

The solution Çelik devised was to split the browser's capabilities into two modes: Quirks mode and Standards (or "compliance") mode. Quirks mode is the implementation of rendering engines in use that manage nonstandard markup (essentially the same forgiving rendering that we've relied on for years). It is forgiving of our shortcomings as well as those of our tools, but can be incredibly inconsistent as a result.

Compliance mode, on the other hand, is a streamlined standards-compliant rendering engine, allowing for faster, more accurate, and more *controlled* rendering of your designs.

Web browsers with DOCTYPE switching technology rely on *specifically formed* DOCTYPE *declarations* for proper switching to occur.

DOCTYPE declarations can be written in any number of ways. The default DOCTYPEs in many visual tools and HTML editors are problematic for the reasons I mentioned earlier in this chapter. There's nothing *wrong* with those DOCTYPEs in any technical sense, but there is something wrong with them in regards to DOCTYPE switching technology. You must use some very specific DOCTYPEs to kick the browser in question into Standards mode. All of the DOCTYPEs in this chapter will do the trick.

Here's how the behavior breaks down:

- Documents with older or Transitional DOCTYPEs, poorly formed DOCTYPES, or no DOCTYPE at all are displayed using Quirks mode, and will be interpreted with the legacy bugs and behaviors of version 4 browsers.
- Documents with properly formed HTML Strict or XHTML DOCTYPEs are displayed using Compliance mode. This mode follows W3C specifications for HTML, CSS, and other layout languages as closely as possible.

Of course, any browser (including Netscape 4) that came along before DOCTYPE switching was conceived will act just as Quirks mode does. In contrast, Opera 6 and earlier does not bother with DOCTYPE switching, but those browsers work more like standards mode does, because Opera has been purposely developed with standards in mind.

> **note**   For an excellent overview of DOCTYPE switching, read "DOCTYPE Switching and Standards Compliance" by Matthias Gutfeldt. The article describes the technical details regarding the switching technology and provides additional resources (http://gutfeldt.ch/matthias/articles/doctypeswitch.html).

Secret #119:   Enclose Inline Elements in Blocks

If you're using XHTML 1.0 Strict or XHTML 1.1, you can't have any widowed inline elements. This means that any inline element must appear within a block.

Listing 7-4 shows a valid XHTML 1.0 Transitional document with an image (which is an inline element) marked up on a line by itself. This is allowed in HTML and XHTML Transitional.

Listing 7-4: Valid transitional document with a widowed inline element

```
<!DOCTYPE html PUBLIC "-//W3C//DTD XHTML 1.0 Transitional//EN"
"http://www.w3.org/TR/xhtml1/DTD/xhtml1-transitional.dtd">

<html xmlns="http://www.w3.org/1999/xhtml">
<head>
<title>block and inline elements in XHTML</title>
<meta http-equiv="content-Type" content="text/html;
charset=iso-8859-1" />
</head>

<body>

<img src="images/molly.jpg" width="250" height="165"
alt="photograph of molly" />
```

(continued)

Listing 7-4: *(continued)*

```
</body>
</html>
```

Listing 7-5 shows the image, an inline element, marked up properly for XHTML 1.0 Strict or XHTML 1.1. Here, I'm using a paragraph element, but you can use any logical block-level element to contain your inline elements. Another good choice for this would be the div element.

Listing 7-5: Proper management of inline elements in XHTML 1.1

```
<!DOCTYPE html PUBLIC "-//W3C//DTD XHTML 1.1//EN"
"http://www.w3.org/TR/xhtml11/DTD/xhtml11.dtd">

<html xmlns="http://www.w3.org/1999/xhtml">
<head>
<title>block and inline elements in XHTML</title>
<meta http-equiv="content-Type" content="text/html;
charset=iso-8859-1" />
</head>

<body>
<p><img src="images/molly.jpg" width="250" height="165"
alt="photograph of molly" /></p>

</body>
</html>
```

Secret #120: name Becomes id

In XHTML 1.0 Strict and 1.1, the name attribute is replaced with the id attribute. In the past, you might have had the following:

```
<a name="intrapagelink">Line 200</a>
```

But in XHTML 1.0 Strict and XHTML 1.1, you must use id instead:

```
<a id="intrapagelink">Line 200</a>
```

In most cases, using id doesn't change the function. However, because some browsers do not properly identify or interpret id, when you need to ensure back-ward compatibility, use a Transitional XHTML DTD and include both, as in the following:

```
<a name="intrapagelink" id="intrapagelink">Line 200</a>
```

note The id attribute becomes very important when using CSS. See Chapter 9, "Laying Out Pages with CSS" for details.

Secret #121: The target Attribute is Unavailable in Anchor

You've been doing it all along—targeting a new window for links. It's an easy option in HTML and XHTML Transitional. However, if you're using XHTML 1.0 or XHTML 1.1, you cannot use the `target` attribute in an anchor element.

Here's what you've been doing:

```
<a href="newpage.html" target="_blank">Opens in new window</a>
```

But what are your options to open links in a new window? The main workaround is to use JavaScript, as in the following example:

```
<a onclick="window.open('http://www.molly.com/newpage.html',
'newWindow');" href="#">Opens in new window</a>
```

However, people sometimes turn their JavaScript off. If you don't want to use JavaScript for any reason, your only alternative is to use a Transitional DTD and the `target` attribute.

Summary

The last two chapters have covered more about HTML and XHTML than the vast majority of working Web designers could tell you. Hopefully, you've found some clarification, insight, or suggestions that will assist you in understanding the why as well as the how of writing markup.

If you've found the last couple of chapters a bit on the technical or dry side, fear not. CSS is up next, so you'll get a chance to learn more about how to add great design and presentation options to your well-formed, valid, and structured documents.

Style Tips for
Type and Design

◆ ◆

Secrets in This Chapter

◆ ◆

C ascading Style Sheets (CSS) have become an area of extreme focus in re-cent years, largely due to the fact that browser support for most CSS is now widespread. CSS helps you eliminate presentational markup from your HTML or XHTML, add visual intrigue and effects to your designs, and aids designers by improving workflow.

This chapter focuses on sharing the best techniques to address the integration of CSS with HTML or XHTML documents, improve the way you style text, and use CSS to style your designs.

Learning CSS

The secrets in this chapter assume at least a basic knowledge of CSS. While new-comers to CSS can certainly use many of the techniques described here, it would behoove anyone interested in contemporary Web design and development to learn the concepts within the language itself. Along with many excellent books, a variety of Web sites and tutorials are available, almost always for free, that will help you learn the theory.

note   **Appendix C, "Helpful Reading, Web Sites, and Resources" provides numerous helpful sites, articles, and courses available to learn CSS.**

Also, many of the techniques described in this chapter (and subsequently in Chap-ter 9, "Laying Out Pages with CSS")are inspired directly by the people who created the techniques. In many cases, I've provided you with actual listings and descrip-tions of a given technique. However, where the techniques were published fairly recently, or have many variations, I've provided an explanation of the techniques, screen shots, and link information to the locations where you can learn the tech-niques directly from their creators.

Secret #122:   When to Use Linked Style

As discussed in Chapter 7, style and scripting is ideally moved to an external document. The reasons for this are practical: You can easily integrate that style sheet or script with one or one million documents, and you can do so in one line of code instead of embedding the style or script in every single document. This way, you can quickly change style or scripts and update the documents automatically, as well as reduce the final page weight of your document. What's more, browsers will cache your linked style, making the information immediately applicable to all pages that use it, speeding up the loading of the page and providing a more seamless user experience.

A linked style sheet is external to documents. It contains the style rules with no HTML markup and is saved with an extension of `.css`. Linked style is then linked to as many documents as you want by using the `link` element within the head portion of the HTML or XHTML page:

```
<link rel="stylesheet" href="border.css" type="text/css"
media="all" />
```

Linked style sheets are very powerful because of their capability to control so many documents at once, making the management of documents far less time-consuming and frustrating (Figure 8-1).

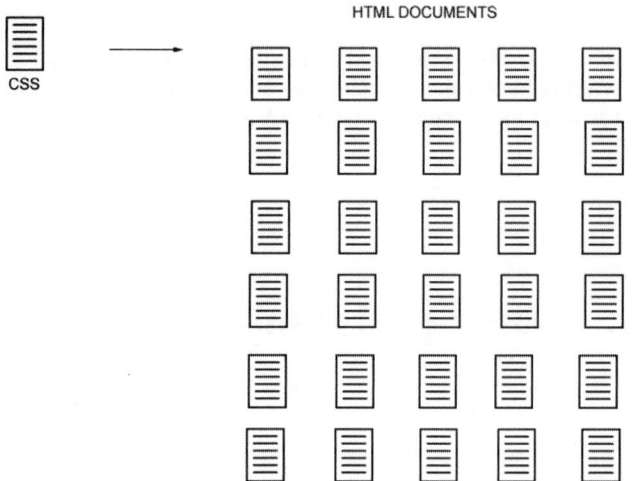

HTML DOCUMENTS

CSS

Figure 8-1: A linked style sheet's relationship to Web documents.

Secret #123:   When to Use Embedded Style

An embedded style sheet is a style sheet that appears in the document head within the style element:

```
<style type="text/css">
p {
border: 1px dashed black;
}
</style>
```

Embedded sheets govern that document only (see Figure 8-2).

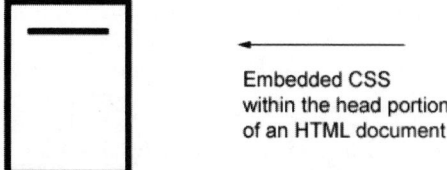

Embedded CSS
within the head portion
of an HTML document

Figure 8-2: Embedded style within a document.

Embedded style sheets override other style sheet types with the exception of in-line and user styles. Although they are extremely useful and clutter a document less than inline styles do, they should still be used sparingly. Linked styles are far more efficient—with embedded styles you have to update all the individual pages that contain them, reducing the efficiency gained by using linked styles. You will see embedded style used throughout this chapter, but that's because using embedded styles enables me to show all that's going on in one listing rather than several.

> **tip** When working on CSS ideas, I start using an embedded style sheet so I don't have to switch between documents each time I add or take away a style. After I'm finished, I remove the embedded style and link to the style information I created.

Secret #124:   When to Use Inline Styles

Inline style is added to an individual element using the `style` attribute, as in the following example:

```
<p style="border: 1px dashed black;">This paragraph will have a 1
pixel black, dashed border around it.</p>
```

Inline style is powerful in that it overrides other styles. It can be very useful for quick fixes or in those cases where you want to style something only once.

However, relying on inline style results in the cluttering up of your documents. Documents become less accessible because various user agents might not recognize inline styles, and the wide range of devices that are emerging might also have difficulty recognizing inline style. What's more, you can't tap into the document management aspects of CSS if you rely too heavily on inline style. So it's best to reserve inline style for occasional, specific use.

Secret #125:   Importing Style

An imported style sheet is an external sheet that uses the `@import` property within an embedded style sheet to import the styles instead of being linked directly to a page:

```
<style type="text/css">
@import border.css
</style>
```

Imported style sheets are somewhat limited in their use because some browsers don't support them. As a result, they are in use today mostly in workarounds, such as the common technique of placing information in an imported style sheet and other styles in a linked style sheet.

Browsers that support some styles but do not support the `@import` property will ignore the layout but apply some style (providing a readable, somewhat styled document to those browsers), but leaving out the positioning and other style information that those browsers read improperly. This technique is described in detail in Chapter 9, "Laying Out Pages with CSS."

Secret #126:   Understand the Cascade

The cascade in style sheets is a *hierarchy of application*. It appears in several places—you already read about how inline styles will override embedded styles, and both will override linked styles. So, if you have an inline style for a paragraph, an embedded style for a paragraph, and a linked style for a paragraph, the inline styles take precedence over the embedded styles, which take precedence over the linked styles. This is referred to as *conflict resolution*, and the cascade is one means of resolving such conflicts.

> **note**   Additional style information that doesn't conflict from one style sheet type to another is also applied to the selector in question.

Another area where the cascade appears is in the ordering of multiple style sheets within a document. For example, say you have three style sheets linked to your document:

```
<link rel="stylesheet" type="text/css" href="molly1.css" />
<link rel="stylesheet" type="text/css" href="molly2.css" />
<link rel="stylesheet" type="text/css" href="molly3.css" />
```

The rules of the cascade say that whichever is last in the list is the style that will be applied. Say you have a style rule for a paragraph that is different in each of these sheets. The styles in molly3.css will be the style that is applied.

People run into trouble with this a lot because there may be conflicting style rules in a given sheet, so the cascade resolves the conflict using this application hierarchy.

If you're struggling to figure out why your h2 element isn't turning blue, the reason might be because that style is in conflict with another h2 style that appears in a style sheet that takes precedence within the hierarchy.

Secret #127:   Work with Inheritance

Inheritance is the relationship of parent elements to child elements. In CSS, most properties are inherited, but some are not. So, if you're finding conflicts in your CSS designs, be sure to look at how the styles for a parent element might be influencing the style of its children or grandchildren.

This harkens back to the tree structure discussed in Chapter 6. If you have a well-structured document, finding these types of conflicts is easy, and avoiding them altogether is easier still.

Listing 8-1 shows a document with inheritance at work.

Listing 8-1: Inheritance within a simple document

```
<!DOCTYPE html PUBLIC "-//W3C//DTD XHTML 1.0 Strict//EN"
     "http://www.w3.org/TR/xhtml1/DTD/xhtml1-strict.dtd">

<html xmlns="http://www.w3.org/1999/xhtml">

<head>
<title>Inheritance Test</title>
<meta http-equiv="content-type" content="text/html; charset=iso-
8859-1" />
<style type="text/css">

body {
    font-family: Arial;
    font-size: 16px;
    background-color: #ccc;
    color: #000;
}

h1 {
    font-size: 22px;
    color: #999;
}

h2 {
    font-size: 18px;
}

p {
    background-color: #fff;
    color: #999;
}

</style>
</head>

<body>

<h1>Header Level 1, inherits font family and background color from
body element.</h1>

<p>Paragraph, inherits font family and font size from body
element.</p>

<h2>Header Level 2, inherits everything but size from body
element</h2>

</body>
</html>
```

As you can see in the document itself, the children of the body: h1, h2, and p, are all influenced in some way by the parent element, body (see Figure 8-3).

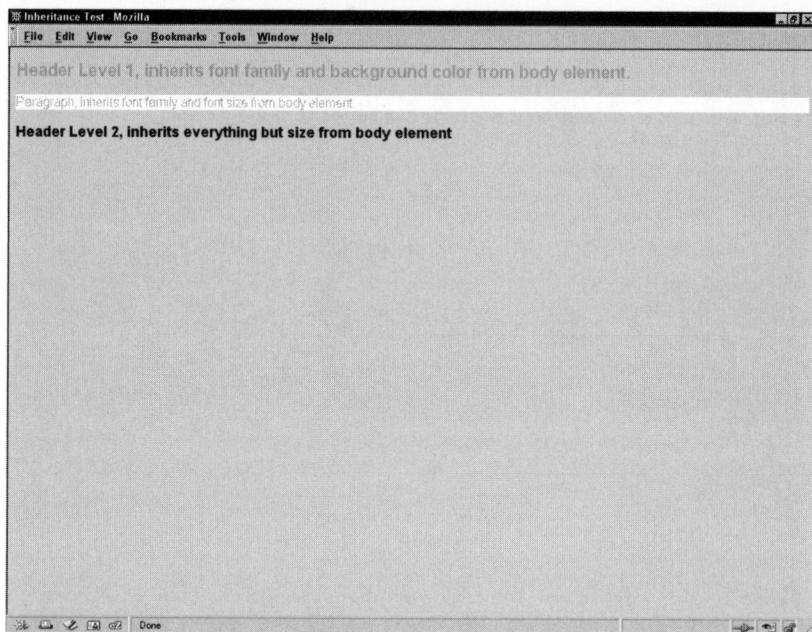

Figure 8-3: Inheritance at work.

Secret #128: Be Aware of Specificity

Although cascade and inheritance are commonly known aspects of CSS and you have probably had some experience with them, one issue that is documented less but is incredibly important in CSS is *specificity*.

Specificity is the weight or importance of a given element and is calculated in a fairly complex way.

> **note**
> See **www.w3.org/TR/REC-CSS2/cascade.html#specified-value** for the actual logic used to calculate specificity. If an element is higher in specificity due to these calculations, the style associated with that element is what will be applied.

A clear example of this is that elements with a class selector will have a higher specificity than a class that can be used anywhere. Listing 8-2 shows this in action.

Listing 8-2: Specificity test

```
<!DOCTYPE html PUBLIC "-//W3C//DTD XHTML 1.0 Strict//EN"
        "http://www.w3.org/TR/xhtml1/DTD/xhtml1-strict.dtd">

<html xmlns="http://www.w3.org/1999/xhtml">
```

(continued)

Listing 8-2: *(continued)*

```html
<head>
<meta http-equiv="content-type" content="text/html; charset=iso-
8859-1" />
<title>Specificity Test</title>

<style type="text/css">

.mylinkclass {
   color: #999;
   font-weight: bold;
}

a.mylinkclass {
   color: #333;
}

</style>

</head>

<body>

<p><a href="http://www.molly.com/" class="mylinkclass">This link is
dark gray because a.mylinkclass has a higher specificity</a>.
However, you'll notice that the link is bold because there are no
conflicts with the font-weight property.</p>

<p class="mylinkclass">This text is light gray and bold.</p>

</body>
</html>
```

Understanding that specificity is a part of conflict resolution in CSS means that you'll be better able to figure out why a given style might be appearing (or not appearing) within your document (see Figure 8-4).

Secret #129:   Creating Multiple Link Styles

One of the earliest supported yet still most highly sought after features in CSS is the ability to have multiple styled links within a given document. Designers love this because they can create link colors and styles of any number and any kind without having to rely on scripting and graphics.

To create multiple link styles, combine a class with each of the pseudo class selectors used to define links. Those pseudo classes include the following:

   ◆ `a:link`
   ◆ `a:visited`
   ◆ `a:hover`
   ◆ `a:active`

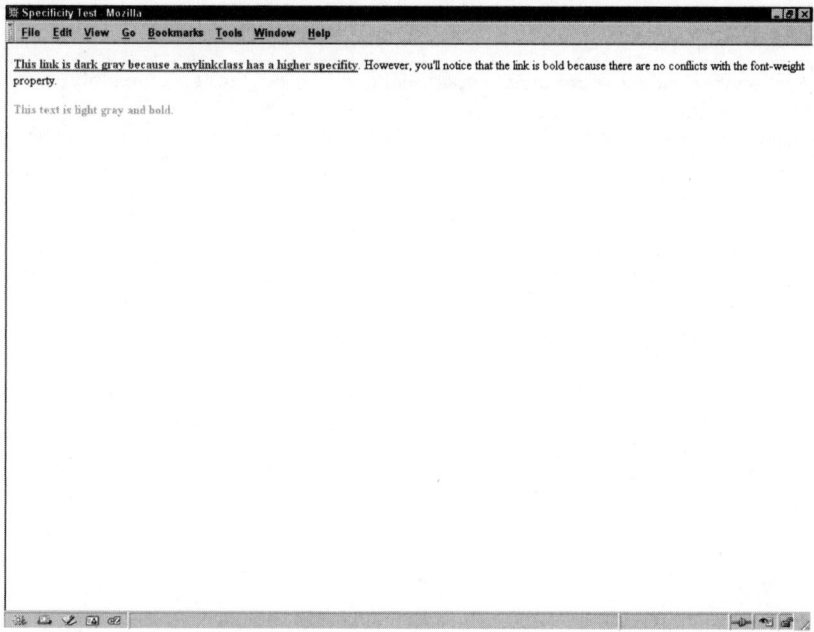

Figure 8-4: Specificity resolves conflict by assigning the rule with the highest specificity to the selector.

Each of these pseudo classes corresponds to a specific state of the link.

- ♦ Link is the normal state.
- ♦ Visited is the state of the link after it's been followed.
- ♦ Hover is the state as the mouse or pointing device hovers over the link.
- ♦ Active is the state when the mouse is clicked on the link.

> **note**
>
> To work properly, your pseudo classes must follow the specific order: link, visited, hover, active (LVHA). Many people remember this using the mnemonic "LoVeHAte."

Listing 8-3 shows a scenario in which I have created two classes: `leftnav` and `rightnav`, and added them to my pseudo class selectors to create two different styles of links for the same page.

Listing 8-3: Multiple link styles in a document

```
<!DOCTYPE html PUBLIC "-//W3C//DTD XHTML 1.0 Strict//EN"
     "http://www.w3.org/TR/xhtml1/DTD/xhtml1-strict.dtd">

<html xmlns="http://www.w3.org/1999/xhtml">

<head>
<title>Multiple Links</title>
```

(continued)

Listing 8-3: *(continued)*

```html
<meta http-equiv="content-type" content="text/html; charset=iso-
8859-1" />
<style type="text/css">

a.leftnav:link {
   color: #333;
   text-decoration: none;
}

a.leftnav:visited {
   color: purple;
}

a.leftnav:hover {
   color: orange;
}

a.leftnav:active {
   color: blue;
}

a.rightnav:link {
   color: #999;
   font-weight: bold;
}

a.rightnav:visited {
   color: purple;
}

a.rightnav:hover {
   color: blue;
}

a.rightnav:active {
   color: red;
}

</style>

</head>

<body>
<p><a class="leftnav" href="http://www.wiley.com/">visit wiley's
site</a></p>

<p><a class="rightnav" href="http://www.wiley.com/">visit wiley's
site</a></p>

</body>
</html>
```

While I've placed both links in the main body for demonstration purposes, the links would be used for left and right navigation, respectively. You can create as many link classes as you like, depending upon your needs. In Figure 8-5, you can see the results of the two different link styles.

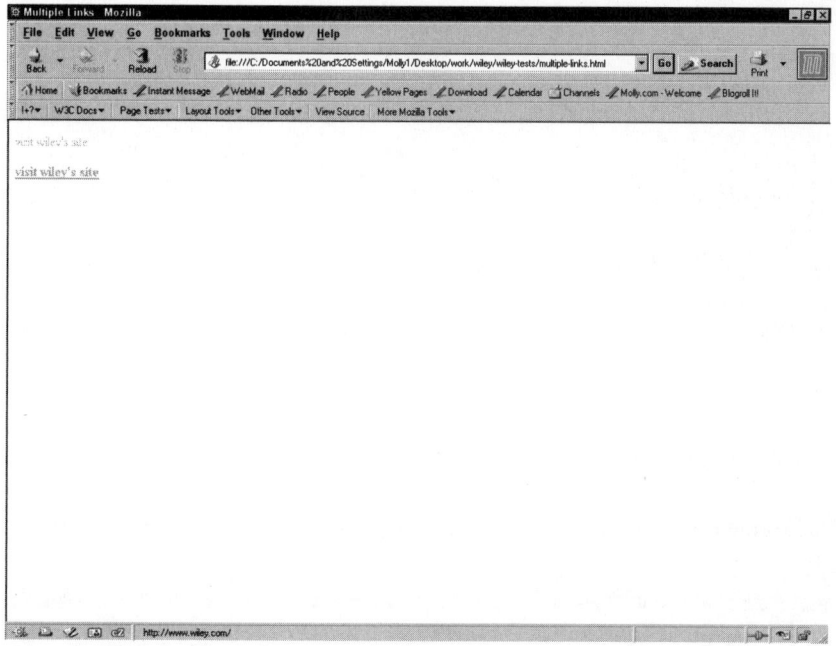

Figure 8-5: Multiple link styles with CSS.

Secret #130:   Link Effects

As you saw in the last secret, the :hover pseudo class is used with links to allow for a hover color as the mouse passes over the link.

It's become conventional to use this to create special effects, such as having an elegant color change upon mouse over, as demonstrated in the following code:

```
a:link {
    color: blue;
}

a:visited {
    color: purple;
}

a:hover {
    color: orange;
}
```

```
a:active {
    color: red;
}
```

Or having the link reverse background and foreground colors, as in the following:

```
a:link {
    color: blue;
}

a:visited {
    color: purple;
}

a:hover {
    background-color: orange;
    color: white;
}

a:active {
    color: red;
}
```

Figure 8-6 shows the reverse effect on mouseover.

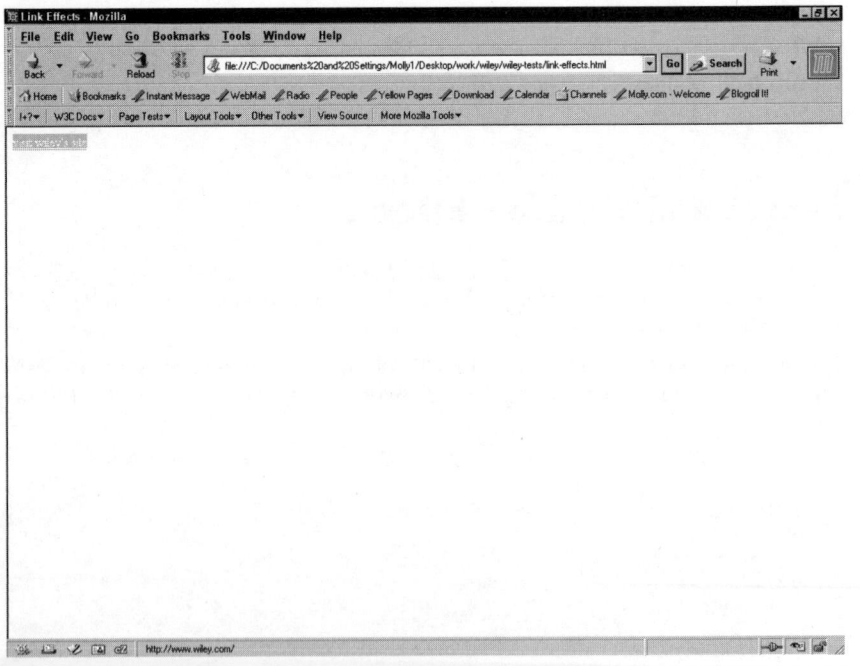

Figure 8-6: Creating a reverse hover effect.

Some techniques even employ adding a background image and using that to create wonderfully rich link effects (see Figure 8-7).

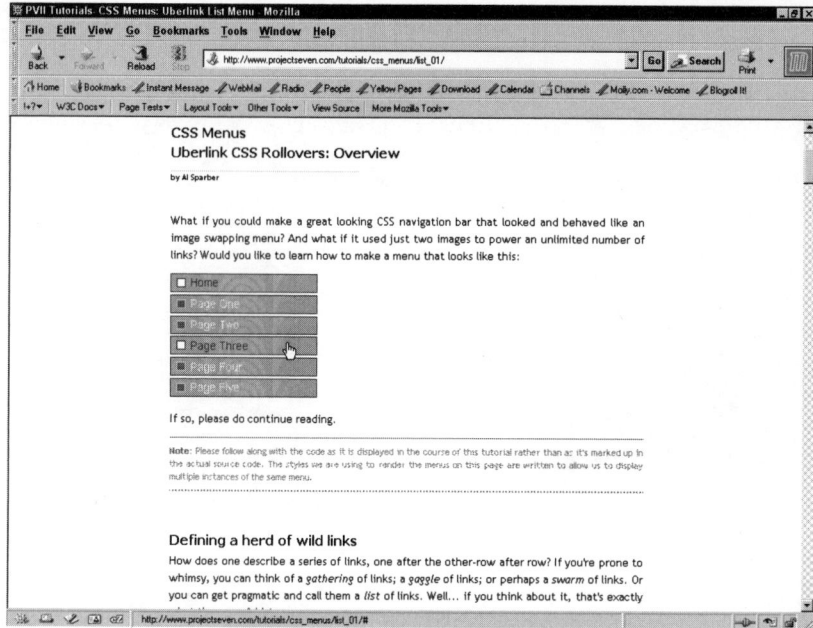

Figure 8-7: Project Seven created these attractive rollovers using background images within the anchor element.

---

warning

Avoid any link effect that dramatically changes upon hover. For example, making the text larger, bolder, or italicizing it upon hover may be visually jarring to the eye and cause problems with the usability of your links.

Secret #131:   CSS Borders and Border Styles

One of the coolest things about CSS is that you can tap into specific portions of a given element. Each element creates a box (you can read more about this in Chapter 9), and you can grab portions of that box and style them with CSS.

One such portion is element box borders. So, for *any* element, you have four borders: left, right, top, and bottom. You can define width, color, and style for any number or combination of borders you wish by simply using the border properties, as in the following example:

```
div.borders {
   border-top: 2px solid black;
   border-bottom: 2px solid red;
   border-left: 2px dotted purple;
   border-right: 2px dotted blue;
}
```

This would create a box with a 2-pixel solid border on top and bottom, and a 2-pixel dotted border to the left and right, with the colors for the borders as defined. One very common application of border styles is to create a thicker section for a box with a header or footer, or to create `blockquote` sidebars (see Figure 8-8).

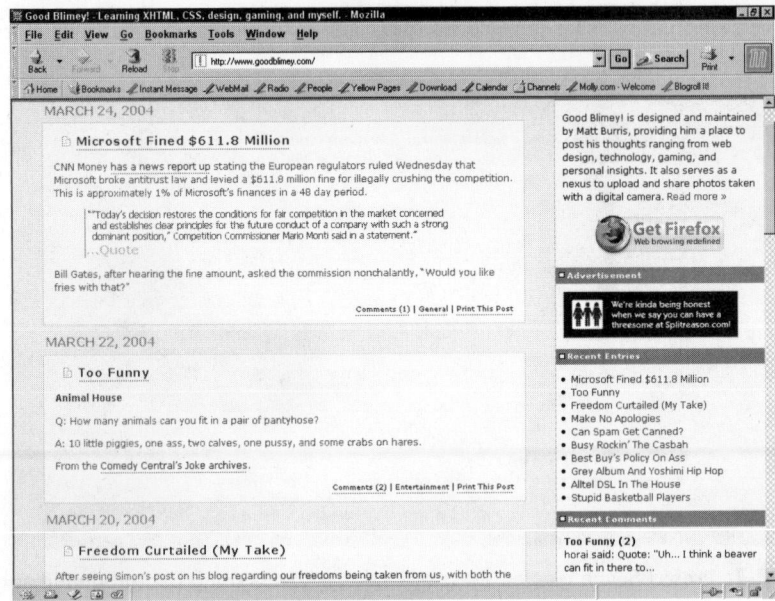

Figure 8-8: Using borders to create an attractive quotation sidebar.

Table 8-1 describes the styles available for borders.

Table 8-1: Border Styles in CSS

Property Value	Description
`dotted`	Creates a dotted border
`dashed`	Creates a dashed border
`solid`	Creates a solid border
`double`	Creates a double-line border, and both lines take on the defined width
`groove`	Creates a 3D grooved effect
`Ridge`	Creates a 3D ridged effect
`Inset`	Creates an inset effect
`Outset`	Creates an outset effect

You can also use a value of `none` should you want no border at all, and to hide borders you can use a value of `hidden`. You can see how the border styles are rendered in Figure 8-9.

If you'd like to add the same border style to all borders, you can use the CSS shorthand property, `border`, as follows:

```
#content {
  border: 2px solid black;
}
```

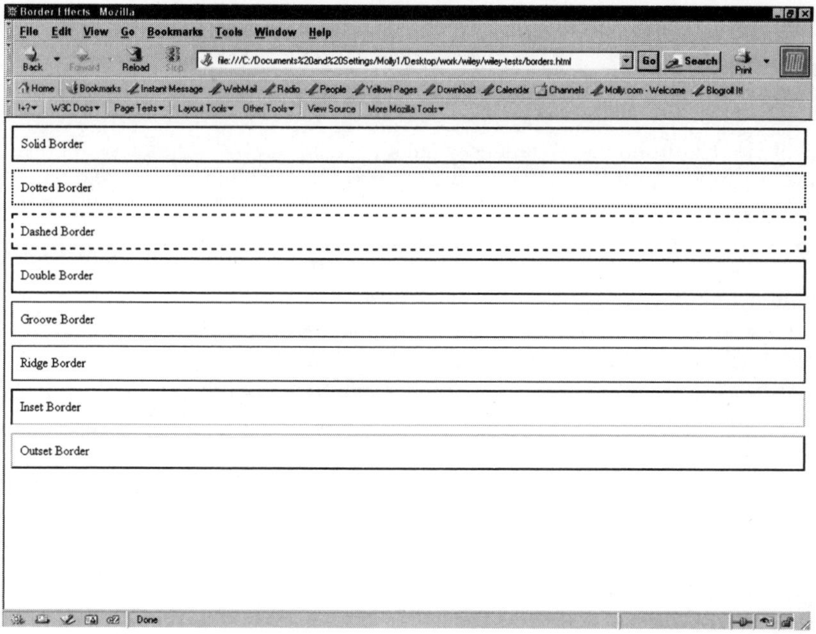

Figure 8-9: Border styles in CSS.

Secret #132:   Gaining Space with Padding

Another amazing CSS feature is the ability to apply padding. As with borders, you can pad any side of a given element box: top, right, bottom, or left. Padding is especially helpful because it allows you to add white space within your designs without having to rely on spacer graphics and tables.

A common use of padding is to add white space around photos and illustrations within the page. Many readers will remember trying to do this using vspace and hspace. Now, you simply apply padding as required:

```
#photo {
  padding-left: 10px;
  padding-top: 10px;
}
```

If you'd like to apply equal padding to an entire box, you'd do so just as you did with borders, this time using the padding shorthand property:

```
#photo {
  padding: 10px;
}
```

> **warning** While padding should work very well in all browsers with contemporary CSS support, there are known problems with the property in Netscape 4.0 and Internet Explorer 5.0. Later browsers within both camps have improved support for padding.

Secret #133:   Understanding Type Sizing Options in CSS

One of the remaining controversies when it comes to CSS and fonts is which value to use when defining font sizes for the screen. The problem is a complex one because there are both philosophical and browser support issues clouding the topic.

Numerous value options exist for font sizing. These include the following:

- percentages
- em (this unit of measurement emerges from the width of the letter "M" within a given typeface)
- ex (this unit of measurement relates to the height of "x" within a given typeface)
- inches
- centimeters
- pixels
- picas
- points
- keywords

So what's appropriate to use? Philosophically, the argument is that screen fonts should be scalable—resizing in proportion to the screen resolution. Let's go with that, and leave out the exs, inches, centimeters, picas, and points for now. While useful for print, these are not typical choices for displaying fonts on screen.

That leaves us with percentages, ems, pixels, and keywords. All of these should be scalable options, but here's where the philosophy and browser support get in the way. Internet Explorer (IE) for Windows, for example, has bugs galore when it comes to font sizing. Owen Briggs, an author and CSS designer has taken 264 different screen shots of rendering problems in browsers (see Figure 8-10). I'll leave you to discover the ugly details on your own.

---

note   Learn about text-sizing problems, view 264 screen shots of text-size rendering bugs, and read one man's solution at `www.thenoodleincident.com/ tutorials/box_lesson/font/index.html`.

What is the solution? It's a difficult call that you must ultimately make based on your target browsers and audience needs. I used to always use pixels; now I find myself using ems and percentages in a lot of cases. A good rule of thumb is that if you're using fixed designs, pixels will work just fine, but if you want dynamic designs that scale, you may need to combine percentages and ems. Fortunately, you can combine text-sizing options within your CSS, which can be of help.

Secret #134:   Type Effects

Aside from figuring out the confusing issues with type sizing, there are a few useful and interesting font- and text-related properties that will help you in your quest to add typographic interest to your sites.

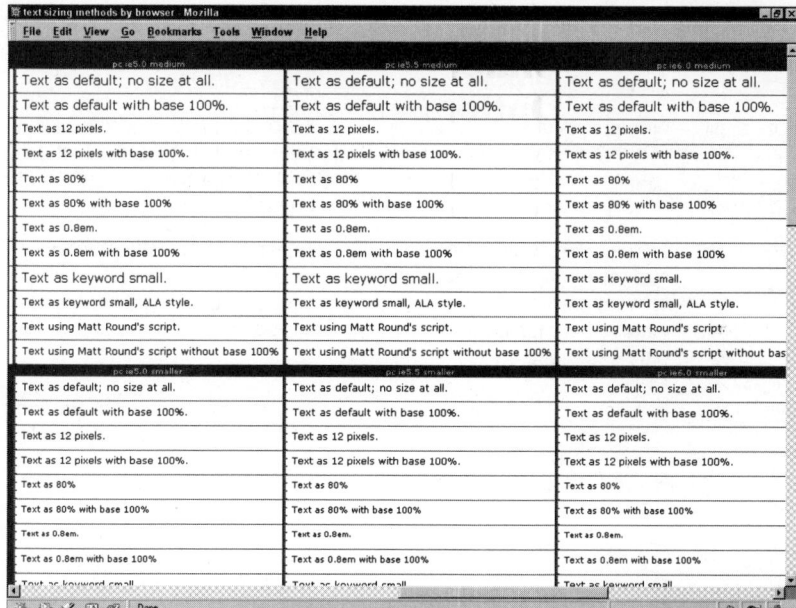

Figure 8-10: Owen Briggs has documented incredibly complicated problems with text-size rendering in CSS.

Unfortunately, some of them have buggy or no support, but some of these properties can be extremely useful, particularly to those designers creating sites for only the latest browsers.

Table 8-2 covers the properties of interest, values you'll want to know about, and what the properties do.

Table 8-2: CSS Type-Related Properties

Property	Values You'll Use	Use and Support
font	Shorthand property that allows you to define style, variant, weight, size, line-height, font-family, and other font-related features	Use shorthand wherever it makes sense to group rules: `h1{font: bold 14px/16px Arial, sans-serif;}` This rule calls for the h1 element to be styled in 14 pixel Arial (or sans-serif if Arial is unavailable) with a bold weight and a line-height of 16 pixels
font-family	A family name, such as Arial. Note that if the family name contains any white space, you must place quotes around it: `"Trebuchet MS"`. A generic name, such as serif, sans-serif, monotype, fantasy, or cursive. The generic name should relate to the family name	Typically, you'll use a font-family name or series of family names along with a generic name: `p{font-family: "Trebuchet MS", Arial, Helvetica, sans-serif;}` The font-family property has very good support

continued

Table 8-2: *(continued)*

Property	Values You'll Use	Use and Support
font-size-adjust	Numeric value	Helps suppress an alternate font to the same height as the first-named font. This property isn't supported anywhere
font-stretch	Absolute keyword values, such as ultra-condensed and semi-condensed, or extra-expanded and ultra-expanded	Expands or condenses a font. This would be an extremely useful property, but font-stretch isn't supported anywhere at this time
font-style	italic, oblique	Creates the italic or oblique form of the chosen font. Very good support
font-variant	small-caps	This font property selects the small-caps variant of your named font, or simulates the effect, making all your text appear in capital letters. Decent support
font-weight	bold, bolder, lighter, 100–900	Allows variations for the visual weight of a font. Very good support
letter-spacing	length	This determines the space between letters *in addition* to the default space. You'll use a length value, such as px or em: `p {letter-spacing: 0.2em;}` Support is limited to contemporary browsers only
word-spacing	length	Word spacing determines the space between words *in addition* to the default space. You'll use a length value: `p {word-spacing: 1.0em;}` Support is limited to contemporary browsers only
line-height	length, percentage, number	Allows you to control the vertical space between lines of text: `p {line-height: 130%;}` Good support in all contemporary Web browsers
text-align	left, right, center, justify	Allows you to align text: `p.right {text-align: right;{` Good support across browsers

Property	Values You'll Use	Use and Support
text-decoration	none, underline, overline, line-through, blink	Allows you to add an underline, overline, strikethrough, or blink decoration to your text. The most common use of this property is to remove underlines from links: `a {text-decoration: none;}` Support for the underline, overline, and line-through values is very good; blink is only a suggested feature in the CSS2 specification, not a required one, so it is not available in all browsers

text-indent	length, percentage	Allows you to indent text:
		
		`p {text-indent: 10%;}`
		
		Or out-dent it if you use a negative value, in which case you should increase the corresponding margin:
		
		`p.outdent {text-indent: -20px; margin-left: 20px;}`
		
		Support for text-indent is very good

text-shadow	color, length	Adds a drop-shadow effect to your text: `p {text-shadow: 3px 3px 3x #333}` Text shadow has very limited browser support
text-transform	capitalize, uppercase, lowercase	Allows you to modify the way text is capitalized. Choosing capitalize will capitalize each word in a sentence. The uppercase value will cause all letters affected by the property to appear in uppercase, even if you entered them as lowercase. Finally, lowercase will force all letters influenced by the property to lowercase. `h1 {text-transform: uppercase:}`

Figure 8-11 displays a number of the properties within this table.

note   For complete descriptions of these properties, their use, and all the values you can assign to them, see http://www.w3.org/TR/CSS2/fonts.html and www.w3.org/TR/CSS2/text.html.

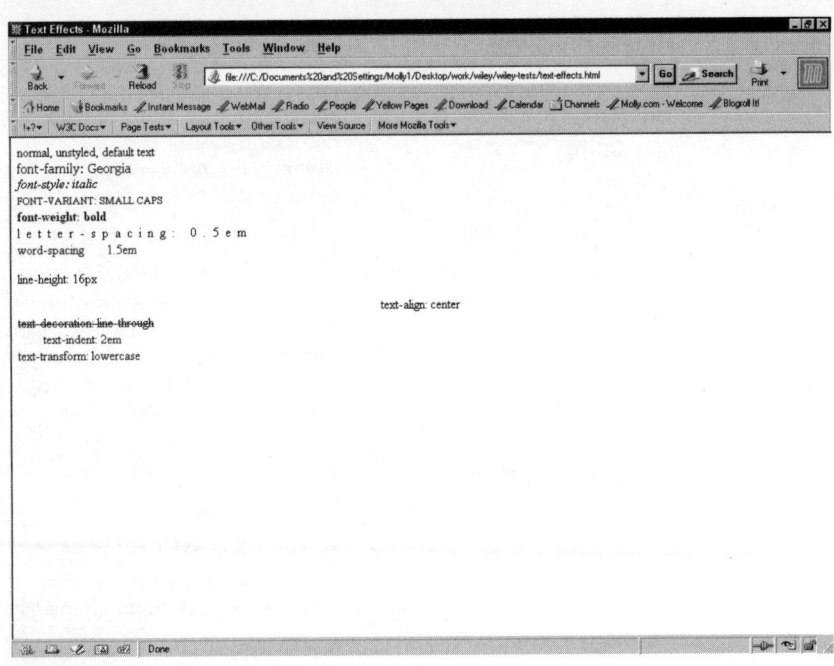

Figure 8-11: Exploring text effects using CSS.

Secret #135:   Styling Lists with CSS

There are a number of cool ways to style lists, too. This secret focuses on list properties (Table 8-3), but the next two secrets show you the popular technique of turning lists into navigation systems.

Table 8-3: List Properties in CSS

Property	Values of Interest	Use and Support
list-style	list-style-type, list-style-position, list-style-image	Shorthand property for all list-related values.
		`ul li {list-style: disc inside;}`
		This creates a disc next to each list item within an unordered list, and places the disc within the element box. Support is very good for the list-style property
list-style-image	url	Allows you to use an image for your list markers:

Property	Values of Interest	Use and Support
		`ul li {list-style-image:url(images/red-dot.gif);}`
		Available in all contemporary browsers
list-style-position	inside, outside	This positions the list marker inside the element box or outside of the element box. It is moderately well supported
list-style-type	disc, circle, square, decimal, decimal-leading-zero, lower-roman, upper-roman, lower-greek, lower-alpha, lower-latin, upper-latin, Hebrew, Armenian, Georgian, cjk-ideographic, hirgana, katakana, hiragana-iroha, ktakana-iroha	The wonderful ability to ensure your lists use the marker you want them to, including using a range of language-related marker types. `ol li {list-style-type: decimal-leading-zero;}` This specifies a numeric list with a leading 0. Support for list-style-type is good, but not all browsers support all available values

Figure 8-12 shows a range of list effects at work.

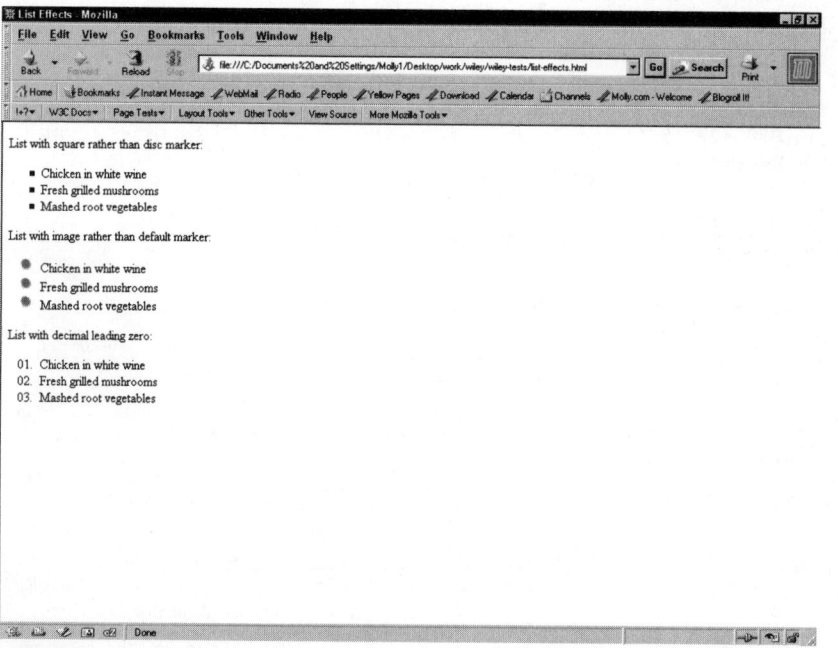

Figure 8-12: Fun with CSS lists.

Secret #136: Using Lists for Vertical Navigation

Lists for navigation make sense, because navigation boils down to being a list of links, no matter how it appears visually on the page.

That, added to the improved support for CSS, provides you with an opportunity to use style to create visually attractive lists that are either completely text-based or use background graphics as a means of providing hover effects.

Listing 8-4 sets up a vertical navigation list.

Listing 8-4: Using unordered lists for vertical navigation

```
<!DOCTYPE html PUBLIC "-//W3C//DTD XHTML 1.0 Strict//EN"
    "http://www.w3.org/TR/xhtml1/DTD/xhtml1-strict.dtd">

<html xmlns="http://www.w3.org/1999/xhtml">

<head>
<meta http-equiv="content-type" content="text/html; charset=iso-
8859-1" />
<title>List-Based Navigation: Vertical</title>

<style type="text/css">

#nav ul {
  margin-left: 0;
  padding-left: 0;
  list-style-type: none;
}

#navlist {
  padding-left: 0;
  margin-left: 0;
  border-bottom: 1px solid #999;
  width: 128px;
}

#navlist li {
  margin: 0;
  padding: 0.25em;
  border-top: 1px solid #999;
}

#navlist li a {
  text-decoration: none;
  color: red;
}

#navlist li a:hover {
  color: #333;
}

</style>
```

```
</head>

<body>

<ul id="navlist">
<li><a href="link1.html" title="Go to Link One">Link One</a></li>
<li><a href="link2.html" title="Go to Link Two">Link Two</a></li>
<li><a href="link3.html" title="Go to Link Three">Link
Three</a></li>
<li><a href="link4.html" title="Go to Link Four">Link
Four</a></li>
<li><a href="link5.html" title="Go to Link Five">Link
Five</a></li>
<li><a href="link6.html" title="Go to Link Six">Link Six</a></li>
<li><a href="link7.html" title="Go to Link Seven">Link
Seven</a></li>
<li><a href="link8.html" title="Go to Link Eight">Link
Eight</a></li>
<li><a href="link9.html" title="Go to Link Nine">Link
Nine</a></li>
</ul>

</body>
</html>
```

Figure 8-13 shows the results.

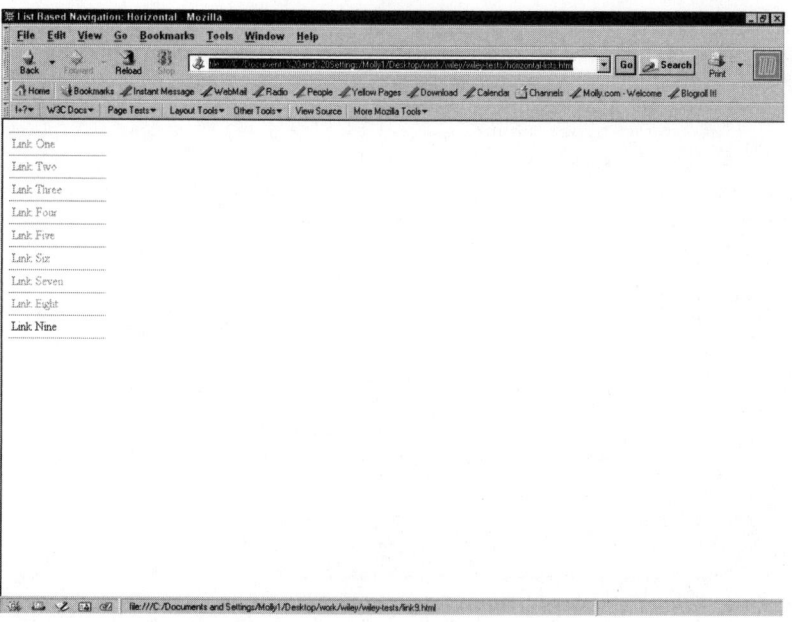

Figure 8-13: Using unordered lists and CSS to create attractive navigation.

> note
>
> **For an excellent tutorial on how to use lists to create beautiful navigation, see**
> **http://css.maxdesign.com.au/listamatic/.**

Secret #137:   Using Lists for Horizontal Navigation

I'm sure you're thinking using a list for navigation is well and good, but what about horizontal navigation, which has become so commonplace in today's design?

Using the `display` property, you can change the list from being a block-level element to being an inline element. As a result, the list becomes horizontal, as shown in Listing 8-5.

Listing 8-5: Horizontal lists using the display property

```
<!DOCTYPE html PUBLIC "-//W3C//DTD XHTML 1.0 Strict//EN"
     "http://www.w3.org/TR/xhtml1/DTD/xhtml1-strict.dtd">

<html xmlns="http://www.w3.org/1999/xhtml">

<head>
<meta http-equiv="content-type" content="text/html; charset=iso-
8859-1" />
<title>List-Based Navigation: Horizontal</title>

<style type="text/css">

#nav ul li {
    font-family: Georgia, "Times New Roman", Times, serif;
    font-size: 14px;
    color: #CC9900;
    display: inline;
    list-style-type: none;
    padding-right: 10px;
    }

</style>

</head>

<body>

<div id="nav">
  <ul>
   <li><a href="home.html">Home</a></li>
   <li><a href="books.html">Books</a></li>
   <li><a href="articles.html">Articles</a></li>
   <li><a href="events.html">Events</a></li>
   <li><a href="courses.html">Courses</a></li>
   <li><a href="consultation.html">Consultation</a></li>
   <li><a href="about.html">About Molly</a></li>
   <li><a href="fun.html">Fun Stuff</a></li>
   </ul>
</div>

</body>
</html>
```

Figure 8-14 displays the horizontal list.

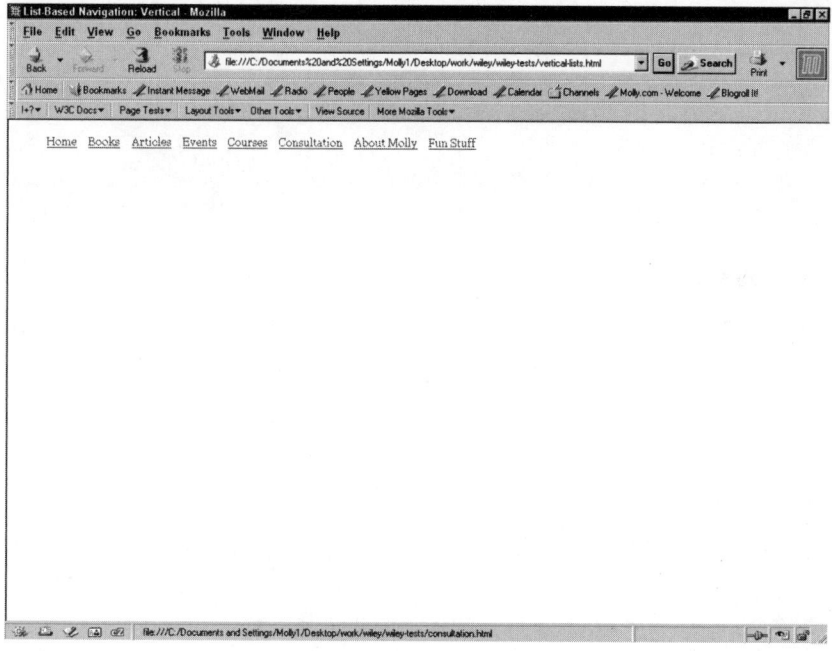

Figure 8-14: Using a list and the display property to create a horizontal navigation bar.

Now, you can add link colors, hover effects, background graphics—whatever you wish to enhance the list's design. You can get any number of great-looking navigation schemes, such as the one under development for my new redesign (see Figure 8-15).

> **note** Want to try some lists out but aren't confident yet about how they work? Try using Ian Lloyd's terrific List-O-Matic (**www.accessify.com/tools-and-wizards/list-o-matic/list-o-matic.asp**), which allows you to input your information and will output both the CSS and XHTML for a number of list styles.

Secret #138:   Spice Up Forms

Creating attractive forms has always been difficult in HTML. With CSS, you can definitely enhance forms because you have far more options to style form controls. By applying background and foreground colors, modifying or eliminating borders, controlling text size, and having better control over the sizing of controls themselves, you can use CSS to create much more attractive and usable forms.

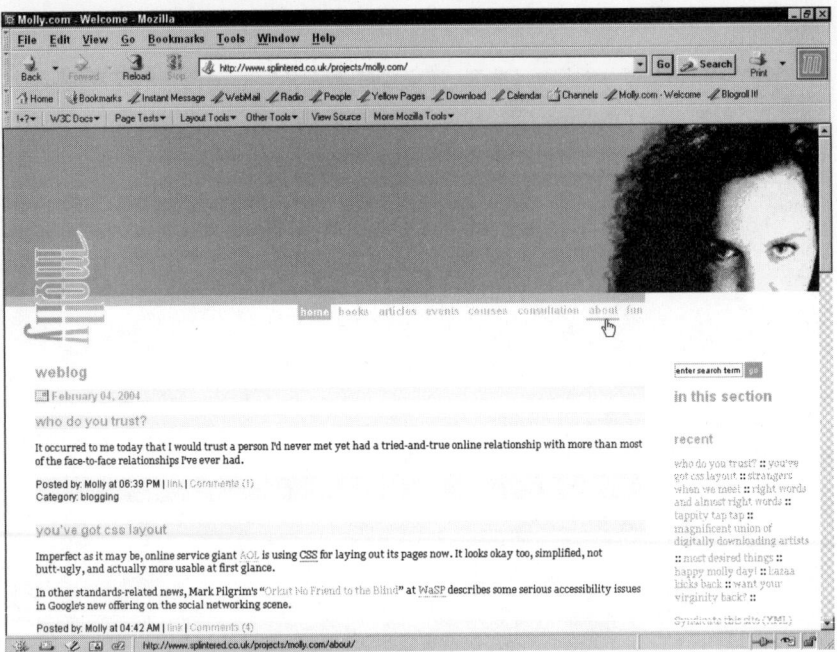

Figure 8-15: Horizontal navigation integrated into the main design.

Listing 8-6 shows a drop-down menu and submit button that've been enhanced using style.

Listing 8-6: Spicing up forms with CSS

```
<!DOCTYPE html PUBLIC "-//W3C//DTD XHTML 1.0 Transitional//EN"
      "http://www.w3.org/TR/xhtml1/DTD/xhtml1-transitional.dtd">

<html xmlns="http://www.w3.org/1999/xhtml">
<head>
<title>Form Control Effects</title>
<meta http-equiv="Content-Type" content="text/html; charset=iso-
8859-1" />

<style type="text/css">

#submit {

  background-color: #333;
  font-weight: bold;
  font-size: 12px;
  color: white;
  border: 2px dotted yellow;
  padding: 2px;
  width: 125px;
  height: 22px;
}
```

```
option, .input {
  background-color: #333;
  color: #fff;
}

.light {
  background-color: #ccc;
  color: #000;
}

</style>

</head>

<body>

<form action="http://www.molly.com/form.cgi" method="get">

<select id="destinations">
<option selected="selected"> -- Destinations -- </option>
<option class="light" value="../photos/">Photo Gallery</option>
<option value="../about/">About Us</option>
<option class="light" value="../education/">Educational
Opportunities</option>
<option value="../jobs/">Job Opportunities</option>
</select>

<input type="submit" value="submit" id="submit" />

</form>

</body>
</html>
```

In this case, I've used alternate background colors in the drop-down menu to highlight choices (see Figure 8-16).

---

tip   **Using CSS, you no longer need to use tables to make your forms attractive. You can find a straightforward tutorial on tableless forms at quirksmode (www.quirksmode.org/css/forms.html).**

Secret #139:   Add Visual Effects to Data Tables

As with forms, you can apply CSS rules to aspects of tables: borders, background color, background graphics, and fonts. This is really good news because in the days of table-and-font-tag design, trying to add fonts to tables meant having to open and close the font element for *every single table cell*. Fortunately, CSS comes to the rescue here, too.

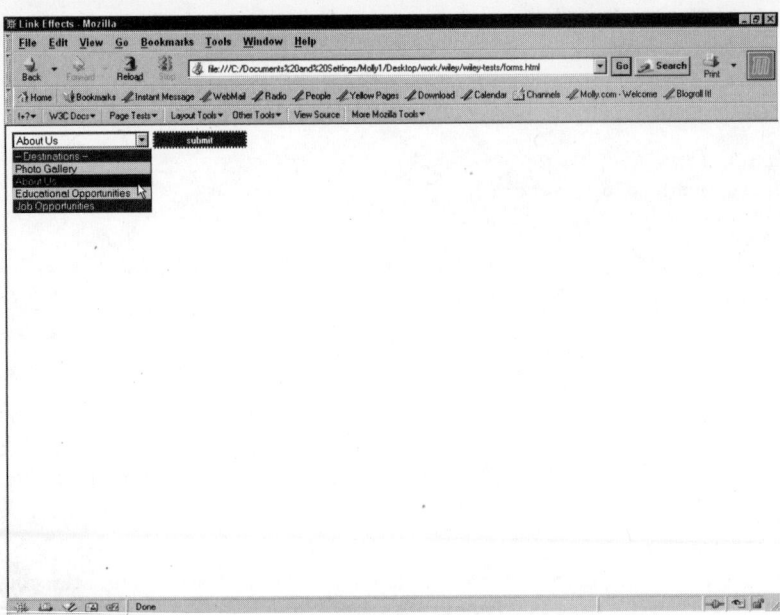

Figure 8-16: Using alternate background colors within a form component.

note Even though it became commonplace to use background graphics in table cells, the attribute was never part of any specification. Fortunately, CSS allows you to place backgrounds into any element you want, circumventing that concern.

Listing 8-7 provides a simple data table with color-coded entries and border effects.

Listing 8-7: A data table with color-coded entries and border Effects

```
<!DOCTYPE html PUBLIC "-//W3C//DTD XHTML 1.0 Transitional//EN"
    "http://www.w3.org/TR/xhtml1/DTD/xhtml1-transitional.dtd">

<html xmlns="http://www.w3.org/1999/xhtml">

<head>
<title>Data Table Effects</title>
<meta http-equiv="Content-Type" content="text/html;
charset=iso-8859-1" />

<style type="text/css">

#data1 {
  color: black;
  font-family: Arial, sans-serif;
  font-size: 14px;
  font-weight: bold;
  width: 450px;
  border: 1px solid #999;
}
```

```
th {
  background-color: #333;
  font-size: 16px;
  color: white;
  padding: 5px;
}

tr.dark {
  background-color: #999;
  color: #fff;
}

tr.light {
  background-color: #ccc;
}

</style>

</head>

<body>

<table id="data1">
<tr class="light">
<th>Value</th>
<td>001-01</td>
<td>001-02</td>
<td>003-03</td>
</tr>

<tr class="dark">
<th>Results</th>
<td>Very Good</td>
<td>Satisfactory</td>
<td>Inconclusive</td>
</tr>
</table>

</body>
</html>
```

You can see the visual results in Figure 8-17.

What thrills me about this table is how simple the markup is in comparison to what would be required to create the same effect without CSS! You'd have to have eight font elements, a `bgcolor` attribute in every cell, you couldn't have controlled the padding for the table headers specifically, and you wouldn't have had control over the thickness, style, and color of your border.

Secret #140: Using Background Graphics in CSS

As you read earlier in this chapter, you can add a background graphic to *any HTML element*. You can attach an image to an element as broad as body, and as specific as a single list item.

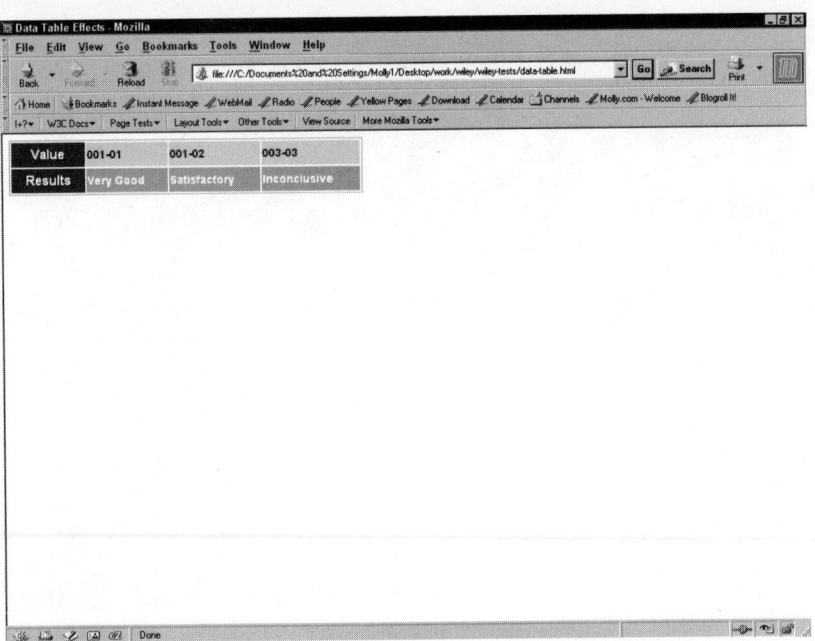

Figure 8-17: Using CSS to improve the look of data tables.

I've heard quite a few CSS designers say that they think about designing CSS using layers of graphics—stacking graphics from the elemental ground up, as it were.

One of my favorite CSS designs within the experimental CSS Zen Garden is Patrick Lauke's Door to My Garden. Not only is it a stunning example of what can be done with CSS in general, but as with all Zen Garden examples, it uses background graphics in a variety of elements to achieve its effect.

Figures 8-18 and 8-19 help point out where the graphics are being used—in the second figure, you can see how the entire text and navigation sections scroll.

> **note** You can view Door to My Garden at `www.csszengarden`
> `.com/?cssfile=041%2F041%2Ecss`. I highly recommend using a
> browser other than IE to get the full effect of the design.

Secret #141: Image Replacement Techniques

Image replacement is a technique that allows designers to place text "underneath" an image and hide the underlying text.

The entire goal with image replacement is to allow text and a graphic to be available for an element. The graphic, of course, will have the text displayed in a beautiful font so you can work within the nature of the design. Ideally, the text hidden below provides ASCII text to those with screen readers or graphics turned off.

Figure 8-18: Top portion of Door to My Garden.

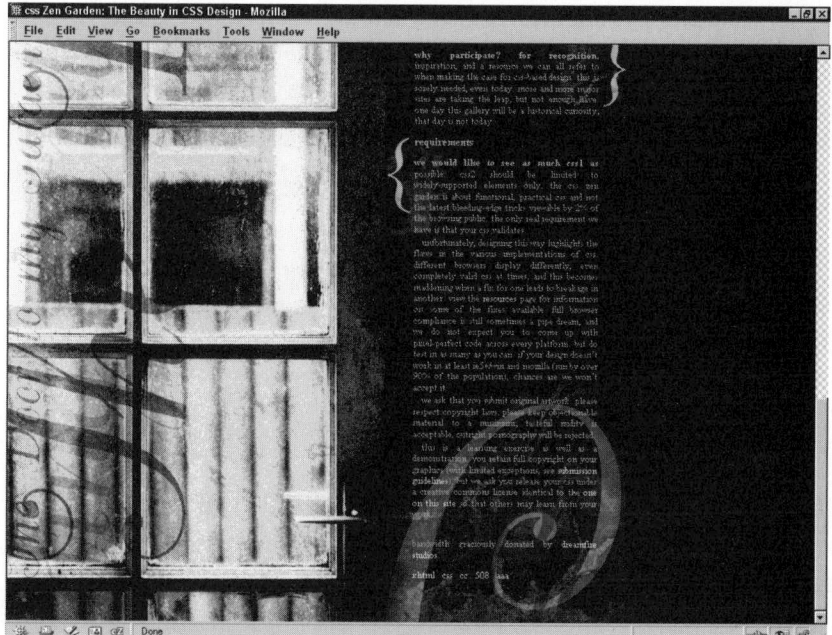

Figure 8-19: Detailed view of Door to My Garden.

The first technique of this kind to emerge has become known as *Fahrner Image Replacement* (FIR), after Todd Fahrner, its creator. First, you create a rule for the image, as in the following example:

```
h1 {
   background-image: url(header1.gif);
   background-repeat: no-repeat;
   height: 25px;
}
```

This CSS rule has `header1.gif` as the background to an h1 element, with no repeating of the image, and a specified height for the image as being 25 pixels. With that taken care of, you add the following rule:

```
span {
display:none;
}
```

Within the HTML, you'd write the following:

```
<h1><span>Header Text</span></h1>
```

So, with full CSS support in a visual browser, the results will render as described.

For some time, it was thought that this simple bit of brilliance worked well because screen readers were able to read the hidden text. However, accessibility specialist Joe Clark did some testing on FIR, and found that it was problematic in some screen readers. That completely blew the top off of the practice, considering the whole reason for doing it is to allow a visual design to be completely accessible.

> **note** For details, read Clark's "Facts and Opinion about Fahrner Image Replacement," at **www.alistapart.com/articles/fir/**.

As a result, a number of alternatives began to emerge, all of them with merit. These were gathered up by Dave Shea at his mezzoblue site, so you can try all the techniques out and determine which, if any, image replacement technique is for you.

> **note** For examples of alternative image replacement techniques, see "Revised Image Replacement" by Dave Shea, at **www.mezzoblue.com/tests/ revised-image-replacement/**.

Secret #142: CSS-Based Text Mouseovers

Want to create a mouseover without using any JavaScript whatsoever? Well, you can, as CSS expert Eric Meyer shows us via his CSS/Edge site (www.meyerweb .com/eric/css/edge/).

The technique is pretty simple, and taps into the use of the `display` property to hide text, and then have that text appear in a specified position upon hover, as demonstrated in Listing 8-8.

Listing 8-8: Text mouseovers using CSS

```
<!DOCTYPE html PUBLIC "-//W3C//DTD XHTML 1.0 Transitional//EN"
      "http://www.w3.org/TR/xhtml1/DTD/xhtml1-transitional.dtd">

<html xmlns="http://www.w3.org/1999/xhtml">

<head>
<title>Text Mouseovers</title>
<meta http-equiv="Content-Type" content="text/html; charset=iso-
8859-1" />

<style type="text/css">

#links {
  position: absolute;
  top: 100px;
  left: 25px;
  width: 150px;
  height: 300px;
  font: 14px Arial, sans-serif;
}

#links a {
  display: block;
  font-weight: bold;
  text-decoration: none;
  text-align: center;
  padding: 10px;
  color: #c00;
  border: 1px solid black;
}

#links a:hover {
  color: #c00;
  background-color: #FFF;
}

#links a span {
  display: none;
}

#links a:hover span {
  display: block;
  position: absolute;
  top: 50px;
  left: 225px;
  width: 150px;
  padding: 5px;
   color: #FFF;
  background-color: black;
}
li {
  list-style-type: none;
```

(continued)

Listing 8-8: *(continued)*

```
    padding: 10px;
}

</style>

</head>

<body>

<ul id="links">
<li><a href="http://www.wiley.com/">Wiley<span>Wiley is the
publisher of this book.</span></a></li>
<li><a href="http://www.molly.com/">Molly<span>Molly is the
author of this book.</span></a></li>
<li><a href="http://www.sidesh0w.com/">Ethan<span>Ethan is the
technical editor of this book.</span></a></li>
</ul>

</body>
</html>
```

Figure 8-20 shows the results.

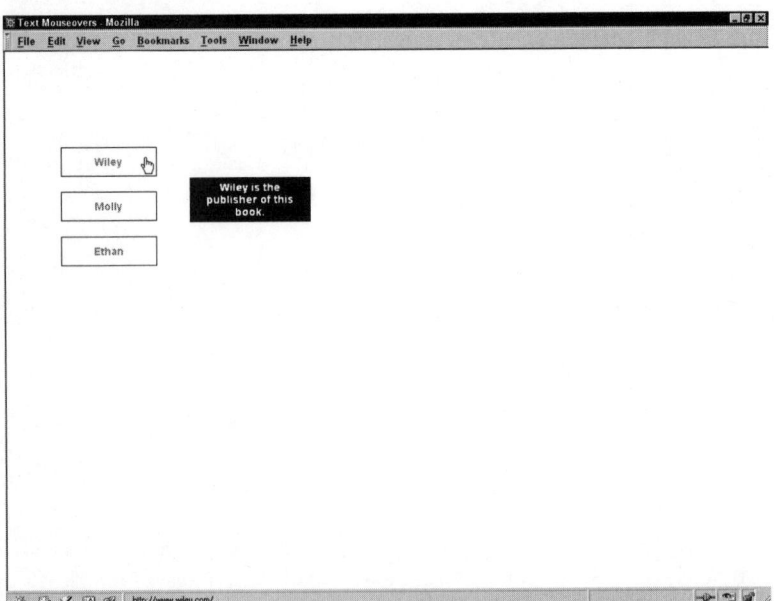

Figure 8-20: Text mouseovers using CSS work well in today's modern Web browsers.

---

tip　　Add additional features to your links styles to enhance the look. Or, create an awesome list-based navigation, as described earlier in this book, to create horizontal as well as vertical navigation options with this technique.

Secret #143:   Text and Image Mouseovers

You can use the same swapping technique using images. In this case, you'll be placing an image element directly into the anchor element and, instead of using the display element to hide and then reveal the image, you'll set the image to have no height and width until the hover state, in which you'll include width and height (see Listing 8-9).

Listing 8-9: CSS mouseovers using images

```
<!DOCTYPE html PUBLIC "-//W3C//DTD XHTML 1.0 Transitional//EN"
      "http://www.w3.org/TR/xhtml1/DTD/xhtml1-transitional.dtd">

<html xmlns="http://www.w3.org/1999/xhtml">

<head>
<title>Text Mouseovers</title>
<meta http-equiv="Content-Type" content="text/html; charset=iso-
8859-1" />

<style type="text/css">

#links {
  position: absolute;
  top: 100px;
  left: 25px;
  width: 150px;
  height: 300px;
  font: 14px Arial, sans-serif;
}

#links a {
  display: block;
  font-weight: bold;
  text-decoration: none;
  text-align: center;
  padding: 10px;
  color: #c00;
  border: 1px solid black;
}

#links a:hover {
  color: #c00;
  background-color: #FFF;
}

#links a span {
  display: none;
}
```

(continued)

Listing 8-9: *(continued)*

```
#links a img {
  height: 0;
  width: 0;
  border-width: 0;
}

#links a:hover img {
  position: absolute;
  top: 75px;
  left: 255px;
  height: 50px;
  width: 190px;
}

li {
  list-style-type: none;
  padding: 10px;
}

</style>

</head>

<body>

<ul id="links">

<li><a href="http://www.wiley.com/">Wiley<img src="wiley.gif"
/></a></li>
<li><a href="http://www.molly.com/">Molly<img src="molly.gif"
/></a></li>
<li><a href="http://www.sideshow.com/">Ethan<img
src="sideshow.jpg" /></a></li>
</ul>

</body>
</html>
```

Figure 8-21 shows the results.

Secret #144:   Dynamic CSS Menus

This technique is an extension of the ideas in the CSS mouseover techniques, but it applies the :hover pseudo class to other elements—this is actually a perfectly acceptable use of :hover, but, unfortunately, IE doesn't support it. As a result, you'll only have access to the primary links.

So, while you can use this effect to create great menus (see Figure 8-22) without JavaScript, you can't do it in IE (see Figure 8-23). However, because you're simply styling lists, they will tend to degrade to nested lists in most browsers without CSS support (as shown in Figure 8-24).

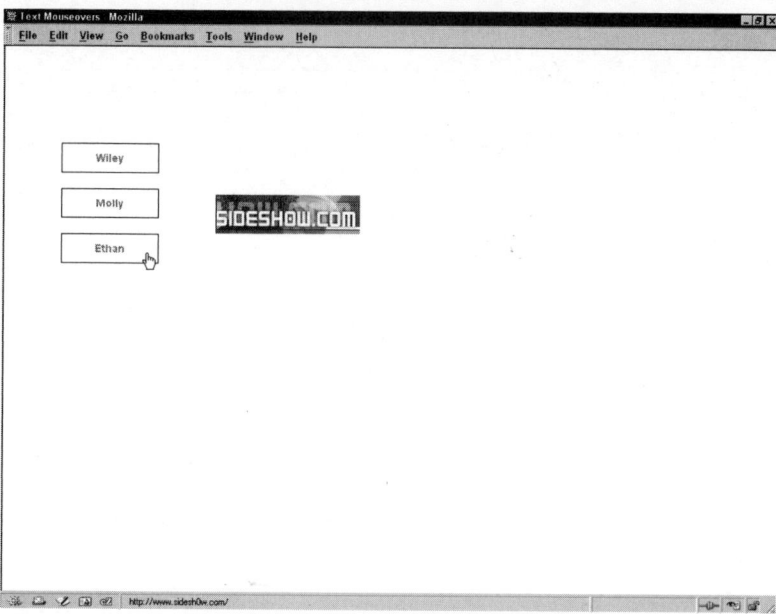

Figure 8-21: CSS-based mouseovers with images.

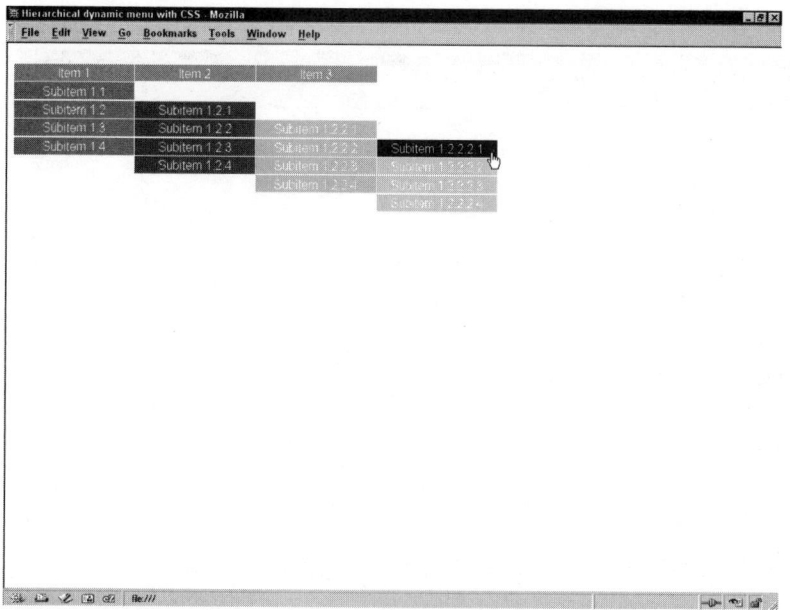

Figure 8-22: A CSS-based dynamic menu in action.

note

For more information about the mouseover and menu techniques discussed here, visit Eric Meyer's CSS Edge, at www.meyerweb.com/eric/css/edge/. A good explanation for hierarchical dynamic menus can be found at www.pixy.cz/blogg/clanky/csshiermenu/.

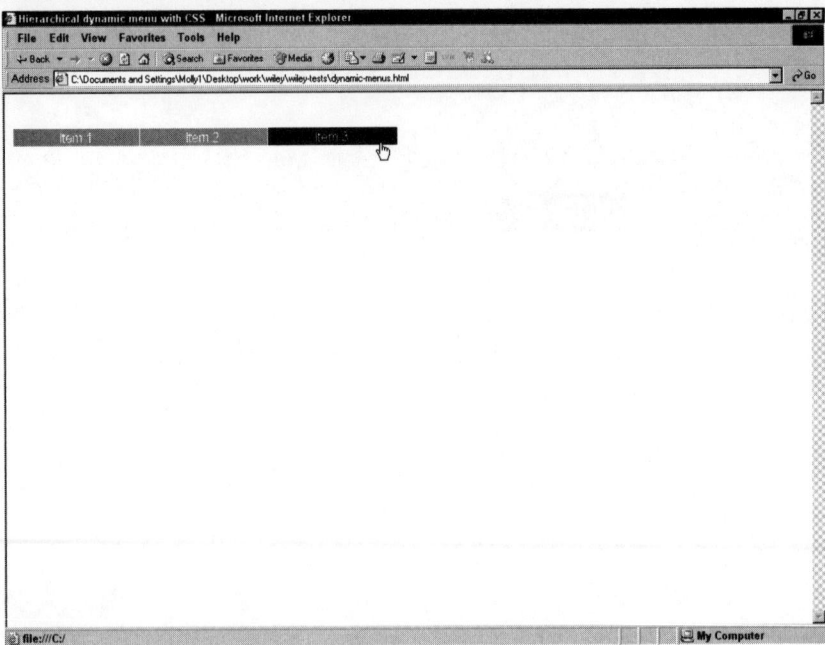

Figure 8-23: IE will only display the top links of the menu.

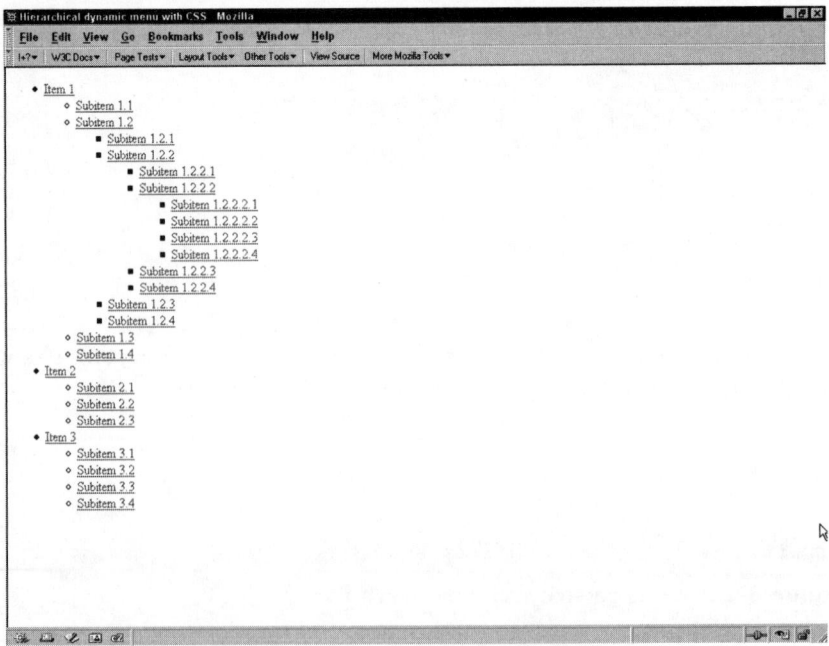

Figure 8-24: The same menu with styles completely disabled.

Secret #145:   Rounded Tabs

Still another interesting effect offered up by Eric Meyer is a technique whereby you can use images to create a rounded tab effect in horizontal list navigation. Rounded tabs are a mainstay of navigation, providing a softer look than square tabs tend to offer.

The beauty of this technique is that it is supported in all contemporary browsers (see Figure 8-25).

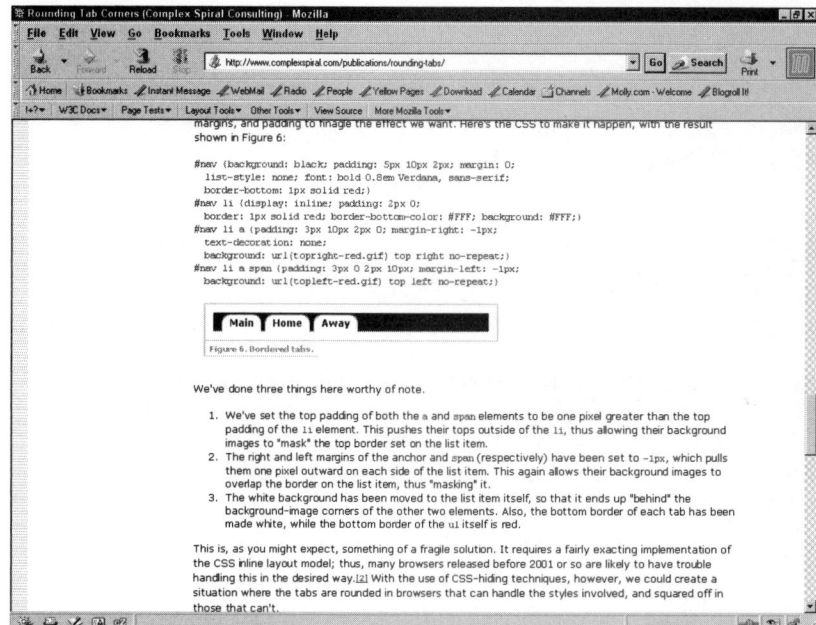

Figure 8-25: Rounded tab technique from complex spiral consulting.

note   This technique is described in a white paper on Eric's consulting Web site, at **www.complexspiral.com/publications/rounding_tabs/**.

Secret #146:   Sliding Doors

Another awesome effect for tabbed navigation is the "Sliding Doors" technique created by CSS designer Douglas Bowman.

In this technique, you use two separate images, one small and one large, to create a sliding effect. This allows you to create dynamic navigation that is far more friendly to the resizing of fonts while maintaining the navigation design. Figure 8-26 shows the concept at work.

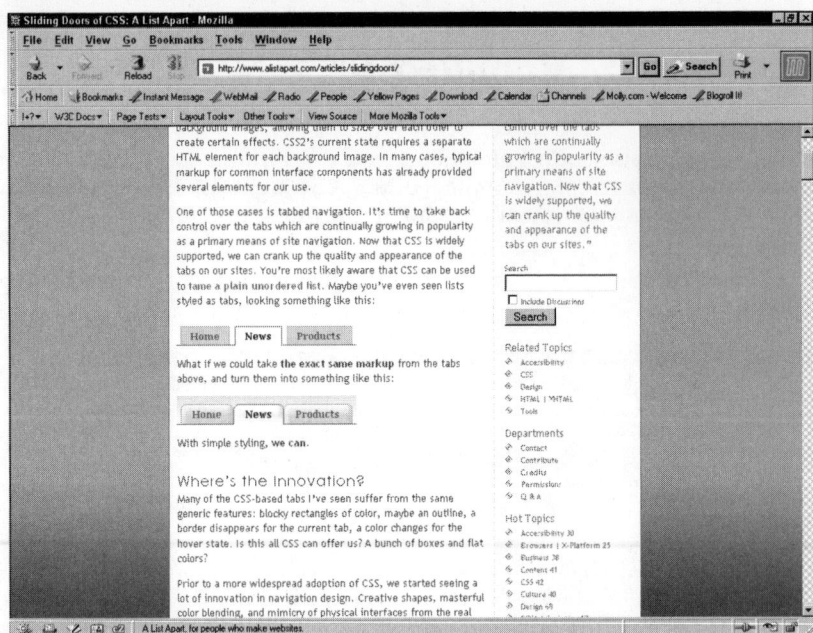

Figure 8-26: The Sliding Doors effect.

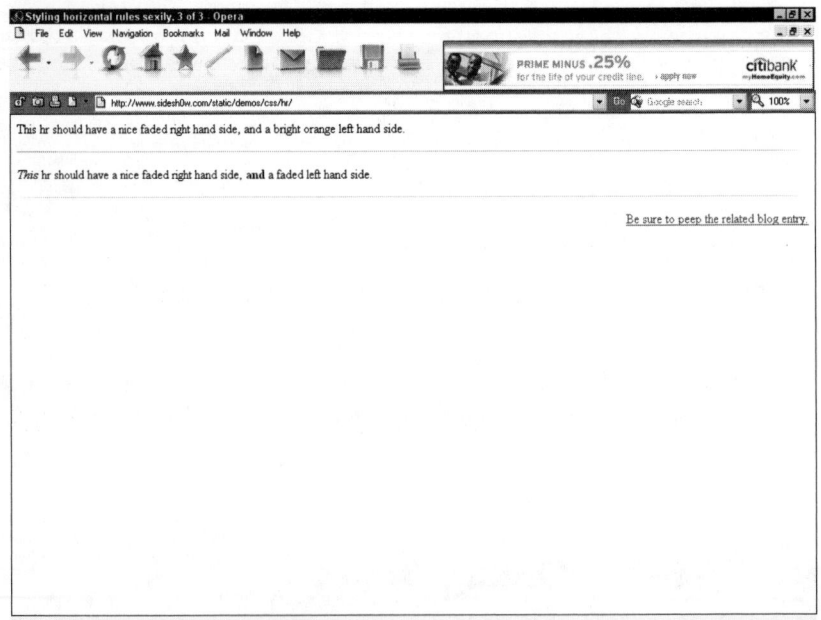

Figure 8-27: Horizontal rule fade effects.

note

To learn the Sliding Doors technique as well as some variants, see
www.alistapart.com/articles/slidingdoors/.

Secret #147:   Cool Rules

I stumbled upon this technique while writing this chapter. Ethan Marcotte (this book's technical editor) and designer Dunstan Orchard worked together to find a means to style horizontal rules using background graphics.

Through a bit of trial and error, Ethan and Dunstan came up with a means to create cross-browser horizontal rule effects including subtle fades. Figure 8-27 shows the results.

note To read more about styling horizontal rules, see `www.sidesh0w.com/ weblog/2004/03/17/sexily_styling_horizontal_rules.html`.

Summary

Obviously, there are still concerns about the role CSS plays for certain audiences, but CSS has truly emerged as more than just a band-aid solution for font and color control. You can now enhance your pages in so many ways, and I really believe we have only just begun to understand where CSS will take us in terms of visual design.

If you're excited about CSS after this chapter—and I hope you are—you'll be happy to know you get to spend another chapter with CSS, examining how CSS works for layout, how to manage workarounds, deal with hacks, and write CSS for other media types.

Laying Out
Pages with CSS

Chapter
9

◆ ◆

Secrets in This Chapter

◆ ◆

A n intriguing development over the past several years has been the move away from table-based design to transitional designs using lighter tables and CSS, or out-and-out pure CSS layouts.

CSS ultimately frees the designer by providing much richer and more diverse means of presenting and delivering designs to various media including, but not limited to, the following:

- Screen
- Print
- Projection
- Audio
- Braille
- Television

But page layout with CSS is in relatively early days yet, so designers need a lot of additional information to work with their layouts effectively.

In this chapter, you'll learn about some of the most practical means of laying out pages. The examples are made simple so you can both begin using them quickly and gain insight into the concepts being employed. Also included in this chapter are numerous hacks to assist you in making sure your CSS layouts are as backward compatible as possible.

CSS Layout Basics

Several terms and concepts are referred to throughout this chapter, so it's good to let you know them up front:

- **Box Model.** Any HTML or XHTML element creates a box, and you can use CSS to access and style aspects of that box, including margins, padding, and borders. There are problems in Box Model implementations—which is one of the reasons that CSS layouts require so much attention to detail and often require hacks to ensure proper cross-browser display.
- **Graceful degradation.** This is the concept that when styles are removed from a design, the actual text content is still available and easily accessed, even if all the visual layout and design elements are gone.
- **Hack.** A hack is any use of code outside its original, intended purpose.
- **Workaround.** A workaround is typically an exploitation of a bug within a browser allowing you to bypass support problems. Hacks and workarounds are very similar, and there's always dissent as to whether a hack is a hack, a workaround, or a technique.
- **Positioning.** In CSS, you can position element boxes either absolutely, via specific coordinates, or relatively, in relation to other elements. You can create complete layouts with absolute positioning, as is sometimes called for.

note   The layouts in this chapter use positioning in conjunction with other methods for maximum flexibility. Many visual editors, such as Dreamweaver, use the term "layers" to refer to absolutely positioned CSS boxes.

◆ **Floats.** Floats in CSS are a means of floating something to the right or left. Intended mostly to float images, floating has become one form of laying out documents.

◆ **Filters.** Filters in this context are a means of bypassing specific browsers while targeting others. Filters are really hacks, but the terminology is used to define specific hacks that are filtering specific browsers.

note   See Appendix C for helpful resources to assist you in your CSS education.

Secret #148:   Two-Column Layout, Positioned Left Navigation

Using absolute positioning, you can create a two-column layout with a left column menu and right content area.

Listing 9-1 shows the CSS and markup used to create the layout.

Listing 9-1: Working with positioning in layout

```
<!DOCTYPE html PUBLIC "-//W3C//DTD XHTML 1.0 Strict//EN"
    "http://www.w3.org/TR/xhtml1/DTD/xhtml1-strict.dtd">

<html xmlns="http://www.w3.org/1999/xhtml">

<head>
<title>Layout Content Right, Navigation Left</title>

<style type="text/css">

#content {
  margin:0px 50px 50px 175px;
  padding:10px;
}

#nav {
  position:absolute;
  top:50px;
  left:20px;
  width:200px;
  padding:10px;
  line-height:17px;
}

</style>

</head>

<body>

<div id="content">
```

(continued)

Listing 9-1: *(continued)*

```
<p>Lorem ipsum dolor sit amet, consectetuer adipiscing elit. In
vestibulum vestibulum elit. Ut porta. Duis vulputate bibendum
tellus. Vivamus dictum egestas mi. Cras justo. Vestibulum nisl
mauris, convallis a, vestibulum et, accumsan vel, lacus. Morbi
mattis viverra turpis. Pellentesque blandit quam in sapien. Proin
pellentesque, purus sit amet mollis sollicitudin, lacus leo
rhoncus enim, nec vestibulum urna tellus at magna. Ut
adipiscing.</p>

<p>Morbi ut sem non diam fringilla tincidunt. Maecenas nunc
tellus, adipiscing eget, tincidunt ut, venenatis ut, enim. Sed
posuere turpis at nisl. Sed at sem. Nullam sagittis tincidunt
magna. Duis tempus. Proin dui turpis, consequat quis, porttitor
ut, molestie vel, libero. Phasellus sodales venenatis urna.</p>

<p>Maecenas ipsum risus, fringilla rutrum, porta id, congue id,
leo. Fusce augue nulla, vestibulum at, euismod ut, ultrices in,
felis. Cras vitae pede ac mi lobortis fermentum. Phasellus
viverra. Ut ultrices, neque ac congue varius, justo quam elementum
mi, at nonummy urna elit quis augue. Praesent feugiat pede a
turpis. Duis libero diam, volutpat id, dictum vitae, aliquet sed,
lorem. </p>
</div>

<div id="nav">
  <ul>
  <li><a href="home.html">Home</a></li>
  <li><a href="books.html">Books</a></li>
  <li><a href="articles.html">Articles</a></li>
  <li><a href="events.html">Events</a></li>
  <li><a href="courses.html">Courses</a></li>
  <li><a href="consultation.html">Consultation</a></li>
  <li><a href="about.html">About Molly</a></li>
  <li><a href="fun.html">Fun Stuff</a></li>
  </ul>
</div>

</body>
</html>
```

Figure 9-1 shows the results.

Secret #149: Float-Based Layout

While not primarily intended for laying out documents, the use of the `float` property in CSS does allow you to create a number of convenient layouts with minimum fuss.

Floating layouts are common because they are functional, flexible, and easy to work with. Floating layouts use the `float` property and a value of `left` or `right` to determine which element gets floated.

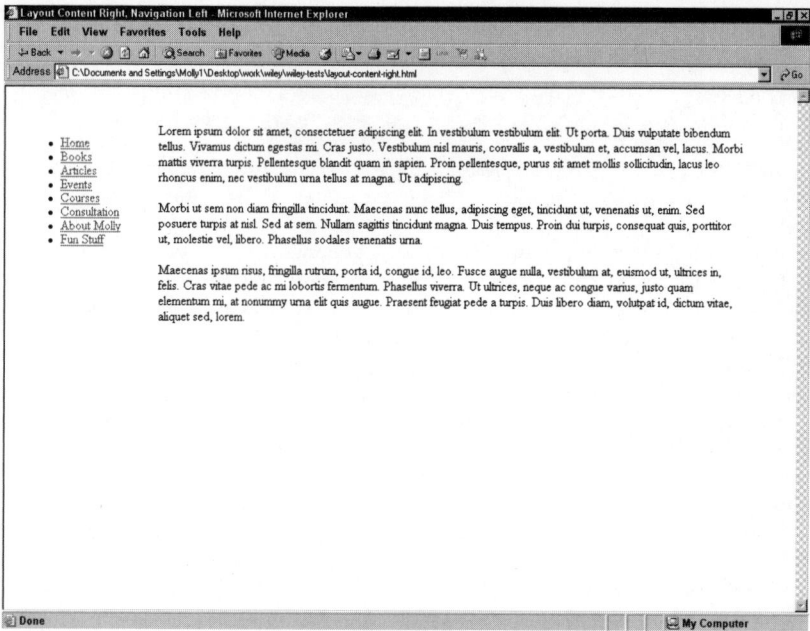

Figure 9-1: A CSS layout using positioning.

Listing 9-2 shows how.

Listing 9-2: Float-based layout, floating left content

```
<!DOCTYPE html PUBLIC "-//W3C//DTD XHTML 1.0 Strict//EN"
     "http://www.w3.org/TR/xhtml1/DTD/xhtml1-strict.dtd">

<html xmlns="http://www.w3.org/1999/xhtml">

<head>
<title>Layout Float Left</title>

<style type="text/css">

#content {
   float:left;
   width:70%;
   background-color:#fff;
   padding: 15px;
}

#nav {
  margin-top: 15px;
}

</style>

</head>
```

(continued)

Listing 9-2: *(continued)*

```
<body>

<div id="content">
<p>Lorem ipsum dolor sit amet, consectetuer adipiscing elit. In
vestibulum vestibulum elit. Ut porta. Duis vulputate bibendum
tellus. Vivamus dictum egestas mi. Cras justo. Vestibulum nisl
mauris, convallis a, vestibulum et, accumsan vel, lacus. Morbi
mattis viverra turpis. Pellentesque blandit quam in sapien. Proin
pellentesque, purus sit amet mollis sollicitudin, lacus leo
rhoncus enim, nec vestibulum urna tellus at magna. Ut
adipiscing.</p>

<p>Morbi ut sem non diam fringilla tincidunt. Maecenas nunc
tellus, adipiscing eget, tincidunt ut, venenatis ut, enim. Sed
posuere turpis at nisl. Sed at sem. Nullam sagittis tincidunt
magna. Duis tempus. Proin dui turpis, consequat quis, porttitor
ut, molestie vel, libero. Phasellus sodales venenatis urna.</p>

<p>Maecenas ipsum risus, fringilla rutrum, porta id, congue id,
leo. Fusce augue nulla, vestibulum at, euismod ut, ultrices in,
felis. Cras vitae pede ac mi lobortis fermentum. Phasellus
viverra. Ut ultrices, neque ac congue varius, justo quam elementum
mi, at nonummy urna elit quis augue. Praesent feugiat pede a
turpis. Duis libero diam, volutpat id, dictum vitae, aliquet sed,
lorem. </p>
</div>

<div id="nav">
  <ul>
   <li><a href="home.html">Home</a></li>
   <li><a href="books.html">Books</a></li>
   <li><a href="articles.html">Articles</a></li>
   <li><a href="events.html">Events</a></li>
   <li><a href="courses.html">Courses</a></li>
   <li><a href="consultation.html">Consultation</a></li>
   <li><a href="about.html">About Molly</a></li>
   <li><a href="fun.html">Fun Stuff</a></li>
   </ul>
</div>

</body>
</html>
```

Figure 9-2 shows the results.

Secret #150:   Nested Float

The nested float layout in Listing 9-3 shows how you can nest div elements to get more interesting layouts. Nesting div elements can be an important part of

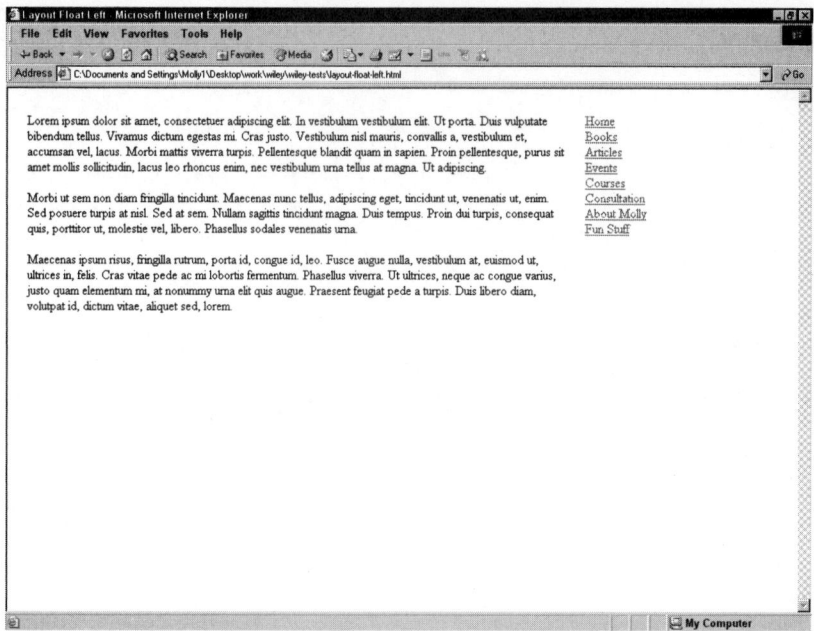

Figure 9-2: A CSS layout using float.

complex layout designs. This simple example will help give you a taste of how it works.

Listing 9-3: Nested Float

```
<!DOCTYPE html PUBLIC "-//W3C//DTD XHTML 1.0 Strict//EN"
    "http://www.w3.org/TR/xhtml1/DTD/xhtml1-strict.dtd">

<html xmlns="http://www.w3.org/1999/xhtml">

<head>
<title>Nested DIV Example</title>

<style type="text/css">

#content {
  border: 1px solid #000;
}
#content #nav {
  border-left: 1px solid #000;
  border-bottom: 1px solid #000;
  float: right;
  width: 250px;
  background: #ccc;
  margin: 0px 0px 10px 10px;

}
```

(continued)

Listing 9-3: *(continued)*

```
</style>

</head>

<body>

<div id="content">

<div id="nav">
  <ul>
    <li><a href="home.html">Home</a></li>
    <li><a href="books.html">Books</a></li>
    <li><a href="articles.html">Articles</a></li>
    <li><a href="events.html">Events</a></li>
    <li><a href="courses.html">Courses</a></li>
    <li><a href="consultation.html">Consultation</a></li>
    <li><a href="about.html">About Molly</a></li>
    <li><a href="fun.html">Fun Stuff</a></li>
  </ul>
</div>

<p>Lorem ipsum dolor sit amet, consectetuer adipiscing elit. In
vestibulum vestibulum elit. Ut porta. Duis vulputate bibendum
tellus. Vivamus dictum egestas mi. Cras justo. Vestibulum nisl
mauris, convallis a, vestibulum et, accumsan vel, lacus. Morbi
mattis viverra turpis. Pellentesque blandit quam in sapien. Proin
pellentesque, purus sit amet mollis sollicitudin, lacus leo
rhoncus enim, nec vestibulum urna tellus at magna. Ut
adipiscing.</p>

<p>Morbi ut sem non diam fringilla tincidunt. Maecenas nunc
tellus, adipiscing eget, tincidunt ut, venenatis ut, enim. Sed
posuere turpis at nisl. Sed at sem. Nullam sagittis tincidunt
magna. Duis tempus. Proin dui turpis, consequat quis, porttitor
ut, molestie vel, libero. Phasellus sodales venenatis urna.</p>

<p>Maecenas ipsum risus, fringilla rutrum, porta id, congue id,
leo. Fusce augue nulla, vestibulum at, euismod ut, ultrices in,
felis. Cras vitae pede ac mi lobortis fermentum. Phasellus
viverra. Ut ultrices, neque ac congue varius, justo quam elementum
mi, at nonummy urna elit quis augue. Praesent feugiat pede a
turpis. Duis libero diam, volutpat id, dictum vitae, aliquet sed,
lorem.</p>
</div>

</body>
</html>
```

You can see the results in Figure 9-3. Figure 9-4 shows a styled version of this design scheme in use.

Reversing the layout is simple, too. All you need to do is modify the float from right to left and change the borders, as follows:

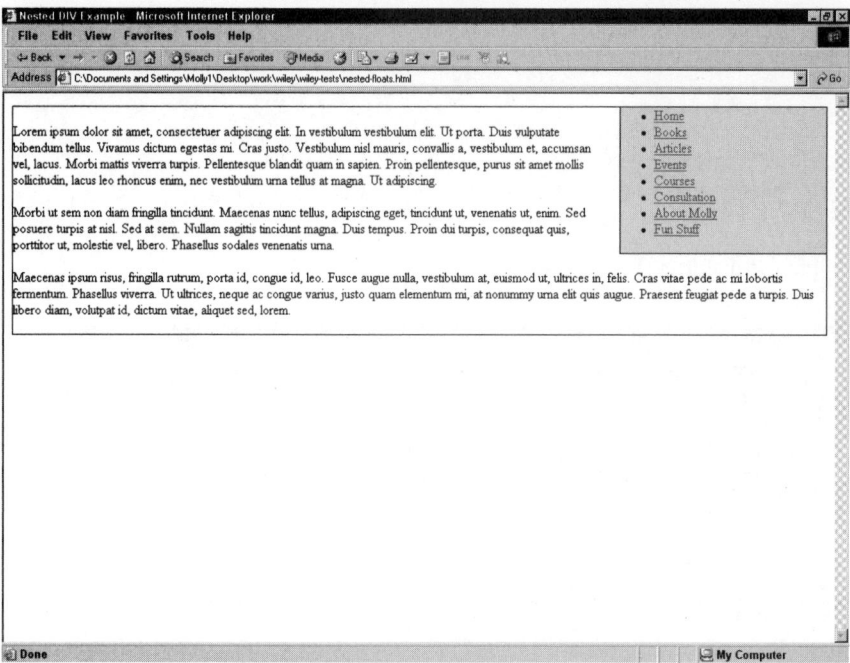

Figure 9-3: The basic layout styles for a nested float.

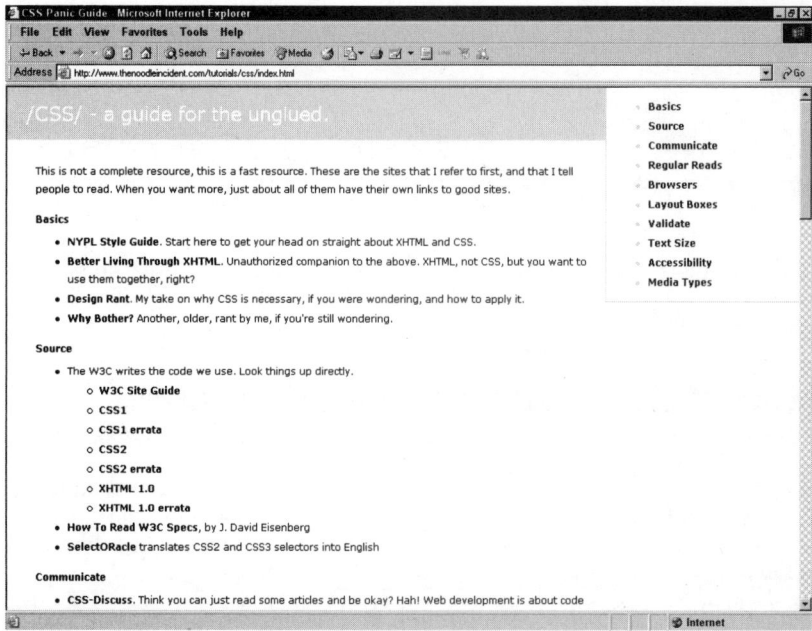

Figure 9-4: A styled example of a nested float from Owen Brigg's CSS panic guide.

```
#content #nav {
  border-right: 1px solid #000;
  border-bottom: 1px solid #000;
  float: left;
  width: 250px;
  background: #ccc;
  margin: 0px 0px 10px 0px;
}
```

Figure 9-5 shows the reverse.

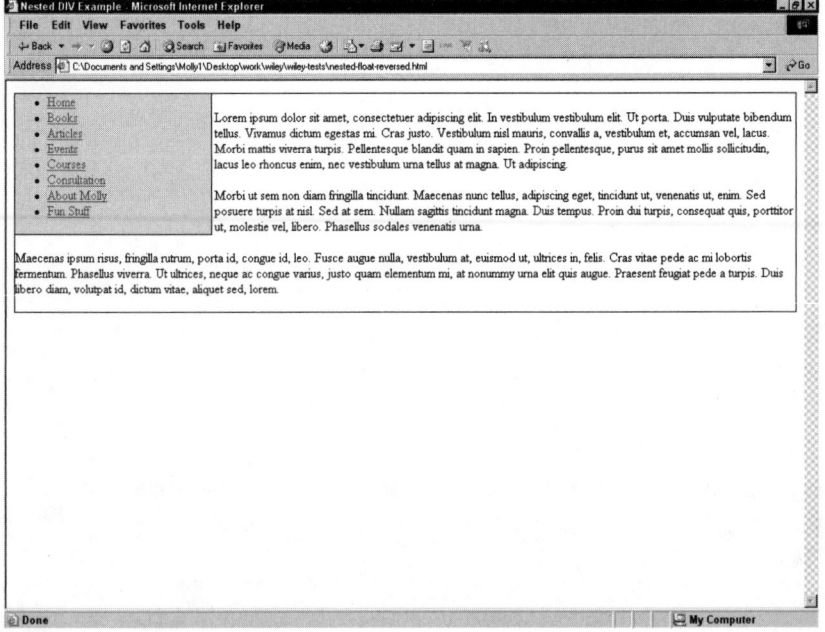

Figure 9-5: Reversing the float.

Add a little style to the page and you've got an easy, useful float-based layout.

Secret #151: Three-Column Layout

This is a very popular layout, used frequently to emulate the three-column layouts to which we're accustomed in table-based designs. In this case, each of the flanking columns is a fixed width, and the center content column will adjust dynamically (see Listing 9-4).

Listing 9-4: Dynamic three-column layout

```
<!DOCTYPE html PUBLIC "-//W3C//DTD XHTML 1.0 Strict//EN"
    "http://www.w3.org/TR/xhtml1/DTD/xhtml1-strict.dtd">
```

```
<html xmlns="http://www.w3.org/1999/xhtml">

<head>
<title>Three-column Layout</title>

<style type="text/css">

#content {
  padding: 10px;
  width: auto;
  position: relative;
  margin: 0px 210px 20px 170px;
}

#nav {
  padding: 10px;
  width: 200px;
  position: absolute;
  left: 10px;
  top: 75px;
}

#right {
  padding: 10px;
  text-align: right;
  width: 150px;
  position: absolute;
  right: 20px;
  top: 50px;
}

</style>

</head>

<body>

<div id="content">
<p>Lorem ipsum dolor sit amet, consectetuer adipiscing elit. In
vestibulum vestibulum elit. Ut porta. Duis vulputate bibendum
tellus. Vivamus dictum egestas mi. Cras justo. Vestibulum nisl
mauris, convallis a, vestibulum et, accumsan vel, lacus. Morbi
mattis viverra turpis. Pellentesque blandit quam in sapien. Proin
pellentesque, purus sit amet mollis sollicitudin, lacus leo
rhoncus enim, nec vestibulum urna tellus at magna. Ut
adipiscing.</p>

<p>Morbi ut sem non diam fringilla tincidunt. Maecenas nunc
tellus, adipiscing eget, tincidunt ut, venenatis ut, enim. Sed
posuere turpis at nisl. Sed at sem. Nullam sagittis tincidunt
magna. Duis tempus. Proin dui turpis, consequat quis, porttitor
ut, molestie vel, libero. Phasellus sodales venenatis urna.</p>
```

(continued)

Listing 9-4: *(continued)*

```
<p>Maecenas ipsum risus, fringilla rutrum, porta id, congue id,
leo. Fusce augue nulla, vestibulum at, euismod ut, ultrices in,
felis. Cras vitae pede ac mi lobortis fermentum. Phasellus
viverra. Ut ultrices, neque ac congue varius, justo quam elementum
mi, at nonummy urna elit quis augue. Praesent feugiat pede a
turpis. Duis libero diam, volutpat id, dictum vitae, aliquet sed,
lorem.</p>
</div>

<div id="right">
<p><em>Maecenas ipsum risus, fringilla rutrum, porta id, congue
id, leo. Fusce augue nulla, vestibulum at, euismod ut, ultrices
in, felis.</em></p>
</div>

<div id="nav">
  <ul>
    <li><a href="home.html">Home</a></li>
    <li><a href="books.html">Books</a></li>
    <li><a href="articles.html">Articles</a></li>
    <li><a href="events.html">Events</a></li>
    <li><a href="courses.html">Courses</a></li>
    <li><a href="consultation.html">Consultation</a></li>
    <li><a href="about.html">About Molly</a></li>
    <li><a href="fun.html">Fun Stuff</a></li>
  </ul>
</div>

</body>
</html>
```

Figure 9-6 shows the results.

Add a little CSS pizzazz, and you end up with a fully styled site, such as that shown in Figure 9-7.

Secret #152:   Vertical Centering in CSS

Recently, designers have got back to fixing their CSS designs. In other words, instead of having the design flow dynamically to the browser size, the design is fixed to a certain pixel width (see Figure 9-8).

> **note**   While some designers prefer fixed designs, other camps strongly advocate "fluid" or "liquid" designs—those designs that flow to fill the browser window. Advantages of liquid design include that no browser space is wasted, and no matter how you size your browser, the design will flow to fit it. Liquid design means less control of aspects of the overall design, and managing text line

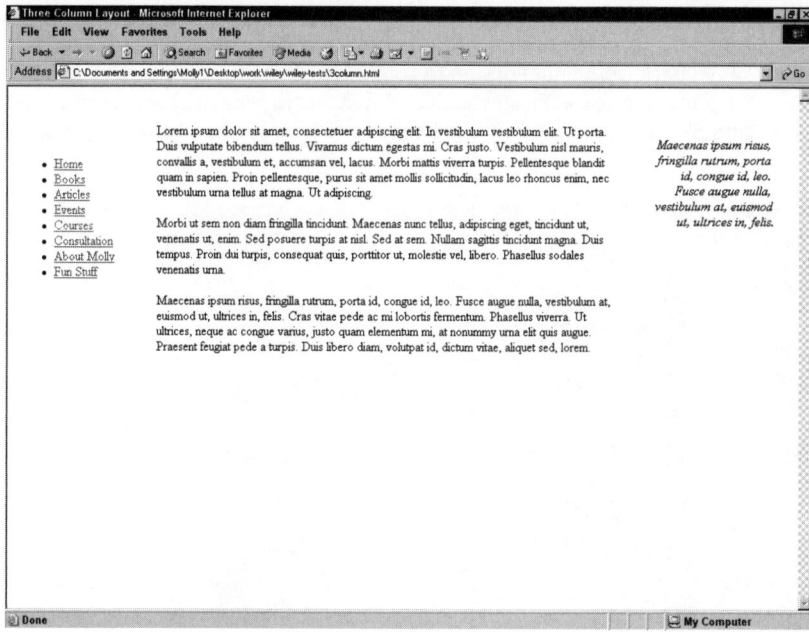

Figure 9-6: The basic three-column layout.

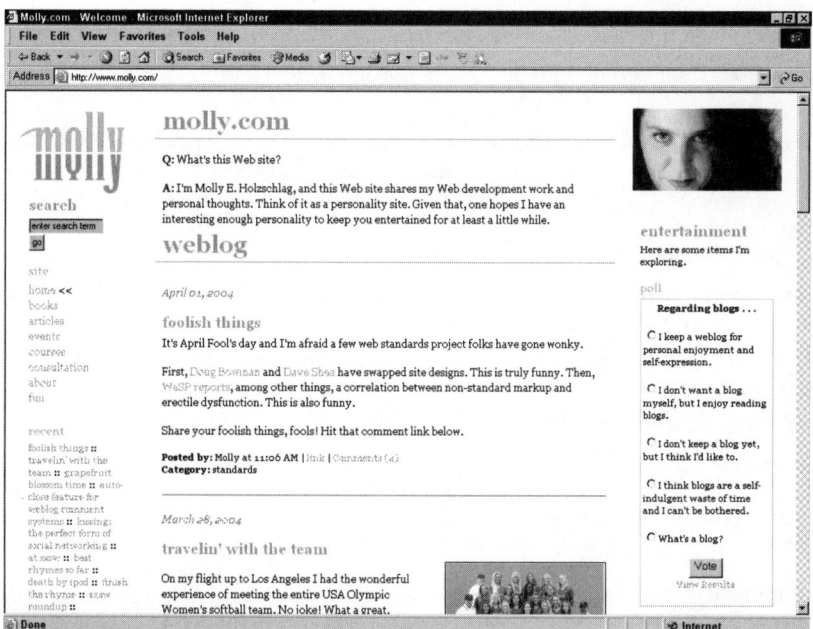

Figure 9-7: Molly.Com uses this three-column layout.

lengths in a fluid design is difficult, if not impossible, without sacrificing some other aspect of the design. These issues most likely are responsible for the move back from liquid design to controlled, centered designs, as we are beginning to see with sites such as A List Apart, www.alistapart.com/, and many of the CSS Zen Garden designs, www.csszengarden.com/.

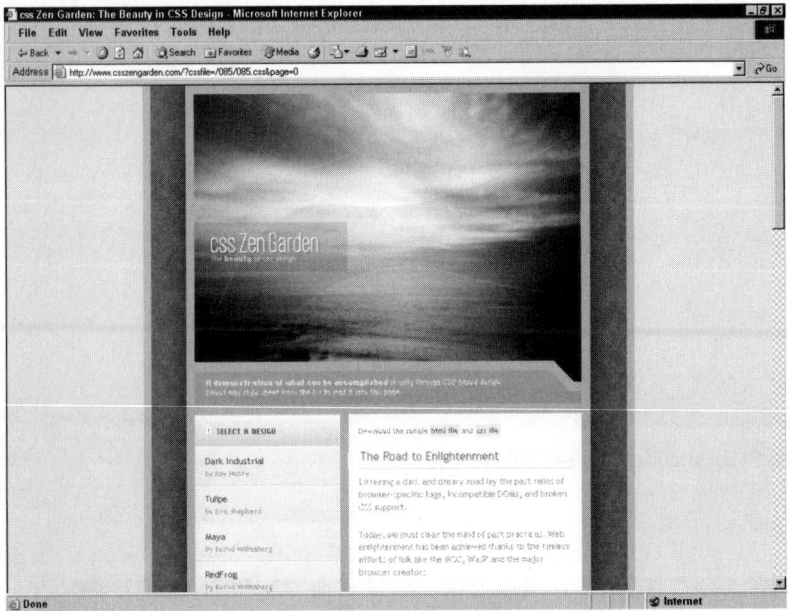

Figure 9-8: Centered designs in CSS are making a comeback.

While CSS offers a logical means to center designs, a problem exists with browser implementation. It's more than a bit frustrating, because with table-based layouts this was very easy, but the same difficulties with accessibility and limited design options exist when using tables. You'd simply use the align="center" attribute to center the containing table, and the entire layout would then be centered.

So how do you achieve the same effect in CSS? You have to employ a workaround to support multiple browsers.

The correct way to horizontally center a box is to set the left and right margins of a given box to a width of auto. This is going to be true of any box within your design, not just the containing box you're using to center the design itself.

```
#mainbox {
  margin-left: auto;
  margin-right: auto;
}
```

By doing this, any box will center neatly, and in complying browsers, it does (see Figure 9-9).

However, because some browsers don't implement the correct CSS to manage your containing boxes, you have to look at workarounds or hacks.

The most common hack in use is to apply the text-align property to the containing box, setting the alignment to a value of center. This technique will

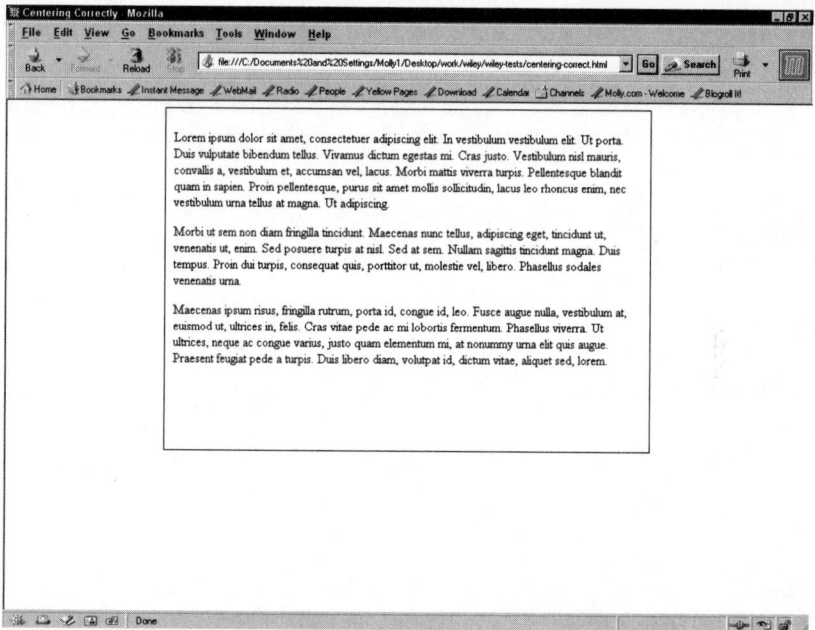

Figure 9-9: Centering a box using the correct method works in complying browsers such as Mozilla.

work in a wider range of browsers. The workaround is controversial for a couple of reasons:

+ You're applying a property meant for text, not for positioning, so you're not using the language correctly, which is why this is considered a hack.
+ You have to write extra CSS to override the `text-align: center` property and value, because you're going to use the `text-align: center` property on the `body` element. So, any text within the body is now going to be aligned to the center, unless you override the `text-align` property elsewhere.

Listing 9-5 shows the CSS and markup for the centering hack.

Listing 9-5: Centering hack

```
<!DOCTYPE html PUBLIC "-//W3C//DTD XHTML 1.0 Strict//EN"
    "http://www.w3.org/TR/xhtml1/DTD/xhtml1-strict.dtd">

<html xmlns="http://www.w3.org/1999/xhtml">

<head>
<title>Centering Hack</title>

<style type="text/css">

body {
```

(continued)

Listing 9-5: *(continued)*

```
    text-align: center;
  }

#content {
  width: 400px;
  height: 400px;
  text-align: left;
}

</style>

</head>

<body>

<div id="content">
<p>Lorem ipsum dolor sit amet, consectetuer adipiscing elit. In
vestibulum vestibulum elit. Ut porta. Duis vulputate bibendum
tellus. Vivamus dictum egestas mi. Cras justo. Vestibulum nisl
mauris, convallis a, vestibulum et, accumsan vel, lacus. Morbi
mattis viverra turpis. Pellentesque blandit quam in sapien. Proin
pellentesque, purus sit amet mollis sollicitudin, lacus leo
rhoncus enim, nec vestibulum urna tellus at magna. Ut
adipiscing.</p>

<p>Morbi ut sem non diam fringilla tincidunt. Maecenas nunc
tellus, adipiscing eget, tincidunt ut, venenatis ut, enim. Sed
posuere turpis at nisl. Sed at sem. Nullam sagittis tincidunt
magna. Duis tempus. Proin dui turpis, consequat quis, porttitor
ut, molestie vel, libero. Phasellus sodales venenatis urna.</p>

<p>Maecenas ipsum risus, fringilla rutrum, porta id, congue id,
leo. Fusce augue nulla, vestibulum at, euismod ut, ultrices in,
felis. Cras vitae pede ac mi lobortis fermentum. Phasellus
viverra. Ut ultrices, neque ac congue varius, justo quam elementum
mi, at nonummy urna elit quis augue. Praesent feugiat pede a
turpis. Duis libero diam, volutpat id, dictum vitae, aliquet sed,
lorem.</p>
</div>

</body>
</html>
```

Your box is now centered. Or is it? In Internet Explorer (IE) 6 and Netscape 4.x it is (even though the height and border styles aren't supported). But in Mozilla and Opera, the box isn't centered (see Figure 9-10).

> **note** The fact that the box does not center properly using this method in Mozilla and Opera is not a fault of those browsers. They're actually rendering the CSS properly. You're using a hack, which more sophisticated browsers tend not to like.

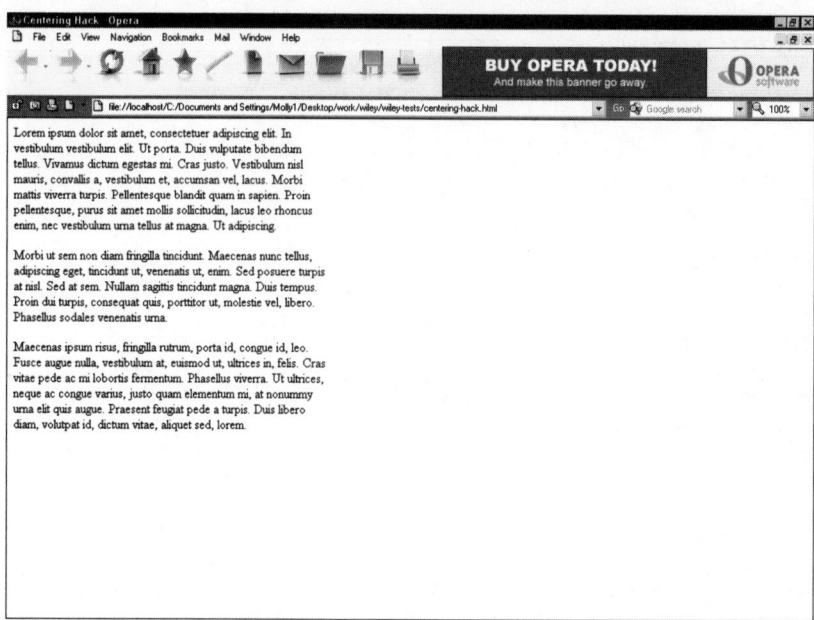

Figure 9-10: Centering using the center hack won't work in some browsers.

So, to make your containing box as cross-browser compatible as possible, you have to use both the right way *and* the hack, as expressed in Listing 9-6.

Listing 9-6: Combining correct vertical centering and the centering hack

```
<!DOCTYPE html PUBLIC "-//W3C//DTD XHTML 1.0 Strict//EN"
     "http://www.w3.org/TR/xhtml1/DTD/xhtml1-strict.dtd">

<html xmlns="http://www.w3.org/1999/xhtml">

<head>
<title>Centering Combo</title>

<style type="text/css">

body {
  text-align: center;
}

#content {
  width: 595px;
  height: 400px;
  border: 1px solid black;
  padding: 10px;
  margin-right: auto;
  margin-left: auto;
  text-align: left;
```

(continued)

Listing 9-7: *(continued)*

```
    }

    </style>

    </head>

    <body>

    <div id="content">
    <p>Lorem ipsum dolor sit amet, consectetuer adipiscing elit. In
    vestibulum vestibulum elit. Ut porta. Duis vulputate bibendum
    tellus. Vivamus dictum egestas mi. Cras justo. Vestibulum nisl
    mauris, convallis a, vestibulum et, accumsan vel, lacus. Morbi
    mattis viverra turpis. Pellentesque blandit quam in sapien. Proin
    pellentesque, purus sit amet mollis sollicitudin, lacus leo
    rhoncus enim, nec vestibulum urna tellus at magna. Ut
    adipiscing.</p>

    <p>Morbi ut sem non diam fringilla tincidunt. Maecenas nunc
    tellus, adipiscing eget, tincidunt ut, venenatis ut, enim. Sed
    posuere turpis at nisl. Sed at sem. Nullam sagittis tincidunt
    magna. Duis tempus. Proin dui turpis, consequat quis, porttitor
    ut, molestie vel, libero. Phasellus sodales venenatis urna.</p>

    <p>Maecenas ipsum risus, fringilla rutrum, porta id, congue id,
    leo. Fusce augue nulla, vestibulum at, euismod ut, ultrices in,
    felis. Cras vitae pede ac mi lobortis fermentum. Phasellus
    viverra. Ut ultrices, neque ac congue varius, justo quam elementum
    mi, at nonummy urna elit quis augue. Praesent feugiat pede a
    turpis. Duis libero diam, volutpat id, dictum vitae, aliquet sed,
    lorem.</p>
    </div>

    </body>
    </html>
```

This method works in a far greater range of browsers, and you can use the technique for creating vertically aligned CSS layouts.

> **note** Be sure to read the "CSS Hacking Strategies" secret later in this chapter for information on how to deal with hacks more efficiently.

Secret #153: Ordering DIVs for Backward Compatibility

When you're creating CSS layouts, the order of your positioned div elements will make a difference in the way in which text is ordered when styles are removed, but won't make a difference in terms of how the CSS is interpreted on-screen.

As a result, you'll want to order your div elements so the content is readable when styles are removed.

Say, for example, you have the following in your document:

```
<div id="navigation">
<!-- navigation elements go here -->
</div>
<div id="content">
<!-- content goes here -->
</div>
```

If you remove the styles, the navigation is going to appear at the top of the page. If you prefer to have the navigation appear at the bottom of the page when styles are removed, simply switch the order of the div elements, as follows:

```
<div id="content">
<!-- content goes here -->
</div>
<div id="navigation">
<!-- navigation elements go here -->
</div>
```

Because the div positioning is based on your CSS, not the order in which the information appears in the document, the visual output in a CSS-compliant browser will be exactly the same.

warning   While this works well for positioned div elements, one of the downsides of using floats for layout is that you can't do this with floated divisions. They must appear in the correct location of the HTML or XHTML document to render properly.

Secret #154:   @import for Graceful Degradation

If you are attempting to gracefully degrade your CSS layouts and have to support Netscape 4.x version browsers, you might want to consider using the @import workaround as a solution to ensure your site degrades the way you'd like it to.

The problem: Netscape 4.x versions have partial support for CSS. Layouts are especially prone to breaking.

The solution: Netscape 4.x versions' impartial CSS support is a partial blessing, because there's no support for the @import rule. This allows designers to split their CSS into two style sheets:

- **Site-wide styles.** This style sheet will contain font, color, and other CSS properties used for just about everything but layout information.
- **Layout styles.** This style sheet contains the layout information for the site.

If you had a site-wide style sheet, styles.css, and a layout style sheet, layout.css, split up in the way previously described, you'd then link to the styles.css, but import the layout styles using @import, as in the following example:

```
<!-- begin link to design styles for screen -->
<link rel="stylesheet" type="text/css" media="screen"
href="styles.css" />
<!-- begin @import for layout styles -->
<style type="text/css" media="screen">@import
"layout.css";</style>
```

Because Netscape 4.x can read the linked style sheet, some style will be applied to the page. But because it cannot read the @import rule or any styles associated with it, the layout style information is ignored, leaving a more gracefully degraded site (see Figure 9-11).

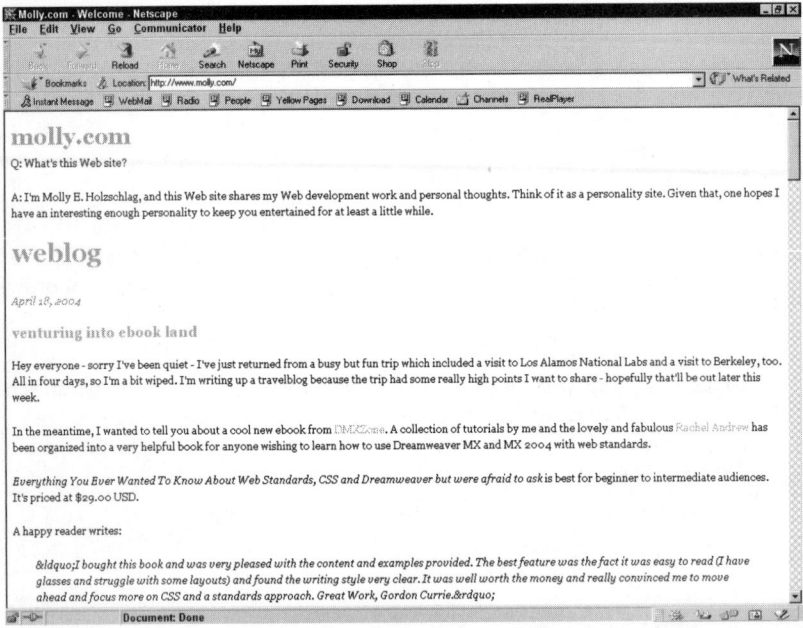

Figure 9-11: Graceful degradation using @import to hide layout styles from Netscape.

Secret #155:   CSS Hacking Strategies

You've already seen the center hack in operation in this chapter. A hack occurs any time you use an element, property, or other syntax within a language for a purpose other than its intended application.

Hacks are in widespread use with CSS because of myriad browser issues. Depending upon your circumstances, you may be able to avoid most hacks, but for most designers and developers, hacks are necessary—especially when it comes to maintaining CSS layout and style across as many browsers as possible.

> **note** In the next few secrets, you'll be learning about a number of hacks to manage layout and design issues across browsers. The majority of these

hacks have been developed by Tantek Çelik, who worked as lead developer on several versions of the Macintosh IE Web browser and is a strong advocate of Web standards, and are presented with his permission. Also of note: all of Tantek's hacks are published under a Creative Commons license, so they are available for you to freely distribute as long as attribution is given. In each hack's case, I've provided the URL specific to the hack's documentation.

Having some strategy in place to deal with hacks can help. Here are a few tips:

- **Avoid hacks if you don't need them.** This means knowing CSS (and CSS hacks) well enough to strip out hacks from CSS that you might borrow from other designers to use as a template or guide.
- **Comment your hacked code.** Any time you add a hack, make sure you place a comment with that hack to notify others who might be working with your code. Let everyone know that it is in fact a hack, and if it has a specific, known name, such as "hi pass filter," include that in your comment, too.
- **Consider using `@import` within your main style sheet to import your hacks.** This way, you can simply remove the hack file and `@import` rules from your main sheet as you find they are no longer required.

If you choose to import your hacks, you must add the rules directly to your primary style sheet:

```
/* begin hacks */
@import "hi-pass.css";
@import "boxmodel.css";
@import "opera.css";
/* end hacks */
```

Figure 9-12 describes the way you would import a hack. By keeping the hacks in separate files, they become easier to remove down the line.

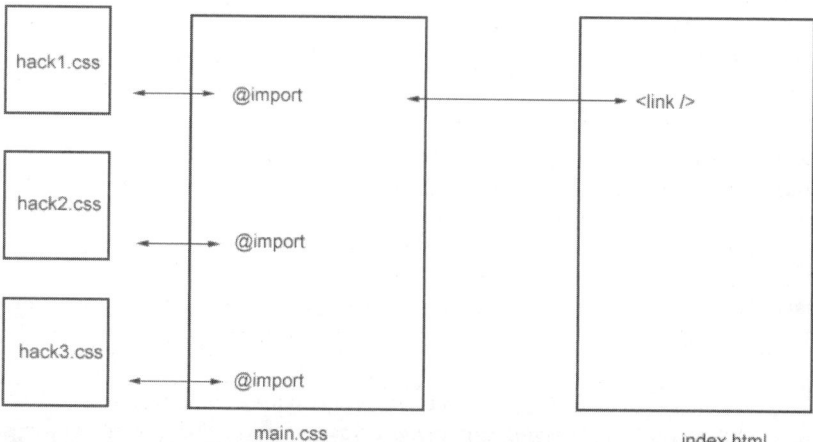

Figure 9-12: Importing hacks into a primary style sheet.

Secret #156: The Box Model Hack

Perhaps the most widely used hack in CSS, the Box Model Hack helps correct problems with positioning. IE for Windows has an incorrect implementation of the Box Model, as described earlier in this chapter. While DOCTYPE switching corrects this problem in IE 6.0, earlier IE versions will misinterpret your CSS badly enough to cause significant layout discrepancies.

note **Read more about DOCTYPE switching technology in Chapter 7, "Moving Ahead with XHTML."**

Begin with a simple box, such as the following:

```
#content {
   border: 10px solid black;
   padding: 10px;
   width:300px;
}
```

The correct interpretation would be to add the borders and padding width-wise as follows:

```
Left border 10px +
Right border 10px +
Left padding 10px +
Right padding 10px +
Box width 300px =
340 pixels total width
```

However, improper Box Model interpretations will place the border and padding *inside* the width of the box, resulting in those widths being subtracted, as follows:

```
Box width 300px -
Left border 10px -
Right border 10px -
Left padding 10px -
Right padding 10px =
260 pixels total width
```

As you can see, this is a significant difference. The Box Model Hack taps into a parsing bug in those problem browsers to work around the problem. Using the `voice-family` property, you first define your desired width, insert the hack, and then apply a width, which gets overridden and tricks the problem browsers into using the correct width of 340 pixels:

```
div.content {
   width: 340px;
   voice-family: "\"}\"";
   voice-family: inherit;
   width: 260px;
}
```

You might consider using some additional hacks along with the Box Model Hack to cover for other browsers that might have problems with the hack itself.

note

To learn more about the Box Model Hack, see visual examples, and read more about additional, useful CSS to help with other browsers at `http://tantek.com/CSS/Examples/boxmodelhack.html`.

The Box Model Hack will now validate at the W3C's CSS validator. For a time it did not, but because the actual syntax is valid CSS syntax, the W3C corrected the validator to support it, even though the way it's being used is inappropriate. Think of the use of a table element to create a layout table. Even though the use of tables for layout is the biggest hack in HTML history, the table element is still a valid element, even though we're misusing it from its original intent.

Secret #157:   The High Pass Filter

This filter is a means of filtering CSS rules to a variety of browsers while ensuring that unwanted styles don't get maligned by those problem browsers. The high pass filter takes into account the idea that we want to move toward as hack-free an environment as possible, but still be able to deliver CSS to browsers in a controlled way.

So while we're still hacking away, we're moving those hacks out of the main HTML and CSS documents, as described in the previous "CSS Hacking Strategies" secret.

In the case of the high pass filter, you'll first create a linked style sheet with @import rules written in such a way as to trick browsers without proper implementation:

```
<link rel="stylesheet" href="highpassfilter.css" />
```

This style sheet itself contains two rules:

```
@import "null?\"\{";
@import "highpass.css";
```

The first rule is a trick using the same technique employed in the Box Model Hack to throw off those browsers that can't parse the escape sequence, "?\"\{", The second style sheet, highpass.css, will contain your actual styles, which will then be imported into the style sheet and carried over into the compliant browser via the link, leaving the hack separate from the main HTML document and from the clean style sheet.

note

For the documentation on the High Pass Filter, see `http://tantek.com/CSS/Examples/highpass.html`.

Secret #158:   The Mid Pass Filter

This filter allows you to provide a style sheet for versions IE 5.0 and 5.5 of Windows without including any other browser. This means you can fix the Box Model and other problems in IE 5.x versions without adding those hacks directly to your main documents.

In the case of the mid-pass filter, you'll trick the browser using the @media rule with a value of tty.

> **note**   The **@media** rule helps specify media types (see Secret 162 later in this chapter). It is similar to **@import** in that you can use multiple instances of **@media** to define different media types within a single style sheet. In this instance, it's being used specifically as a hack.

Consider the following:

```
@media tty {
 i{content:"\";/*" "*/}} @import 'midpassbefore.css'; /*";}
}/* */
p.test { color:green; padding:1em }
strong { color:black; background:#fff; padding:0 2px; margin:-2px
}
@media tty {
 i{content:"\";/*" "*/}} @import 'midpassafter.css'; /*";}
}/* */
```

Because of the filtration process based on bugs with the @media rule, both the first and last @media tty rules will be seen *only* by IE 5.x browsers for Windows, and will be ignored by all other browsers. All browsers will interpret the style information in the middle.

> **note**   See **http://tantek.com/CSS/Examples/midpass.html** for documentation on the mid-pass filter.

Secret #159:   IE 5.0 Windows Band Pass Filter

This filter works on the same premise as the mid-pass filter, but is specific to IE 5.0 for Windows *only*. Every other browser before or after is filtered out.

```
@media tty {
 i{content:"\";/*" "*/}}; @import 'ie50winbandpassbefore.css';
{;}/*";}
}/* */
p.test { color:green; padding:1em }
strong { color:black; background:#fff; padding:0 2px; margin:-2px
}
```

```
@media tty {
 i{content:"\";/*" "*/}}; @import 'ie50winbandpassafter.css';
{;}/*";}
}/* */
```

In this case, the styles you place in an imported style sheet using the @media tty rule and the associated syntax will be picked up by IE 5.0 only:

```
i{content:"\";/*" "*/}}; @import 'ie50winbandpassbefore.css';
{;}/*";}
}/* */
```

Any browser that supports the other CSS in the sheet will pick up those styles.

note   **The IE 5.0 Windows Band Pass Filter documentation can be found at** `http://tantek.com/CSS/Examples/ie50winbandpass.html`.

Secret #160: IE 5.5 Windows Band Pass Filter

By now you've got the hang of what these filters are doing. In this case, you're filtering for IE 5.5 specifically. Anything you put into the imported style sheet using the IE 5.5 filtration syntax will be used by IE 5.5 only, with no other browsers able to access that style.

```
@media tty {
 i{content:"\";/*" "*/}}@m; @import 'ie55winbandpass.css'; /*";}
}/* */
```

Any additional normal style information within the style sheet will be picked up by those browsers supporting the styles therein, but only IE 5.5 will pick up the styles in the ie55winbandpass.css file.

note   **The documentation for the IE 5.5 Windows Band Pass Filter is available at** `http://tantek.com/CSS/Examples/ie55winbandpass.html`.

Secret #161: Opera Hacks

A number of hacks exist to work with the Opera browser. Despite very good support of CSS from its early days, Opera still has some bugs that require a bit of hacking to work.

There are several Opera hacks and hack versions. Both are used in rather opposite ways to filters—they allow you to hide CSS *from* Opera so it doesn't parse that particular code. This way, you can write CSS, then add the hack to those styles that Opera won't manage properly.

note

You can read about Opera hack techniques online. The following documentation is copyrighted, but you can implement the techniques should you need to manage support for Opera browser versions.

The Owen hack hides CSS from Opera versions 6.0 and earlier, as well as hiding the same CSS from IE for Windows (`www.albin.net/CSS/OwenHack.html`).

The "Be Mean to Opera" Hack hides CSS from Opera versions 5 and earlier, so it is more specific to the problems inherent in Opera only, prior to the 6.0 version (`www.albin.net/CSS/beMeanToOpera.html`).

Secret #162: Understanding CSS Media Types

Now we move onward to the available media types within CSS.

Media types are useful when creating alternate style sheets for various types of media, such as creating an alternate design for your site specific to print.

In CSS, there are ten recognized media types in CSS2, and more to come. Table 9-1 describes the media value and its associated use.

Table 9-1: Media Types in CSS

Media Type/Value	Use
all	For all media: `<link rel="stylesheet" src="all.css" media="all" />`
aural	For use with speech synthesizers: `<link rel="alternate stylesheet" src=" aural.css" media="aural" />`
Braille	For tactile Braille devices: `<link rel="alternate stylesheet" src=" braille.css" media="braille" />`
embossed	For paged Braille printers: `<link rel="alternate stylesheet" src=" embossed.css" media="embossed" />`
handheld	For small-screen devices such as PDAs: `<link rel="alternate stylesheet" src=" handheld.css" media="handheld" />`
print	For paged printing, or for print preview on-screen: `<link rel="alternate stylesheet" src=" print.css" media="print" />`
projection	For projection media: `<link rel="alternate stylesheet" src=" projection.css" media= "projection" />`

Media Type/Value	Use

screen	For the computer screen specifically:
	`<link rel="alternate stylesheet"`
	`src=" screen.css" media="screen" />`

tty	For fixed-width, limited-display terminals:
	`<link rel="alternate stylesheet"`
	`src=" tty.css" media="tty" />`

tv	For television devices:
	`<link rel="alternate stylesheet"`
	`src=" tv.css" media="tv" />`

note Use the "alternate stylesheet" value when the media type in question is not the primary style sheet type.

Of course, user agent support for many media types is sketchy, but you can see the value here, especially as support for media types increases. You can create a single, clean HTML document and then link to numerous style sheets, allowing a different display on screen, via projector, via print, and so forth—a "write once, play anywhere" concept, if you will.

note The CSS specification notes that more media types will be added over time. It's important to use media types that are well supported, unless you are delivering to a specific device and know that you are able to support it using CSS.

Secret #163:   Alternate Style Sheet for Print

This and the following two secrets demonstrate how alternate style sheets can be used along with primary style sheets to provide for other media types.

If you'd like to add an alternate style sheet for print, you first create your site styles. Then, you create another style sheet specifically for print, and link to it from the documents for which you want the print styles available:

```
<link rel="alternate stylesheet" src="print.css" media="print" />
```

Here are some guidelines to think about when creating styles for print:

 ◆ Use proper font sizing options. Pixels are great for screen, but aren't appropriate for print. Points, ems, exs, inches, and centimeters are all reasonable choices, with points probably being the most useful sizing option for fonts.

 ◆ Consider hiding navigation and links. You can leave out any navigation or links by setting their display to a value of none. Use only what will be appropriate for print—navigation and linking are useless on the printed page.

 ◆ Consider hiding background graphics, ad banners, and any other unnecessary graphic images. Getting rid of unnecessary images for your print version makes your documents more information-centric and appropriate for the printed page. Of course, any logos, relevant illustrations and photos, and graphic-based charts would remain in the print style sheet.

♦ Consider recoloring your background and foreground colors to standard white background/black text for maximum readability.

---

note For an excellent article on print style sheets, see "Going to Print" by Eric Meyer, at **www.alistapart.com/articles/goingtoprint/**.

Secret #164: Alternate Style Sheet for Small-screen Media

While still problematic because of lack of device support, creating alternate style sheets for handheld devices will become more and more useful as device manufacturers create support in their user agents.

Because the handheld, small-screen media market is a growing concern, it's good to be aware that you can create CSS styles specifically for handheld devices (see Figure 9-13)—even if it's too early in the game to actually be using them right now.

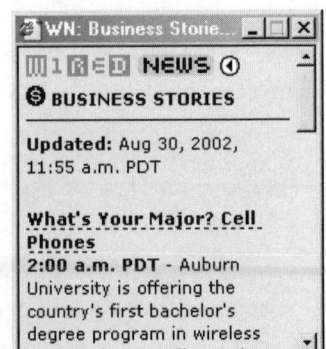

Figure 9-13: Doug Bowman prototyped these CSS-driven small-screen designs of Wired News for handheld devices.

Typically, you will strip out almost everything for a handheld device, leaving very simple styles for headers, paragraphs, and navigation. Depending upon the target device or devices, you may or may not wish to include images. You'll use the link element to link your documents to the alternate style sheet:

```
<link rel="alternate stylesheet" src= "handheld.css"
media="handheld" />
```

> **note**   Opera is in the process of building and distributing CSS-compliant user agents for handheld devices. For more information, see **www.opera.com/ products/smartphone/smallscreen/**.

Secret #165:   Alternate Style Sheet for Projection

Another area where the Opera browser has done some excellent implementation of CSS media is with projection. Using a feature known as OperaShow, you can create a presentation using HTML, style it with CSS for as many media types as you want, and create a special style sheet for use in projection mode.

I found this technique after years of using PowerPoint for presentations. PowerPoint is simple to use and practically ubiquitous, but one day I did a presentation on Web accessibility using PowerPoint, and then I placed that file on my Web site for people to download and enjoy. Within a few hours I was rather brutally flamed on the Webdesign-l list for having posted something about accessibility that is, in and of itself, not accessible.

After taking a bit of a beating for that, I began to research alternatives, and I stumbled across the then-recently-released OperaShow feature. I now only use this method, because I can create that one document, offer it up as an attractive projection (see Figure 9-14), print (see Figure 9-15), and screen (shown in Figure 9-16) alternatives.

> **note**   For more information on OperaShow, including how to implement projection styles, see **www.opera.com/support/tutorials/operashow/**.

Secret #166:   CSS Best Practices

As you get deeper into CSS, you're going to find that it's a pretty complex language that requires you to not only pay close attention to details, but also improve your workflow and apply the wisdom of others to avoid problems within your own code.

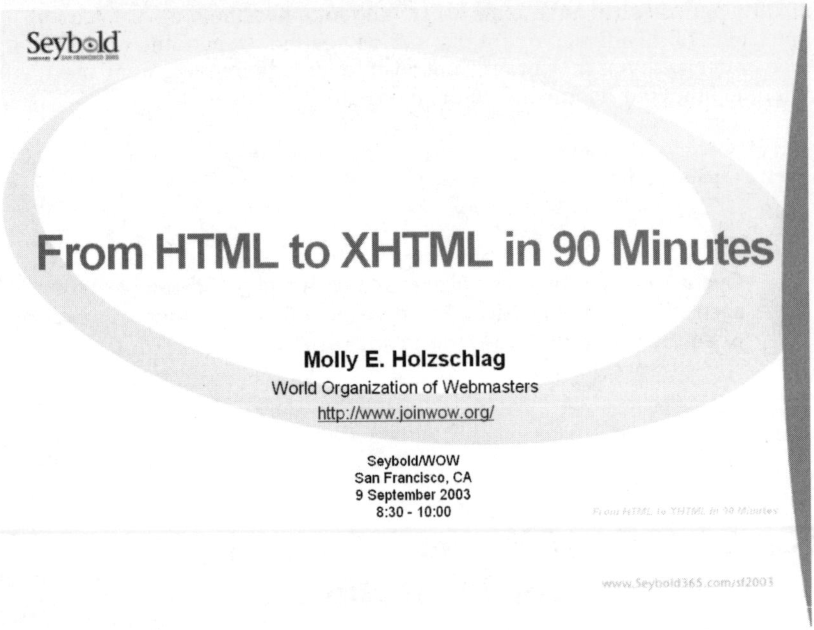

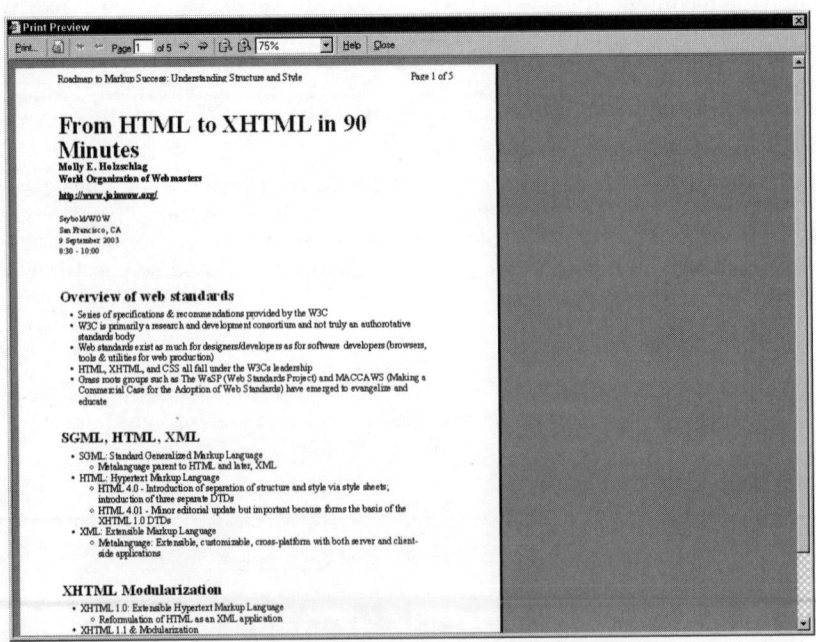

Figure 9-14: Looks like PowerPoint, you say? It's HTML with a CSS style sheet for projection in OperaShow.

Figure 9-15: The same document as viewed in print preview.

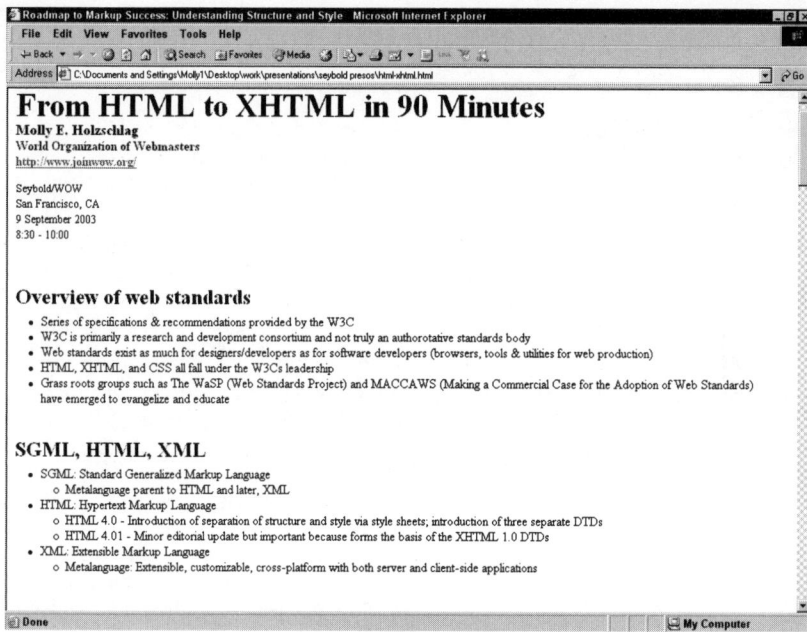

Figure 9-16: The same document, with some minor differences for screen display.

Table 9-2 describes some of the primary best practices and the rationale behind them.

Table 9-2: CSS Best Practices

Suggested Practice	Rationale
Build and test in the most advanced CSS browser available, then work backwards to accommodate other browsers	Starting from perfection and then adding hacks means that your core styles are written elegantly and effectively. You can then choose to add hacks and workarounds, as necessary, to accommodate your individual browser based on the tips in this chapter. This will also enable you to remove those hacks when the time comes, leaving pristine, well-written CSS
Clear floats properly to avoid layout hassles	While floats in layout are very useful, their results can be problematic if not dealt with properly. If you'd like to learn more about the problems and solutions related to floats, see Eric Meyer's "Containing Floats," www.complexspiral.com/publications/containing-floats/

continued

Table 9-2: *(continued)*

Suggested Practice	Rationale
Remember "LVHA" or "LoVe/HAte" linking styles	When creating link styles in CSS, be sure that your styles are in the proper order: Link Visited Hover Active. If they are in any other order, you may get inconsistent results. If you're using the `:focus` pseudo class too, the order is LVHFA
Remember "TRBL" or "TRouBLe" for margin value orders	If you're using the margin shorthand property, your margin order must be Top, Right, Bottom, Left (TRBL)
As you're building your style sheets, consider starting with embedded sheets and then moving them out of the document later	This helps workflow because you have immediate access to your results and don't have to switch between multiple documents while editing. Another issue is that when you work with embedded style, you avoid running into caching problems while testing in some browsers. After you've worked out any bugs or problems and your CSS is pristine, you can move it on out to a linked sheet
Stick to effects within the specifications, except for experimental purposes	Lots of effects exist that are IE- or Mozilla-only, such as styling scrollbars or applying CSS filters. These are proprietary features and are not valid; avoid them to ensure cross-platform viability
Avoid "Flash of Unstyled Content" (FOUC) when using `@import` alone	If you're importing style, you might experience a quick flash of unstyled content in IE before the actual layout styles are interpreted. For information on how to avoid this, see `www.bluerobot.com/web/css/fouc.asp`
Name custom classes and IDs based on function, not appearance	If you name a class `.smallblue` and later you need a color change, you have to change the class name. You can avoid that by naming by function, such as .quote or #footer
Combine selectors wherever possible	If you can use shorthand, rely on inheritance and group selectors: you'll have leaner, meaner CSS
Validate your CSS	Validation of both your markup and your CSS can help you quickly find errors and ensure compliance

note   The best practices described here are based on Dave Shea's CSS Crib Sheet, which is an ongoing compilation of CSS best practices, and are used here with permission. See `www.mezzoblue.com/css/cribsheet/` for the documentation as well as updates and a means to add your own suggestions to this ongoing document.

Summary

While certainly no replacement for a ground-up education in CSS, these past two chapters should provide you with a well-rounded understanding of the primary concepts, applications, and best practices being used in today's progressive CSS designs.

In the next chapter, "Adding Accessibility Features," you'll learn how to add markup and CSS to your site that will assist those with disabilities or using special devices to access your content to better get to that content. You'll explore legal and ethical issues surrounding accessibility, and find out how using the concepts you've explored in the markup and CSS chapters here assist in achieving accessible designs.

Adding Accessibility Features

Chapter

10

♦ ♦

Secrets in This Chapter

♦ ♦

Accessibility has become a critical component of Web design. This is especially true for those designers working in government and education, where specific laws may require those designers to implement accessibility features.

Creating accessible Web sites is not a difficult thing to do, really, if you have developed sound markup practices and reduced or removed the use of tables for layout from your designs. After that, it's a matter of applying certain elements and attributes to your documents, providing alternatives to aural or visual media, and properly testing your documents for accessibility compliance.

What is Web Accessibility?

The term "accessibility" is used to describe a specific problem within Web design: how to make Web sites available to those who have disabilities that might prevent them from seeing, hearing, and moving through Web pages.

A significant number of disabilities impact use of the Web, including those related to vision, hearing, and mobility. Some visually challenged individuals rely on large-type, high-contrast operating system and Web browser features to access pages. Many visually challenged people use screen reader technology, a combination of hardware and software that reads screen content aloud. Braille printers are also common, where screen data is interpreted by the printer and then printed out. People with mobility impairments may use special keyboards, mice, and pointing devices (such as special sticks held in the mouth or placed on the forehead for tapping out keyboard commands). Other devices exist as well, but in all cases, using these devices (referred to as *assistive* devices) on the types of Web pages dominating the Web is no easy task.

> **note** For an excellent overview of this topic, see "How People with Disabilities Use the Web" from the W3C, at `www.w3.org/WAI/EO/Drafts/PWD-Use -Web/`.

Another accessibility concern is comprehension. Even a physically healthy, bright person requires clear communication on the Web, where making a quick yet lasting impression counts. Whether a person has a learning disability or is extremely literate, your site should have clarity and context to communicate its message.

The Advent of Accessibility Challenges

The field of accessibility on the Web has an intriguing history. Remember, the Web was introduced as a text-based environment, not the predominantly visual environment that most people experience it as being. After all, in only a decade the Web has become a platform that supports almost every conceivable media type.

However, back in the day, the Web was just text. You could include a link to an image or other object, but that object would have to be downloaded and viewed in an external application, because the user agents at that time, such as Lynx, did not have graphical user interfaces (GUIs, pronounced "gooey"). The markup in use was very simple: just headers, paragraphs, text, lists, a horizontal rule to break up sections of text. See Figure 10-1 for a view of a text-only browser.

You might think that in comparison to what we have today, the text-based Web was extremely limiting. After all, there was no Flash, no QuickTime, Real Audio and

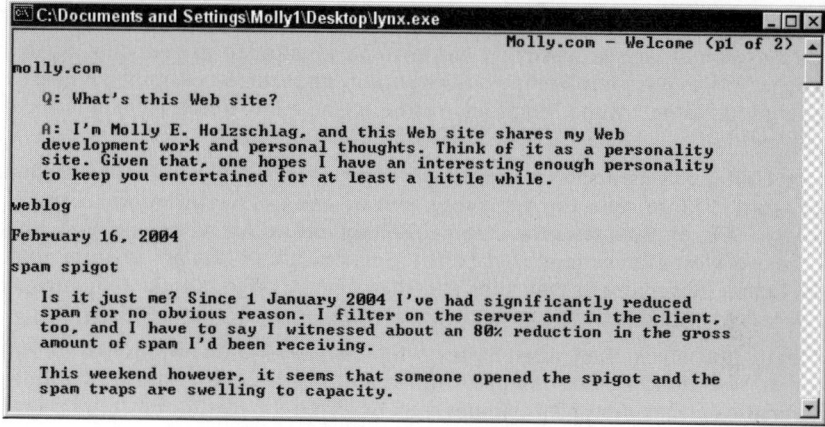

Figure 10-1: A Web page as viewed in the text-only browser, Lynx.

Video, not even inline GIFs or JPEGs to make the site visually interesting, and no ready means of using color, except whatever your monochrome monitor used for display.

If I'd not witnessed the Web's growth from birth to its current state, I would think that these were limitations too. But from a historical standpoint, a text-only environment was far more accessible than most of the sites we have today. Early text-based sites were easier for screen reader technology to interpret for blind users, because screen readers were simply reading directly from the text, with no browser GUI causing a barrier. There were no images to deal with and no complex table layouts to confound and frustrate. For the mobility impaired, there were no fly-out menus or drop-down toggles to contend with.

When the transition to a GUI-based environment via visual Web browsers occurred, many disabled people who were using Internet-related services, such as e-mail, Gopher, and the World Wide Web, were suddenly left out in the cold.

For several years, Internet resources such as Gopher had been a source of empowerment for many disabled, and suddenly that empowerment was gone because the GUI Web browser was so effective that it became the application of choice for accessing other Internet services via the Web, too. And existing assistive devices simply weren't advanced enough to handle the complex demands that the visual Web began placing on them. To this day, screen reader technology is several steps behind, but advances have been made. With the implementation of accessibility features in operating systems and Web browsers, many barriers are finally coming down.

Fortunately, we now have enough awareness and techniques to begin seriously addressing these issues in our design and development tasks. The good news is that it's not really that difficult to make a Web site accessible, especially if you're adhering to Web standards and best practices. While you can have a standardized site and still not meet accessibility guidelines, following standards, especially in terms of creating structured, valid markup, and removing presentational elements and attributes from a document, makes that document inherently more accessible.

Best practices in document authoring means writing conforming documents that are also accessible. These practices are interdependent, even if they have exclusive features.

Accessibility and Law

One reason that Web accessibility has become so popular an area of study is that many countries have implemented laws pertaining to the accessibility of Web sites. The United States, United Kingdom, Australia, and many European countries have implementations of accessibility legislation and guidelines.

In the United States, accessibility laws emerged as legislation with the Rehabilitation Act in 1973. In 1990, the Americans with Disabilities Act (ADA) was signed into law. By 1998, an update to the original Rehabilitation Act was published, known as the Workforce Investment Act (WIA). Section 508 of this act *requires* that all U.S. federal government Web sites and sites developed with federal monies *must be accessible* in accordance with the guidelines set out by this section.

Other institutions in the United States, while not necessarily required to create accessible Web sites, are beginning to implement policies. Many state governments, universities and community colleges, and other public institutions are reviewing policies and creating accessibility guidelines for their Web sites.

> note
>
> **Complete documentation for the Rehabilitation Act of 1973 is available at `www.icdi.wvu.edu/files/file20.htm`.**
>
> **The full text of the ADA can be found at `www.usdoj.gov/crt/ada/pubs/ada.txt`.**
>
> **Read the Workforce Investment Act at `www.usdoj.gov/crt/508/508law.html`**
>
> **For a wide range of information regarding Section 508 and its implementation, see the U.S. Section 508 Web site at `www.section508.gov/`.**

Similar laws and guidelines exist worldwide and, in some cases, are far more aggressive than U.S. laws. For example, Portugal (incidentally the first European nation to institute a formal policy on Web accessibility) mandates accessibility *for all Web sites*.

> note
>
> **Many wonder about the enforceability of accessibility legislation, especially when accessibility features are just starting to be implemented on a grand scale.**

The W3C tracks and manages international implementations of Web accessibility. In fact, the W3C offers the most explicit specifications for Web accessibility via the Web Accessibility Initiative (WAI), which includes a number of important specifications and activities, such as the Web Content Accessibility Guidelines (WCAG). The W3C's involvement in accessibility is largely due to the many issues discussed here: accessibility's relationship to markup, the international scope of accessibility needs, and the continued improvement and evolution of the Web.

> note
>
> **For more information on laws pertaining to countries other than the U. S., please see the WAI International Program Office page, at `www.w3.org/WAI/IPO/Activity.html`.**
>
> **The WAI home page (`www.w3.org/WAI/`) provides details regarding all activities within the W3C related to accessibility.**

Accessibility and You

In many disabled communities, there's a term for nondisabled people, "TAB." TAB stands for "Temporarily Able Bodied" and is an ironic way to express a very real truth: Most people will become disabled to some degree and for some period of time at some point in their lives.

Whether you sustain a bad injury from a snowboarding accident, find yourself battling a long-term illness, or suffer side effects of old age, none of us get a free pass when it comes to physical vulnerabilities.

Making Web sites accessible is important because the Web should be available for *all* people. Creating accessible sites makes for a better Web that can enrich and empower us all.

Secret #167:   Describing Visual and Aural Content

Imagine that I have a video on a page that is a capture of a class I taught. For those individuals who can see and hear (and have broadband), the full experience of watching me teach might be preferable to just reading a transcript. However, for those who cannot or prefer not to view and listen to the presentation, making a transcript available is a perfect option.

As simple as it seems, one of the major challenges when dealing with Web accessibility is to accurately provide enough information to describe what's happening on a page that contains components that might not be accessible to persons with a given disability.

Any time you have graphic, audio, video, or other nontext content on a page, provide a description either inline or using additional accessibility features found within this chapter. The point, however simple, is to author your documents well enough so they would be completely understandable without the graphic, audio, or video content.

Secret #168:   Providing Alternate Content

One means of ensuring access to Web sites is to provide alternate content wherever necessary. This may be as simple as providing a clear link on your home page to an accessible version of your site, linking to alternative pages using the `link` element, or using the `longdesc` attribute to provide access to pages with a longer description.

If you've got a Web site that is simply not accessible for some reason (such as the fact that it's built in Flash), consider offering a simple link to text-based content from the home page.

---

warning

In today's practices of using streamlined, structured markup with CSS, the need to provide alternative pages for most sites should be unnecessary. The exceptions to this are whenever your document is primarily Flash, or uses audio, video, or other objects that might be inaccessible.

Another way to offer alternative information is to place a link element in the head portion of your document with a relationship defined as an accessible site link, as in the following code:

```
<head>

<title>Acccessibility Techniques</title>

<link title="Text-only version" rel="accessible"
href="textpage.html" media="aural, Braille, tty" />

</head>
```

You'll end up creating two documents—one with the Flash or graphical informa-tion and one that is text-only for accessibility purposes. Browsers that support the alternative media specified by the link element will automatically provide access to the linked document via a user-agent feature.

Interestingly, you can create fully accessible navigation schemes using the link element, as shown here:

```
<link href="index.html" rel="home" title="home page">
<link href="feb2004.html" rel="prev" title="previous article">
<link href="apr2004.html" rel="next" title="next article">
<link href="translations.html" rel="up" title="translations">
<link href="mailto:molly@molly.com" rel="author" title="Mail the
author">
```

The rel attribute is used within the link element to indicate the text that will be displayed within the compliant browser, with a hyperlink assisting users to navigate to those pages directly (see Figure 10-2).

Figure 10-2: Mozilla offers a menu that will appear when link elements are found in a document.

> tip
>
> You can set the site navigation bar in Mozilla to never show, show when needed, or show always. To modify these settings, select View ⇨ Show/Hide ⇨ Site Navigation Bar, and select your option from the menu.

Another technique for providing additional information is the longdesc attribute. This attribute provides text descriptions on another page related to the object. The attribute is placed within the img element itself. The value is the URL to the alternate page, as demonstrated in the following:

```
<img src="breeds.jpg" alt="chart of cat breeds by country"
longdesc="accessible/breeds.html" />
```

You would then create a page with details about the image, such as the color of the cat, its age, qualities of the breed, and so forth.

As smart as longdesc is and as much as you should use it in those cases where you have complex images, maps, and graphs, browser support is a serious issue. Most accessibility specialists therefore suggest using a technique known as "D link" along with the longdesc attribute. This is a descriptive link denoted by a

"D" inside square brackets, as follows:

```
<img src="breeds.jpg" alt="chart of cat breeds by country"
longdesc="accessible/breeds.html" /><a
href="accessible/breeds.html" title="text description of cat
breeds by country">[D]</a>.
```

This way, any browser or user agent that can support the `longdesc` attribute will, and a link will be available in either case to the additional descriptive information.

Secret #169:   They're NOT alt "Tags!"

The `alt` attribute is one of the first accessibility features to have found widespread support early on in terms of specifications and browsers. And somehow the term "alt tag" became part of our professional gloss.

It's very important to learn proper terminology, to use it, and to continue learning it and modifying the way we speak to foster better communications between ourselves, fellow team members, and our clients.

The `alt` attribute is available for use with a number of nontext elements, including `applet` (which is deprecated in HTML 4.0), `area`, `img`, and `input`. The goal of the text is to provide a replacement description of the object in question, as in the following example:

```
<img src="images/abyssinian.jpg" width="300" height="200"
alt="photo of an adult Abyssinian cat" />
```

If the image is of a complex nature, such as a graph or chart, and a short description is not possible, you can provide alternate content by following the guidelines discussed previously in this chapter.

---

warning While you shouldn't be using spacer graphics at this point, if you do, you may wish to include the `alt` attribute but leave the value empty, `alt=" "`. This way, your document will conform and no unsightly [image] placeholder will appear. Using the term "spacer" is a poor choice because screen readers will read the `alt` text, so if you have a lot of spacer graphics in your document identified that way, the visitor will hear "spacer spacer spacer spacer" instead of your content!

Secret #170:   Use the title Attribute in Links

The `title` attribute allows you to add extra context to your links without detracting from the flow of your content. In Chapter 4, "Making Sites Usable and Persuasive," I discussed how important it is for links to be descriptive. But descriptive links alone, while helpful, can be limiting. The `title` attribute lets you add more information about the link so the site visitor can have more contextual information should it be required.

Listing 10-1 shows how.

Listing 10-1: Adding the title attribute to links

```
<!DOCTYPE html PUBLIC "-//W3C//DTD XHTML 1.0 Transitional//EN"
     "http://www.w3.org/TR/xhtml1/DTD/xhtml1-transitional.dtd">

<html xmlns="http://www.w3.org/1999/xhtml" lang="en">

<head>

<title>Linking Techniques</title>
<meta http-equiv="Content-Type" content="text/html; charset=iso-
8859-1" />

</head>

<body>

<p>The new cat owner must be prepared to <a href="feeding.html"
title="feeding your cat">feed</a>,
<a href="training.html" title="training your cat">train</a>, <a
href="playing.html" title="playing with">play with</a> and give
plenty of love to their new pet.</p>

</body>
</html>
```

Figure 10-3 shows a sample of this markup with the mouse passing over one of the links. The tool tip appears with the additional information. This feature exists in all contemporary browsers.

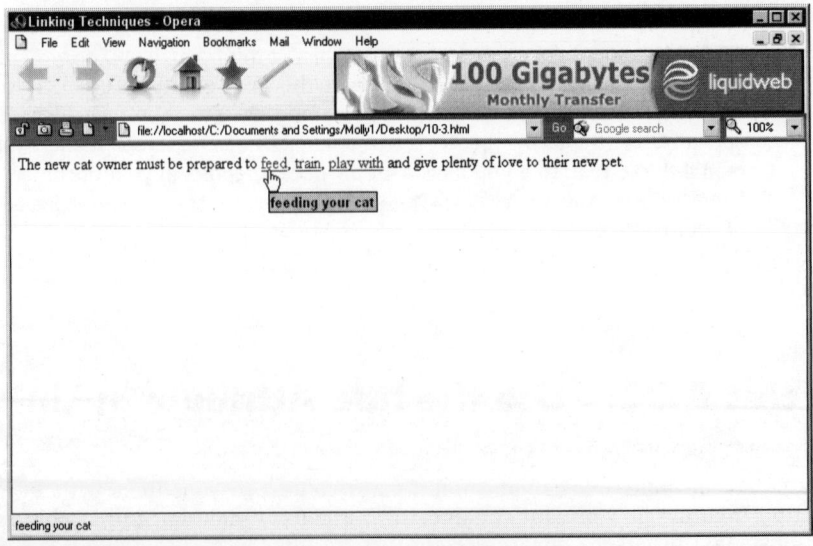

Figure 10-3: Additional `title` attribute information within a tool tip. Note how the Opera browser also displays the `title` attribute information in the browser status bar upon mouseover.

tip

Using the `title` attribute not only helps with accessibility, but helps with search engine ranking too. A happy side effect of using `title` attribute descriptions is that you can have additional keywords within a `title` attribute, helping leverage your site rank effects. For more information on search ranking, see Chapter 14.

Secret #171: Using the abbr Element for Abbreviations

Acronym? Abbreviation? What's the difference? This is an area of great debate as it pertains to markup. Both elements emerged at around the same time but were implemented differently between browsers during the addition of accessibility elements in HTML 4.0.

So you now have two elements: `abbr` and `acronym`. You use them in exactly the same way, but have to determine which is an abbreviation and which is an acronym in a given circumstance.

Abbreviations are typically defined as a shortened word formed from a complete word, such as Win for Windows. Acronyms are typically defined as being formed from letters or components of a compound term, such as OS for Operating System.

To use the `abbr` element, simply place the content in the tags, and use the `title` attribute to write out the abbreviation, as shown in Listing 10-2.

Listing 10-2: Using the abbr element

```
<!DOCTYPE html PUBLIC "-//W3C//DTD XHTML 1.0 Transitional//EN"
    "http://www.w3.org/TR/xhtml1/DTD/xhtml1-transitional.dtd">

<html xmlns="http://www.w3.org/1999/xhtml" lang="en">

<head>

<title>Abbreviations</title>
<meta http-equiv="Content-Type" content="text/html; charset=iso-
8859-1" />

</head>

<body>

<p>I was in the middle of writing this chapter on my  <abbr
title="Windows" >Win</abbr> machine when it crashed.</p>

</body>
</html>
```

When the user's mouse passes over the term "Win", a tool tip will appear with the complete term. Many Web browsers also provide a dotted underline, bringing attention to the fact that the term is an abbreviation and more information is available (see Figure 10-4).

I was in the middle of writing this chapter on my Win machine when it crashed.

Figure 10-4: Abbreviations tagged with the `abbr` element will appear with a dotted underline.

---

tip   You can modify the style of the default underline using CSS.

Secret #172:   Using the acronym Element for Acronyms

The acronym element is applied exactly as the abbr element is, but is reserved for use with acronyms, as illustrated in Listing 10-3.

Listing 10-3: Using the acronym element

```
<!DOCTYPE html PUBLIC "-//W3C//DTD XHTML 1.0 Transitional//EN"
    "http://www.w3.org/TR/xhtml1/DTD/xhtml1-transitional.dtd">

<html xmlns="http://www.w3.org/1999/xhtml" lang="en">

<head>

<title>Acronyms</title>
```

```
<meta http-equiv="Content-Type" content="text/html; charset=iso-
8859-1" />

</head>

<body>

<p>I get so frustrated with my Windows 2000  <acronym
title="operating system">OS</a></acronym> sometimes.</p>

</body>
</html>
```

This will result in the same dotted underline and tool tip containing the `title` attribute text (see Figure 10-5).

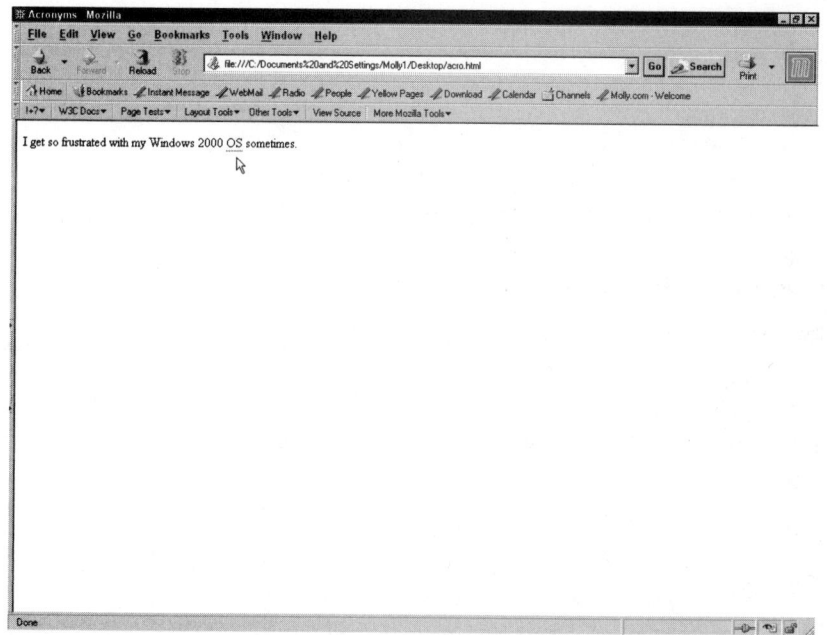

Figure 10-5: Acronyms tagged with the `acronym` element will result in the tool tip appearing upon mouseover.

---

warning

Internet Explorer 6.0 does *not* support the `abbr` element. As a result, many accessibility specialists suggest using the `acronym` element in all cases. Of course, this is problematic because it goes against the semantics and is therefore a hack. Furthermore, `acronym` is going to be deprecated in XHTML 2.0.

For an interesting discussion on the issue, including some excellent advice about using CSS along with acronyms and abbreviations for accessibility purposes, see Craig Saila's article "HTML is Not an Acronym" at `www.evolt.org/article/HTML_is_not_an_acronym/17/35750/`.

Secret #173: Understand the accesskey Attribute

The accesskey attribute makes it easier to navigate from the keyboard than from a pointing device such as a mouse. Essentially, you're creating keystroke combinations to provide a keyboard shortcut to a given element or form control. Your site visitors will hold down the *Alt* key and press the assigned accesskey value to get to the element or form control in question.

The accesskey attribute can be used with the following elements:

- a
- area
- input
- button
- textarea
- label
- legend
- caption

Listing 10-4 shows the accesskey attribute at work:

Listing 10-4: Using the accesskey attribute

```
<!DOCTYPE html PUBLIC "-//W3C//DTD XHTML 1.0 Transitional//EN"
    "http://www.w3.org/TR/xhtml1/DTD/xhtml1-transitional.dtd">

<html xmlns="http://www.w3.org/1999/xhtml">

<head>

<title>Using accesskey</title>
<meta http-equiv="Content-Type" content="text/html; charset=iso-
8859-1" />

</head>

<body>

<p><a href="http://www.molly.com/books.php"
accesskey="b">Molly's book list (Alt-B)</a></p>

</body>
</html>
```

> **note**
>
> You'll have noticed that I included a text reference (*Alt+B*) to indicate to my visitor that the link has been assigned an access key and can be reached quickly by using the keystroke combination.

Secret #174:   Index Link and Form Controls Using tabindex

The tabindex attribute allows you to add a specific order to links and form controls. Many people who use assistive devices tab to links and form controls rather than using a mouse, as fewer movements are necessary.

If you have a logically ordered document in terms of each link and form element following the next in a natural sequence, you won't have to use tabindex. However, should you wish to allow a site visitor fast access to links or form controls outside of a sequential flow, such as making navigation items on the page last in the list even though they might appear first, tabindex is the solution.

The tabindex attribute can be used along with the following elements:

- a
- area
- button
- input
- object
- select
- textarea

You then will assign a numeric sequence to each item on your page, and when the user presses the tab key, the tab will go to the next item in your sequence. Listing 10-5 shows a document using tabindex.

Listing 10-5: Indexing tabs using tabindex within a series of links

```
<!DOCTYPE html PUBLIC "-//W3C//DTD XHTML 1.0 Transitional//EN"
     "http://www.w3.org/TR/xhtml1/DTD/xhtml1-transitional.dtd">

<html xmlns="http://www.w3.org/1999/xhtml" lang="en">

<head>

<title>Adding Tab Indexing</title>
<meta http-equiv="Content-Type" content="text/html; charset=iso-
8859-1" />

</head>

<body>

<p>The new cat owner must be prepared to <a href="feeding.html"
tabindex="1">feed</a>,
<a href="training.html" tabindex="2">train</a>, <a
href="playing.html" tabindex="3">play with</a>
and give plenty of love to their new pet.</p>

</body>
</html>
```

When using `tabindex` in form controls, the process is the same: simply add the `tabindex` attribute and value in the series you prefer, such as the following:

```
<input type="checkbox" id="feeding" tabindex="2" />Yes, send me
information about feeding techniques.
<input type="checkbox" id="training" tabindex="3" />Yes, send me
information about training techniques.
<input type="checkbox" id="playing" tabindex="1" />Yes, send me
information about exercise techniques.
```

Anyone tabbing through the preceding markup will tab to the last item first, the top item second, and the middle item last.

Secret #175: Group Form Selections with select and optgroup

The `optgroup` element helps you group form selections into logical chunks. This assists with the clarity of a document, which is generally helpful as well as especially important when authoring documents for the learning disabled or those with other cognitive problems. In this example, I've broken down the breeds of cat by location. The element relies on the `label` attribute (note that this is significantly different from the `label` element) to define the group name.

The resulting menu provides greater clarity for the site visitor (refer to Listing 10-6).

Listing 10-6: Grouping form selections

```
<!DOCTYPE html PUBLIC "-//W3C//DTD XHTML 1.0 Transitional//EN"
    "http://www.w3.org/TR/xhtml1/DTD/xhtml1-transitional.dtd">

<html xmlns="http://www.w3.org/1999/xhtml">
<head>
<title>Working with optgroup</title>
<meta http-equiv="Content-Type" content="text/html; charset=iso-
8859-1" />
</head>

<body>

<div align="center">

<form action="submit" method="post">
<p>Which cat breeds have you considered?</p>
<select name="breeds" multiple="multiple">
<optgroup label="american">
<option>American Shorthair</option>
<option>California Spangled Cat</option>
<option>Main Coon</option>
</optgroup>

<optgroup label="european">
```

```
<option>Scottish Fold</option>
<option>European Burmese</option>
<option>European Shorthair</option>
</optgroup>

<optgroup label="asian">
<option>Singapura</option>
<option>Asian Shorthair</option>
<option>Bengal</option>
</optgroup>
</select>
<p><input type="submit" value="submit" /></p>
</form>

</div>
</body>
</html>
```

Figure 10-6 shows how any `optgroup` within a menu is neatly and clearly organized.

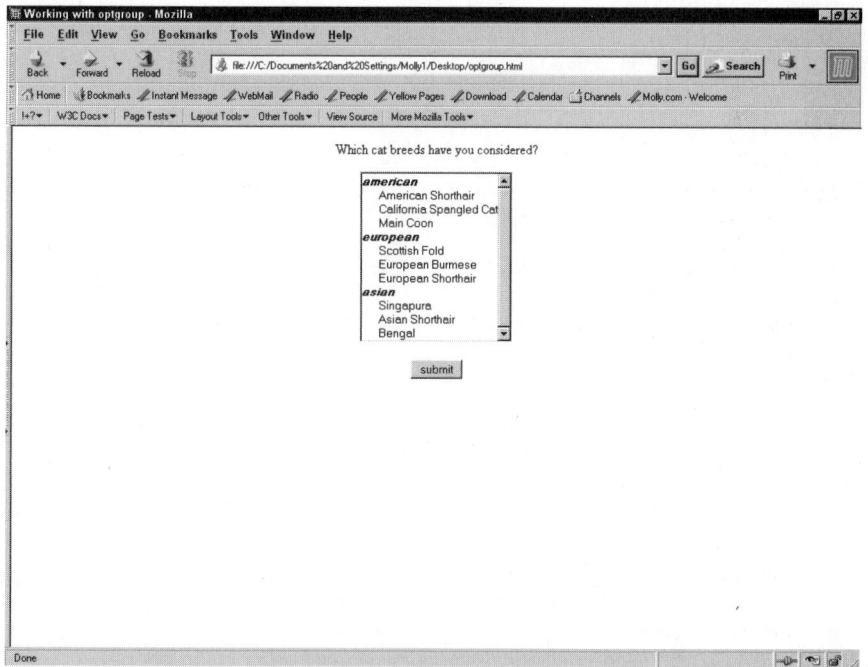

Figure 10-6: Using **optgroup** in menu selections helps organize those sections into logical groupings.

---

tip   Keep your **label** attribute values clear and simple to avoid any confusion.

Secret #176: Add fieldset and legend to Forms

The fieldset element combines your form controls into logical groups. The legend element defines the group. Separating form sections in this way helps increase the comprehension of the form.

Listing 10-7 shows how fieldset and legend are used.

Listing 10-7: Combining form controls into logical groups

```
<!DOCTYPE html PUBLIC "-//W3C//DTD XHTML 1.0 Transitional//EN"
    "http://www.w3.org/TR/xhtml1/DTD/xhtml1-transitional.dtd">

<html xmlns="http://www.w3.org/1999/xhtml">

<head>

<title>Your New Kitten</title>
<meta http-equiv="Content-Type" content="text/html; charset=iso-
8859-1" />

</head>

<body>

<form action="submit" method="post">
<fieldset>
<legend>Information About Your Kitten</legend>
Name of kitten:
<input type="text" name="name-puppy" />
Age of kitten:
<input type="text" name="age-puppy" />
Breed of kitten:
<input type="text" name="breed-puppy" />
</fieldset>

<fieldset>
<legend>Information About You</legend>
Your Last Name:
<input type="text" name="owner-lastname" />
Your First Name:
<input type="text" name="owner-firstname" />
</fieldset>
<input type="submit" name="submit" />
</form>

</body>
</html>
```

Figure 10-7 shows the visual results with the cues that help enhance understanding of the form sections.

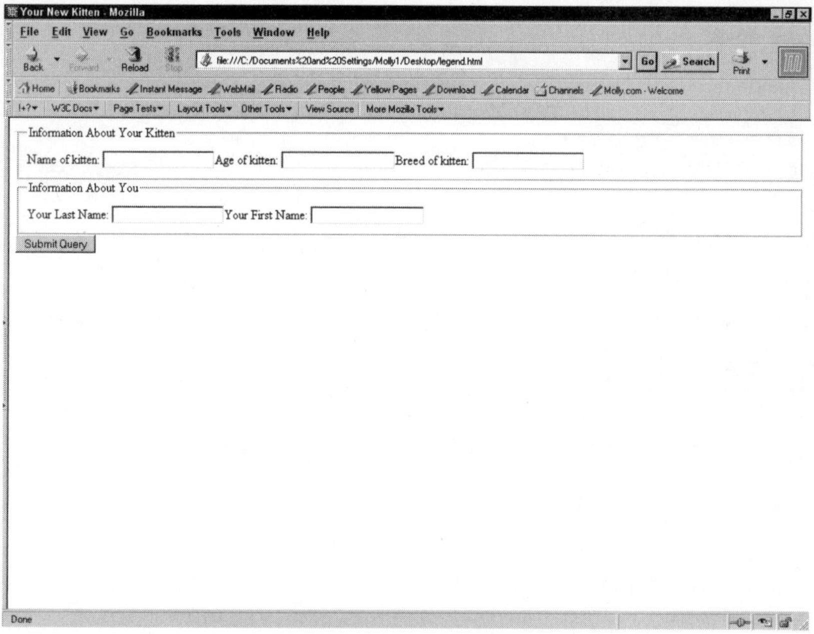

Figure 10-7: `Fieldset` and `Legend` help provide visual cues to assist users in understanding and navigating forms more effectively.

> **tip** Always group your form sections logically, clearly identifying which section belongs to what type of questions.

Secret #177:   Using the label Element with Forms

The label element (not to be confused with the label *attribute* discussed earlier) assists with the accessibility of forms by labeling form controls. This additional labeling provides information for screen readers and other assistive devices so they can more adequately describe the context of each form control.

The label element works in tandem with the for attribute, in which you describe the purpose of the form control (see Listing 10-8).

Listing 10-8: Using the label element

```
<!DOCTYPE html PUBLIC "-//W3C//DTD XHTML 1.0 Transitional//EN"
    "http://www.w3.org/TR/xhtml1/DTD/xhtml1-transitional.dtd">

<html xmlns="http://www.w3.org/1999/xhtml">
```

(continued)

Listing 10-8: *(continued)*

```
<head>

<title>Your New Kitten</title>
<meta http-equiv="Content-Type" content="text/html; charset=iso-
8859-1" />

</head>

<body>

<form action="submit" method="post">
<fieldset>
<legend>Information About Your Kitten</legend>
<label for="id-kitten">Name of kitten: </label>
<input type="text" id="id-kitten" />
<label for="age-kitten">Age of kitten: </label>
<input type="text" id="age-kitten" />
<label for="breed-kitten">Breed of kitten: </label>
<input type="text" id="breed-kitten" />
</fieldset>

<fieldset>
<legend>Information About You</legend>
<label for="owner-lastid">Your Last Name: </label>
<input type="text" id="owner-lastid" />
<label for="owner-firstid">Your First Name: </label>
<input type="text" id="owner-firstid" />
</fieldset>
<label for="submit"><input type="submit" id="submit" /></label>

</form>

</body>
</html>
```

note   The value of the `for` attribute must have a corresponding id value within the
control being labeled.

Secret #178:   Summarize and Caption Data Tables

Whenever you use data tables, provide a summary and caption for those tables
using the caption element and summary attribute.

The caption element describes the nature of the table, as shown in Listing 10-9.

Listing 10-9: Summarizing and captioning data tables

```
<!DOCTYPE html PUBLIC "-//W3C//DTD XHTML 1.0 Transitional//EN"
     "http://www.w3.org/TR/xhtml1/DTD/xhtml1-transitional.dtd">

<html xmlns="http://www.w3.org/1999/xhtml" lang="en">

<head>

<title>Adding a Caption</title>
<meta http-equiv="Content-Type" content="text/html; charset=iso-
8859-1" />

</head>

<body>

<table>
<caption>Feeding Schedules for Kittens</caption>
<tr>
<td>Column content</td>
<td>Column content</td>
</tr>
</table>

</body>
</html>
```

The element contents appear above the table (as shown in Figure 10-8), adding more information and clarity as to the purpose of the table.

The summary attribute is used within the table element and is a means of summarizing the table's purpose and structure. This assists those users who can't see the table to understand how it's laid out and what its purpose is (refer to Listing 10-10).

Listing 10-10: Summarizing a data table

```
<!DOCTYPE html PUBLIC "-//W3C//DTD XHTML 1.0 Transitional//EN"
     "http://www.w3.org/TR/xhtml1/DTD/xhtml1-transitional.dtd">

<html xmlns="http://www.w3.org/1999/xhtml" lang="en">

<head>

<title>Adding a Summary</title>
<meta http-equiv="Content-Type" content="text/html; charset=iso-
8859-1" />

</head>

<body>
```

(continued)

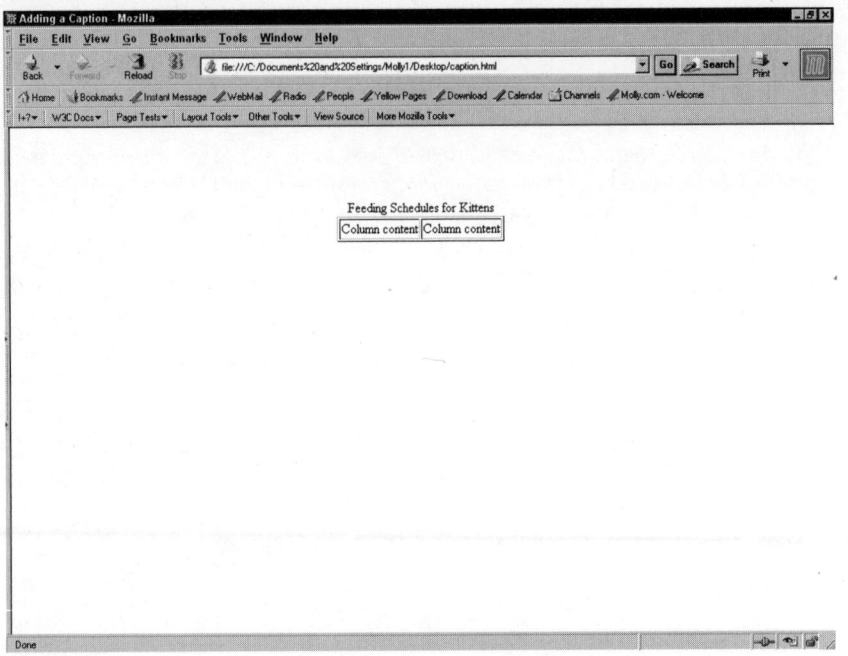

Figure 10-8: Captions will always appear above the table. Here, I've added borders to the table so you can see the relationship more effectively.

Listing 10-10: *(continued)*

```
<table summary="This table describes a weekly feeding
schedule for kittens">
<caption>Feeding Schedules for Kittens</caption>
<tr>
<td>Column content</td>
<td>Column content</td>
</tr>
</table>

</body>
</html>
```

While summaries do not appear as text on the page, as captions do, they are used by supporting screen readers and other accessibility software, and in some browsers summary values will appear when the mouse hovers over the table.

tip	While ideally you'll use both captions and summaries to make your data tables more accessible, most experts feel that if you decide not to use the `caption` element because it displays text you might not wish to have displayed on your page, you should at least include the summary attribute and table description.

Secret #179:   Consider Using Skip Links

Skip links are a technique that allows users (not just those interested in accessibility) to skip over navigation systems that might appear between the user and the main content. This gets the user directly to the content.

If you view your site in a text-based browser or with style sheets turned off and find that your navigation appears prior to your content (as shown in Figure 10-9), you may wish to consider using skip links.

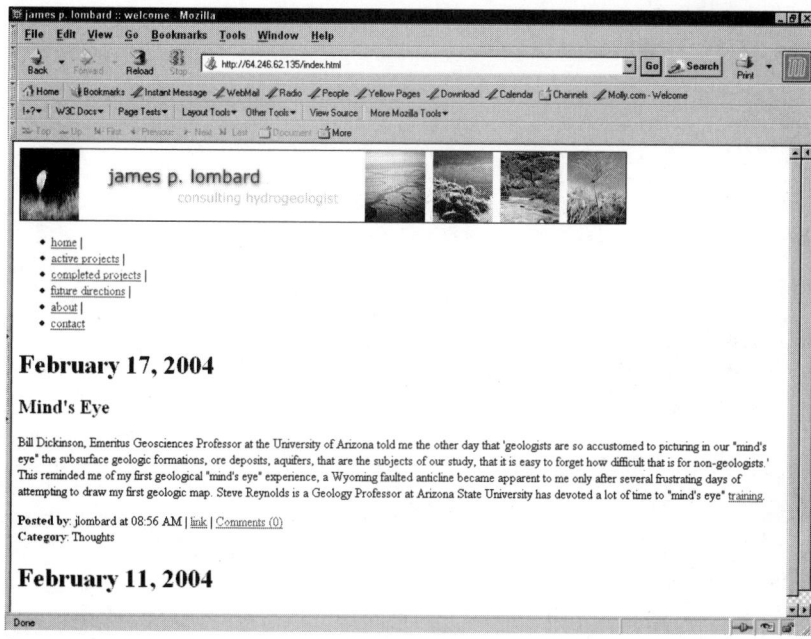

Figure 10-9: Navigation in this instance appears before the content.

In skip linking you use a standard anchor link referenced to an intrapage link. Then, you add some CSS to hide the link. Screen readers will read the skip link first, allowing users to jump ahead to content at their discretion.

First, create the skip link and name the target. The skip link should appear first in the body portion of your documents:

```
<a href="content" class="skiplink">Skip to Content</a>
```

Then, create the intrapage link target, placing it right above where content starts:

```
<a name="content"></a>
```

> **note** If you're using HTML 4.0, the `name` attribute for your anchor is fine. However, in XHTML 1.0, it's recommended to use both the name and id, such as `<a name ="content" id="content"></a>`. In XHTML 1.1, the `name` attribute has been replaced completely by id, so you'd write `<a id="content"></a>`.

In your CSS, add the class for the skip link, and hide the link, as follows:

```
.skiplink {

  display: none;

}
```

This hides the link completely from the visual display, but those accessing the site using assistive devices will be able to choose it. Listing 10-11 shows a mockup page with everything in the correct order. I've used embedded style to add the style class; ordinarily, this will likely be placed in an external or imported sheet.

Listing 10-11: Ordering skip links

```
<!DOCTYPE html PUBLIC "-//W3C//DTD XHTML 1.0 Strict//EN"
     "http://www.w3.org/TR/xhtml1/DTD/xhtml1-strict.dtd">

<html xmlns="http://www.w3.org/1999/xhtml">

<head>

<title>skip links</title>
<meta http-equiv="Content-Type" content="text/html;
charset=iso-8859-1" />

<style type="text/css">
.skiplink {
    display: none;
}
</style>

</head>

<body>
<p><a href="content" class="skiplink">skip links</a></p>

<!-- navigation is here -->

<p><a name="content"></a></p>

<!-- content begins here -->

</body>
</html>
```

Because of varying browser support for the display property in CSS, some accessibility specialists say you should try to leave the link visible, as this will allow all users to access it. Other designers add a hover feature so that a link becomes visible when the mouse passes over it. Whether you choose to use skip links, and how you choose them, will be based on your site's needs.

---

note   **If you do use skip linking, be sure to implement it on every page of your site consistently. What's more, learn about potential problems with hidden** elements and how they react in some screen readers at **http://simon. incutio.com/archive/2003/09/13/screenReaders**.

Secret #180:   Making Frames Accessible

I was reading my friend Matt Mullenweg's site the other day. Matt is the developer of the WordPress Weblogging system and a co-author of the XHTML Friends Network (XFN), an extension of XHTML used in social networking.

cross ref	See Chapter 13, "Keeping Sites Fresh and Engaging," for more information.

He had a few personal points on the site, the first one being, "I have done some terrible things in my life but I have never made a site with frames."

After I picked myself up off the floor from laughing so hard, I gave the issue some consideration. When frames first became available, they were browser-based, proprietary constructs. Since we'd never seen anything like that for the Web, for a time framed sites were all the rage. I myself have built more framed sites than I can count, but all prior to 1998.

Part of the problem with frames is that they go against the very premise of markup— their job is presentational. Other problems concern the ability to properly bookmark frame-based pages, navigate back and forth using browser controls, and limiting screen space even further by breaking available space into smaller boxes. While there are some reasonable applications for frames, they are limited and are in very minimal use at this point despite the fact that frameset and frame elements are standardized within HTML and XHTML frameset DTDs.

The best advice when it comes to making frames accessible, take Matt's sarcastic comment and places it in a cold, harsh light: don't use them. For the most part, the Web will be a better place if you avoid them altogether.

Should you decide to use frames, you can make them accessible by including noframes content. This allows for browsers without frame support to display a complete page's contents without the frames, but you have to set this content up, essentially maintaining multiple versions of a given document to achieve your goal.

Listing 10-12 shows a sample frameset with the noframes content.

Listing 10-12: Using noframes in a frameset document

```
<!DOCTYPE html PUBLIC "-//W3C//DTD XHTML 1.0 Frameset//EN"
      "http://www.w3.org/TR/xhtml1/DTD/xhtml1-frameset.dtd">

<html xmlns="http://www.w3.org/1999/xhtml">

<head>
```

(continued)

Listing 10-12: *(continued)*

```
<title>frameset with accessibility</title>
<meta http-equiv="Content-Type" content="text/html; charset=iso-
8859-1" />

</head>

<frameset cols="200, *">
<frame src="menu.html" name="menu" />
<frame src="content.html" name="content" />

<noframes>
<body>
<p>Your web browser does not support frames. This site also has <a
href="accessible.html"
title="go to the accessible content">alternative, accessible
content</a>.</p>

</body>
</noframes>
</frameset>
</html>
```

> **note**
> The only time a **body** element can appear within a frameset document is *within* the **noframes** element.

Of course, a browser that supports frames will, unless otherwise configured by a site visitor, interpret the frameset whether the noframes content is there or not, making that content pretty darned inaccessible anyway.

While you can enhance accessibility using attributes such as title and name (or id) for every frame, and using additional elements and attributes for accessibility described in this chapter, the general rule of thumb is to avoid frames altogether.

Some designers choose to have an entry page where they offer a link to nonframed, alternative content.

> **note**
> For more information about frames and accessibility, see
> www.wac.ohio-state.edu/wac/webaim/frames.htm.

Secret #181:   Testing with Accessibility Validators

Using validators for accessibility checks is an important part of the testing process. However, some controversy exists as to whether these validators are as intuitive as they need to be.

For example, I passed a page through one validator only to be considered invalid because I'd used the words *blue* and *pink* in the document. The validator thought I was using color to convey information, when I was actually writing about color.

So, use these validators as you would grammar or spell-checking—as a tool to expand on your existing knowledge.

Table 10-1 describes the most common accessibility validators and their features.

Table 10-1: Accessibility Validators and Common Features

Accessibility Validator	Features	URL
Bobby	Very widely used, easily configurable products for online validation as well as standalone products for accessibility tests	`http://bobby.watchfire .com/bobby/html/en/index .jsp`
A-Prompt	Free, downloadable testing tool. Configurable for W3C performance and Section 508	`http://aprompt.snow .utoronto.ca/`
LIFT	Collaborative, team-based accessibility software that tests for accessibility and helps manage workflow, complete with plug-ins for programs such as Dreamweaver and FrontPage	`www.usablenet.com/`
Cynthia Says	Designed to detect problems with Section 508 compliance and WCAG guidelines. Test online or buy the standalone validator.	`www.cynthiasays.com/`

Secret #182:   Testing with Lynx

Another quick, handy way to test for accessibility is to test with Lynx, a completely text-only browser. It is available for multiple platforms, including Windows, although it does require some setup. Lynx runs from a prompt and displays Web pages as text, as you saw in the introduction to this chapter.

You can download Lynx from `http://lynx.browser.org/`. You'll also find some online help available to assist you with setting up Lynx on your system.

> **note**   If you want a GUI-based "sorta-like-Lynx" look at some pages while online, check out the Lynx Viewer at `www.delorie.com/web/lynxview.html`.

Secret #183:   Testing with Screen Reader Software

Ever wonder what a Web page sounds like to your visually challenged viewers using screen reader software? If you're working on a Windows machine, you can install a free demo of JAWS. It's a full-featured product, but you can only use it for 40 minutes at a time.

Checking out your sites using the software is a very sobering experience, so I highly recommend it. The pricing on professional JAWS is upwards of U.S. $1,000.00, and the standard version is just under that price.

> **note** For the free JAWS demo, see `www.freedomscientific.com/`
> `fs_downloads/jaws_form.asp`. Additional information on professional screen reader software and other assistive software and hardware is available on the site, too.

Summary

While this chapter covered many techniques that will enable your sites to be more accessible, it is in the testing phase that you will ultimately learn more about how to be effective at accessibility.

One of the strongest criticisms about accessibility testing and validation is that a lot is still left to the discretion of the designer: Use of color, for example, is rarely tested or validated, yet we all know that colors can cause all kinds of problems for people who are color blind. Creating accessible sites is ultimately a balance between technique and practicality.

If you're a little weary of code, it's time to brighten things up a bit. The next several chapters deal with visual design, rich media, and keeping Web sites fresh.

Part III

Designing Sites for Long-Term Success

Sophisticated Visual Design in a Global Market

Chapter

11

◆ ◆

Secrets in This Chapter

◆ ◆

The World Wide Web is in fact a global environment, with many languages as well as religions, customs, and ways of life. Creating visually stimulating designs that work for your clients—no matter how near or far they might be—requires an understanding of a variety of practices: excellent Web graphic design skills and an awareness of the psychology of color and space.

While this chapter can't make you a designer, it can point out some of the most critical issues of the day and provide solutions to some of the more problematic issues with visual design and Web sites.

Secret #184:   Visual Design and Site Intent

Your site's visual design must always match the intent of your site. We've discussed a lot about how to define intent and goals, as well as how to define your audience. By doing that very important preliminary work (and occasional re-evaluations of the same), you should be able to clearly define exactly what it is your site does and what it is you want your site visitors to do once they get there. I refer to this relationship as *appropriate* site design, because you want the visual design to appropriately meet your goals and your audience's needs.

Unfortunately, many jump in and start designing without working through these considerations. The lack of preliminary work can result in flawed sites.

Other problems can include the following:

- Designers designing for themselves
- Designers having to accommodate the whims of superiors who often want a feature that is inappropriate to the site
- Clients wanting to determine the site's visual design according to their tastes and not the audience's

Frustrating scenarios, but certainly all of us have run into these problems. So, how do you solve them? Certainly, in a well-run project (see Chapter 2, "Managing Your Web Project") the majority of these problems should be solved, right from the start. If you're on your own, make sure that you do a comprehensive assessment of the situation, and explain to your clients the choices you are making and why.

Finding the right balance and keeping interferences at bay are no easy tasks, and there is no single answer. It is up to the designer to weigh the issues within design. The use of color, type, iconography space, size, and proximity of objects and text content must be balanced between the need to properly serve your audience and help them achieve what they came to your site to do.

Secret #185:   Defining and Maintaining Your Brand

A brand is the means by which your company or organization is identified. This can be in the form of its name, such as IBM, or its memorable logo, such as GE, or a slogan, such as "It's the real thing", which most readers will know is Coca-Cola.

Depending upon the way your site—or the site you're working on for someone else is set up in terms of trademark and other legal aspects, it may fall to you as the designer to ensure that the company's brand is well-defined and maintained throughout the site.

For trademarked names, logos, and slogans in the United States, it is up to the holder of the mark to ensure its strength and safety. This is one reason some companies, such as Disney, are notoriously litigious when it comes to anyone trying to mess with their brand materials.

If it's up to you to help the client define the brand for his or her Web site, here are some time-honored tips to help:

+ Consider a brand name that has existing and related meaning to your goods or services. A well-known example of this is Nike, a brand known worldwide. Nike is the Greek Goddess of Victory, a perfect choice for athletic goods.

+ Build your visuals based on the symbology of your brand. Images should reinforce the message behind the brand, not dilute it in any way.

+ Write slogans that are catchy and relevant.

+ Integrate your strategies into the long-term Web site plan.

+ Test early. If the brand name, images, or slogans do not test well early in the design process, it may be time to go back to the drawing board and gain more insight as to why.

+ Be sure to place your branding consistently throughout your site. The company logo should appear on every page, as should any slogans. Imagery related to the brand should be used consistently, too.

tip
Many designers create a larger logo for the home page, and use a smaller logo on subsequent pages. Linking logos on subsequent pages to the home pages is also a very common, recommended practice (see Chapter 4 for more details).

Secret #186:   GIFs and JPEGs: Still Your Secret Graphic Weapon

Interestingly, one area where very little change has occurred is in the use of GIFs and JPEGs as the primary file choices for the Web. Where advancements have been made is in the software used to generate these file formats—especially in Adobe Photoshop, which now offers a very helpful interface in which you can make great decisions about which file type is going to best suit your needs (see Figure 11-1).

Another place where advancements have been made is in how we use Web graphics. The move toward standards-based design with CSS has helped designers learn to use images in highly creative ways. Instead of the heavy slice-and-dice graphic techniques used in the table-based layouts of the past, you can now attach graphics to any HTML or XHTML element via CSS. What's more, you can apply color to any element, allowing you to reduce the use of graphics to create areas of color. As a result, you have a much richer ability to apply graphics in compelling ways (see Figure 11-2).

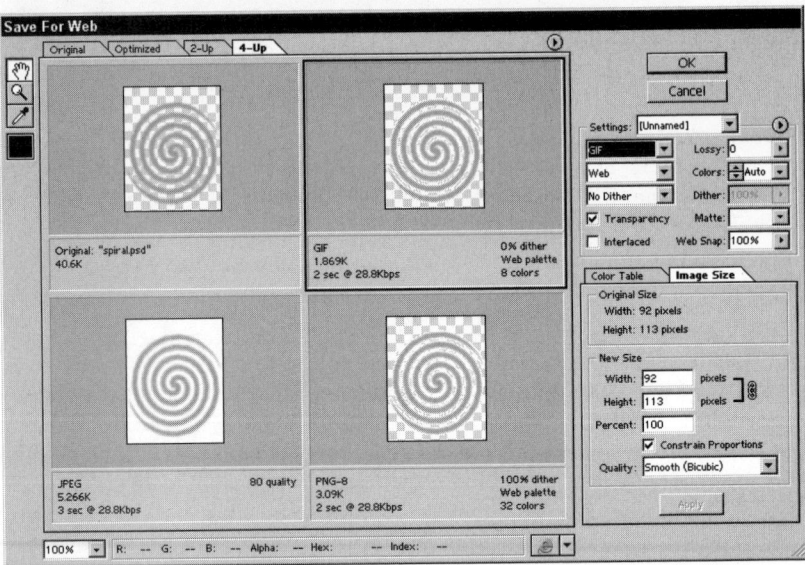

Figure 11-1: Working with graphics in Adobe Photoshop's "Save for Web" interface.

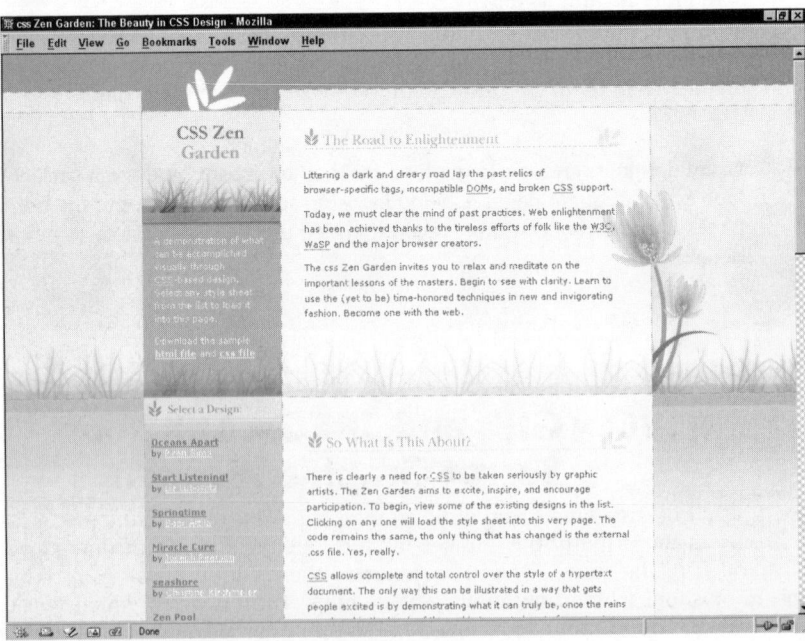

Figure 11-2: Today's CSS-based designs give you more control over how you use Web graphics.

No tool can replace knowledge born of experience, so it's important to have a little knowledge about the file types in order to best work with them.

Prior to having the more advanced compression utilities available today, knowing how and why to choose a specific file type was a major step in creating good graphic compression while retaining high visual quality. Table 11-1 points out the

Table 11-1: GIF and JPEG Features

Feature	GIF (Graphic Interchange Format)	JPEG (Joint Photographic Expert Group Format)
Compression Type	GIF compression is based on limiting the amount of colors to 256 or less. It is considered a *lossless* compression method because, while restrictive, the compression does not remove data. The fewer colors used the better the compression results. GIFs are typically best for those images or line drawings with flat color, few colors, grayscale images, and no gradients. Restricting the number of colors too much can result in very pixilated, jaggy images	JPEG compression is known as *lossy*. This means that unlike GIF, actual data is lost in the compression process. JPEG can support millions of colors, so it's a far better choice for most photographs, images with subtle light sources, and gradients. If too much compression is applied to a JPEG file, the lost data will show up as faded or blurry blocks referred to as *artifacts*
Transparency	Transparency is the ability to define certain areas of a graphic as being transparent so the background color or pattern can be seen through those transparent areas. GIF supports transparency	JPEG does not support transparency in any way
Progressive Rendering	Progressive rendering is a technique that allows portions of the graphic file to be seen as it loads, becoming increasingly more clear as data arrives to the Web browser. Very helpful in those situations where low bandwidth is expected, GIFs support progressive rendering with a feature known as *interlacing*. All common compression utilities allow you to interlace a GIF	Progressive rendering wasn't available in the earliest days of the JPEG format, but has been around for many years and is supported in all contemporary browsers. Depending upon your compression software, you can use a number of options to determine how you'd like your JPEGs to render
Animation	GIF animation became all the rage around 1995, and is now used so much on the Web as to cause some controversy—largely due to overuse. But a GIF animation can be practical, as in a banner ad, or fun, as in adding a tasteful or subtle movement to a logo or other visual object on the page. Many utilities exist to create animation. (See Chapter 1, "Setting Up a Master Toolbox" for more details)	There is no support for animation in the JPEG format

features of GIF and JPEG formats to assist you in using today's tools to their best end.

An interesting outcome of having more sophisticated tools to apply compression to Web graphics is that sometimes you find that the general guidelines, such as using GIF for line drawings and JPEG for anything with light source and color gradation, do not apply.

> **tip**　For excellent graphic results, use a compression utility that allows you to apply numerous options and preview the resulting look, file size, and download time. Most good compression utilities (check Chapter 1) have features like this, and, of course, Photoshop's Save for Web feature supports this. Balancing the visual quality of the resulting image with its file size will get you the best possible results.

Secret #187: Refinding the Lost Promise of PNG

Portable Network Graphics (PNG) appeared in 1995 as a reaction to the fact that Unysis, owner of the patent for GIF compression, began to seek licensing fees for use of GIFs. PNG was created to provide a royalty-free means of providing all of the features of GIFs and then some to those wishing to have high-quality graphics that are flexible and well-compressed.

PNG has many rich features that appeal to Web designers, including the following:

◆ Combined features of JPEG and GIF compression: Ability to limit colors, to compress grayscale palettes, and compress true colors. This means that you don't have to choose between JPEG or GIF, because PNG takes care of both approaches.

◆ Alpha channel support in PNG allows for transparency, something formerly only available in GIF. The transparency technology in PNG is superior to the GIF format, but limitations in browsers have prevented it from becoming widespread for this application.

◆ Advanced progressive rendering

So, if PNGs provide such flexibility, why have they been so slow to be adopted? Well, the problem is not with the PNG format, nor is the problem support within graphic applications. PNG is available in all major compression utilities these days, and users are convinced, too.

It won't come as a surprise that the issue is browser support. It was the major thorn in PNG's side in the years since it was developed, and remains a major thorn when it comes to one browser—Internet Explorer (IE). The problem isn't that the file format itself isn't supported, but that the alpha support—the portion of the technology required to mask aspects of the image or make them transparent—is broken, requiring people to use GIFs for transparency anyway. As a result, PNG has yet to fully achieve its promise—through no fault of its own.

Can you use PNG confidently? It depends on the browser base you'll be addressing. Typically speaking, if you aren't using transparency in PNG and are aiming at contemporary browsers, you can use PNG freely with confidence that PNGs will look good in most of those browsers, including IE.

Unfortunately, if you do attempt to use PNG for transparency, you'll get good support for it just about everywhere but IE (see Figures 11-3 and 11-4 for comparison of transparency-rendering abilities).

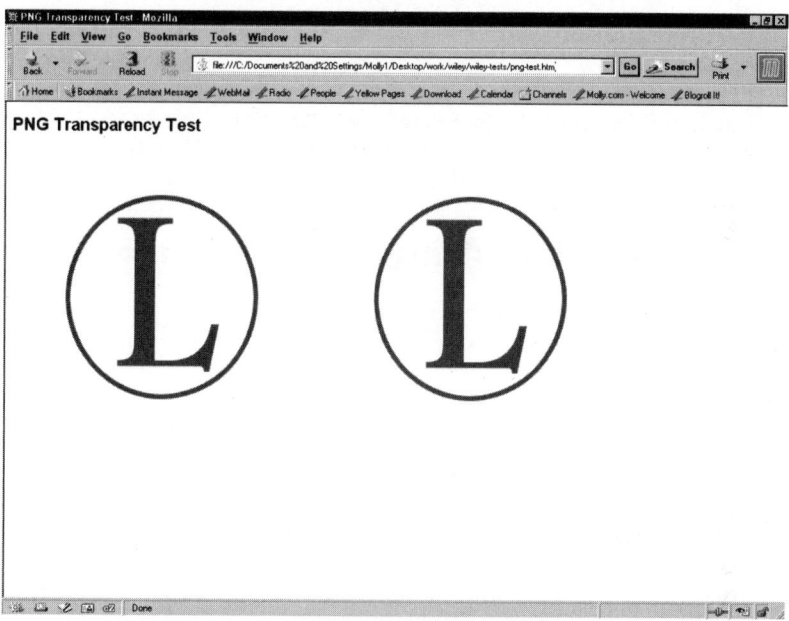

Figure 11-3: The logo on the left is a transparency but renders perfectly well as the nontransparent version on the right in the Mozilla browser.

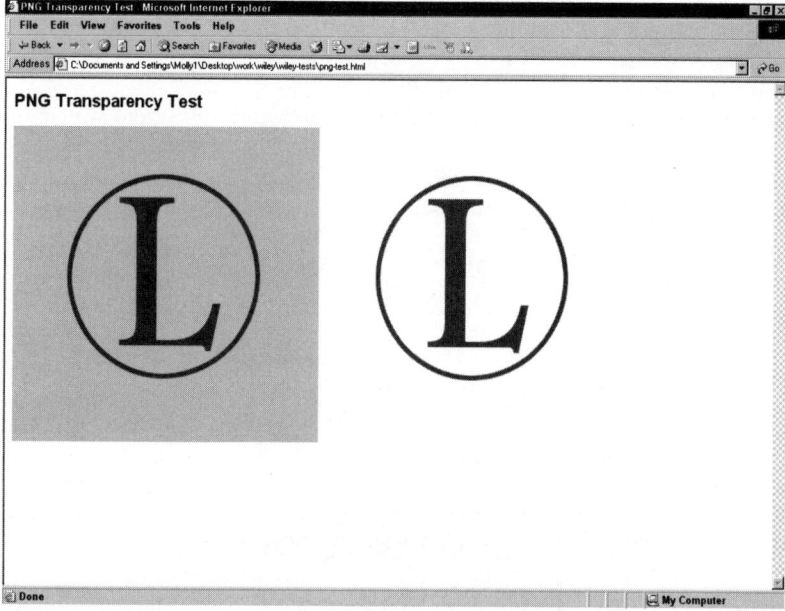

Figure 11-4: The same logos within the IE 6.0 browser—you can see that the left logo has large areas that should be transparent showing up as a dark area.

note For coverage on PNG browser support, see `www.libpng.org/pub/png/pngapbr.html`.

A related technology, Multiple Network Graphics (MNG), offers animation capabilities. You can learn more about this format at `www.libpng.org/pub/mng/`.

PNG is a recommendation by the W3C. To read more about the standardization of PNG, see `www.w3.org/Graphics/PNG/`.

Secret #188:   GIF Animation Do's and Don'ts

GIF animations are a great way to add movement and fun to a Web page. They are also useful for Web-based ads. However, there are certain problems and limitations of which you should be aware when using GIF animations.

Here are some guidelines to help:

♦ Don't overuse animations on a single page. This often occurs when newcomers to the Web get overenthusiastic. Usually, one animation per page is fine; more is only warranted in those cases where the designer has more experience and is applying the technique purposefully.

♦ Do optimize your GIFs well. To do this, you'll need a good GIF animation program, such as Ulead's GIF Animator, that allows you to optimize specifically for GIF animation. Refer back to Chapter 1 "Setting Up a Master Toolbox" for more information.

♦ Don't make animations blink too fast. This can cause serious problems in epileptics and others prone to seizures. Animated GIFs in general cause accessibility and usability problems—you can't stop and start them easily, and you can't rewind or fast-forward. Make sure you consider your audience's needs at all times.

♦ Describe animations using `alt` text, inline descriptions, and consider using `longdesc` along with GIF animations for accessibility reasons. See Chapter 10, "Adding Accessibility Features" to learn more.

♦ Do try for subtlety. Sometimes the most interesting GIF animations are those that are very subtle, such as someone's eye blinking every once in a while. For me, these are the most fun animations—they aren't overly obvious and yet they provide an eye-catching bit of intrigue for your page.

note   The Opera Web browser, located at `www.opera.com/features/access/visual/`, allows users to disable animated GIFs.

Secret #189:   Image Maps: To Use or Not to Use

Image maps are one of the Web's oldest forms of navigation. They can be extremely useful, as anyone using mapping sites for directions can see. However, in general use, they don't always serve a purpose that couldn't be more efficiently handled using a different method, such as standard text linking enhanced with style, or dynamic menu systems.

The main problem with using image maps is accessibility. Should you choose to go with an image map, here are a few guidelines that will help:

- Always use `alt` text inside the `img` element and all coordinate areas. This helps improve understanding of the purpose of a given area within the map.
- All the colors used in your map should be readable.
- Consider using `longdesc` to describe your map more effectively. For example, if it's a map of the United States and you can get state information by clicking on a state, you should describe that clearly to your visitors.
- Always have alternative, accessible navigation available.
- Never use server-side image maps. They aren't accessible to people who are using non-GUI browsers, whereas client-side maps can be.

Despite these problems, image maps are extremely well supported browser-wise, can be written to standards, are easy to create, and can sometimes be esthetically impressive and useful (see Figure 11-5).

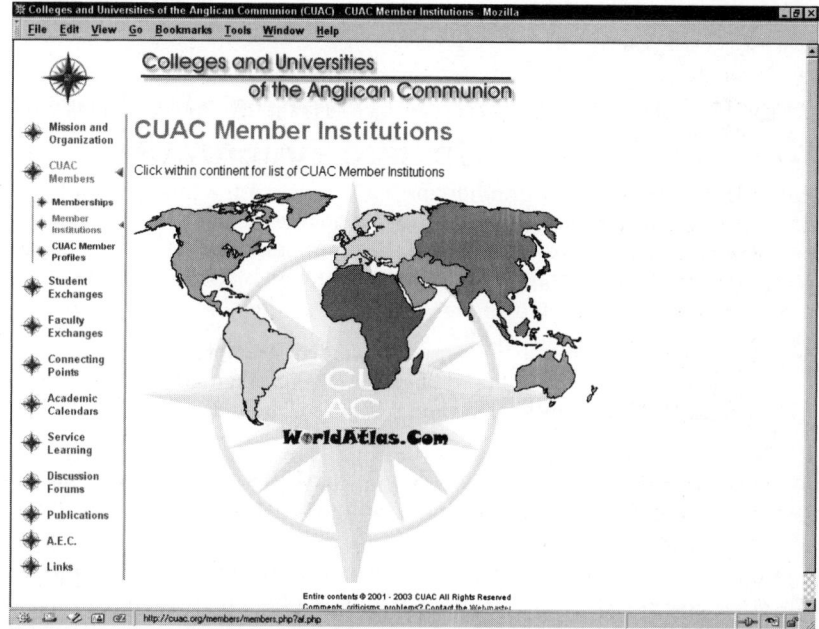

Figure 11-5: Image maps are often very useful.

Secret #190:   Make the Most Out of Text-Based Type

Typography remains an area of Web design that frustrates designers to no seeming end. Even with the text sizing and formatting options that CSS provides, the reality is that you're still limited by the font faces that you can use—a carryover problem from the days of HTML presentation, due not to the technologies but rather the fact that a font must be present on a site visitor's machine in order for that font to be properly displayed by a browser.

But this doesn't mean you can't do clever things with the available fonts and come up with combinations, text effects, and other techniques to achieve interesting looking type for your pages.

Here are a few tips:

- ◆ **Try type family contrast.** Use serif fonts for headers and san-serif fonts for body text or vice-versa.
- ◆ **Try contrast by weight and color.** Use the same font for headers and body text, but contrast them using different color and weight.
- ◆ **Using CSS, you can modify line height, word spacing, and even transform case.** Learn these techniques and use them to create interesting text effects without ever touching a graphic.

> **note** See Chapter 8, "Style Tips for Type and Design," to learn more about using CSS to enhance HTML-based text.

Secret #191: Combine Graphics and Markup for Effective Typography

While the technique of using graphic images to create attractive type along with markup-based styled text has been in use for a long time, the advances in CSS have given rise to new techniques and approaches that empower designers to create visually beautiful designs that rely on a combination of text and graphics.

> **note** Image replacement techniques are an excellent example of advanced methods growing out of the combination of CSS and markup-based text. See Chapter 8, "Style Tips for Type and Design" for more details.

Figure 11-6 shows a design for the CSS Zen Garden by its creator, Dave Shea. In it, he uses a combination platter of styled text and graphics to achieve an extremely progressive design.

In Figure 11-7, I've highlighted portions of the page. Everything that is highlighted clearly is text-based, and those portions not highlighted are graphical (with the exception of the left navigation). This way, you can see how Shea has applied this technique.

Secret #192: What Is White Space and Why Do I Care?

White space is space within a visual design, also referred to as *negative* space, in which no text or image appears. Despite its name, white space isn't always white—it is whatever the color or design of the background is.

Figure 11-6: Blood Lust, a design by Dave Shea, uses a combination of text and graphics.

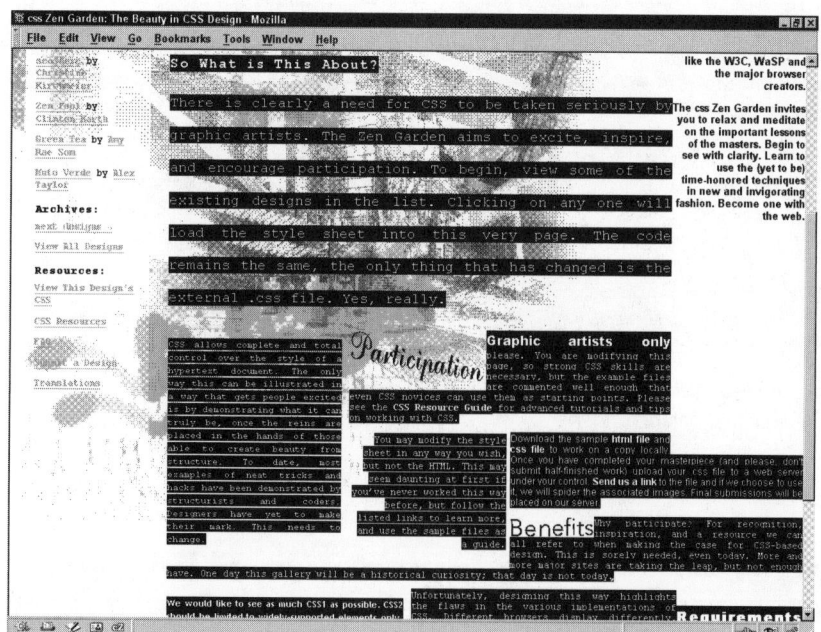

Figure 11-7: Comparing the text and graphic sections in the Blood Lust design.

White space is incredibly important for readability and for balance in design. Some of the advantages of white space include the following:

♦ White space can be used to lead the eye.

♦ Space allows the eye to rest at intervals.

♦ Appropriate use of white space will help strengthen your message— sometimes what isn't in a design can be as important as what is.

Interestingly, designers have studied white space in the context of culture. Keith Robertson, in an essay titled "On White Space: When Less is More" claims that white space symbolizes intelligence, class, and refinement, whereas the lack of it in a design is a "symbol of vulgarity, of crassness, of schlock, of bad taste."

While that might seem to be a radical statement, the bottom line is that white space helps us keep our sites from being too cluttered, busy, and confusing. From a practical standpoint, good uses of balanced, visual space can be very helpful for users and make a design more appealing (see Figure 11-8).

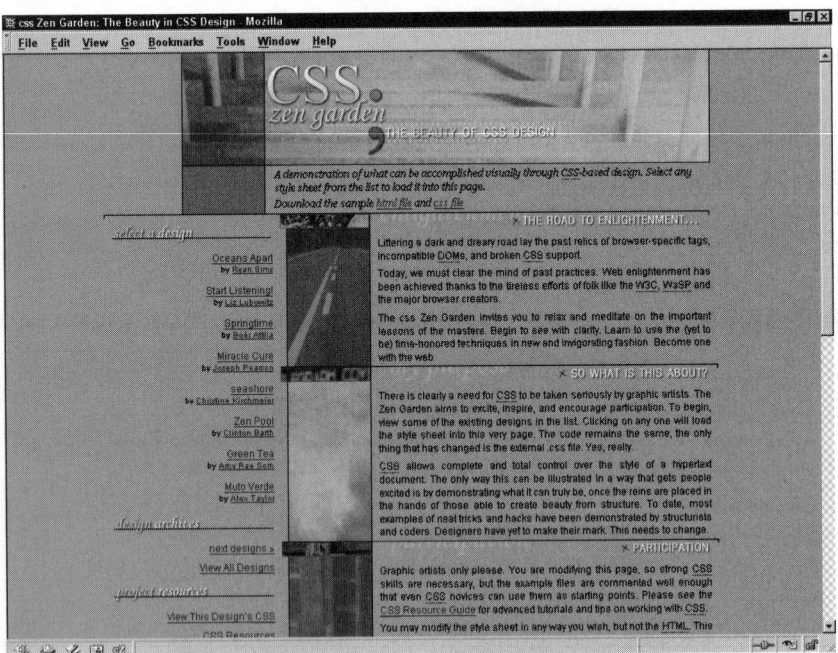

Figure 11-8: White space in design is an essential element to enhance readability and provide visual balance.

Secret #193:   The Importance of Proximity

One problem novice designers face is balancing page elements such as images, menus, and content in terms of proper proximity and visual weight. As users, we have specific responses to elements that are out of visual harmony.

Proximity is how close or how far a given component might be from another. Figure 11-9 shows a diagram where page elements are too far from one another. This space can cause confusion in site visitors on a subtle level, kind of like walking through the doors of an enormous shopping mall and not knowing where to start.

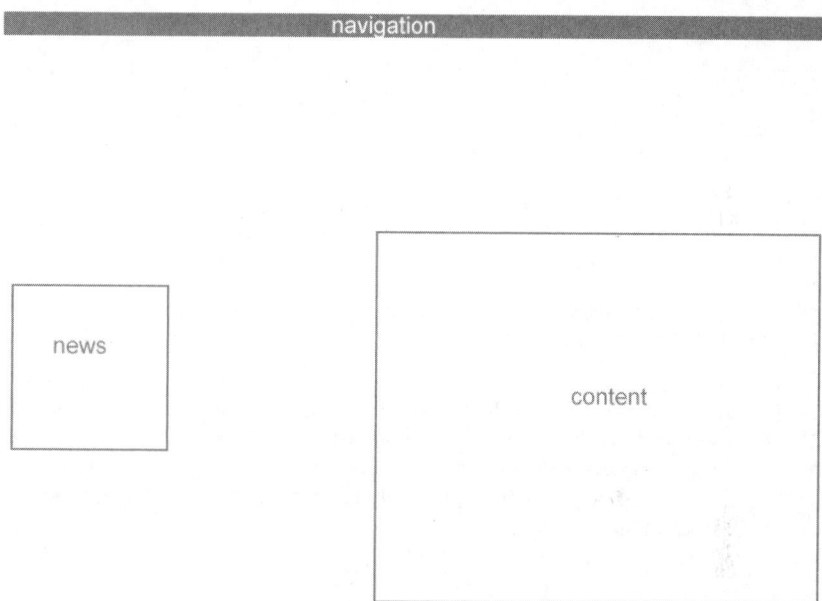

Figure 11-9: Page elements are too far from one another.

You can also have elements too close to one another (see Figure 11-10). This causes a sense of claustrophobia and nervousness in site visitors.

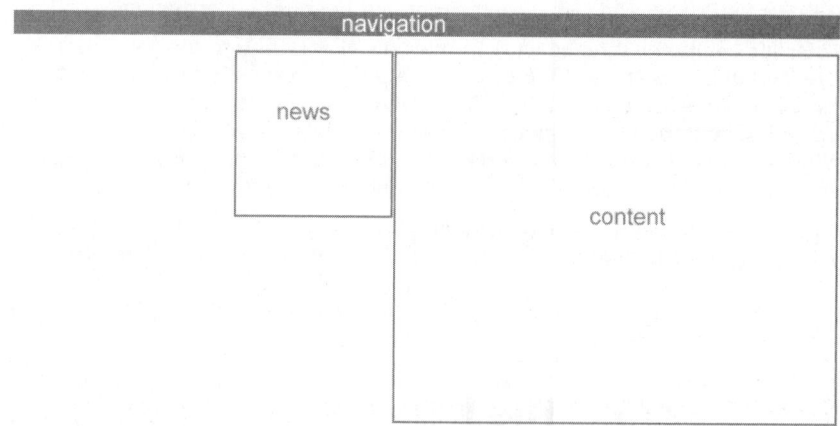

Figure 11-10: Page elements are too close, leaving too much unbalanced white space.

Normal balance of page elements makes your sites more precise and contained, easier for visitors to comprehend and use (see Figure 11-11).

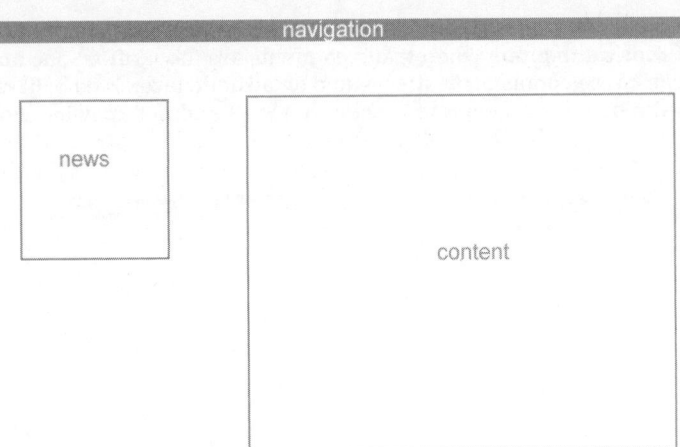

Figure 11-11: Page elements are better balanced with white space.

note

Another issue is weight. This refers to the visual "heaviness" of an object. For example, if you have a very heavy black box on the right side of the page, it will drag the eye to it because it's not balanced with other page elements. Along with being in normal proximity to each other, page elements should balance in terms of visual weight.

Secret #194:   There's No Such Thing as Web-Safe Color

Perhaps that's a bit of a radical statement, but hear out my argument.

Color for computer screens works under the theory of *additive synthesis*. You're already familiar with the RGB color management system, which is used by computers to create screen color. By firing variegated amounts of red, blue, and green, we end up with potentially millions of screen colors. Think about a television set. When you look at a picture onscreen, you are really looking at thousands of tiny phosphor dots firing light that to the human eye make up a given color.

Additive synthesis relies on the computer's hardware and software to numerically determine how much of a given light is added based on a set of situations. If I mix a bit of red light, a bit of blue light, and a bit of green light, I can end up with yellow light. If I use no light at all, the result is black, and complete amounts of red, green, and blue light result in white.

Now, if a computer's hardware and software are responsible for the resulting color, it's very easy to imagine why colors *never* look precisely the same from computer to computer. There are so many variations of video cards, operating systems, and computer monitors that there is simply no realistic way of creating absolutely consistent color from configuration to configuration.

During the Web's earlier days, the variation of these configurations along with the limitations of individual operating systems and Web browsers running on those systems was even more confusing than it is today. Many people were still using systems severely limited in color display—nowadays almost everyone with a computer purchased in the past five years can support millions of colors. But at that time, the desire to create some consistency and avoid a phenomenon called *dithering* was necessary. Dithering is when the software program attempts to find the closest color available to the one you intended—which could end up in some very inconsistent results, such as a nice pastel yellow rendering as a neon yellow. The 216 Websafe palette emerged as a result of this disparity.

note

To view the Websafe palette, visit `www.molly.com/molly/webdesign/colorchart.html`.

In 1999, Bob Stein from VisiBone performed color tests using the 216 Websafe palette. His results suggested that of the 216 colors, only 125 colors were truly "safe." A later study by David Lehn and Hadley Stern for WebMonkey in 2000 looked at colors across systems, browsers, and computers and ended up with the frightening conclusion that there were only 22 colors that could be considered more or less "safe."

Nowadays, unless you are designing for an extremely limited audience, the 216 palette is not only potentially useless in providing consistency color-wise, but very limiting to designers who wish to find colors outside of that palette. So what do you do? My advice is to *use any color you want* whether it is Web-safe or not.

warning

Of course, if you know that you are dealing with audiences that have very limited color support due to older computers and browsers, you may wish to stick to the Websafe palette.

Secret #195:   Making the Most Out of Web Color

Even prior to the widespread support of CSS, using browser-based color was a helpful way of getting more color into your design without relying on graphics. In early conventional Web design, this could be accomplished by coloring fonts or adding background color to table cells.

Nowadays, we have a lot more control over what we can add color to because of CSS. We can literally embellish any HTML or XHTML element with numerous applications of color, including the following:

- Foreground (text) color of any element
- Background color of any element
- Right, left, top, and bottom border colors (and style) for any element
- Hover colors for any element using the pseudo selector:hover applied to that element

To exemplify this, I've created a listing with inline style so you can see how each color is applied independently. Ideally, you'd use linked style for your completed design.

Listing 11-1: Applying color to element components using CSS

```
<!DOCTYPE html PUBLIC "-//W3C//DTD XHTML 1.0 Strict//EN"
    "http://www.w3.org/TR/xhtml1/DTD/xhtml1-strict.dtd">

<html xmlns="http://www.w3.org/1999/xhtml">

<head>
<title>Color Example</title>
</head>

<body style="background-color: #000; color: #fff;">

<p>This text within the body inherits the body style.</p>

<div style="background-color: #fff; color: #000; border-left: 20px
solid #ccc; border-right: 20px solid #ccc; border-top: 20px solid
#999; border-bottom: 20px solid #999;">

<p>Background, foreground, and border colors within the division.
You could style this paragraph or any other elements, and those
styles would also be applied, providing a lot of areas where color
can be used without ever having to touch a graphic.</p>

</div>

</body>
</html>
```

Figure 11-12 shows the results.

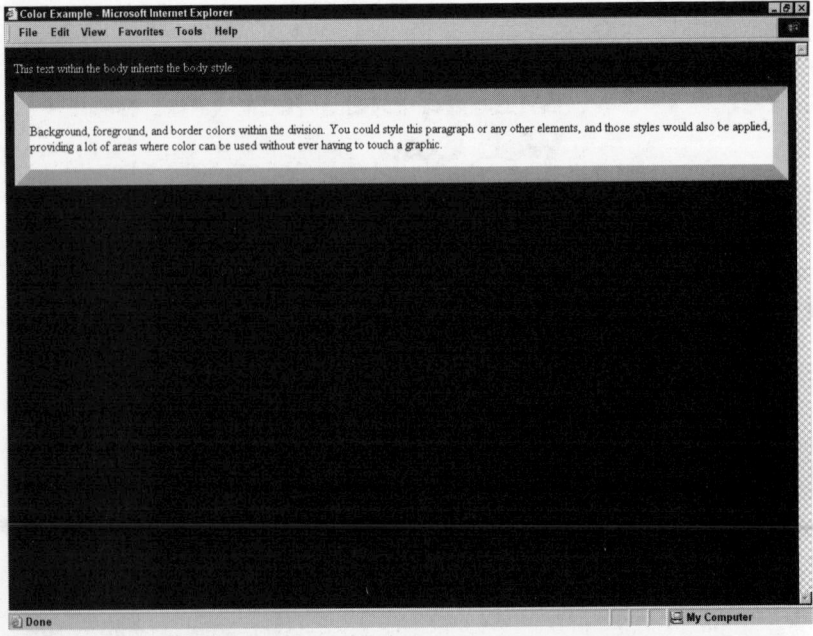

Figure 11-12: Applying color to elements.

The trick now is to combine your graphics along with CSS-driven colors to create designs that are innovative and colorful, yet download quickly because you're using CSS wherever possible to manage color rather than weighty graphics.

Secret #196: The Symbolic Meaning of Shapes

Shapes play an important role in conveying information without words. Shapes have specific psychosocial meanings that can be helpful when creating logos, icons, or other expressive visual components within a design.

Table 11-2 shows three basic shapes and defines their general conveyed meaning.

Table 11-2: The Symbolic Meaning of Shapes

Shape	Meaning
Rectangle	Rectangles and squares typically represent authority, stability, and strength. Many designs attempting to convey reliability and consistency of a product will use lines, rectangles, and squares
Circle	Circles typically represent community, fluid movement, and the feminine. Many community Web sites, sites oriented toward women, or designs wishing to convey flexibility and expression will use curves and circles
Triangle	Triangles represent action, movement, and direction, and are associated with the masculine. Designs wishing to express movement and purpose may use angles, arrows, and triangular shapes

note For interesting examples of shapes in world symbology, see **www.symbols .net/**.

Of course, shapes can be combined to extend a meaning. A clear example of this is the famous FedEx arrow, which is a combination of a rectangle and a triangle, indicating stable, forward movement.

Secret #197: The Psychology of Color

As with shape, colors have specific psychosocial responses. What's especially interesting is that a single color can have paradoxical responses. If you see red on a stop sign, it's a warning, signifying potential danger. But a red heart means love and passion.

Color values are going to make a difference, too. A neon green will elicit a different emotional response than a deep forest green. Also, as with shapes, the combination of colors means even more complex emotional results.

So, designers interested in making sure that they are using correct colors to convey their meaning to audiences must have awareness both of general color psychology and the social implications that colors and color combinations might have to use color appropriately.

Table 11-3 describes common colors and common psychological responses. While by no means comprehensive or inclusive of combinations and color value, understanding the general significance of a given color—and any related paradoxes—can help you make better color choices for your designs.

Table 11-3: Common Colors and Related Meanings

Color	Meaning
Red	Power, energy, love, warmth, passion, aggression, danger
Blue	Trust, conservative, security, technology, cleanliness, sorrow, order
Green	Nature, earth, health, good luck, jealousy, renewal, money
Yellow	Optimism, joy, hope, philosophy, dishonesty, cowardice, betrayal
Purple	Spirituality, mystery, royalty, power, transformation, cruelty, arrogance, homosexuality
Orange	Energy, balance, warmth
Brown	Earth, reliability, comfort, endurance
Gray/silver	Intellect, futurism, elegance, modesty, sadness, decay
White	Purity, cleanliness, precision, innocence, sterility, death
Black	Power, sexuality, sophistication, mystery, fear, unhappiness, death

Pretty interesting to see the disparities in meaning for individual colors, I think.

Secret #198: Color and Culture

Much of the paradox of color psychology comes out of the mixing of cultural perceptions. In Table 11-4, I've provided you with color quirks born of social issues. This can help you select or avoid colors based on your audience and the cultural influences within that audience.

note   For an amazing Web site resource on color, including color and the Web, visit www.colormatters.com/. The site is maintained by J. L. Morton, a color expert who has influenced my own writing and research on color, culture, and the Web for many years.

Table 11-4: Cultural Significances and Color

Color	Cultural significance
Red	In China, red is used to express celebration and good luck. Combined with white, the power of both colors increases the significance. In the United States and many parts of Europe, red can represent prostitution, as in "red light" districts
Blue	Interestingly, blue is considered the most safe color to use around the globe because there are no known negative cultural connotations. In China, the color represents immortality. For the Jews, blue is a holy color. In Hinduism, blue is the color of the god Krishna
Green	In many cultures, green is seen as very calming and uplifting. One caution for U.S. designers using color for global audiences is to not associate green with money—which of course is common in the United States because all of our paper money is green. This is actually quite rare, as most countries around the world use multicolored paper money and do not associate green with wealth or finance
Yellow	In China, yellow is an imperial color. In Western cultures, yellow is often associated with happiness, children, and joy
Purple	Purple is a problematic color. In Catholic Europe, it has had a long association with mourning and death. In the United States and many other cultures, purple is related to mysticism, new age, and alternative religions. In parts of the Middle East, purple is associated with prostitution. Designers should use purple with great care. It's not surprising to learn that purple is found in nature very infrequently.
Orange	In product packaging, particularly in the United States, orange is used to express cheap or inexpensive. As a result, it should be avoided in sites attempting to express luxury and elegance
Brown	While not as widespread in positive connotations as the color blue, brown is a very neutral color and is almost always associated with nature
Gray/silver	Gray is used worldwide as a neutral color. Silver tones tend to express sophistication and technology, at least at this time in history.
White	While so very commonly used for contrast in design, white has paradoxical cultural significance of a rather profound nature. In most western cultures, white is a symbol of salvation, holiness, and purity. But in some western and many eastern cultures, white represents death and mourning
Black	Black also has a profound cultural paradox: it is the color of death and mourning in many cultures, representing also the dark spirit world and evil. In contrast, black has long been associated with elegance and sophistication, especially in cosmopolitan, prosperous, and progressive areas of the world

Secret #199:   Color and Gender

The perception of color is not only influenced by our own psychology and culture, but by our gender too. Men's and women's reactions to color are significantly different and, when combined with cultural issues, the challenge becomes quite complex.

A few interesting items about gender and color follow:

- Blue stands out for men much more than for women.
- Men prefer blue to red, women red to blue.
- Men prefer orange to yellow, women yellow to orange.

It's also believed at this point in our understanding of color perception that women's color identification and awareness of color subtlety tends to be more diverse than men's.

In color studies where men and women were asked to list all the colors they could think of, women were able to consistently list more colors than men could.

While it's far too early to come to conclusions about whether these are actual differences in perception or merely cultural influences on women resulting in the ability to cite a color as being peach rather than pink, it's certainly interesting to think about.

More importantly, that gender plays a role in the perception of color indicates that to communicate effectively Web designers must know their audience as well as possible.

Secret #200:   Color Tips

Because of the complex relationships humans have with color, a few guidelines as to what to avoid or use in a given circumstance can be helpful. Here are a few tips to help you make good decisions when it comes to color in the context of global design.

- First and foremost, know your target market. Knowing demographic information about your site visitors will help you make decisions regarding color and psychology, color and gender, and color and culture.
- Because blue is the most universally acceptable color, you can use it in almost any situation.
- Pink is an odd color with which to work in a global environment. East Indian men, for example, will likely see pale pinks or other pastel colors as being feminine. Yet, for the Japanese, pastel colors are very popular for both sexes.
- Remember that adding texture will change a color. So if you're creating a graphic from a blue-green and add a texture that makes it look more blue than green, work from the resulting color, not the initial color.
- A phenomenon referred to as *simultaneous contrast* is the result of one color being placed on different backgrounds, and as a result, the

perception of the same color is different. Be aware of this issue when you choose contrast colors.

- Speaking of contrast, make certain any important text content on your site contrasts well with the background colors in use. While subtle contrast can make for interesting design, you want to take care to ensure that the content is readable.

- Typically speaking, you do not need to restrict color in graphics to Web-safe color. If you have few colors and are saving to GIF format, you can use the Websafe palette should you choose to do so. Don't attempt to save photos as Web-safe colors.

Secret #201: Exploring Scalable Vector Graphics

Scalable Vector Graphics (SVG) is an application of XML. Via markup, graphic images, animations, and interactive graphic designs can be designed and implemented for Web viewing. Of course, browsers must support the technology, which is one reason that many Web developers haven't looked into it too seriously, or perhaps haven't heard of it at all.

SVG is being developed under the auspices of the W3C. As a result, much work has been done to make it compatible with other standards, including the following:

- XML
- XSLT
- CSS2
- Document Object Model (DOM)
- SMIL
- HTML
- XHTML
- Sufficient accessibility options via the Web Accessibility Initiative (WAI) and Web Content Guidelines (WCAG)

Perhaps the most important concept when studying SVG is that it is *scalable*. This means that any graphic is not limited by a fixed pixel. Like vector graphics, a scalable graphic can be made larger or smaller, without distortion of the graphic. This is especially important for designing across resolutions. Scalable graphics adjust to the available screen resolution. This alone makes SVG very attractive to designers, as it solves one of the most frustrating issues we face: creating designs that are as interoperable yet visually rich as possible.

SVG elements are based on standard graphic design elements. They are as follows:

- **Geometric shapes.** A geometric shape is a line, combination of lines, a curve, or combination of curves, or a combination of curves and lines.
- **Text.** Text elements are represented as characters and combinations of characters.
- **Raster (also referred to as *bitmapped*) images.** Raster graphics are those that are mapped to bits. This means that they do not contain scalable methods. Raster graphics are typically used in combination with scalable graphics, and are comprised of photographs and specialty filters.

The rendering of SVG is based on a paint model. Color, gradients, and patterns are painted onto the screen to gain the end results. Shapes and text can be filled or stroked. Other graphic techniques, such as masking and opacity, can all be applied.

SVG also allows access to scripting and to the DOM, which is how SVG supports animations and interactive graphics.

An interesting aspect to SVG is that the scalable methodology is rendered via XML, rather than using a binary graphic file. The exception to this is whenever a bitmapped graphic is used within an SVG environment, the image is included using the SVG `image` element.

SVG is, as one can imagine, quite complex in its syntax. And the more complex a design becomes, the more complex the resulting markup becomes. As a result, the development of graphical user interface (GUI) tools for SVG began early.

Several of these tools are available that offer a standard drawing environment but export to SVG for use in supported browsers. In addition, many familiar graphic companies and graphic design products are adding SVG export support to their product lines.

> *note*   To read the current SVG specification and updates about SVG at the W3C, visit **www.w3.org/Graphics/SVG/**.
>
> The Adobe SVG Zone, at **www.adobe.com/svg/main.html**, has excellent examples, tools, tutorials, and up-to-date SVG browser plug-ins.

Summary

While it may seem that not much has changed in visual design for the Web, significant advances have been made in the tools we use: better compression for graphics and more options too, with improved PNG support and the emerging SVG implementations. Techniques have advanced—largely because of CSS and our ability to rely on it to improve how we use graphics and color within our sites. Finally, understanding the psychology, culture, and gender issues involved in visual design and color, we can gain better control over how our sites are perceived by others.

Next, you'll learn how to work with JavaScript, DHTML, and other media to make your sites more expressive.

Spicing It Up with Dynamic Content and Rich Media

Chapter

12

◆ ◆

Secrets in This Chapter

◆ ◆

O ver the years, lots of scripting and multimedia have been used on the Web, but in often haphazard ways—lots of cut-and-paste scripts, no attention to professional practices, and not much consideration as to the why and when of integrating scripting and media into a site. Still, there are very powerful reasons to use scripting, audio, and video—in some cases, entire sites are dependent on these forms of interactive technologies to properly serve their audience needs and the site's goals.

This chapter focuses on some of the most common and sensible approaches to scripting and media, when and why you should script, and how to ensure that your documents remain as clean, well-structured, and standardized as possible.

All about Scripting and Rich Media

Scripting is typically used to refer to JavaScript, although I cover other, related topics in this chapter as well, including standardized scripting and the Document Object Model (DOM). I also discuss Rich Media, a popular term used to describe media with "rich" features, such as Flash, animations, video, and audio.

JavaScript, ECMAScript, and DOM

Netscape set out to create an interactive scripting environment for its browser. Originally known as LiveScript, Sun Microsystems, who at the time was developing its Java language, decided to work with Netscape to package the two together. This resulted in the name change from LiveScript to JavaScript.

The interest in scripting within browsers in turn spawned movement on Microsoft's part to come out with its own variant, JScript. Microsoft also promoted Visual Basic Script (VBScript) for a while to be used like JavaScript within Web documents, but that fell out of favor because it wasn't cross-browser compatible. With the emergence of interest in standards came ECMAScript, which is considered the standardized form of scripting for the Web.

> **note**   To read more about ECMAScript, see `www.ecma-international.org/`. ECMA is a fast-track standards body working on a range of standards related to communications technology.

Even though much of the work going on with scripting today has its roots in EC-MAScript, we will likely be referring to this form of scripting, whether standardized or not, as "JavaScript" for a very long time to come.

> **note**   It's important to understand the difference between Java and JavaScript. Unlike Java, which is a complex programming language with applications both on the Web and beyond, JavaScript is an interpreted script that integrates with Web documents. JavaScript, unlike Java, which is compiled, is interpreted line-by-line by the browser.

Today, JavaScript is used to accomplish a range of Web-based techniques, including the creation of pop-up windows, mouseover animations, as well as browser detection and pre-caching of images, all in hopes of making the user experience more interactive.

JavaScript works by connecting scripting to (X)HTML elements via DOM. DOM is the interface that allows a browser to bind scripts to elements, resulting in more dynamic options for the page designer.

JavaScript is also one of the cornerstones of Dynamic HTML (DHTML). Contrary to its name, DHTML is not a language, it is a combination of technologies: (X)HTML, CSS, sScripting, and DOM.

> **note**
>
> **DOM is standardized, too, but incorrect support for DOM in browsers has caused a lot of cross-browser difficulties. The W3C oversees standardization of DOM is at www.w3.org/DOM/.**

Some general JavaScript rules to remember include the following:

* JavaScript is case sensitive.
* It's possible that even if someone is using a JavaScript-enabled browser the JavaScript is turned off, so you need to plan your designs to degrade gracefully.
* JavaScript code can be commented out so older browsers don't try to display the code.

In both HTML and XHTML, JavaScript can be placed as follows:

* Embedded in a script element in the head element of a document
* JavaScript is placed in an external document with a suffix of .js and is referenced from the document using the script element.
* Portions of JavaScript may appear within script elements inside the body of your document, or attached to intrinsic events.

> **note**
>
> **Remember that in XHTML, intrinsic events must be written in lowercase, such as onclick, instead of other case forms including the commonly used camel case, onClick.**

To embed a script, you place the script in between the script elements in the head portion of an HTML or XHTML document, as follows:

```
<head>
<script type="text/javascript">
</script>
</head>
```

You'll notice that I've included the type attribute with the text/javascript value. This is required, but often left out. On the other hand, you'll often see the language="javascript" attribute in the script element. This is okay in HTML and XHTML Transitional, but not in strict document type definitions (DTDs) or in XHTML 1.1. So, I just leave out the language attribute in all cases, but always include the type attribute. This practice should cause no change in the behavior of the script in any contemporary browsers.

If you'd like to hide code from those browsers not supporting JavaScript, you can do so using the following comment style around your script. Note that this is slightly different than conventional HTML comments, which do not use the double slash (//) prior to closing the comment:

```
<head>
<script type="text/javascript">
```

```
<!-- Hide script from old browsers

// End hiding script from old browsers -->
</script>
</head>
```

Finally, if you'd like to comment your JavaScript, you can use // before any single-line comment. For multiline comments, you'll use the same type of comments you've seen used in CSS, as follows:

```
<head>
<script type="text/javascript">
<!-- Hide script from old browsers

/* the following script is a simple name prompt. It will display a
dialog box for the user to enter his or her name. */

var namePrompt=prompt("What Is Your Name","");
function dispname(namePrompt) {
document.write(""+namePrompt+"");

}
{dispname(namePrompt);
}

// End hiding script from old browsers -->
</script>
</head>
```

If you wanted to link to the JavaScript, you would place the script itself, without any HTML tags (although you can use comments) into a separate text file and name it, using .js as the suffix.

In your (X)HTML page, place the script element and include the source to your JavaScript file, as follows:

```
<head>
<script src="scripts/testing.js" type="text/javascript"></script>
</head>
```

note   While it is recommended that you place most scripts external to your source HTML files (and I heartily agree), I've shown many scripts in this chapter in embedded form. I did this for the sake of clarity, so you could see the script and corresponding XHTML in one location. If you'd like to move a script out of the document, you can do so by using the means described earlier this chapter.

Using Rich Media

The term "rich media" has emerged to define enhanced media on the Web. Typically, this means the media runs inline, such as Flash, or via a Java applet, audio, or video file. Rich media often uses markup, scripting, and client-server technologies to enhance and extend what we typically think of as multimedia.

Flash has become very widespread; at one time it was felt it might even "take over" as the de facto means of creating Web sites. Flash has become a very sophisticated tool that goes far beyond simple animations. With the addition of ActionScript and the continued progress and development of Flash-related tools, Flash is the rich media of choice for a wide range of applications and design solutions.

Audio and video have seen an incredible surge of interest in the past few years, particularly since broadband is becoming so widespread. There are a variety of means of including audio and video in a site, including the following:

- ◆ Offering media for direct download
- ◆ Offering a link to media for inline viewing (provided the client has the proper plug-in to support that media type)
- ◆ Streaming media via a number of streaming technologies, including Real and QuickTime

Even in those cases where broadband isn't in use, streaming has become efficient enough a technology to deliver lower-quality files to low-bandwidth users.

Secret #202:   Providing the Current Date

Greeting visitors is a nice way to welcome them to your site and to create a warm and active relationship with them. Listing 12-1 offers you a little script that provides a simple way to add today's date and time onto your page to keep your site looking fresh.

Listing 12-1: Providing the current date

```
<!DOCTYPE html PUBLIC "-//W3C//DTD XHTML 1.0 Strict//EN"
        "http://www.w3.org/TR/xhtml1/DTD/xhtml1-strict.dtd">

<html xmlns="http://www.w3.org/1999/xhtml">
<head>
<title>Dynamic Date Display</title>

<script type="text/javascript">
<!-- Hide script from old browsers

dayName = new Array
("Sunday","Monday","Tuesday","Wednesday","Thursday","Friday",
"Saturday")
monName = new Array ("January", "February", "March", "April",
"May","June", "July", "August", "September", "October",
"November", "December");

now = new Date;
// End hiding script from old browsers -->
</script>

</head>

<body>
<script type="text/javascript">
```

(continued)

Listing 12-1: *(continued)*

```
<!-- Hide script from old browsers

document.write("<h1>Today is " + dayName[now.getDay()] + ", " +
monName[now.getMonth()] + " " + now.getDate() + ".</h1>")

// End hiding script from old browsers -->
</script>

</body>
</html>
```

In this case, you can see how the `script` element is being used in the `body` element to generate the display. You can place that portion anywhere within your design that you'd like the day and date to display.

What's more, you can control the output with HTML elements and style. You'll notice that the display text code is contained within an `h1` element. You can change this element to anything you want, and add CSS to present it to your linking.

Figure 12-1 shows the results after I've added the script to a client page.

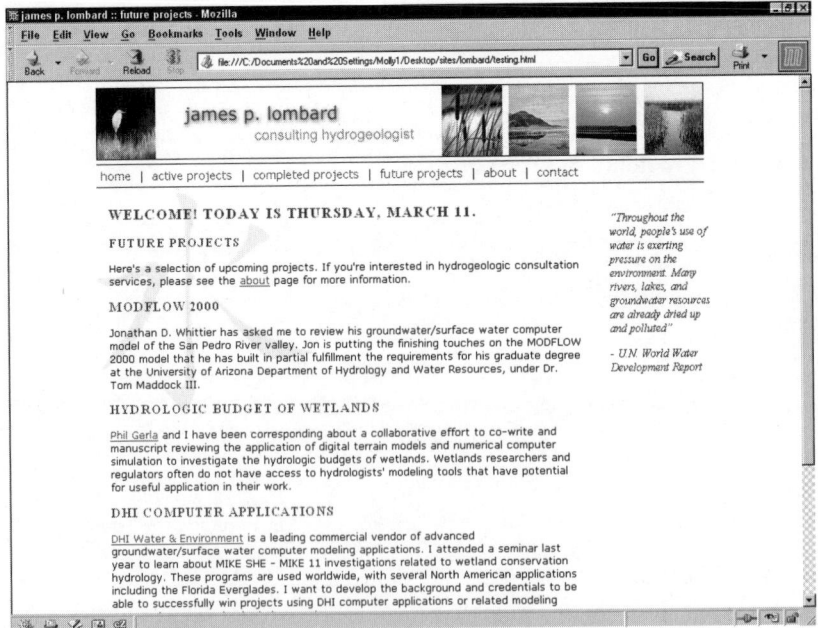

Figure 12-1: Using JavaScript to display time and date.

Secret #203: Doing Popups Properly

As mentioned more than once before in this book, popups are problematic. The reasons are numerous, most related to usability and accessibility. But there are some good uses for popups and helpful ways of making them accessible.

Popups are very easy to create, and you can also easily ensure that they are both usable and accessible.

Listing 12-2 shows a link to a code sample. By clicking on the link, the site visitor is able to see the code within a browser window.

Listing 12-2: Creating a simple, accessible, usable pop-up window

```
<!DOCTYPE html PUBLIC "-//W3C//DTD XHTML 1.0 Strict//EN"
      "http://www.w3.org/TR/xhtml1/DTD/xhtml1-strict.dtd">

<html xmlns="http://www.w3.org/1999/xhtml">
<head>
<title>accessible pop-up windows</title>

<script type="text/javascript">
<!-- Hide script from old browsers
function popitup(url)
{
   newwindow=window.open(url,'name','height=400,width=450,resizable
=1,toolbar');
   if (window.focus) {newwindow.focus();}
   return false;
}

// End hiding script from old browsers -->
</script>

</head>

<body>

<ul>
<li><a href="code1.html" onclick="return
popitup('code1.html')"> Link to code sample 1</a></li>
<li><a href="code1.html" onclick="return
popitup('code2.html')">Link to code sample 2</a></li>
<li><a href="code1.html" onclick="return
popitup('code3.html')">Link to code sample 3</a></li>
</ul>

</body>
</html>
```

Place the file name and location in the head portion of the script. Here, I've included variables to ensure that the window opens, is resizable, and has the toolbar available—all important elements to make the pop up accessible. Finally, if a person has no JavaScript or it is disabled, the pop-up information will just load into the current window. Figure 12-2 shows the link and the pop-window results.

You can always place an image or other object in the pop up as well. In this case, it's recommended you don't just link to the image, but rather to an HTML page containing the image so you can include alternate text within the img element as well as any additional text necessary to describe the image (see Figure 12-3).

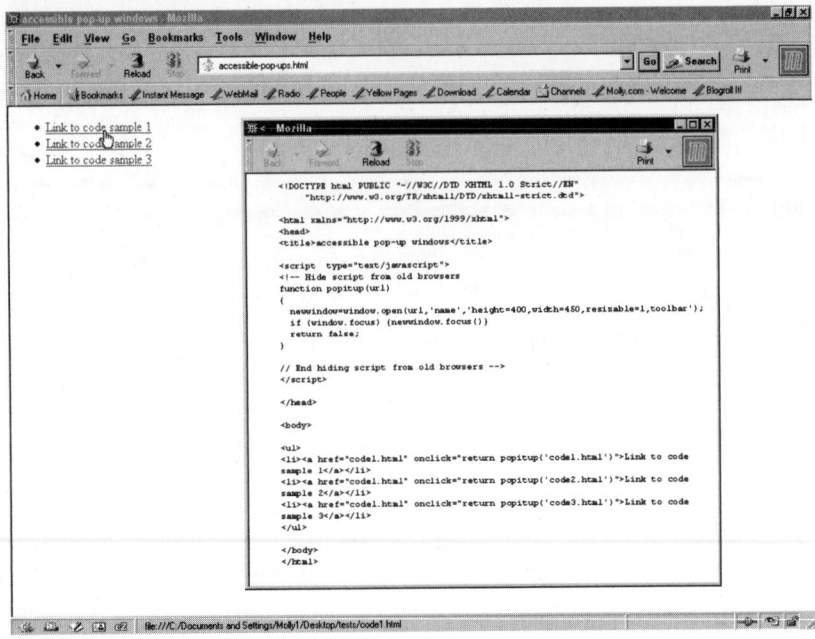

Figure 12-2: Code sample in a JavaScript pop-up window.

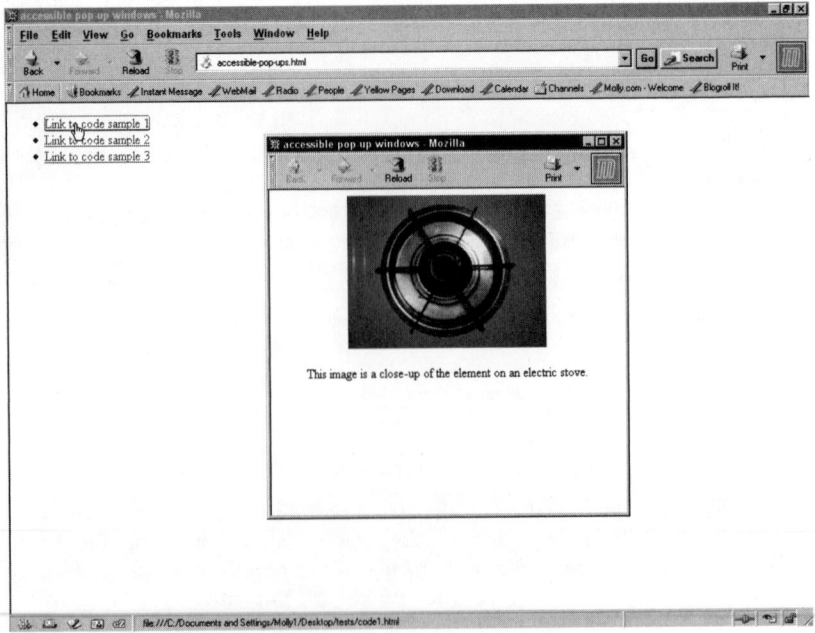

Figure 12-3: Using an image in the pop-up window.

warning

Try to keep the number of pop-up windows you use to a minimum. They are problematic, as is evidenced by the surplus of pop-up blocker software available these days. However, there are certainly very good uses for pop-up windows, such as for code samples and detail images.

Secret #204:   Randomize Images and Text

Randomizing images and text can really help keep your site fresh (see Chapter 13). You can use a number of approaches to randomization features; here, I'll show you straightforward JavaScript solutions that will work for most situations.

note

If you have concerns about JavaScript being disabled or unavailable in large amounts of your population, or you simply prefer to tap into the power of application languages, you can provide randomization features using Perl, PHP, ColdFusion, ASP.NET, and more. See Appendix B for more information on server-side application languages.

Listing 12-3 demonstrates a randomized, linked image script that's placed in the body of your document. You'll need to get a few things in order to make this script work:

- A number of images. They should be all the same size because you'll be placing them in the same location on a given page.
- You'll want to replace the number *6 (as I've got it here) with the number of images you're actually using.
- Change the location and image name in each if statement.
- To add more images, copy the if statement and add the subsequent image number in the statement (img = = #).
- Adjust the output HTML to contain the proper width, height, and alternative text image for your images.
- Be sure to rename the link files (link1.html, link2.html, and so on) to your actual link locations.
- Add or modify the border properties using CSS.

Listing 12-3: Linked, accessible, random image generation

```
<!DOCTYPE html PUBLIC "-//W3C//DTD XHTML 1.0 Strict//EN"
     "http://www.w3.org/TR/xhtml1/DTD/xhtml1-strict.dtd">

<html xmlns="http://www.w3.org/1999/xhtml">
<head>
<title>Random Image Script</title>
</head>

<body>
<script type="text/javascript">
```

(continued)

Listing 12-3: *(continued)*

```
<!
var imgTotal = 6;
var rnumb = Math.floor(Math.random()*imgTotal);
var str = "<a href=\"";
str += "page" + rnumb + ".html";
str += "\"><img src=\"";
str += rnumb + ".gif\"";
str += " width=\"250\" height=\"188\" alt=\"random photo image\"
style=\"border:0\" /></a>";

document.write(str);
var b1dis = "<a href=\"";
var bdis = "\"><img src=\"";
var edis = " width=\"250\" height=\"188\" alt=\"random photo
image\" style=\"border:0\" /></a>";
var rnumb = "";
var img = "";

rnumb += Math.floor(Math.random()*6);
img = rnumb;

if (img == "0") {
document.write(b1dis+ "page1.html" +bdis+ "1.gif\"" +edis);
}

if (img == "1") {
document.write(b1dis+ "page2.html" +bdis+ "2.gif\"" +edis);
}

if (img == "2") {
document.write(b1dis+ "page3.html" +bdis+ "3.gif\"" +edis);
}

if (img == "3") {
document.write(b1dis+ "page4.html" +bdis+ "4.gif\"" +edis);
}

if (img == "4") {
document.write(b1dis+ "page5.html" +bdis+ "5.gif\"" +edis);
}

if (img == "5") {
document.write(b1dis+ "page6.html" +bdis+ "6.gif\"" +edis);
}

// -->
</script>
</body>
</html>
```

Figure 12-4 shows figures of my images prior to randomization.

Figure 12-4: All of my images prior to adding the script.

I optimized this script to output XHTML. If you're using HTML, simply remove the space and trailing slash from the **img** element.

Figures 12-5, 12-6, and 12-7 show three visits to the page with a different image in place each time.

In the case of randomizing text, Listing 12-4 shows a script that can be used right inline to generate as many text sayings as you want. Simply replace the sayings within the quotes, or add additional ones as you see fit.

The text will then be displayed in a random fashion on your page upon each visit. You can use style to control the appearance of your text.

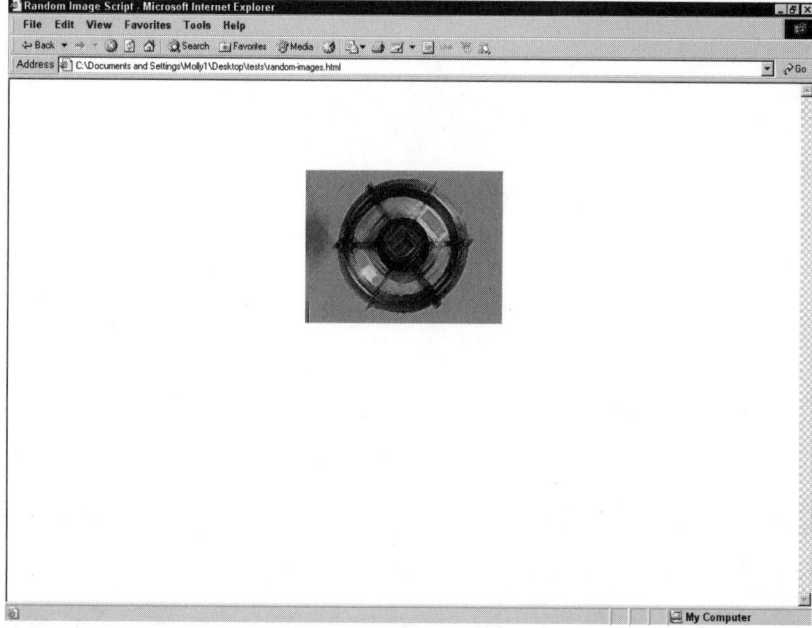

Figure 12-5: One of my images loads on the first visit.

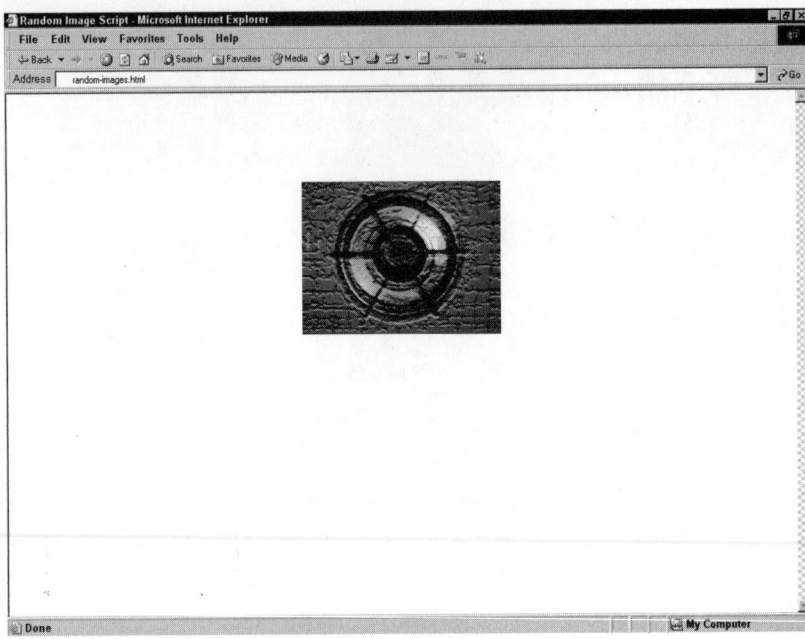

Figure 12-6: Another image loads on page refresh.

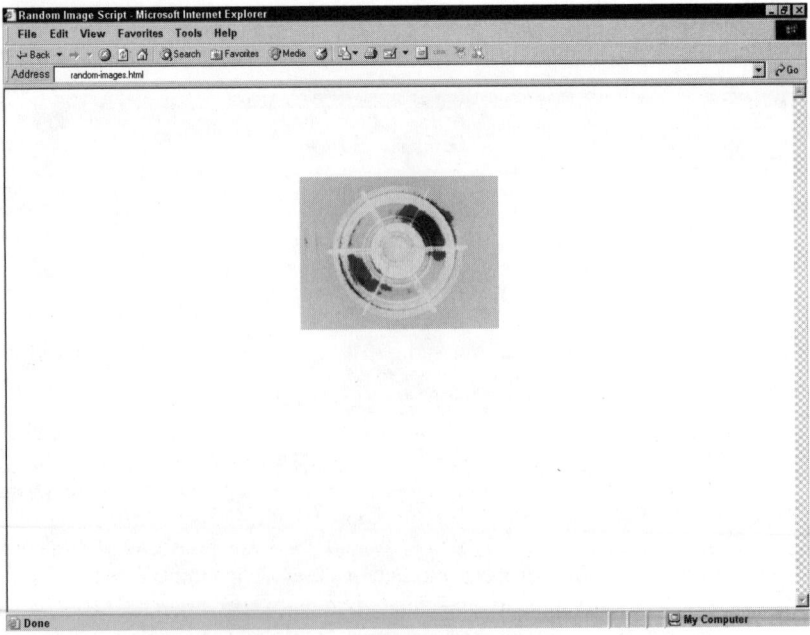

Figure 12-7: On my next visit, still another image loads.

Listing 12-4: Random text script

```
<!DOCTYPE html PUBLIC "-//W3C//DTD XHTML 1.0 Strict//EN"
    "http://www.w3.org/TR/xhtml1/DTD/xhtml1-strict.dtd">

<html xmlns="http://www.w3.org/1999/xhtml">
<head>
<title>Random Text Script</title>
</head>

<body>

<script type="text/javascript">
<!--
function text() {

var text = new Array();
var number = 0;

text[number++] = "My mother buried three husbands, and two of them
were just napping. - Rita Rudner";
text[number++] = "I never know how much of what I say is true. -
Bette Midler";
text[number++] = "Sometimes I worry about being a success in a
mediocre world. - Lily Tomlin";
text[number++] = "I base my fashion taste on what doesn't itch. -
Gilda Radner";
text[number++] = "Marriage is a fine institution - but I'm not
ready for an institution. - Mae West";

var increment = Math.floor(Math.random() * number);
document.write(text[increment]);
}
//-->

</script>
</body>
</html>
```

Figures 12-8 and 12-9 show random visits to a page where I've used the script.

> **tip**
>
> To place this script externally, simply copy the script itself (none of the HTML or comments to hide the script) in a separate file, name it randomtext.js, and link to it from the location where you'd like your random text to appear using the script element: `<script src="randomtext.js" type="text/javascript"></script>`. This is especially helpful for a script of this nature, because you may want to have 1000 text entries to choose from, and you certainly don't want them residing in the HTML document itself.

Again, these script solutions can be very helpful to you, but you may very well find more advanced, customizable, and flexible scripts of almost any denomination—JavaScript, Perl, CGI, PHP and so on.

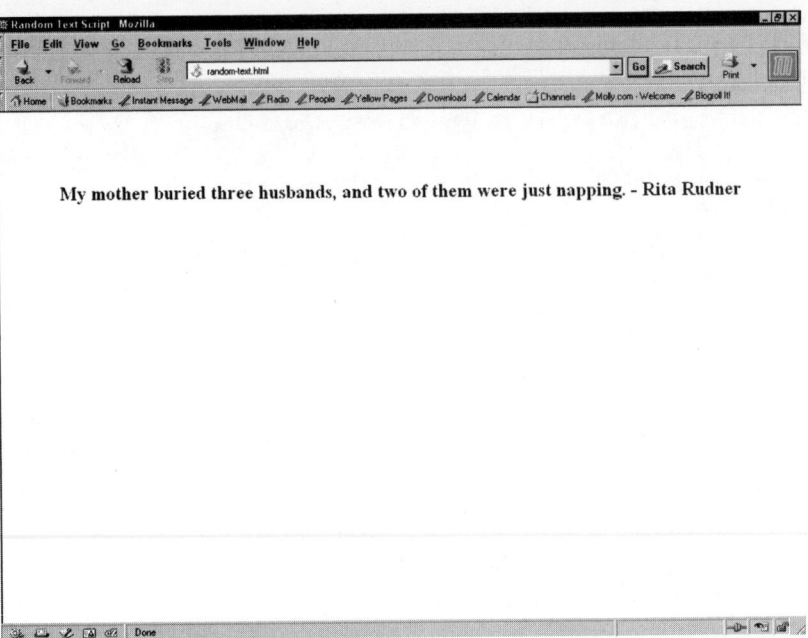

Figure 12-8: First visit to the page with the random quotes.

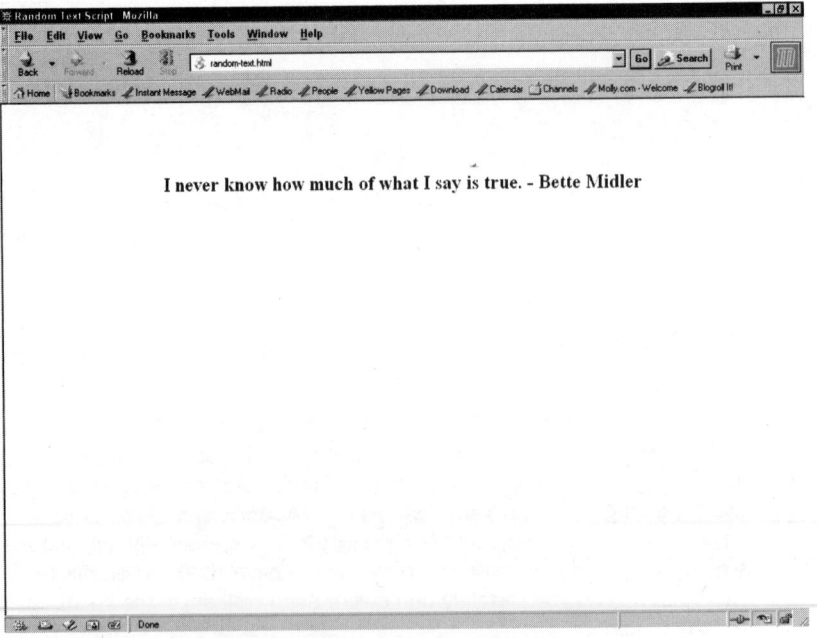

Figure 12-9: A subsequent visit to the random quote page.

Always consider your environment and audience before committing to a long-range option. In the meantime, you might find these scripts do exactly what you want them to, or at the very least, provide a means for you to find out if you'd like to have randomization features on your site.

Secret #205: Open a New Window Without target

As many readers may be aware, the `target` attribute in links is not available for use anymore when using XHTML Strict or XHTML 1.1.

Because many people like to have external links open in a new window, this causes a problem for those developers working in those forms of XHTML. You can use JavaScript to circumvent this problem.

If you want to only apply this from time to time, you can add some JavaScript directly to the link in question, as in the following example:

```
<a href="http://www.wiley.com/" onclick="java_script_:
this.target='_blank';">
```

Another approach is to embed the following JavaScript into pages where you'd like the feature to work (see Listing 12-5).

Listing 12-5: External linking for multiple links

```
<!DOCTYPE html PUBLIC "-//W3C//DTD XHTML 1.0 Strict//EN"
    "http://www.w3.org/TR/xhtml1/DTD/xhtml1-strict.dtd">

<html xmlns="http://www.w3.org/1999/xhtml">

<head>
<title>Link in New Window</title>

<script type="text/javascript">
<!-- Hide script from old browsers

function externalLinks() {
 if (!document.getElementsByTagName) return;
 var anchors = document.getElementsByTagName("a");
 for (var i=0; i<anchors.length; i++) {
   var anchor = anchors[i];
  if (anchor.getAttribute("href") &&
       anchor.getAttribute("rel") == "external")
    anchor.target = "_blank";
 }
}
window.onload = externalLinks;
// End hiding script from old browsers -->
</script>
```

(continued)

Listing 12-5: *(continued)*

```
</head>

<body>

<h1>Links will open in new window</h1>

<p><a href="http://www.wiley.com/" rel="external">Wiley's Web Site
</a></p>
<p><a href="http://www.molly.com/" rel="external">Molly's Web Site
</a></p>

</body>
</html>
```

Now, every link to which you've added the `rel="external"` attribute will open in an external window. Figure 12-10 shows the results—note that I've resized the resulting window so you can see the relationships, but normally when you use this script, the window will open as a full, complete, new browser window.

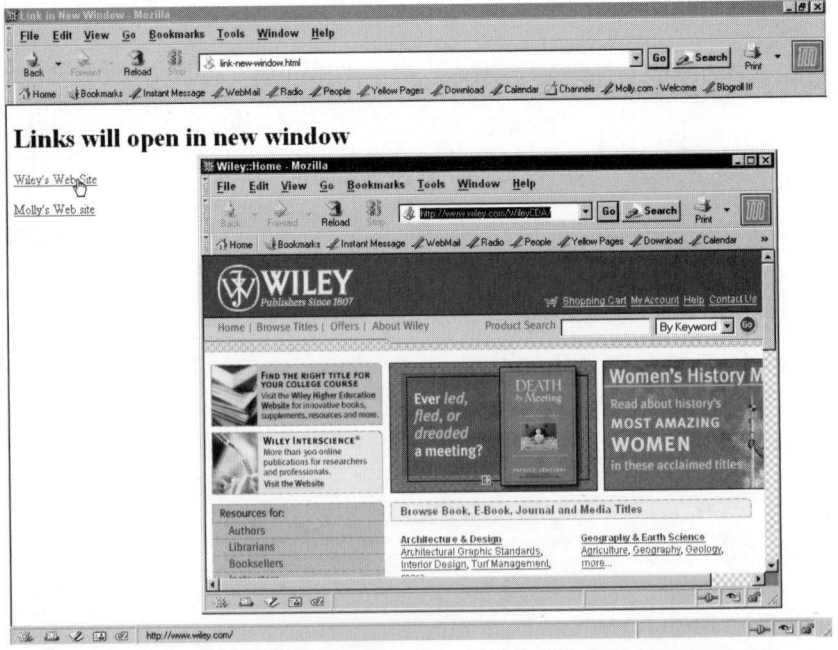

Figure 12-10: Opening an external link in another browser window using JavaScript.

> **tip**
>
> Placing a script of this nature externally makes great sense, too, because you can control thousands of pages from that one script instead of having to embed it in every document you'd like to have this useful feature.

Secret #206:   Check for Plug-Ins

The existence of plug-in applications on a visitor's machine is important if you're tapping into multimedia. Almost all rich media plays in some type of plug-in application, so testing for the application can be helpful for your visitors.

You can use Apple's completely free browser plug-in for Flash, Shockwave, QuickTime, RealPlayer, and Windows Media Player—they are included in the script.

> **note**   The script is really, really long so please retrieve it from the Apple Web site at
> `http://developer.apple.com/internet/webcontent/examples/`
> `detectplugins_source.html`. You'll likely need to modify it for your
> needs (such as making sure elements are in lowercase and the type rather
> than the language attribute is being used).

In Figure 12-11 you'll see the output of the test results after running the script in my browser. I added some JavaScript in the body of the element to have this information print out on screen.

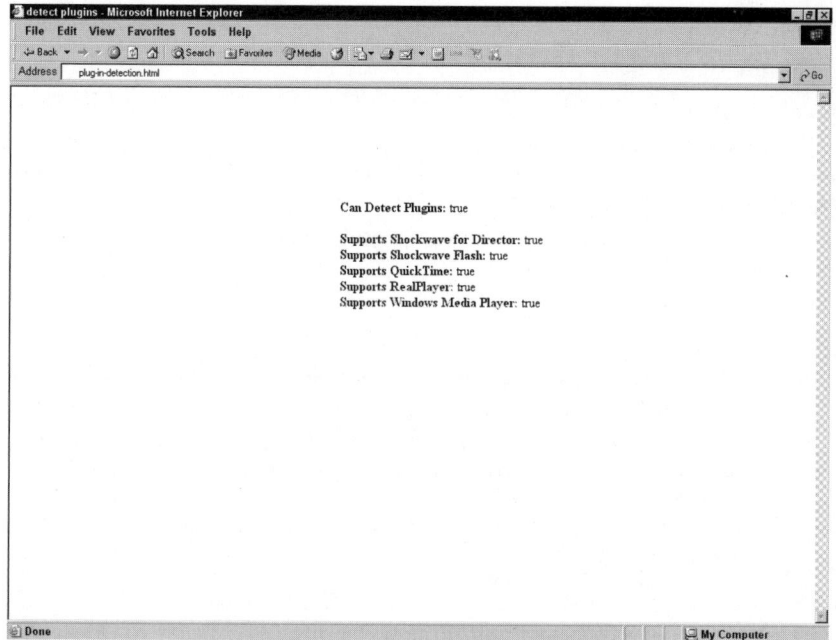

Figure 12-11: Printing the output of my plug-in test to file.

Obviously, you don't want this information to display. Instead, you want to provide some action once you have the script embedded in the document containing your media (or preferably have referenced it externally). You can do the following:

+ Modify the script to send a message if the plug-in in question wasn't found.

+ Automatically redirect the page to an alternate page with a description of the content. This is useful for accessibility, and can also be used as a means of explaining to your site visitors that they don't have the required plug-in, but if they follow the link you've provided to the download site, they can make the choice to download the plug-in and return to view your content.

+ Redirect the page to the plug-in download page immediately so the site visitors can download the plug-in to view your content.

For more information on customizing the script, see Apple's coverage of this topic, at `http://developer.apple.com/internet/webcontent/detectplugins.html`.

> **note** Any way you slice it, the use of plug-ins is a difficult issue that causes usability problems. Testing and redirecting isn't a magic solution, but at least it gives your site visitor the opportunity to get to your information.

Secret #207: Text Size Switching

Text-size switching has been appearing on Web sites for well over a year now, it's not just a fad. It's incredibly helpful for those individuals who might need assistance reading things on-screen.

By providing sizing options, you add a helpful, custom feature that makes your site more legible to your visitors.

> **note** Many browsers contain text sizing and zoom options, too. Using a switching method won't interfere with that and also provides a more customized, controlled means of resizing text based on your sizing options rather than those offered by the browser. And many users don't seem to realize they can change text size via their Web browser, so offering them the feature directly can circumvent that little problem. You can also add other features to assist with the page's readability, such as a higher contrast version.

Text resizing is done by combining three techniques: HTML (or XHTML), CSS, and JavaScript. Here's what you do:

1. Create the style sheets that contain the text sizing options. You can have as many options as you want.

2. Link these styles sheets to the documents where you'll offer the text-size switching, using the `link` element with the `rel` attribute, the `title` attribute, and the `alternate` style sheet attribute value.

3. Link the style-switching JavaScript (Listing 12-6) found in this secret to the documents using the style-switcher using the style element.

4. Add your text or graphic links representing the style switch into your (X)HTML document.

Listing 12-6 shows the JavaScript you'll use. Simply place it in a text editor and name the file `styleswitcher.js`.

Listing 12-6: Style switch JavaScript

```
function setActiveStyleSheet(title) {
  var i, a, main;
  for(i=0; (a = document.getElementsByTagName("link")[i]); i++) {
    if(a.getAttribute("rel").indexOf("style") != -1 &&
a.getAttribute("title")) {
      a.disabled = true;
      if(a.getAttribute("title") == title) a.disabled = false;
    }
  }
}

function getActiveStyleSheet() {
  var i, a;
  for(i=0; (a = document.getElementsByTagName("link")[i]); i++) {
    if(a.getAttribute("rel").indexOf("style") != -1 &&
a.getAttribute("title") && !a.disabled) return
a.getAttribute("title");
  }
  return null;
}

function getPreferredStyleSheet() {
  var i, a;
  for(i=0; (a = document.getElementsByTagName("link")[i]); i++) {
    if(a.getAttribute("rel").indexOf("style") != -1
       && a.getAttribute("rel").indexOf("alt") == -1
       && a.getAttribute("title")
       ) return a.getAttribute("title");
  }
  return null;
}

function createCookie(name,value,days) {
  if (days) {
    var date = new Date();
    date.setTime(date.getTime()+(days*24*60*60*1000));
    var expires = "; expires="+date.toGMTString();
  }
  else expires = "";
  document.cookie = name+"="+value+expires+"; path=/";
}

function readCookie(name) {
  var nameEQ = name + "=";
```

(continued)

Listing 12-6: *(continued)*

```
   var ca = document.cookie.split(';');
   for(var i=0;i < ca.length;i++) {
     var c = ca[i];
     while (c.charAt(0)==' ') c = c.substring(1,c.length);
     if (c.indexOf(nameEQ) == 0) return
 c.substring(nameEQ.length,c.length);
   }
   return null;
}

window.onload = function(e) {
  var cookie = readCookie("style");
  var title = cookie ? cookie : getPreferredStyleSheet();
  setActiveStyleSheet(title);
}

window.onunload = function(e) {
  var title = getActiveStyleSheet();
  createCookie("style", title, 365);
}

var cookie = readCookie("style");
var title = cookie ? cookie : getPreferredStyleSheet();
setActiveStyleSheet(title);
```

Listing 12-7 shows my XHTML document, which includes the links to the alternative style sheets I created, the script source reference, and the links I created to allow users to make the switch.

Listing 12-7: An XHTML document employing the style sheet switch

```
<!DOCTYPE html PUBLIC "-//W3C//DTD XHTML 1.0 Strict//EN"
     "http://www.w3.org/TR/xhtml1/DTD/xhtml1-strict.dtd">

<html xmlns="http://www.w3.org/1999/xhtml">
<head>
<title>Text-size switching</title>
<meta http-equiv="Content-Type" content="text/html;
charset=iso-8859-1" />

<!-- this style sheet is the default style -->
<link rel="stylesheet" type="text/css" href="css/black-style.css"
media="all" />

<!-- this style sheet defines the normal size via the title
attribute -->

<link href="css/black-style.css" rel="alternate stylesheet"
type="text/css" title="normal" media="all" />

<!-- this style sheet contains the styles for the large size text
-->
```

```
<link href="css/large-type.css" rel="alternate stylesheet"
type="text/css" title="large" media="all" />

<!-- here is the link to the style switching script -->
<script type="text/javascript"
src="scripts/styleswitcher.js"></script>

</head>

<body>

<div id="content">

<h1>Welcome!</h1>

<p>Lorem ipsum dolor sit amet, consectetuer adipiscing elit. Nam
adipiscing interdum diam. Proin porta. Sed aliquam lectus
consectetuer tortor. Mauris vel tellus. Nullam rutrum, metus ut
mattis molestie, pede lacus dictum lorem, eget pellentesque enim
leo eget pede. Nam felis wisi, malesuada ut, commodo eget,
vestibulum ac, nunc. </p>

</div>

<div id="menu">
  <ul>
    <li id="top"><a href="home.html">Home</a></li>
    <li><a href="aboutus.html">About Us</a></li>
    <li><a href="contactus.html">Contact Us</a></li>
  </ul>

<!-- note links below, using the value defined in the title
attribute to select the style sheet -->

  <ul>
  <li><a href="#" onclick="setActiveStyleSheet('normal'); return
  false;">normal type</a></li>
  <li><a href="#" onclick="setActiveStyleSheet('large'); return
  false;">make type larger</a></li>
  </ul>
</div>

</body>
</html>
```

Figure 12-12 shows the normal text size as I load the page, and Figure 12-13 shows the large text size when I click the switch.

---

tip   You may wish to add the media type using the **media** attribute and an appropriate value. You'll see that in my markup, I've used "all" so these styles will be applied to all media including the screen. If you wanted to have an alternate style sheet for print or projection, you could define that using the **media** attribute accordingly.

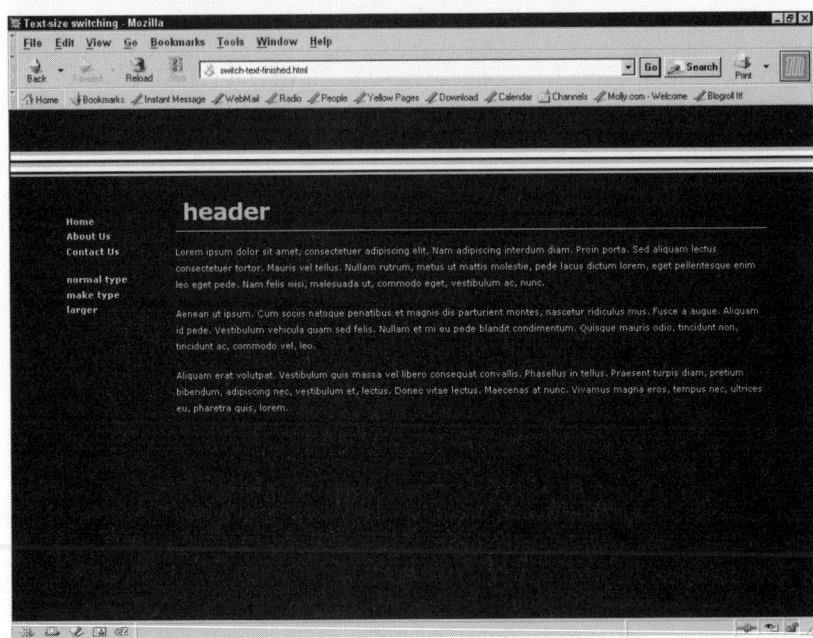

Figure 12-12: Default text size upon visit to the page.

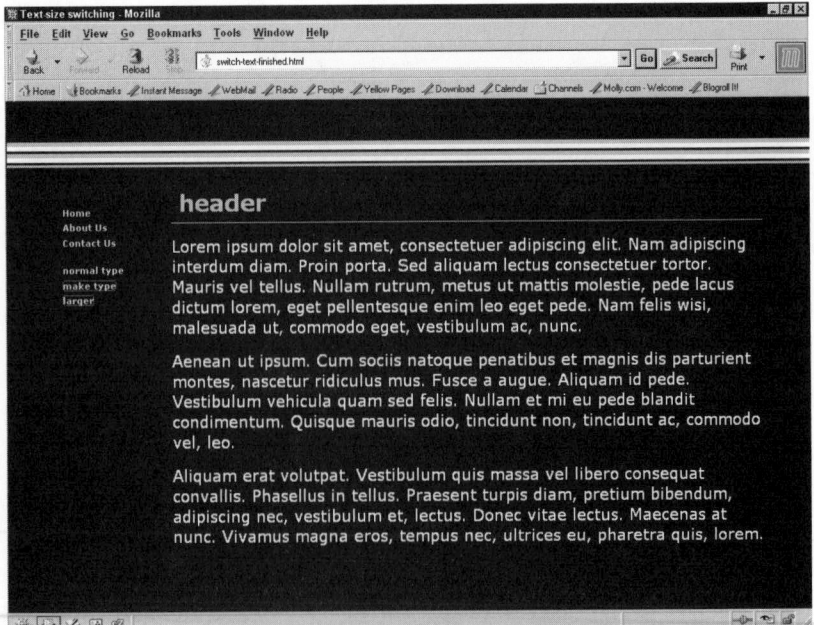

Figure 12-13: Enlarged text size upon switching the style.

Secret #208: Style Sheet Switching for Visual Design

Along with switching text styles, you can use the same technique to switch entire visual designs. This allows your site visitors to customize the way they see your site.

The process for switching styles for entire designs is exactly the same as with text switching. You're tapping into the rel and title attributes, using alternate style sheets and the style switcher JavaScript.

Listing 12-8 shows my XHTML document configured for multiple style sheets. The switching script is exactly the same script used in the preceding secret.

Listing 12-8: XHTML document showing options for changing entire site Style

```
<!DOCTYPE html PUBLIC "-//W3C//DTD XHTML 1.0 Strict//EN"
     "http://www.w3.org/TR/xhtml1/DTD/xhtml1-strict.dtd">
<html xmlns="http://www.w3.org/1999/xhtml">

<head>
<title>Style Switching</title>
<meta http-equiv="Content-Type" content="text/html; charset=iso-
8859-1" />

<link href="css/black-style.css" rel="stylesheet" type="text/css"
media="all" />

<link href="css/black-style.css" rel="alternate stylesheet"
type="text/css" title="black" media="all" />

<link href="css/flower-style.css" rel="alternate stylesheet"
type="text/css" title="flower" media="all" />

<link href="css/pastel-style.css" rel="alternate stylesheet"
type="text/css" title="pastel" media="all" />

<script type="text/javascript"
src="scripts/styleswitcher.js"></script>

</head>

<body>

<div id="content">
<h1>Welcome!</h1>

<p>Lorem ipsum dolor sit amet, consectetuer adipiscing elit. Nam
adipiscing interdum diam. Proin porta. Sed aliquam lectus
consectetuer tortor. Mauris vel tellus. Nullam rutrum, metus ut
mattis molestie, pede lacus dictum lorem, eget pellentesque enim
leo eget pede. Nam felis wisi, malesuada ut, commodo eget,
vestibulum ac, nunc. </p>
```

(continued)

Listing 12-8: *(continued)*

```
</div>

<div id="menu">
  <ul>
    <li id="top"><a href="home.html">Home</a></li>
    <li><a href="aboutus.html">About Us</a></li>
    <li><a href="contactus.html">Contact Us</a></li>
  </ul>

  <ul>
  <li><a href="#" onclick="setActiveStyleSheet('black'); return
false;">black style</a></li>
  <li><a href="#" onclick="setActiveStyleSheet('flower'); return
false;">floral style</a></li>
  <li><a href="#" onclick="setActiveStyleSheet('pastel'); return
false;">pastel style</a></li>
  </ul>
</div>

</body>
</html>
```

You can refer back to Figure 12-12 to see the default style. Figure 12-14 shows the "flower style," and Figure 12-15 shows the "pastel style" after using the style switch links.

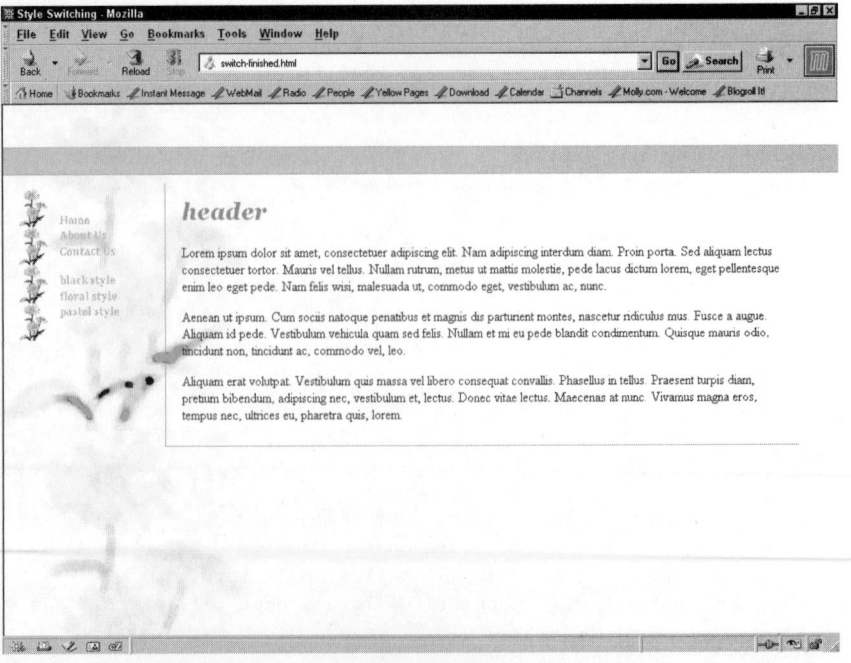

Figure 12-14: Style switch to a flowery look.

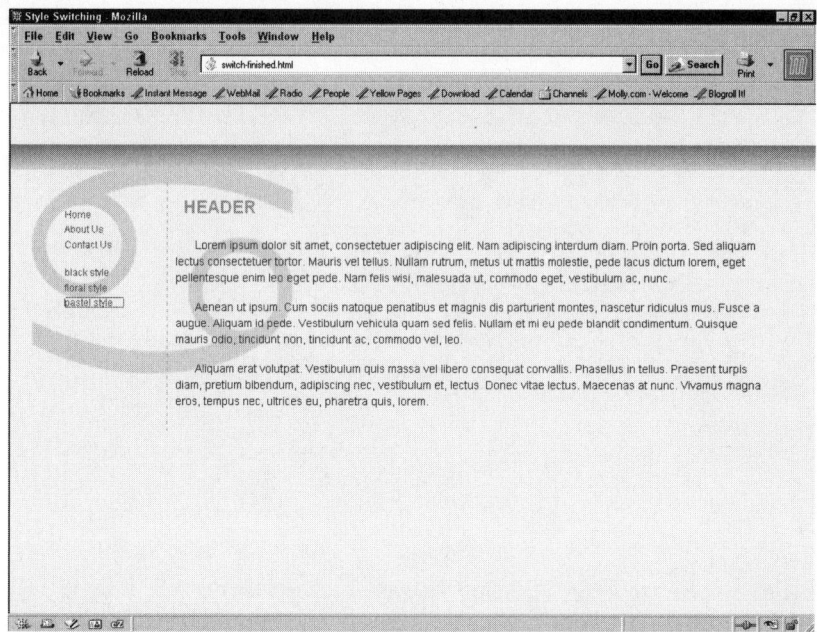

Figure 12-15: Switch again for a different style completely.

> note
>
> There are other means to implement style switching, such as with PHP and other server-side solutions. Server solutions are best when you believe you have a significant audience with JavaScript disabled. To read more about implementing style switching, see "Alternative Style: Working with Alternate Style Sheets" by Paul Sowden (who also authored the switching script used here) at **www.alistapart.com/articles/alternate/**.

Secret #209:   Dynamic Menu Systems

One of the most useful applications of scripting is the ability to create a range of menu systems, including drop-down menus, fly-out menus, and sliding menus.

To show all the types of menus available here would be very difficult, so Listing 12-9 provides one simple example. You'll note that it uses an XHTML Transitional DOCTYPE. This is because the name attribute is in use. Feel free to research a variety of scripts to help you configure dynamic menu systems of your own.

Listing 12-9: JavaScript Drop-down menu navigation

```
<!DOCTYPE html PUBLIC "-//W3C//DTD XHTML 1.0 Transitional//EN"
    "http://www.w3.org/TR/xhtml1/DTD/xhtml1-transitional.dtd">

<html xmlns="http://www.w3.org/1999/xhtml">
<head>
```
(continued)

Listing 12-9: *(continued)*

```html
<title>JavaScript Drop-down Menu</title>
<meta http-equiv="Content-Type" content="text/html; charset=iso-
8859-1" />

<script type="text/javascript">
<!-- Hide the script from non-JS browsers

function goToLink(form)
   {
location.href = form.options[form.selectedIndex].value;
   }
//-->
</script>
</head>

<body>

<div class="center">
<form name="URLmenu" action=''script.cgi''>
<select name="choices">
<option value="http://www.molly.com/">molly.com</option>
<option value="http://www.wiley.com/">Wiley Web Site</option>
<option value="http://www.webstandards.org/">Web Standards
Project</option>
<option value="http://www.webopedia.com/">Webopedia</option>
</select>
<input type="button" value="Go!"
onclick="goToLink(this.form.choices); " />
</form>
</div>

</body>
</html>
```

This script is referred to as a drop-down, pull-down, or "jump" menu. When the user clicks the Go button, he or she will end up at the selected URL. This kind of menu system is very handy for "jumping" from section to section within a site, or as shown here, to other related sites.

Figure 12-16 shows the menu.

> **tip** You can use style sheets to add visual interest to your menu.

Dynamic menu systems can be very handy when you have a particularly large site and want to offer numerous navigation options to site visitors. It is very important, however, to follow some simple guidelines to ensure that the menu systems you implement using JavaScript and DHTML are useful:

♦ For accessibility purposes, be sure that your users can easily navigate the site if JavaScript is unavailable. This means providing accessible options to the menu (see Chapter 10, "Adding Accessibility Features").

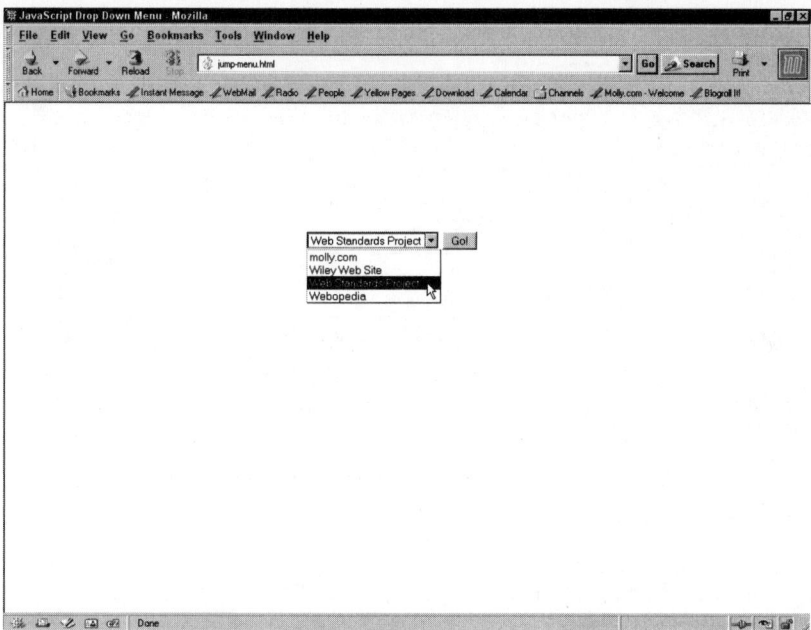

Figure 12-16: Simple JavaScript jump menu.

♦ For both usability and accessibility concerns, be sure that any dynamic menus do not overlap or cover up important content, such as other links or menu options.

♦ Be sure to test your menus aggressively in those browsers that you will be required to support—the lack of consistent DOM support in browsers causes compatibility problems with some scripting.

♦ Use clear and common language for menu options (see Chapter 4, "Creating and Managing Fantastic Content").

Dynamic menu systems can get quite complex (see Figure 12-17) with all kinds of added features, such as fly-outs and mouseover popups with additional information about the link.

---

note
For free dynamic menu scripts, see the Dynamic HTML Lab at www.webreference.com/dhtml/ and at JavaScript.com, www.javascript.com/.

You can see Milonic's product at **www.milonic.com/.**

Secret #210: Forms Validation with JavaScript

Validation of forms is an important step that many Web designers aren't aware of early on. Validation of forms provides several helpful usability features, including making sure the information that the user inputs is correct, and that the user doesn't leave any required information out.

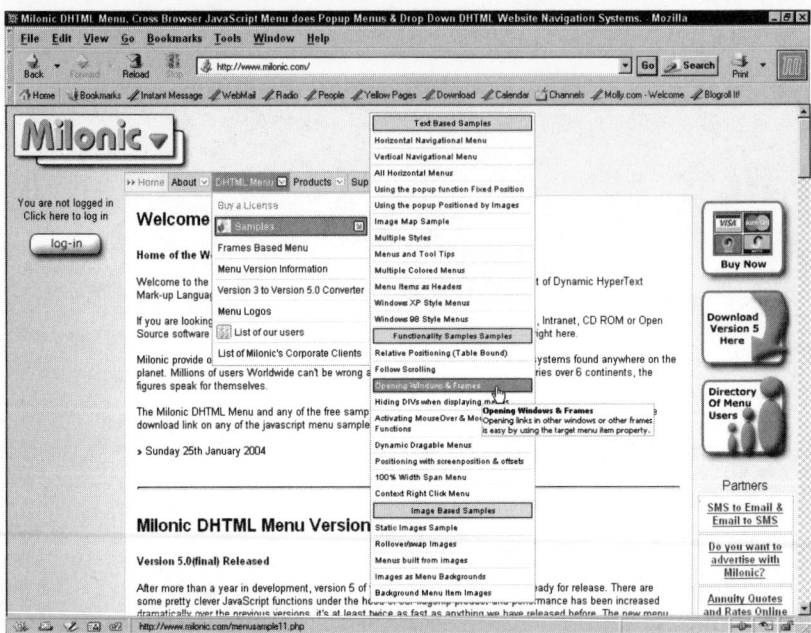

Figure 12-17: Milonic has created a very useful cross-browser menu system.

You can validate forms on the server using PHP, Perl, CGI, ASP.Net—and there are certainly advantages to that, especially because the validation is not dependent upon JavaScript being present or enabled.

However, the primary reason for using JavaScript to validate forms is that it all happens *within the browser*. This means that the feedback to the user is immediate and no trip to the server and back is required.

> **note**
>
> There are many ways to validate aspects of forms using JavaScript, and the code is usually quite detailed. For an excellent tutorial including the necessary script, see "Form Validation Step-by-Step" by Robert Dominy, at
> `http://javascript.about.com/library/weekly/aa070901a.htm`.

Secret #211: The Trouble with applet, object, and embed

If you've been using media on the Web for a while, no doubt you are familiar with the rather awkward history of how we've come to manage media.

First, there's the `applet` element, used to embed Java applets in Web pages:

```
<applet codebase="http://www.molly.com/library/classes"
code="basicApplet.class" width="50" height="100" alt="Basic
Applet"></applet>
```

While it's still acceptable to use the `applet` element in HTML 4.0, 4.01, and XHTML 1.0 Transitional, the element was formally deprecated in HTML 4.0 in favor of the `object` element.

Then Flash began to emerge as the hottest thing on the Web—add to that the desire to embed objects into browsers, and the proprietary `embed` element emerged. Even though the `embed` element doesn't exist in any public DTD, its use on the Web is extremely widespread as a result:

```
<embed src="media/mysong.mp3" width="50" height="100">
```

Not only is `embed` widespread, but despite its nonstandard status, it has terrific browser support.

Enter `object`. The `object` element is a standard, forward-compatible markup element available to you in all contemporary DTDs—and all contemporary Web browsers. Its job is to take care of *any* object that's being attached to an HTML or XHTML document. This includes applets, Flash files, audio files, and video files.

> **note**
>
> The XHTML 2.0 specification (still being developed) is attempting to make the use of **object** ubiquitous, meaning it will be used for all objects including images (bye, bye **img** element). Backward compatible it won't be, but it's certainly sensible for the long-term needs. It's possible that the final version will still include the **img** element for backward compatibility, as it's currently an area of great controversy.

For those browsers not supporting the `object` element, or more importantly, those browsers with bugs or incomplete support, there are very few, if any, real alternatives to present media. The bottom line is that managing media without the proprietary `embed` element has been one of the most hair-pulling, frustrating bits for all of us who are trying to create compliant, cross-browser, cross-platform, backward- and forward-compatible Web documents.

This means you have only a few options when dealing with media:

- ♦ Use `applet` for Java applets with a transitional DTD.
- ♦ Use `embed` and `object` combined. This technique ensures backward compatibility and is the most widely used approach. However, because `embed` is not a valid element, this technique will not be valid, and therefore the document is not standard. Some people don't care, as long as it works. My only thoughts about this is that if you're going to do it, use a transitional DTD, try to keep everything else valid, and add a comment in the document that you've made the choice to use an invalid element. This way, anyone viewing your source code will be able to learn from you.
- ♦ Use `object` alone for all embedded media. This is the standard approach, but it's fraught with compatibility problems.
- ♦ Use a specialty approach (such as the "Flash Satay" method described in the next secret).
- ♦ You can write your own DTD to include the `embed` element. Because XHTML conceptually allows you to do this, it's not as insane as it sounds. IBM, for example, creates their own DTDs (see Chapter 6, "Crafting Pages with HTML" for more on DTDs) to include the `embed` element. Creating your own DTD means that instead of validating against the public DTD, the document can be validated against your

custom DTD. You can add the embed element for backward compatibility and use it on those pages that require the element.

note

Interested in writing your own DTDs? A short tutorial is available at www.vivtek.com/xml/writing_dtd.html.

An excellent test suite for browser behavior for objects can be found at www.student.oulu.fi/%7esairwas/object-test/.

Secret #212:   Adding Flash and Complying with Standards

In an effort to achieve better performance and compliance, Drew McLellan worked on a means of extracting the embed element from the combo-platter use of both object and embed most people using Flash had been employing to achieve backward compatibility.

He started with this sample code:

```
<object
classid="clsid:D27CDB6E-AE6D-11cf-96B8-444553540000"
codebase="http://download.macromedia.com
/pub/shockwave/cabs/flash/swflash.cab#version=6,0,0,0"
width="400" height="300" id="movie" align="">
<param name="movie" value="movie.swf">
<embed src="movie.swf" quality="high" width="400"
height="300" name="movie" align=""
type="application/x-shockwave-flash"
plug inspage="http://www.macromedia.com/go/getflashplayer">
</object>
```

As you can see, both the object and embed elements are in use. McLellan then began to withdraw problematic elements and attributes, and benchmark each modification. One very important piece was to remove the codebase attribute and replace it with the data attribute. He was able to get the code down to this:

```
<object
type="application/x-shockwave-flash" data="movie.swf"
width="400" height="300">
<param name="movie" value="movie.swf" />
</object>
```

This markup now worked in Netscape and Mozilla, and while the Flash movie would play in Internet Explorer (IE) after downloading fully, it wouldn't stream properly. This wasn'tnoticeable for small files at high speeds, but enter a larger file, and it became very noticeable. Therefore, McLellan and designer Jeffrey Zeldman put their heads together and cooked up a solution involving creating a "container" movie in Flash, and loading the movie via ActionScript.

By the time the Satay method is employed, the markup looks like this:

```
<object type="application/x-shockwave-flash"
data=" c.swf?path=movie.swf"
width="400" height="300">
<param name="movie"
```

```
value="c.swf?path=movie.swf" />
</object>
```

You can see the `c.swf?path` code, which is the container movie. With this in place, the file streams in IE, works in numerous browsers, and is completely valid markup.

note

To cook up a Flash Satay, you'll need to add a dash of ActionScript. For the complete recipe, see "Flash Satay: Embedding Flash While Supporting Standards" by Drew McLellan, at **www.alistapart.com/articles/ flashsatay/**.

Another approach is simply to use the `object` element as follows:

```
<object type="application/x-shockwave-flash"
data="media/movie.swf" width="300" height="130">
<param name="movie" value="media/movie.swf" />
</object>
```

This works well in some contemporary browser, but is not supported well by those browsers with partial or no implementation of the `object` element.

Secret #213:   Adding Audio

You can place and access most Web-based audio files in a couple of standardized ways: by using the `anchor` element or the `object` element to embed media.

Using the `anchor` element is the same as placing any link within an XHTML document:

```
<a href="media/rocksong.mp3" title="audio version of my new
rocksong">New tune available today</a>!
```

If you use this method, your users will either save the file to their desktops, launch a plug-in application, or load a new browser page, depending on which browser they're using and how they have set their preferences.

If you want the audio control interface to be embedded with the rest of the content, ideally you will choose to embed the clip in the page by using the `object` element:

```
<object data="media/rocksong.mp3" type="audio/mp3" width="200"
height="200">Warning: Your browser can't embed the
object.</object>
```

Take notice of these items:

+ I'm using the data attribute described in the Flash Satay method rather than the `codebase` attribute.
+ The text in between the opening and closing `object` tags will only render if the requested object doesn't display.
+ I've included the `width` and `height` attributes. These are required for most browsers if you're using the `object` element.
+ I've included the MIME type attribute with a value of `audio/mp3`.

You can also combine the `object` and `a` elements so that if, for some reason, an individual's browser doesn't render the media inline, you can include a link to the media instead:

```
<object data="media/damien-rice-volcano.mp3" type="audio/mp3">
</object>
<a href="media/damien-rice-volcano.mp3" title="download audio
file">If file does not display please follow this link</a>
```

Figure 12-18 shows audio playing in the IE browser.

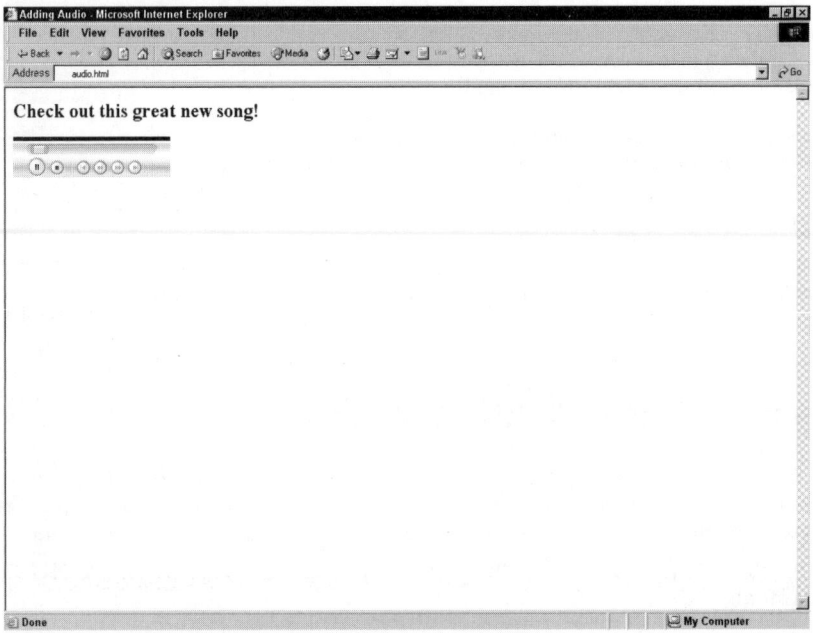

Figure 12-18: Playing an embedded media file in IE.

---

tip	Numerous other workarounds might be of assistance to you in trying to manage cross-browser compatibility for audio, video, and other plug-in technologies. See "Using the Right Markup to Invoke Plugins" by Arun K. Raganathan, at `http://devedge.netscape.com/viewsource/2002/markup-and-plugins/`. You may also wish to take a look at the "Standards Compliant Method to Add MP3s to Pages" which offers four potential solutions, at `http://realdev1.realise.com/rossa/rendertest/mp3.html`.

Secret #214: Adding Video

You can add video in several ways as well, but the same frustrations exist in terms of browser bugs and implementation of the `object` element.

Of course, you can always just link directly to your video, as in the following example:

```
<a href="media/heyyacb.mov" title="hey ya charlie brown">View the
Hey Ya Charlie Brown Movie</a>
```

Adding video via the `object` element can be done as you set up your audio in the last step. The difference is going to be in the file name and MIME type, and the support concerns.

You must make sure you include the proper file name and file type:

```
<object data="media/heyyacb.mov" type="video/quicktime"
width="200" height="200">
<param name="autoplay" value="true" />
<a href="media/heyyacb.mov">Heya Charlie Brown!</a>
</object>
```

This is a standards-based approach and will work in some browsers, but it will *not* work in IE, which is a big problem. Fortunately, some workarounds are available.

> **tip**
>
> To learn an approach that nests object elements to achieve better support, read "Standards Compliant method to add QuickTime movies to pages," which covers other forms of video as well, at **http://realdev1.realise .com/rossa/rendertest/quicktime.html**.

Figure 12-19 shows an embedded video in Mozilla using the standardized approach.

Figure 12-19: An embedded video in Mozilla.

Secret #215: About Digital Storytelling

It's time to switch out of the heavy issues and into something a little more creative. Digital Storytelling is a movement that began in the early 1990s with the late Dana Atchley and several other co-founders. The idea was to use digital art forms to tell stories from life. The point was to go deeper into a story than just the verbal— using digital imagery, audio, video, and other multimedia to express the story in a multifaceted, highly personal, and very creative way.

Interestingly, as the Web emerged, many digital artists interested in storytelling came to the Web. Like-minded groups of Web designers and artists using the Web as a means of expression came together at such gatherings as South by Southwest Interactive, various digital storytelling festivals, and events related to other conferences and gatherings—even Burning Man, an extremely popular artist and artisan gathering held each year in the Nevada desert.

Before long, a philosophy emerged that has resulted in rich opportunities to apply the concepts within digital storytelling to both personal and professional Web design applications. The most overt application of these ideologies is the Weblog itself, which is often a very obvious form of digital storytelling, using images and media as well as words to convey the process of a life (see Figure 12-20).

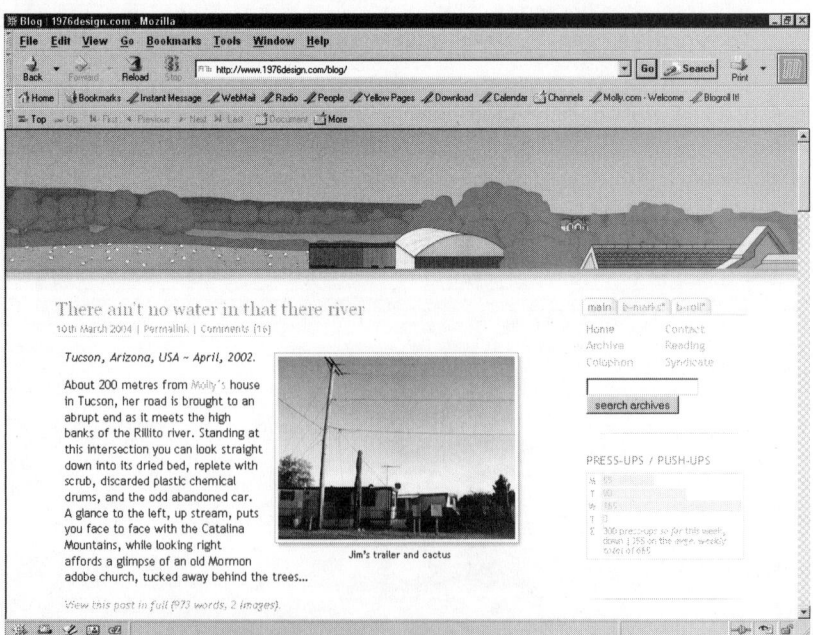

Figure 12-20: Weblogs are a form of digital storytelling.

But digital storytelling can come into play to make professional sites more engaging, interesting, and compelling content. By tapping into dynamic technologies and rich media applications, great stories can be told on what might typically be a dry and boring Web site.

Every corporation, organization, industry, government, or education institution has interesting historical, political, and social issues associated with it. A way that digital storytelling can spice up a site would be to use multimedia and storytelling as a means of telling the corporate history.

Just think of the fascinating stories that could be described about Ford Motor Company, Coca Cola, or the American Civil Liberties Union.

One case study describes how the Kansas City Symphony put together a program for local schools to understand the issues surrounding war. By reading stories enhanced with music and images via a Web site, students are able to become very engaged in the history and emotion of war, leaving a far more lasting impression than just having read pieces of history in plain text.

By adding digital storytelling of this nature to a site, it becomes a destination of interest, a means to educate and inform, and ultimately a means whereby you can establish trust, understanding, and camaraderie with your audience members.

note   For more information, history, methodology, and a sampling of case studies, see the Center for Digital Storytelling Web site, at `www.storycenter.org/`.

Summary

From adding a day and date welcome to including a story via multimedia, you can make any Web site spicier using a range of solutions both old and new. By following a few simple changes in terms of approach, you can widen your horizons—and the enjoyment of your site's visitors—by making your scripts and media accessible, usable, fun, and practical.

The next chapter, "Keeping Sites Fresh and Engaging," shows you how to keep people engaged and involved in your Web site, creating a loyal, lasting, and always interesting relationship between you and your audience.no

Keeping Sites Fresh and Engaging

Chapter
13

◆ ◆

Secrets in This Chapter

◆ ◆

There's nothing like a static Web site to disappoint a site visitor. How do you keep visitors coming back to your site, staying at your site longer, and spreading the word about how effective your site is?

There are simple ways to achieve this, and while many Web designers already tap into many of these approaches, there's a lack of consistency in how they do it. This chapter offers clear, straightforward approaches to keeping sites lively.

Secret #216:   Use Personalization

I rarely use the United States Post Office anymore. Instead, I prefer to pay a little extra for mail and shipping services and go to a privately owned shop such as Mailboxes, Etc. and others of its kind. Why pay more? Well, snail mail and shipping remain an important part of my work, and I want more personal service than the crowds and confusion U.S. post offices usually provide.

When I walk into my mail shop now, I'm greeted personally by the owner or one of her employees. They all know me by first name, and I receive a much more personalized and quality service as a result of this smaller environment.

Like the U.S. post office, many web sites can appear cold, crowded, and confusing. Upon arriving at the site, you may wonder, "What am I doing here?" This is especially true if the site offers products or services that could easily be available elsewhere.

Personalization has become a cornerstone of making sites fresh and engaging. Especially appropriate for any kind of portal or community web site, being able to greet users personally and provide personalized services has become all the rage. If you question that, just think about the services being made available at shops such as Amazon: Favorites lists, personal recommendations, one-click shopping, and (my personal personalization favorite) wish lists. All of these features customize the site to my needs, which makes using the site very easy, fast, and interesting.

> note A report from Jupiter Communications (http://www
> .jupitercommunications.com/) in 2001 shows that personalized sites
> can see annual revenue increases of up to 52 percent.

You can add personalization using several different approaches. Personalization on the scale of Amazon can cost millions of dollars to implement, so obviously adding complex personalization features is no easy choice.

For those with deep pockets and good rationale for adding complex personalization, you can either purchase out-of-the-box solutions or hire programmers to custom-design your own solutions.

For those sites with a more moderate budget, open source software can provide more affordable solutions.

Finally, for small sites, adding some simple personalization features such as a personalized greeting as a user enters the site can be very inexpensive to implement yet provide a bit of warmth for your visitors (see Figure 13-1).

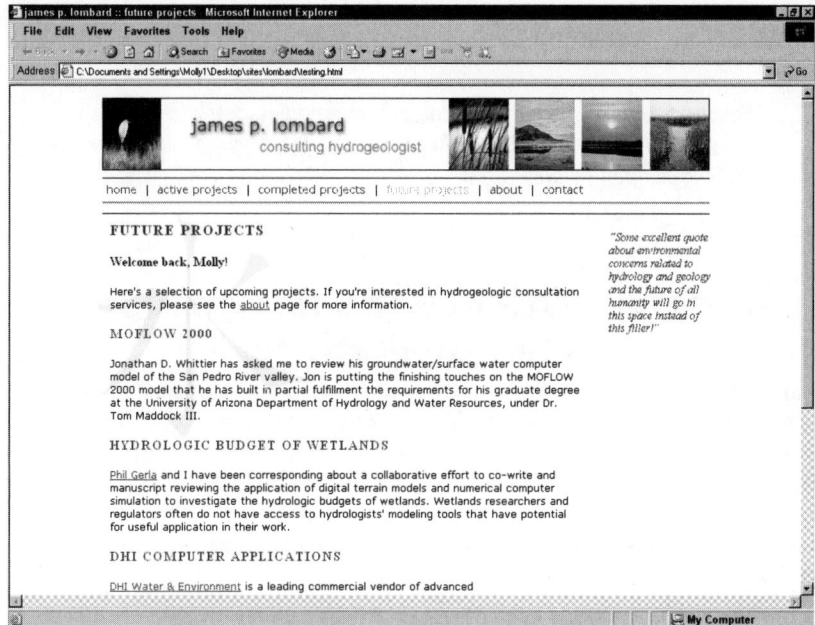

Figure 13-1: Even a simple, personal welcome can add warmth to your site.

A number of scenarios could conceivably benefit from the implementation of a complete, high-end or custom-developed personalization system, as follows:

+ Your web site offers recommended items, and those items are stored in a database.
+ You need to clearly demonstrate return on investment (ROI) for the site. Personalization products can assist with high-level tracking of customer behavior, so ROI can be tracked more efficiently.
+ Your site offers a large number of products (500 or more).
+ Your site is an e-commerce site.
+ Your site offers customer support.
+ You are running a portal site.
+ You are running an auction site.

> **note**
>
> Personalization technology at this level definitely raises concerns about consumer safety, identity, privacy, and security. The Personalization Consortium is an international advocacy group promoting the advancement of personalization technologies but with a strong emphasis placed on ethical practices and responsibility. Visit the Personalization Consortium at http://www.personalization.org/.

Technologies used in personalization run the gamut. You can choose from full-on server packages with included personalization features from such heady providers as IBM, Oracle, BEA Systems, Broadvision, and Vignette.

In the mid-range, Java and open source languages and products are emerging to contend with the high-end.

Finally, on the low end, simple applications using PHP, Perl, and even JavaScript can provide you the ability to greet visitors and make them feel more welcome.

> **note**   For more information on application technologies, databases, and programming languages, see Appendix B, "Overview of Application and Database Technologies."

Secret #217:   Offer Useful Information and Applications

Along with regularly updated, quality content, you should consider adding appropriate information to your site that will be of use to your visitors. Table 13-1 provides a list of some site scenarios and the types of information you might wish to provide to make your site more engaging and useful to your visitors.

Table 13-1: Types of Information You Can Add to Make a Site More Useful

Site Type	Useful Information and Applications Ideas	Specific Site Examples
Real Estate Agency	Local time and weather, neighborhood tracker application, mortgage calculator.	A site with numerous features to enhance home buying can be found at http://www .realtor.com/.
Auto	Customize your car feature, payment calculator, feature comparisons between cars of a similar class, online car-care tracker.	For an example of a customization application on an auto site, see the "Build Your Own" feature on Mercedes Benz USA's web site, at http://www .mbusa.com/brand/index.jsp
Financial	Stock feeds, up-to-the-day interest rate feature, broker tracking, bill-pay features.	A great example of a financial site offering numerous applications and tools for its site visitors is the Motley Fool, found at http://www .fool.com/.
Health-and-Beauty	Self-help quizzes, randomized health and beauty tips.	Emode (now known as "Tickle") is a popular health, beauty, and community-related site with many rich and engaging features for site visitors. Find it at http://web .tickle.com/.
Inspirational/ Religious	Quote of the day feature, religious history quiz.	Beliefnet is a widely used religious and inspirational web site with incredibly useful information and applications for those seeking to learn more about world religions and spirituality. Find it at http://www.beliefnet.com/.

Site Type	Useful Information and Applications Ideas	Specific Site Examples
Portal	Portals benefit from a wide range of information and applications, including everything listed here for other site types, news headlines, horoscopes, this-day-in-history features, and so on.	For an excellent portal example, see Excite, at http://www.excite.com/, which not only offers a lot of great information and useful, fun applications, but also allows you to customize exactly what you see on your home portal page.
Children's	Games for fun, interactive educational presentations, word-a-day for vocabulary building.	KidSites, at http://www .kidsites.com/, is a colorful, upbeat portal site with approved content for kids. Lots of ideas for value-added, helpful offerings can be found here.

Figure 13-2 shows an updated weather feature on a Real Estate agent's web site. This feature adds not only warmth, but demonstrates to visitors that the content is being kept up-to-date and customized for them, ultimately creating a better relationship between the site and the visitor.

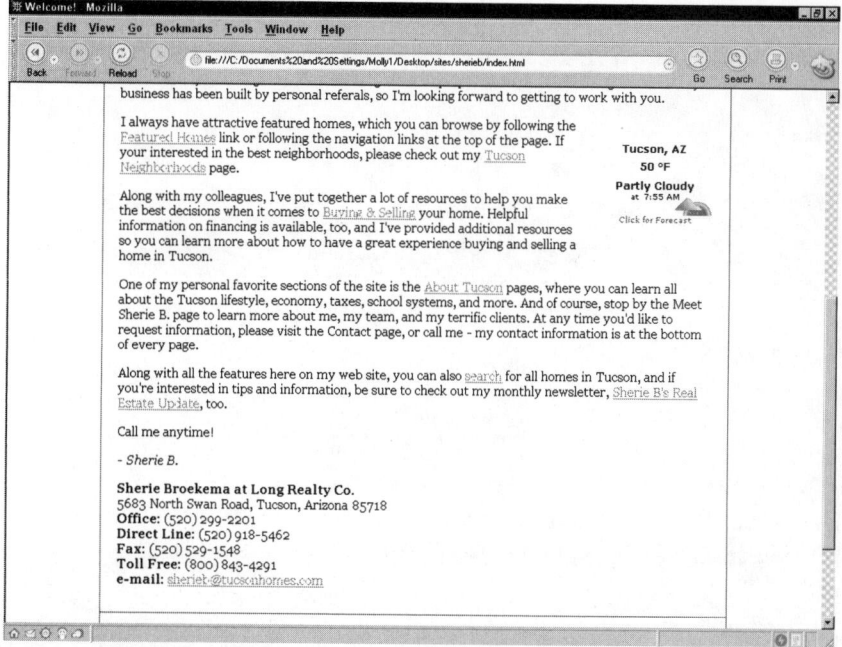

Figure 13-2: Updated local weather information makes this site more visitor-friendly.

Secret #218: Provide Random or Frequently Changed Features

Being able to randomize links and images on the web is something we've been able to do for a long time. Web enthusiasts and designers will remember one of the first major implementations of randomization—Yahoo!'s random link feature.

Later, Google emerged with its impossibly simple interface and an "I'm Feeling Lucky" button. This feature thrills many users because you simply never know what you're going to end up with.

Adding randomization can be very simple. Common approaches to creating random items on a page include the following:

◆ Using a proprietary application and scripting such as .NET
◆ Using PHP randomization scripts
◆ Using Perl scripts
◆ Using JavaScript

---

cross ref

Refer to Appendix B for more information on where to find resources for .NET, PHP, and Perl. For more information on JavaScript, see Chapter 12, "Spicing it Up with Dynamic Content and Rich Media."

You can randomize different types of content, too. Consider the following:

◆ Different graphic image each time the page loads

Figure 13-3: A visit to Dunstan's site shows it being daytime and sunny.

- ◆ Randomized favorite quote
- ◆ The ever-popular random link

A fantastic example of a frequently changed feature can be found on Dunstan Orchard's weblog. He has taken a number of images that reflect the local time and weather conditions on the farm where he lives in Dorset, England. Using PHP and other technologies, each time a visitor goes to the page, the image reflecting current time and temperature conditions is displayed. Figures 13-3 and 13-4 show the effect.

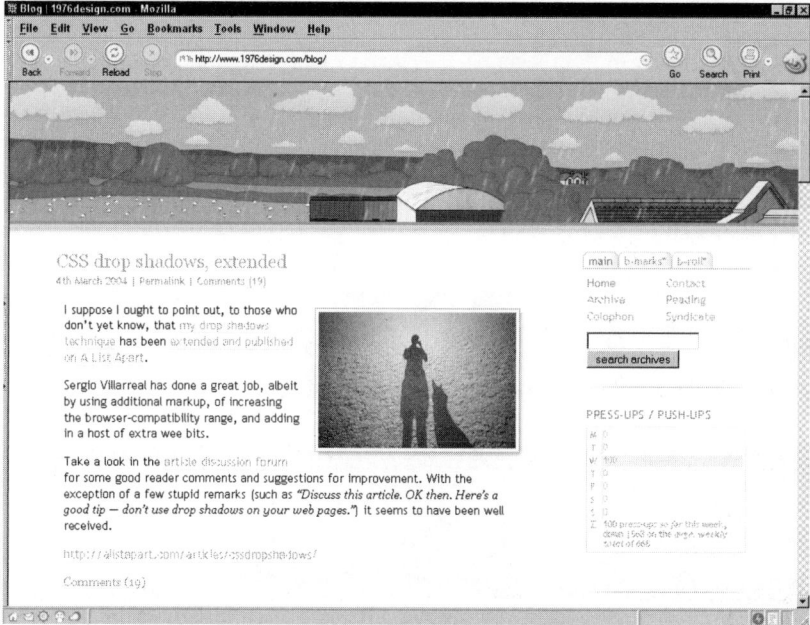

Figure 13-4: A subsequent visit shows rain showers.

Secret #219:   Add a Weblog

Weblogs (also referred to as "blogs") often offer so many rich features that adding them to a site—whether personal (see Figure 13-5) or related to career, profession, or campaigns, (refer to Figure 13-6) is usually a very good idea for a number of reasons.

You might wish to add a weblog for the following reasons:

- ◆ Keeping a weblog for regular news and updates keeps your site active and your content brand new. With the proliferation of weblogs on the web, site visitors are coming to expect these features, and it puts a contemporary face on your work.
- ◆ Blogging software offers a number of site features including commenting systems (discussed later in this chapter), specialty linking features, and calendars that can be used effectively to bring current information to your users.

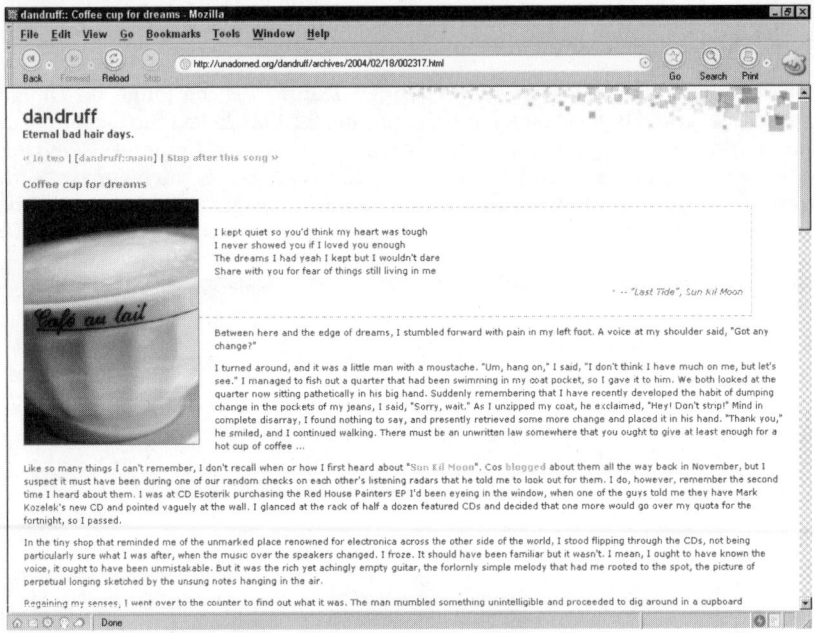

Figure 13-5: Personal weblogs keep sites engaging.

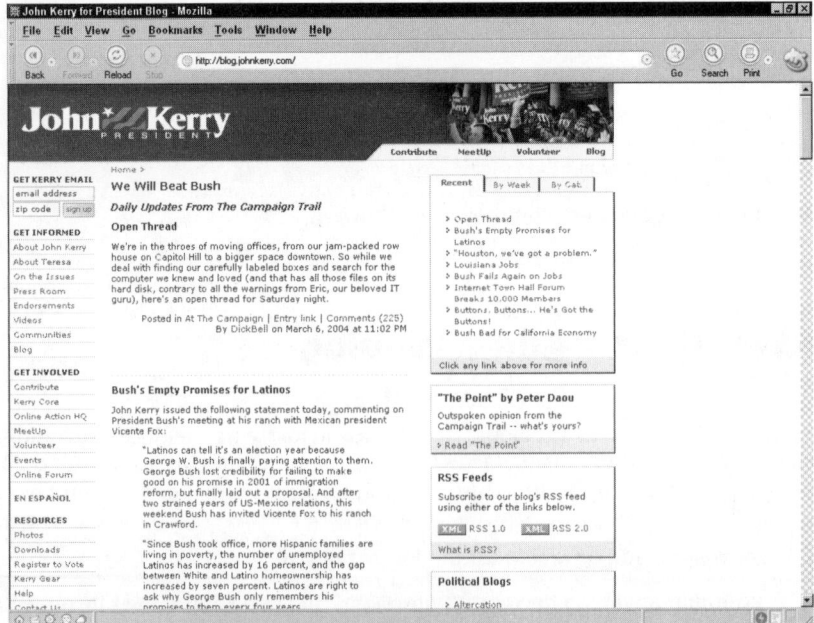

Figure 13-6: John Kerry's weblog offers news, a comment system, and other features.

> ◆ Automatic and multiple-option archiving within most pro weblogging
> software effectively expands the content on your site by keeping your
> entries, articles, and comments according to your preferences, and in
> more ways than one. For example, you can archive by day, week, month,
> category, custom archive type, or any combination thereof.

◆ Automatic aggregation (discussed later in this chapter) in pro weblogging software allows you to distribute your content to newsreaders using contemporary aggregation technology. This brings your message to those people who want it—which not only keeps people up-to-date with your site, but also allows you to reach new visitors via weblog portals and related networks.

> **note** If you're never going to have the resources to keep it updated, don't include a weblog. If you aren't sure, don't make it a primary feature. Keeping up-to-date news and related content on a weblog takes time and resources. There's nothing like getting to a site that looks great only to find that the last weblog entry was six months ago.

Professional quality weblogging software can be used to achieve many of these features. It's important to realize that some of the hobby-related software available, such as Blogger, may be suitable for simple needs but does not typically provide the advanced features in the professional software now available.

> **note** Movable Type (http://www.movabletype.org/) is my personal favorite professional-level blogging software. I've used it on personal as well as professional weblogs.
>
> Another very good choice is Greymatter, a completely free, open-source blogging system by Noah Grey. Find it at http://www.noahgrey.com/greysoft/.
>
> An upcoming contender is WordPress (http://www.wordpress.org/), which offers a lot of features and easy installation, as well as more robust support for social software.
>
> Take a look at additional weblogging software on Yahoo!, at http://dir.yahoo.com/Computers_and_Internet/Internet/World_Wide_Web/Weblogs/Software/.

Secret #220:   Consider Weblog Commenting Systems

No matter which blogging system you choose to use, a commenting system is something you can consider adding. In all professional systems, comment systems allow site visitors to respond directly to your weblog entries.

There are, of course, some significant pros and cons to weigh prior to making the choice whether to comment or not.

On the upside, comment systems can assist you to keep site content fresh in the following ways:

◆ Allowing others to post comments. This boosts the amount of site content available to your visitors.

◆ Comment posting can spawn discussions, increasing the content even more and potentially making it very engaging and interactive (see Figure 13-7).

◆ Comments offer a unique means of personal feedback for site visitors, far warmer than a contact form or e-mail link.

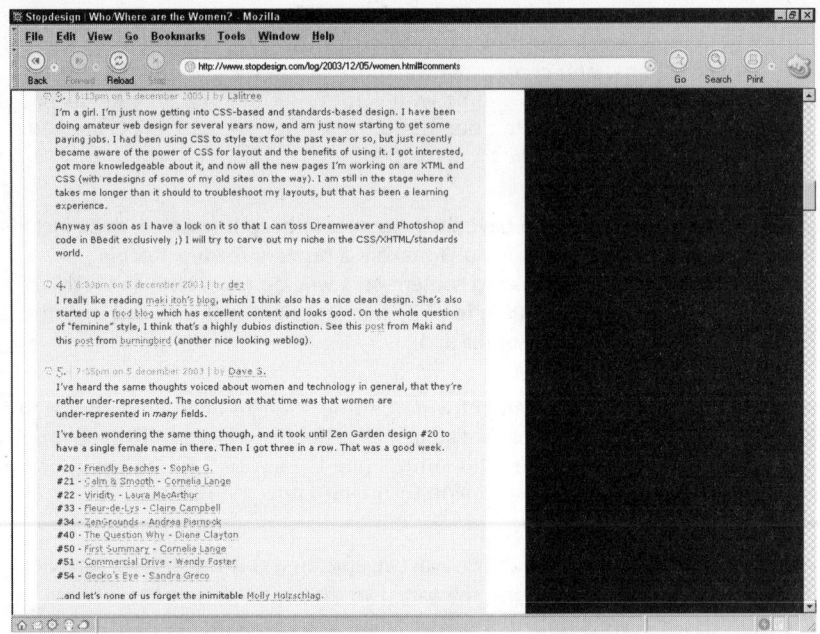

Figure 13-7: Comments in response to designer Doug Bowman's post about women in web design created great discourse as well as long-lasting, important content.

There are some significant downsides to comment systems. Be sure to consider the following:

♦ Comment systems can be abused by angry customers or people who just want a soapbox, so in professional situations they must be monitored. This means human resources, which translates to financial cost.

♦ Comment systems can generate more content and use more bandwidth and space than you might wish to manage. Even though your publishing software will handle archiving of your comments, if you have a lot of feedback, you may want to restrict or eliminate comments altogether to avoid overhead.

♦ Comment systems are highly vulnerable to spam (refer to Figure 13-8). This recent, disturbing trend involves companies sending URLs to your comments. As you can imagine, this can be not only a maintenance concern but embarrassing to boot. Fortunately, there are a growing number of ways in which to reduce or eliminate comment spam from your comment system. Still, the problem is a serious one and requires careful consideration.

Secret #221: Offer Site Registration

Offer site visitors the opportunity to register at the site under a unique name and password. This is used a great deal for e-commerce sites where registrants can access private and secure information and receive updates and promotions directly.

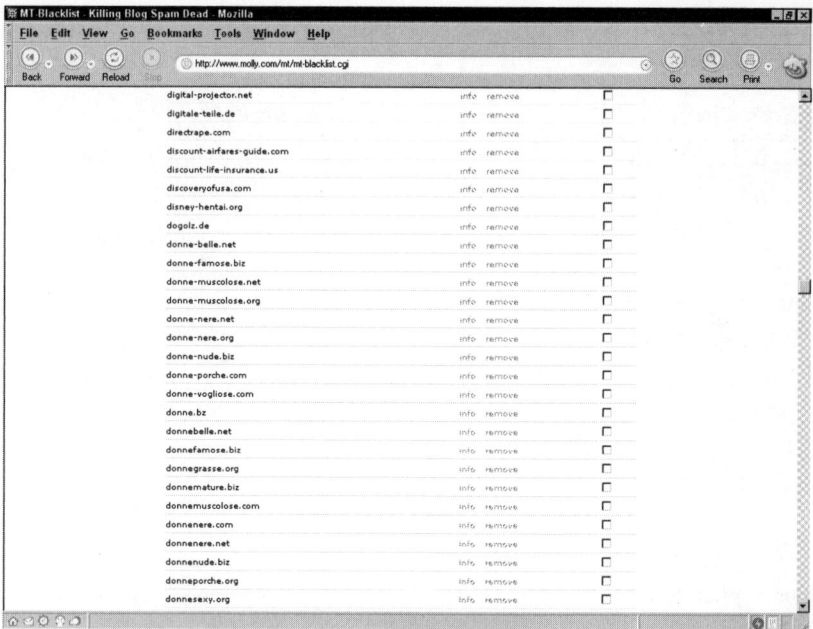

Figure 13-8: Comment spam is an unfortunate problem. Here, you see a portion of known comment spammers from my Movable Type blacklist, which currently contains 853 entries.

However, site registration isn't just for e-commerce and may be of benefit in your situation.

Benefits include the following:

- ◆ You can more readily track the behavior of registered site users—where they go, what they buy, which newsletters they opt for, and so on. This is invaluable demographic information that can be put to market research use to improve your site's bottom line.

- ◆ You can make it easier to customize features for your visitors, offering them personalized services once they are registered, such as credit card and personal information management, purchase or service tracking, and a range of personalized services.

- ◆ Some companies increase profit by reselling their registered user lists to e-mail and direct mail marketers. While this is a practice that is often frowned upon, the ethical question can be avoided by clearly offering registrants the ability to choose whether they go on the list or not.

Along with e-commerce sites, there are other scenarios where registration can be effective or even necessary. Table 13-2 provides some insight.

note   Many people do not want their privacy invaded in any way, which is completely understandable and should be respected. This is why offering the option to register on most sites is considered the ethical thing to do. Consider if registration can benefit your site, and if you see that it cannot, or the risk of turning off your particular audience is high, don't offer site registration.

Table 13-2: Different Site Types and Potential Benefits of Offering Registration

Site Scenario	Benefits of Registration
Political party registration	The ability to register online with your political party can allow you to access to news, features, private planning and discussion forums, and, eventually, you might even be able to vote via the safety and comfort of your own home.
Intranets for government and industry	An intranet might require access from workers in the field. This allows private, protected communication for intranet users, especially if the intranet is framed within a public web site. Through registration, authorized users can have access to the site features that others cannot.
Dating web site	Typically, these sites offer some level of privacy and anonymity to their users, but with known registrants a company can provide additional, more accurately targeted resources and services.
Product support forum	Forums tend to be potential problem areas due to angry customers and poor online etiquette. Registration can help you filter out those individuals looking for a quicker fix, and provide better response to those users who have legitimate product support needs.
Online software registration	By registering purchased software via vendor web sites, better service can be provided for the customer. You can track purchases, ship dates, downloads and offer opt-in newsletters or updates at the registrant's discretion.

Another concern is poorly designed registration and login interfaces. Janice Fraser at AdaptivePath has designed an excellent for-pay report, including templates and samples to address this issue successfully. Find this report at http://www.adaptivepath.com/publications/reports/registration/.

Secret #222:   Consider Cookies to Track Usage

A simpler way to track user behavior on your site is to use a cookie. Cookies are generated in a number of ways but are stored *on the user's* machine. They are saved by the browser and sent back to the server when the site visitor returns.

Tracking your visitors means you can keep your site fresh and engaging by focusing on the specific documents they are requesting, what they are doing on your site, and how they are doing it. You can then target your newest content and information very specifically.

Cookies can be used for a number of beneficial purposes along with tracking, including the following:

- Keep login information recorded on the user's local machine for future automatic login.
- Record any preferences the site user might have set, such as choosing a text size or color for the site if they are being offered.
- Restrict access on one-time events such as polls or contests.
- Add a personal message.
- Track purchases within a shopping cart.

Cookies are controversial because they track personal information, but while there's a dark side to them, they can be extraordinarily useful. What's more, you can set it up so the user is aware that a cookie is being offered, and they can choose to not use it, giving them more control over their level of participation on your site.

> **note** Cookies are built using a number of technologies, including JavaScript. For a comprehensive look at cookies, the controversy and concerns about them, a commonly used JavaScript cookie resource, and additional links can be found at Cookie Central, http://**www.cookiecentral.com/**.

Secret #223:   The Power of Polls

Some months ago I added a poll to my web site, and I was blown away by the increase in activity to the site as well as the number of people who were taking the poll in comparison to doing other activities on the site.

I suppose I shouldn't have been so surprised because polls are hugely popular all around the web. Entire sites are dedicated to building and displaying polls, and numerous freeware, shareware, and low-cost technologies are available to implement them on your site.

> **note** Quizilla is a web site that allows registered members to create quizzes and polls of their own as well as take them. Visit Quizilla at **http://quizilla.com/**.

Typically, you'll want your polls to be relevant to the nature of the site. If you're building a financial site, for example, you might create polls that focus on the way users might be saving (or not saving) money, investment habits, and concerns about financial news. Polls can also help you create a better relationship with your users by asking them direct questions about what they'd like to see on the web site or which features they like or dislike.

Why people are so fascinated with polls is a bit of a mystery, but it may have something to do with the ability to interact anonymously with a site and still see where you fit into the greater picture. What's more, voting in a poll only takes a few clicks at most, whereas comments must be composed.

I compared comments on my site to a poll on the same subject, and the poll had been answered a total of 124 times (see Figure 13-9), whereas only 20 comments were entered (see Figure 13-10).

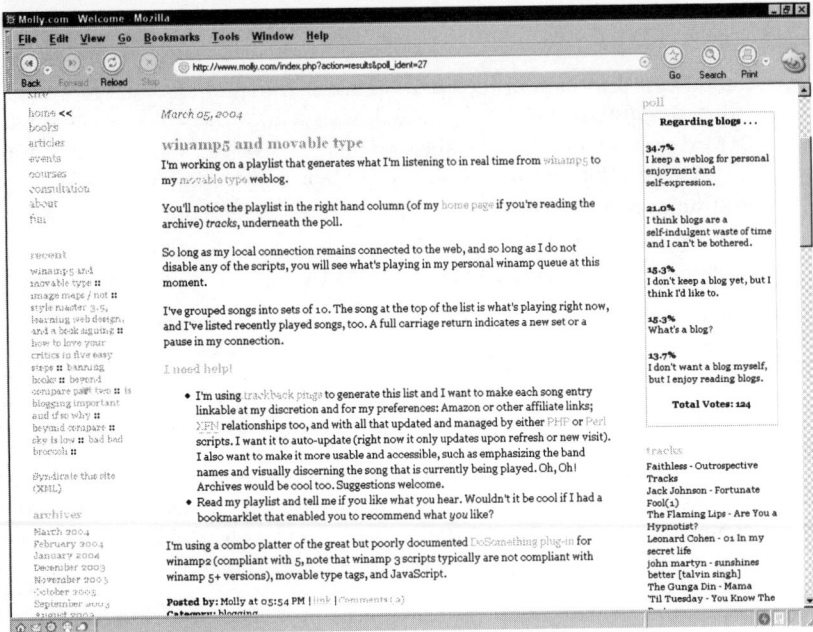

Figure 13-9: Polls seem to be a popular interactive addition to a site. This poll on blogging has 124 responses.

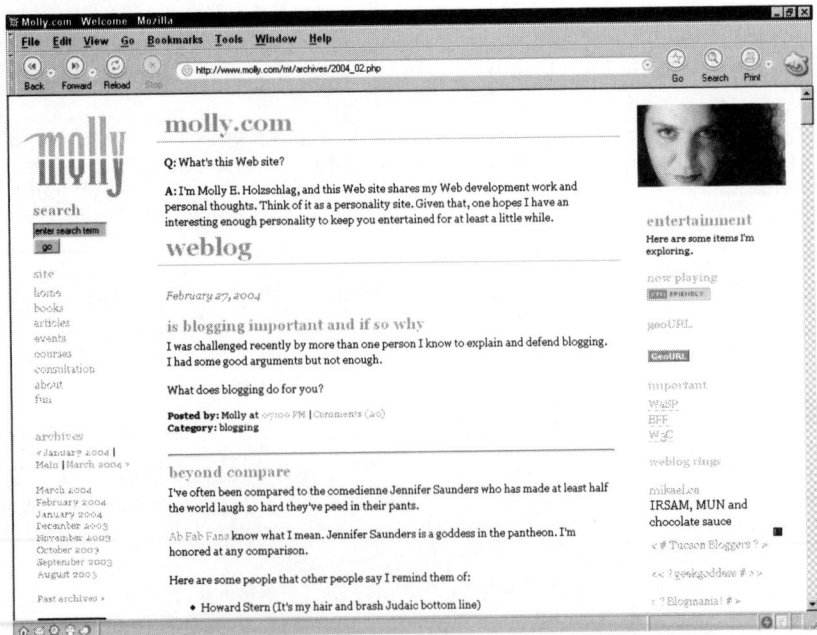

Figure 13-10: Comments tend to be less anonymous and require more interaction. The corresponding post on blogging has 20 comments, almost 1/6 of the participation of the poll.

The style and frequency of your polls are important considerations. Here are some tips to help you write great polls:

- Be sure your question is written in a clear way.
- Avoid double negatives in your poll answer; this can confuse readers.
- Avoid using incomplete sentences.
- Avoid jargon and local sayings if you have a widespread, international, multilingual audience.
- Answer choices should be approximately the same length.
- Have at least 3 answers and at most 7. A happy medium is 5.

note   For an excellent tutorial on polls, see "Creating Online Polls" by Joseph Gannon, at http://www-106.ibm.com/developerworks/usability/library/us-polls/.

Secret #224:   Add Discussion Groups

Another great way to provide helpful services for your site visitors as well as keep your site actively generating new content is to have discussion groups, also referred to as *forums*.

As with commenting, forums can attract the folks you don't want as much as the ones you do. So before even considering forums for your site, assess whether you have the human resources available to manage and moderate.

Table 13-3 describes some situations where forums can be very useful.

Adding a forum to your site can be technically quite easy, as many solutions for forums exist, spanning the range of technologies and pricing.

Open source solutions, such as those built with PHP or Perl, are often free or very low cost. Numerous ASP.NET scripts and services are available for free or low cost, too (see Figure 13-11).

Some service providers also offer forum software already installed and ready to go, there are pre-packaged software products for forums, and you can custom-build forums for your specific needs using a range of application languages including PHP, Perl, .NET, and Java.

note   An excellent, independent listing of forum software and services is available at http://www.thinkofit.com/webconf/forumsoft.htm. The site also contains related tutorials, articles, and product reviews.

Secret #225:   Use Web-based Chat

As with discussion forums, chat can be used to extend a hand to your community and create a longer lasting relationship with them as a result. The scenarios where you might wish to use chat are very similar to those where you'd have a discussion

Table 13-3: Site Types that Can Benefit from Discussion forums

Site Type	Forum Use
Gaming site	Users share game strategies and game "cracks" to help them solve specific issues in their playing, and find other gamers to challenge. Gaming forums are some of the most actively used on the web.
Software development company site	Support forums can be an excellent means of getting fast, helpful support for technical and other problems related to software. These forums can be public, allowing anyone to post their problems and responses in a communal fashion, or they can be restricted. Restricted forums would be for posting technical problems and awaiting a designated moderator's answer. Some companies use both options at the same time, largely because community support tends to be faster and sometimes even more reliable.
Health support group site	Community forums that allow people to share their health-related challenges can be an extremely helpful and humanitarian offering, allowing people who might otherwise be unable to attend live support groups to find information and get help. The American Cancer Society and Alcoholics Anonymous are two organization examples that offer support forums to extend their message and to provide a real service via the forum support.
Job search site	Forums on a job search site can be helpful for jobseekers to exchange strategies, successes, and experiences with various companies.
Special interest web sites	There are thousands of special interest groups. There are coin collectors, art collectors, and wine collectors. There are senior knitters, male knitters, and even gay knitting groups. If you can think of an interest, certainly there are interesting people pursuing that interest online. A wine site can offer forums for its visitors to discuss wines, and a site specializing in excellent quality and choice wool and supplies could benefit from a forum on their site, helping develop brand loyalty as well as community strength.

forum: for feedback, customer service support, special interests, and support group meetings (see Figure 13-12).

note

A resurgence of interest in Internet Relay Chat (IRC) is occurring. IRC is an extremely useful, multiplatform Internet protocol that has been around longer than the web. Depending upon the software you use to access it, it can be extremely easy to use and is completely free. For more information on IRC including FAQs, beginner's guides, operator guides, and links to useful software, go to http://www.irchelp.org/.

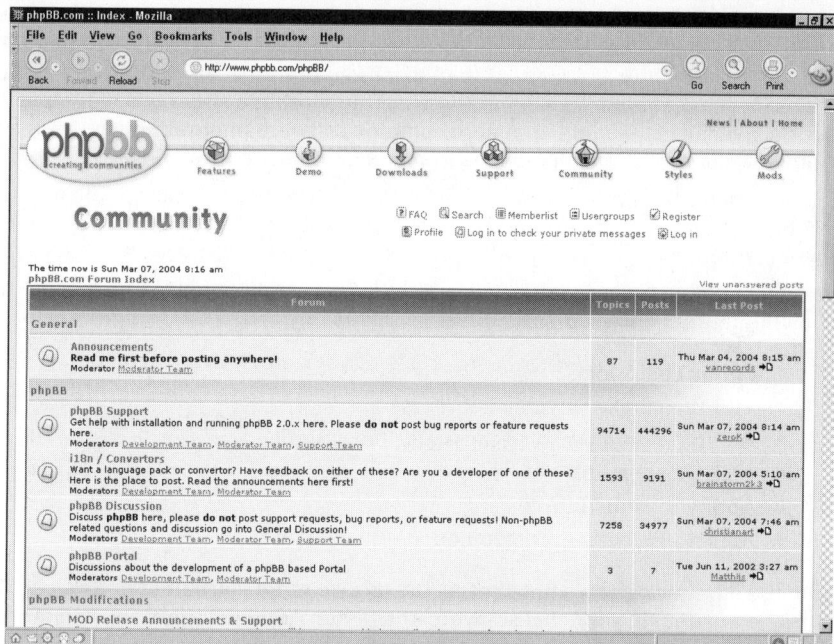

Figure 13-11: Using PHPBB, a popular and inexpensive means to add forums.

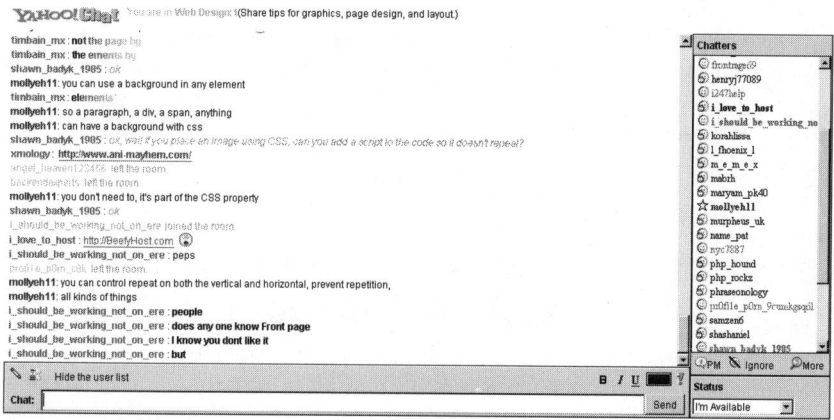

Figure 13-12: Using web-based chat.

Another area where chat is coming into play is via Peer to Peer (P2P) and related technologies. You'll be most familiar with this via your Instant Messaging (IM) program such as AOL AIM, MSN Messenger, and Yahoo! Messenger. All of the popular IM clients have chat software that can be used for group chats. Multisystem messaging software such as Trillian (http://www.ceruleanstudios.com) offers clean interfaces for chat across peer networks. As with IRC, this form of chat is free or very low cost depending upon the software you are using.

And as with discussion forum software, chat software is available in a wide variety. However, because chat is as close to real time as it gets, chat services generally demand more technical resources than discussion forums. So, while you can find free or low-cost options all around the web, high-volume situations will typically require specialized servers and more complex software integration with your site to provide the best service possible. That can get expensive.

If you do determine that chat is a feature you feel would be appropriate for your site, the next thing to determine is the features you want both for your users and from an administrative standpoint.

Some considerations for features your site visitors might benefit from include the following:

+ Public chat rooms
+ Ability to make private chat rooms
+ Ability to send personal messages (as with IM)
+ Ability to send files
+ Ability to embed links
+ Ability to block other members

From the administrator's point of view, the more control you can provide any community manager via your chat software, the better. Administrators and community managers need to be able to restrict a member, ban a member, create rooms, and delete rooms. So, you'll want to look for rich features, balancing that with the realities of budget and appropriateness of chat for your site.

> **note** Learn more about web-based chat software and enjoy helpful articles that can assist you in determining whether chat is for your site, and if so, which application might be best at **http://webdesign.about.com/cs/ chatsoftware/**.

Secret #226: Refresh Your Page Style Regularly

Every few months or so I become completely unhappy with my web site. So, I redesign it. For a personal site where it's natural to experiment with technology and layout, it's fine to completely redesign your web site with some regularity. However, while complete redesigns are essential from time to time, in this case I'm only talking about adding aspects to your page that are visually fresh.

> **note** For more information on when to implement redesigns, see Chapter 15, "Dealing with Growth and Redesigns."

An excellent example of refreshing visual style occurs with certain portal sites such as Google and Yahoo! who change their main logos based on seasonal events.

For example, on Valentine's Day a special Google Valentine logo is created and used for the duration of the day. Similar restyling occurs at Halloween, Christmas, New Years, Easter, and the Fourth of July in the U.S. (see Figure 13-13).

Figure 13-13: Clever Google logos refresh the page style according to the time of year.

Regularly refreshing some aspect of your web site keeps the look fresh, can be amusing and enjoyable for your site visitors, and is simple to implement, because you're only changing one or two visual pieces of the site at a time.

Secret #227:   Style Sheet Switching for Customization

Style switching using CSS and JavaScript is not only a fun way to add interactivity to your site, but very practical. If you've ever wanted to give your site visitors a little more control over the way they view a site without spending big money on personalization software, as well as offer techniques that make the site more usable and accessible, this technique might just do the trick.

Switching styles is a common practice used by many web designers who offer site visitors a preselected default style. Then, the site visitor can choose a style once there, giving the site a different presentation, and a cookie can be implemented to keep the user preference until he or she changes it (refer to Figures 13-14 and 13-15).

This technique is as practical as it is fun. Not only does it provide an enjoyable, enhanced experience for the site visitor, but it can allow you to provide versions of the site that suit different audience needs, such as a high-contrast version for those with vision impairments, or, if your site's layout is all CSS-based, you can provide an alternate design for browsers that do not support CSS, allowing site visitors to get a better visual experience on their terms.

In a similar vein, the style-switching technique can be used to create text-size switching effects. For example, if your site uses small or normal text sizing, you might want to allow your visitor a one-click option to make their text size larger

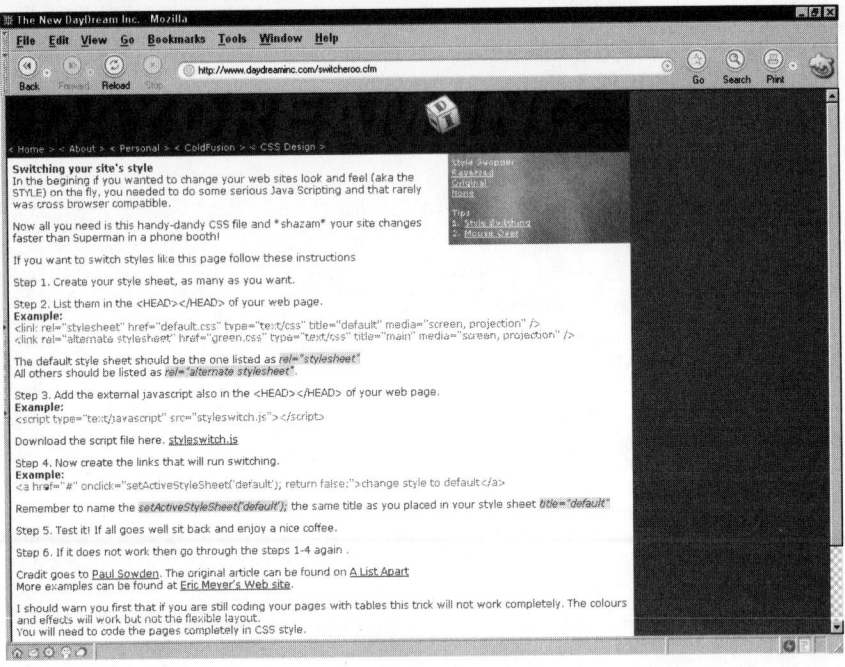

Figure 13-14: Default style upon entry to the site.

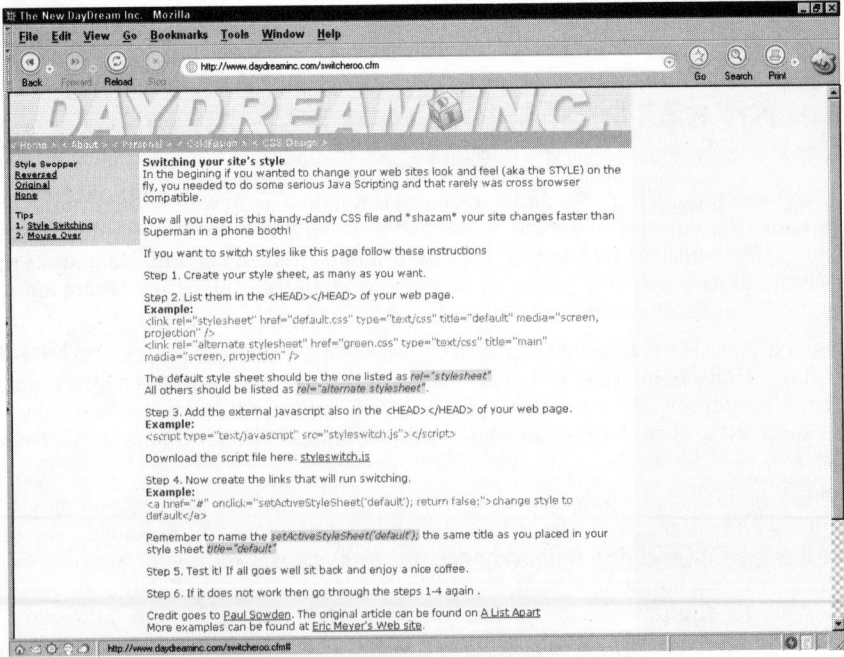

Figure 13-15: New style as applied via a style switch.

(always helpful for aging eyes). This is also an important feature for accessibility, and is in use on many web sites.

Switching styles with CSS is a fairly easy process once you've got all the pieces in order. Style switching requires the following:

- A contemporary web browser with CSS, JavaScript, and cookies turned on
- A basic style sheet for the page's design
- Additional, alternate style sheets
- A style switching script

Of course, because this technique requires JavaScript, your site visitors will have to have JavaScript enabled on their browsers to tap into the switch. If they do not, it will not interfere with your site's performance; visitors simply won't be able to use the feature.

> **note**
>
> To learn how to implement style switching, see Chapter 8, "Style Tips for Type and Design."
>
> There are also server-side alternatives to JavaScript style switching, including PHP alternatives. You may wish to consider alternatives if you have a high frequency of people visiting your site without JavaScript.

Secret #228:   Add Search Technology

As sites begin to grow, search becomes imperative. Fortunately, there are numerous ways to add search to a site. Table 13-4 describes some of the most common ways to add search.

> **note**
>
> To learn more about search, what you should look for, and some ideas to implement it, see Avi Rappoport's "Implementing Effective Site Search" from a presentation at the WEB2001 conference, at http://www.searchtools.com/slides/web2001sf/.
>
> Search and usability are two concepts that go great together. Many usability leaders scrutinize search because it is an extremely important feature for most web site visitors. Nielsen Norman Group offers a report, "E-Commerce User Experience: Design Guidelines for Search" for $45.00 USD, available for download from http://www.nngroup.com/reports/ecommerce/search.html. 37signals offers an Ecommerce Search Report as well, at http://37signals.com/report_search_0103.php.

Secret #229:   Aggregate Content

Content aggregation is a means of using XML-based technology to easily send your updated content across the wire and into the newsfeeds and newsreader software of those individuals who have signed up to receive your content.

Table 13-4: Strategies for Adding Search

Strategy	Description
Homegrown scripting	You can find search scripts in just about every application language known to the web: Perl, PHP, Python, and ASP.NET. You can then implement these into your web site on your own as is, or modify them to your needs. This is typically the least expensive way to go; it provides the opportunity to customize features, but it also requires program-savvy folks to implement and test the scripts.
Professional Search Application Software	A wide range of professional search engines and support is available from familiar companies such as Google. These solutions can be expensive but can be far easier to implement and support as a result of the increased support available via the company you contract or purchase your search product from.
Professional Web Search Service Provision	In this scenario, you contract with a search service (Atomz, at http://`www.atomz.com/`, is a good example), and that service provides you with the code necessary to manage your search. Then, instead of installing software on your own servers, your service provision company handles everything. So, you get a very rich featured search for a reasonable price. This is an excellent choice for mid-range sites. Downsides include limitations in modifying templates to work seamlessly within your site. This will depend upon the provider you choose.
Custom search programming	If you have very detailed needs and are working on specialty documents such as within a medical intranet or other institutional setting, having custom search in place may be more effective than commercial search solutions for such a site. In custom programming, the most important choice is the programmer or team that you put together or hire to accomplish the goal. The search requirements must be clearly organized and planned, giving the programmers as much to work with as possible going in. If you have the human resources, this could be a very good option for you. If you have to outsource, it could be an added expense and other alternatives might accomplish your needs more effectively.

Many sites have little buttons or syndication comments (see an example in Figure 13-16) indicating the availability of syndication.

> **note** Syndication formats are almost always automatically generated by a weblogging tool or related scripting process, and are rarely authored by hand. All major weblogging tools contain some method to aggregate content.

"Really Simple Syndication" or "Rich Site Summary" (RSS for either) are terms used to describe a number of XML-related aggregation technology versions that grew out of a project at Netscape geared to manage news headlines for portal web sites.

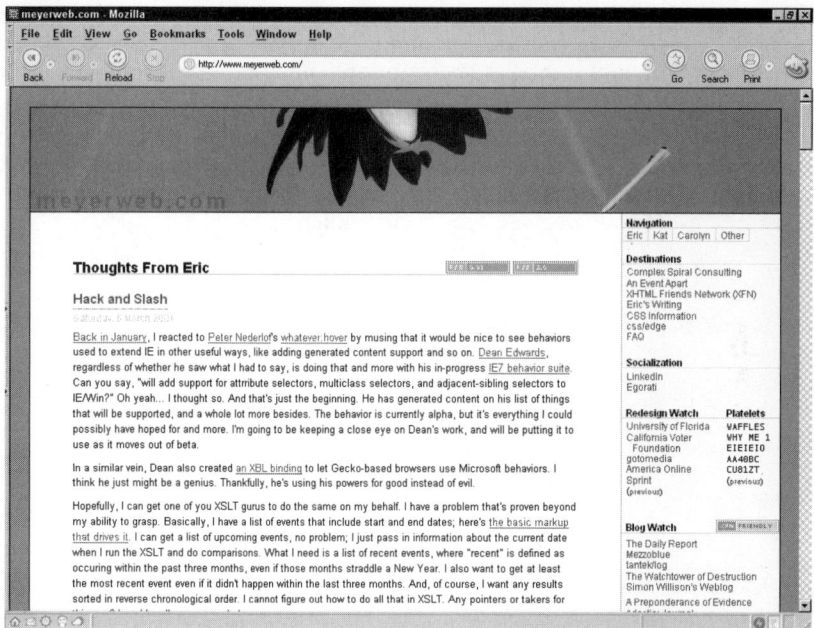

Figure 13-16: Sites display a flag of some sort if they offer syndication.

Within a short time, about nine different RSS formats emerged from different vendors, making it difficult to figure out which is best to use.

You may have also heard the term Resource Description Format (RDF), a more formal XML language being developed at the W3C. RDF, as all aggregation technologies, is very concerned with metadata and how to use that to connect people to information and vice-versa.

Atom is an emerging next-generation format for content syndication and additional features, such as creating and editing posts. Its goal is to provide a more stable, standardized platform for aggregation and offer developers more choice and flexibility than in RSS.

Fortunately, many weblogging tools generate more than one form of RSS, including Atom, and you can manually create RSS and Atom documents, too.

> **note**
>
> To learn more about RSS, see Mark Pilgrim's "What is RSS?" article at http://www.xml.com/pub/a/2002/12/18/dive-into-xml.html.
>
> The RDF specification is available at http://www.w3.org/RDF/.
>
> Information for Atom, including developer tutorials, is published at http://www.atomenabled.org/.

Summary

Keeping your sites fresh and engaging can be as simple as adding a bit of script and a fresh image at timely intervals, or as complex as adding advanced registration and personalization software. Certainly, each site with which you are involved will have different budgets, technical concerns, human resource limitations, and so on. As with everything in web design, making good decisions means researching the options and weighing the various factors prior to jumping into any commitment.

Many of the techniques used in this chapter have crossover with marketing and promotions, because they provide visitor tracking and other means of determining user behavior. In the following chapter, "Improving Site Ranking and Managing Promotions," you'll learn more about how to take such information and use it in the best interest of your web site—and your audiences.

Improving Site Ranking and Managing Promotions

Chapter
14

♦ ♦

Secrets in This Chapter

♦ ♦

W hat if you created a Web site and nobody came? You don't want your sites to end up obscure and unused.

No doubt you've read about meta tags and how they can help your sites get ranked better; and just about everyone using the Web is aware of the annoyances related to Web advertising. But these issues are just the tip of the iceberg.

Read any Web site dedicated to Web promotions and you'll see all kinds of topics, often controversial ones.

This chapter lets you in on the insider's view of why so many Web marketing methods are problematic, and shows you the right way to use common techniques such as keyword and description tagging, how to expand and extend keywords within your content, how to get submitted to search engines in a timely fashion, how to get the word out to interested parties, and how to increase interest via sponsored links and offline promotional opportunities.

I will not teach you how to spam, use annoying ads, or compromise the integrity of the products and services you represent. Just apply a balance between great Web site design and customer service and you will never have to rely on gimmicks.

About Web Site Marketing

There's a book that sits on my shelf, copyright 1995. In it, a couple of marketers decided to take their "guerrilla marketing" tactics to the Internet, persuading a lot of newcomers that aggressive marketing would make them profitable.

In 1995 the Web itself was very young, and we were all trying to sort out the best way to do things. Some of these guerrilla ideas caught on in a big way, but almost always in detriment to the comfort and prosperity of all.

Guerrilla marketing tactics encouraged (and still encourage) e-mail spam, browser hijacking, overuse of ads (especially popups), and a range of adware that's become a scourge to the good users of the Web.

From a management and team perspective, marketing is often considered the most difficult aspect of a successful Web site team, as they tend to have conflicting goals. Marketing goals often conflict with technology goals, and there also tends to be a different focus in marketing. Their job is the sale, and while designers and developers seek to support that, sometimes the two conflict in their goals.

On the Web, no practice can work without the technology necessary to make it work. Technology and how well we use it makes up a significant portion of a site's success.

Of course, marketing and promotional methods are not all bad, and certainly many methods, such as regular specials or Web-specific coupons, can end up being extremely useful in successfully promoting your site. The best of marketing and promotion savvy, in my opinion, are those that relate to successful business strategy, great management, and workflow—all topics found elsewhere in this book.

Now Focus Is on Structure and Content

While you will see how to use long-existing techniques such as meta keyword and description in this chapter, the real focus for today's Web sites is to ensure that they are structured and written so that search engine computers can successfully rank them.

By getting rid of deeply nested tables for layout, ensuring that style is handled with CSS, and making your sites accessible for the disabled, you open up your site to be quickly and easily catalogued by a search engine. Add to that effective titling of your documents, clear language use, and many other cues related to readability and usability, and the rest of the job is pretty straightforward.

A lot of information will try to steer you otherwise—toward paying money for additional software or services to help you get ranked. This is only one of the many myths that exist regarding most search engines and how they rank you. Other myths include the following:

- ◆ **A competitor can ruin your ranking.** A competitor cannot purposely sabotage your ranking or remove you from a search engine under normal circumstances. However, if they have done a better job than you with the design of their site, or they have a very large amount of relevant links to their site, or they have a domain name that is very close to the main concept of the site, they might get a higher ranking (molly.com, for example, will rank higher on most search engines when people search for "molly").

- ◆ **You can pay your way to the top of Google.** No, you can't. You can buy sponsored links and advertising that will appear alongside or above searches of relevance to your site, but there are numerous factors that get sites "to the top."

- ◆ **Paid inclusion services are the way to go.** No, they're not. With very few exceptions, inclusion services are scams, and finding those exceptions is very difficult (see the next section).

No matter what your site's promotion goals, in the immortal words of rapper Chuck D, "Don't believe the hype."

Avoid Unscrupulous Marketing Techniques

Here's a fact: No one can promise you top rankings on all major engines by doing *anything* to your site. I take that back! They *can* promise, and they *do* promise, but they don't deliver.

In the past few years, a rash of Search Engine Optimization (SEO) companies has emerged to "help" us optimize the code on our site and fix problems related to search engine rankings. Many SEOs are straight-out frauds, doing nothing for their clients or doing very little and calling it a day.

Of course, some of these companies aren't fraudulent, but the proliferation of the bad guys is such that you as a consumer *must be hyper-vigilant* if you decide to use any of their services.

note   Google has an excellent overview of SEOs that provides guidance in how to choose one, and how to report complaints about any SEO in the United States or abroad. See `www.google.com/webmasters/seo.html`.

Thankfully, the techniques in this chapter, along with your well-designed and structured Web site will alleviate all of those woes. In fact, in just a few short pages, you'll learn enough to open your own SEO should you desire a little time on the guerrilla-marketing front.

Secret #230: Targeting Keywords for meta Elements

By placing keywords into a meta element within your documents (a common practice), you enable search engines looking for this information to catalog your keywords quickly.

Keywords can help with ranking because you are able to catalog your site based on descriptive words or series of words that define your site as well as reflect the kind of word combinations that users will be inputting into search engines:

```
<meta name="keywords" content="molly, molly.com, html, xhtml, css,
design, web design, development, web development, perl" />
```

Unfortunately, this method, while easy to implement (just add as many keywords as you'd like, separated by commas, to the meta element), has been misused over time.

Instead of sticking to those keywords relevant to their sites, some unscrupulous but imaginative folks decided to add keywords to a site that might have nothing to do with its relevance.

For example, say you're working for a site that sells baby clothing and related items, and the person doing the meta keywords adds in words such as "sex" or "porn"—completely irrelevant and inappropriate for your site. Because sex-related keywords remain extremely popular search words, they often end up where they shouldn't be.

Another unscrupulous bit is the addition of multiple instances of important words numerous times so that in a keyword value, the word "baby" might appear alone (rather than in various reasonable combinations) 100 times.

Search engines got savvy to this behavior and put their foot down by creating stricter rules and sometimes blocking any sites that were using poor practices. This action has actually helped many working in Web development to be more aware of exactly the kind of keyword and keyword combinations they want.

A good exercise is to sit down at your computer with a text editor at the ready, and just begin to write out words and word combinations that might be things you would search for if looking for the given product or service your Web site represents.

You may also wish to have other members of your team add to the list. You can even ask people who use Web sites but do not necessarily know anything about making them to come up with keywords and keyword combinations. Collect, review, and edit these down to the most descriptive and relevant options for use on your site.

---

tip
While repeating a single keyword on its own within the **meta** element is considered a no-no, using the keyword in various combinations is not. For example, I might use "Web design" and follow it up with "Web development" and "Web usability." I've used the word "Web" three times but in relevant, applicable ways. This helps with ranking and clarifying the types of work you do.

Another important means of refining keywords within your site is to match your keywords to actual data reported via the search engine in use on your site (if you have a search engine, that is). Many search applications provide reporting services so you can see your top requested searches and add terms to your `meta` element as necessary.

Figure 14-1 shows a listing of search entries on Molly.Com. I can see that there are several instances of suitable terms to add to my `meta` element, such as "php" and "css."

February 22, 2004

20 total searches, 15 phrases (1 to 15)

Graph	Count	Phrase	Results Count
▬▬▬	3	enter search term	3
▬▬	3	quiznos	6
▬	2	136 colors htlm	73
▪	1	bla	0
▪	1	boxes	19
▪	1	css	55
▪	1	eddie	4
▪	1	editor	27
▪	1	free	45
▪	1	javascript	20
▪	1	jim summer	3
▪	1	no	145
▪	1	php	142
▪	1	webdesign	12
▪	1	webdesign 136 colors	0

Figure 14-1: Local searches assist me in matching common searches on my site to `meta` keywords for major search engine listings.

Secret #231:   Writing Effective meta Descriptions

The next most common `meta` element to define is the site description. This is typically a short description of about 25 words that describes your site simply and effectively.

Numerous search engines look to this data for help with categorizing a site. Consider the `meta` description that appears on my site:

```
<meta name="description" content="I'm Molly E. Holzschlag, and
this Web site shares my Web development work and personal
thoughts." />
```

Now look at Figure 14-2, which is an exact reproduction of the search results found on such search engines as Excite, MSN, and AltaVista.

Molly.com - Welcome
I'm **Molly** E. Holzschlag, and this Web site shares my Web development work and personal thoughts.
molly.com. Q: What's this Web site? ...
http://www.molly.com/

Figure 14-2: An example of how a wide number of major search engines implement the `meta` description.

As you can see, the search engine has catalogued my description. Without an effective description in place, you may end up with other components falling into the ranking first, as shown in Figure 14-3.

Star-Telegram.com
Search: Articles-last 7 days Articles-older than 7 days The Web for News | Business | Sports | Entertainment | Living | Travel | Shopping | Classifieds | Jobs | Cars | Homes News 2 Use Fort Worth ...
www.dfw.com/mld/startelegram/news/columnists/molly_ivins

Figure 14-3: Without a `meta` description in place, the navigation appears before any discernable content.

Follow these general guidelines when creating descriptions:

- Include a "call to action" that encourages users to select your site. This will vary depending on the product and services you want. My description might be more effective if I used this approach, which might read "Visit Molly E. Holzschlag and learn the most current topics and techniques in Web design."
- Be brief. Stick to 25 words or less.
- Be clear and meaningful. "Beautiful Web sites" doesn't mean much, really. Follow that link and you might find a site designer, or someone's personal list of favorite sites.

tip

Including top-level meaningful keywords in your description is a helpful way of improving your document's keyword optimization.

Secret #232: Using Targeted Words in Headers

Not too long ago, many major search engines began looking at content either right away, or after grabbing a `meta` description (should one exist). `H1` level headers get a lot of attention from many engines, because from a structural standpoint they are meant to describe the most important topic on the page.

Once again, in the frenzy to increase ranking, suddenly pages were appearing with multiple `H1` headers packed with keywords. This practice is not only considered bad form and just plain rude, but it doesn't sit too well with those search engines using it as a legitimate means of addressing descriptions.

But the proper use of `H1` elements can still help. That means one `H1` element per page, tops. Add your keywords in an appropriate and clear manner, and you're helping everyone, not just the site's potential rank.

Bad example:

```
<h1>Welcome!</h1>
```

Good example:

```
<h1>Welcome to Tucson Homes, Tucson's Luxury Real Estate Site</h1>
```

> **tip** Sprinkling keywords liberally throughout all headers is helpful. Just be sure you aren't going overboard to the point of losing the real meaning in your headings.

Secret #233:   Using Keywords in Text

After looking at headings, many search engines will begin grabbing your text for descriptions. For sites that aren't built structurally and use tables for content, you're really playing Russian roulette trying to assume which content the engine will grab.

However, if you are following well-structured markup practices, the first place most engines will look after headings is text formatted as being a paragraph. So, when you are preparing your content for the Web, be sure that there are plenty of keywords worked into your content, again following a balanced approach where you are enhancing the keyword count but not diminishing the content's importance.

Here's a welcome paragraph on a client's Web site:

```
I specialize in luxury homes in the Tucson foothills and
University of Arizona area. I am also very knowledgeable about
Tucson golf course properties and retirement neighborhoods. My
business has been built by personal referrals, so I'm looking
forward to getting to work with you.
```

Note some of the powerful keywords and combinations in use:

- luxury
- luxury homes
- homes
- Tucson
- Tucson foothills
- foothills
- University
- University of Arizona
- Arizona
- Tucson golf
- Tucson golf course
- golf
- golf course
- golf course properties

- ◆ Tucson golf course properties
- ◆ retirement
- ◆ retirement neighborhoods.

Naturally, all these keywords and terms should be included in your keyword meta element, too.

Secret #234:   Keeping URLs Short and Relevant

This is a topic that's popped up throughout the book, and for good reason. Whether you're approaching it from the perspective of information architecture, usability, or ranking and promotions, the shorter and more logical your Web site address is, the easier it's going to be to promote and to catalog.

For example, www.molly.com/books/ is going to be a fairly easy URL to promote, whereas www.readallofmollysbooks.com/ is going to have numerous pitfalls.

So, keep URLs as short and sweet as you possibly can.

> **tip**
>
> It's also highly recommended that when you have a www within your domain name that a visitor is able to resolve your site with or without the initiating "www"—www.molly.com *and* molly.com resolve to the same location.

Another problem with URLs and promotion is dynamically created URLs or those that display a session ID.

Consider the following URL, a real URL to an article of mine:

```
http://www.informit.com/content/index.asp?product_id={F41929EF-
0DCC-444C-AE9C-EA20A98C3853}&session_id={6C98C46C-F571-4647-890D-
AB05E18223DD}
```

Anyone who takes this URL and copies it into their browser window may encounter problems when the browser tries to resolve to the correct page. The reason is due to the session ID being added to the URL. That ID is specific to my session, not yours, and will cause problems when another person tries to resolve the URL.

Experienced Web developers and programmers will know that they should remove the session ID, but these issues can and should be dealt with on the server-side. URLs of this nature go against most usability guidelines and cause serious problems when it comes to trying to promote specific pages within Web sites.

> **note**
>
> Did you catch the other problem with the extended URL? If you drop it as is into an XHTML document, it will not validate unless you escape the ampersand within the URL.

Secret #235:   Solicit Reciprocal Links

The more people link to your site, the more "important" that Web address will appear to many search engines, with the site ranking improving based on its popularity. This is called *reciprocal linking*.

One scam you should be aware of is that some SOEs and marketing firms will try to convince you that you need to populate "entry" pages—pages that link to your Web site—on other Web servers to increase links to you, thereby boosting your rank by tricking search engines into thinking that relevant Web pages have links to your site.

The best way to increase linking to you is to solicit it—especially from *relevant* and related Web sites. For example, the more Web sites related to Web development, Web design, and computer book topics that I have linked to molly.com, the better my ranking is going to be.

You can increase linking a number of ways beyond frank solicitation. Today's Weblog software can be applied to businesses too, adding features with rolling "blogrolls"—links to related sites. For topically related sites, there are often *Webrings*—groups of related sites with links from one to the next—and these can be a great way to drive traffic to your sites.

I've added my Web site to a number of rings in the past few years and have been astonished at the resulting increase in visitors to my site. Webrings are grouped by like interest (or geography, such as "Tucson Web sites"), so the people who come to your site as a result are likely going to have a pre-existing interest or need that your site can accommodate.

tip	**Do a search for <yourtopic webring> on any search engine and you'll probably find an assortment of Webrings related to your topic, too.**

If for some reason you do decide, or are told, that you need to research SOEs or other groups that can assist you with linking strategies, be as careful as you can to check out who you are working with. Who knows, you might be surprised and actually find someone who will help you with resources and actually contribute to your goals, but again, the likelihood of that is very low.

Secret #236:   Consider Affiliate Programs

If it's appropriate for your site, you may wish to consider affiliate programs. Amazon.com offers the most famous of these programs.

Here's how affiliate programs work. You create coded links on your own site of recommended products, sign up for the affiliate program to get the various coded links you'll need, and then you will receive a percentage of money from any affiliate sales.

The better you manage to drive people to purchase products via your affiliate program, the more money you can make.

For example, for computer book authors, affiliate programs can make a lot of sense. All books I've written can be linked from my site to an affiliate such as Amazon. Therefore, not only do I get the royalties I'm due from each sale, but I also make a percentage, boosting my earnings a little bit.

There are pros and cons to affiliate programs, just as with anything. I used to manage an affiliate program on my Web site, but eventually took it off because I was getting far too many queries personally. Amazon is better equipped to provide wide-scale customer service and keep information up-to-date than I am without a concentrated effort. For me, the cons outweighed the pros.

Table 14-1 shows some of the pros and cons to consider before jumping into an affiliate program.

Table 14-1: The Pros and Cons of Affiliate Programs

Pros	*Cons*
You have very little overhead in day-to-day management of business logistics and inventory	No hands-on control over product quality, shipping and delivery, and other logistics, yet you may be held accountable by your clients anyway
You can focus on one thing—marketing your product via your Web site	Affiliates do not provide any marketing assistance for the most part. *You* have to sell the goods. So, unless you are a born salesperson or have a good one on your team, an affiliate program might not be in your best interest
You'll learn a lot about selling products online! This makes affiliate programs a good way for many folks to get started in e-commerce	You may become so locked in to the learning curve involved with managing your program and Web site that you neglect other important aspects of Web site and product promotion
You make money	You could make more money in some instances by not relying on an affiliate, who may take as much of 50 percent of your gross sales
You have autonomy to design and develop your site and display your products as you see fit. If you do this very well, you may end up with great leverage against your competitors	You are relying on another company to pay you. Payments can take time, rates can change, and you don't have much recourse except to stop the affiliate program

The most important issue is to be sure the affiliate program with which you are working is on the up-and-up. Check with other people who have used the service, and you can even find out where the company resides, whether it is licensed, and so on.

note   **You may be able to check with the local consumer office or chamber of commerce to see if any complaints have been lodged against the company.**

Secret #237: Use Opt-In E-mail Newsletters to Drive Traffic

Despite the scourge of spam and viruses that have hit e-mail users in the past years, e-mail remains the killer application. E-mail newsletters are undeniably powerful tools to build audience and encourage real relationships between you and your site visitors and customers.

The key to avoiding guerrilla tactics in e-mail advertising is to make all e-mail newsletters optional. You will have people opt in mostly via your Web site, which means they have to get to your Web site in the first place. Once visitors do opt in, you can begin building a personal mailing list, which in turn encourages return visits to your site.

> **tip** There are numerous directories to which you can post announcements about new e-mail lists. These directories can be helpful because they provide a means of getting interested readers and promoters together.

Some of the important factors to consider when initiating opt-in e-mail newsletters are as follows:

- What are the specific results you want from the e-mail? (Sales? More eyes on your site?)
- Do you want to offer HTML e-mail? Many e-mail experts say that HTML e-mail is the only way to go, but HTML e-mail may be problematic or undesirable for certain audiences.
- What kind of content are you going to offer (such as articles, reviews of products, tips and tricks, interviews, and polls)?
- How long will your newsletter be? Most e-mail experts say that keeping content short and to the point wins the day.
- How often will you send the newsletter out to subscribers?

> **note** Most e-mail newsletter services offer reasonably priced assistance for managing HTML versus text e-mail, tracking e-mail responses, statistics, demographics, and additional helpful tools that you can use to increase your awareness of how well your e-mail campaign is working.

Experts do suggest that you spend time creating a plan to start e-mail newsletters, and also build in a way to assess how effective your plan is working. This way, you can adjust to the needs of your audience as time goes on.

> **tip** Generally speaking, you should send your e-mails during the week. Some studies suggest that most people open newsletters between Tuesday and Thursday. While weekends are often considered bad times to send newsletters, it really will depend upon your audience. If you are selling sports products, movies, or other recreational products, the weekend might be the perfect time to grab some attention.

I have an opt-in newsletter on my site, and I have several thousand people on that list. One of the things I do regularly is to focus special promotions and giveaways to those readers as a means of rewarding their ongoing loyalty and interest in my work. Figure 14-4 shows a significant spike in site visits after a newsletter campaign.

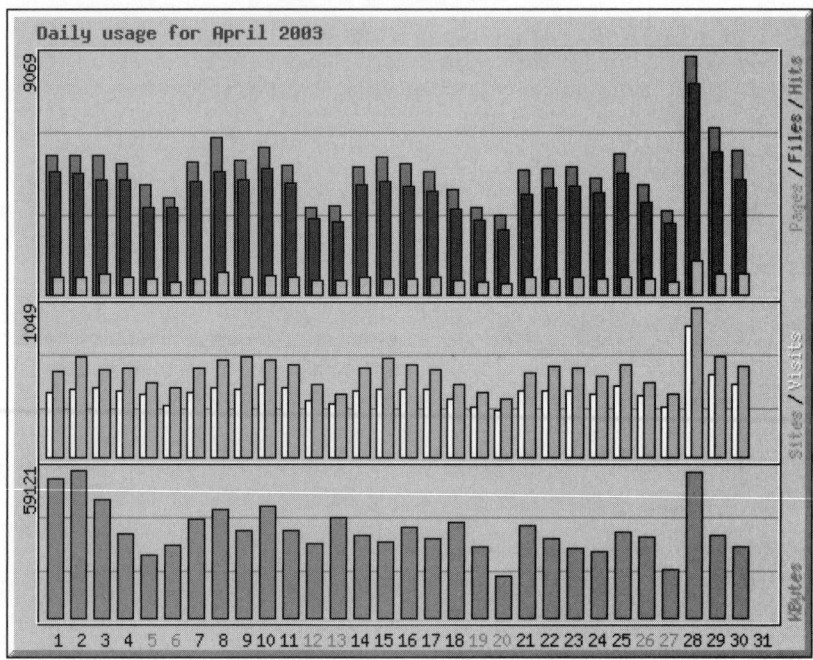

Figure 14-4: A spike in site visits occurred after a newsletter campaign.

Secret #238: Run Regular and Seasonal Promotions

To create interest in your site and brand or build personal relationships, regular promotions can really help. People like getting a break, or even better, free stuff.

Depending upon what you're promoting and to whom, the type of promotions you want to run will vary. Table 14-2 describes several scenarios and suggestions for regular and seasonal promotions.

Table 14-2: Regular and Seasonal Promotion Ideas

Site Type	Promotional Possibilities
DJ Web site	CD giveaways, trivia contests with prizes, show ticket giveaways, yearly concern promotion event.
Heart disease information Web site	Health-related book giveaways, monthly promotions for "heart health," healthy cooking recipe contests, exercise equipment promotions, discount vouchers for healthy heart testing

Site Type	Promotional Possibilities
Dating site	Romantic getaway contests, seasonal promotions for Valentine's day, grand prizes for successful matches who meet and marry
Weather Web site	Weather trivia polls, seasonal promotions, such as "Sensational Spring" or "Sizzling Summer" promotions with contests and prizes such as weather trivia and vacation getaways

The key is to match your promotions to your audience and product or service. This is one part of promotions I really happen to like, because it can be great fun and extremely creative to sit down with friends or team members and come up with great ideas. Even if you're limited in budget, there's usually some way to provide innovative, interactive contests and promotions that engage your clients.

Secret #239:   Learn More About Web Ads

The controversy around Web ads rages on, and there remains very little real evidence as to their success. Sometimes they are effective, sometimes not. The key is to determine for your own site whether buying ads to promote your site or hosting Web-based advertising as a means of enhancing revenue for your site is a reasonable choice.

Some issues to consider include the following:

◆ **Ad placement.** This issue refers to both cases of hosting ads, and buying them. If you are hosting, you want to make clear which areas of your site have ads, and how they will be managed. Similarly, research your placement options if you are buying placement elsewhere.

◆ **Provision.** Numerous vendors manage Web ads. Find one with a good track record and good customer support.

◆ **Ad types.** Whether buying or hosting ads, find out what kinds of ads are considered conventional in terms of dimension, weight, location, and file type (animated GIFs, rich media advertising via Flash).

◆ **Integration into design.** If you are going to be placing ads on your site, you'll want to successfully integrate them. Ads can be an eyesore—but they need to be placed so that your visitors can see them, or they're not going to be worth much. You must find a balance. Fortunately, there are some helpful conventions you can use, but knowing that you want to support ads going into a design is a lot easier than trying to retrofit a design around advertising. Ads are best managed earlier on in the site design process or during a site redesign (see Chapter 15, "Dealing with Growth and Redesign").

◆ **How to manage ad code.** If you are hosting ads on your site, the ad management software or host that you choose is going to be sending you the ad markup. Usually, this markup is filled with problem code, and as you try to clean up your code, the frustration level can get a little out of hand. Plan to test or research the actual code so you know what you're getting into.

✦ **Reporting.** If you're buying ads, you're going to want regular, comprehensive reports to see how the advertising is working. Similarly, if you are hosting ads, you may want to track which ads seem to be influencing your site visitors' behavior. Most companies offering advertising also offer extensive reporting.

✦ **Cost.** Web ads can vary greatly in cost and type. Research to decide which advertising type is best for you.

Along with ad hosting services, you can also consider running your own ad server software.

note | There are a large number of advertising services. The oldest and most well known is DoubleClick (`www.doubleclick.com/`), whose site offers a lot of helpful information covering a wide range of promotion and marketing for Web sites.

For a good article on running your own ad server software, see "Evaluating Ad Management Software" by Bruce Morris, at `www.webdevelopersjournal.com/articles/ad_management.html`.

Secret #240: Add Sponsored Links

Sponsored linking is a phenomenon that's taken off like crazy and seems to be one of the few new ideas to hit Web advertising.

A sponsored link is a text link that can appear in the form of an ad or a simple link. You pay for the sponsorship, and the link is then extremely well targeted to appear on search engines or Web sites *based on relevance*. That relevancy seems to be a key component of sponsored link popularity.

An excellent example of a sponsored link program is Google AdWords. Do any search on Google and you'll wind up seeing several links on the top and to the right side of the search results page. These are sponsored links, and if you compare the topic of your search to the resulting links, you'll see that the relevancy is pretty exacting. I put in the search term "dog breeds" and the sponsored links that appeared were both for breeder directories.

You can purchase AdWords to run on Google (pricing structure is very sensible and guided by your budget needs), or use Google's AdSense, which allows you to build revenue by running others' ads on your site—all targeted by relevance (see the example in Figure 14-5).

note | To learn more about Google AdWords, see `https://adwords.google.com/select/`. To read more about AdSense, see `www.google.com/adsense/`.

For bloggers or other sites where a wide range of topics might be freely discussed, this approach has been found to be controversial, largely due to Google policy. If you'd like to read about the controversy, see `www.kottke.org/03/10/google-adsense-sucks`. The issues described pertain specifically to personal blogs rather than professional sites, but it's always good to be informed.

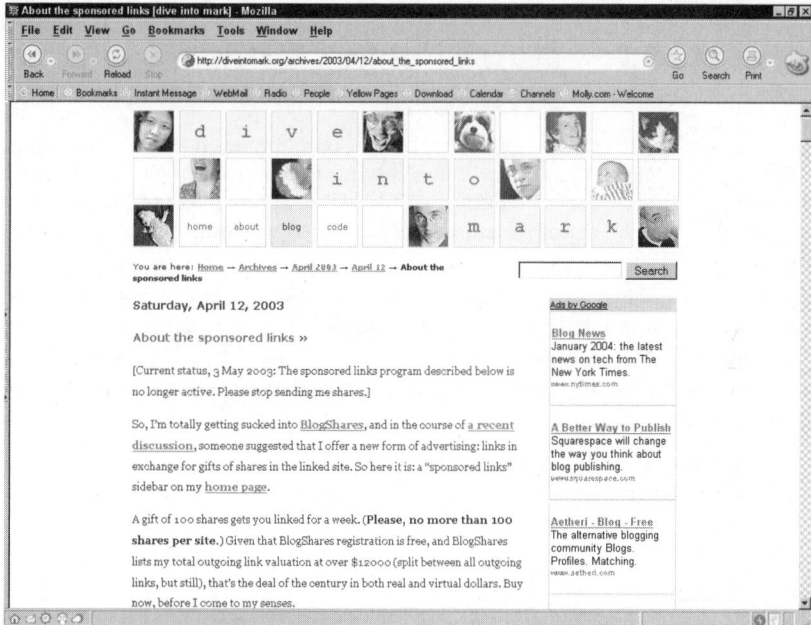

Figure 14-5: Google AdSense helps build revenue. Notice the relevancy of the ads being served—this is Mark Pilgrim's Weblog, so the ads are all about blog-related news and software.

Secret #241: Search Engine Submission

Here's the lowdown on search engine submission. You can do it manually for free. The only problem there is going to be time—you may have to wait for your site to show up, or you may have to submit more than once to ensure that your site shows up. So, you might wish to use a company that does the site submissions.

> **tip**
>
> Getting listed at a major search engine, such as Google, will get you listed in other search engines faster and vice versa.

Once again you're faced with having to choose a vendor to help. Paid submission will get your site ranked faster, and many search engines now offer fast additions and improved ranking for pay.

> **note**
>
> One well-known, affordable vendor for search engine submissions is Microsoft. Their bCentral service, at www.bcentral.com/, provides all kinds of helpful promotion and marketing tools for Web sites.

Secret #242: Don't Forget Offline Promotions!

I'll never forget the first time I saw a URL in a TV commercial. It was 1995 and the commercial was for Subway Subs. I was tidying my bedroom and had the TV on, and when I overheard the URL being read I had to sit down as the impact of what was happening hit me. I knew instinctively that this was only the beginning.

Now, we see URLs in all kinds of unusual places. I remember standing on an upper floor in San Francisco's Argent Hotel and looking out of my window as a bus passed below. A local radio station had its URL painted on top of the bus! Crazy—but certainly fun and memorable.

You want to get your URL on everything you use within your organization, such as the following:

- Letterhead and envelopes
- Business cards
- Company t-shirts, caps, bags, and so on
- Pens
- Checks
- Any promotional collateral

You also want to consider other forms of media cross-promotions, including the following:

- Television commercials
- Radio ads
- Magazine ads
- Billboards
- Direct mail marketing.

Promotions specialists point out that you want to be coordinated in your efforts—build your offline promotion plans in an integrated way with your online promotions and other marketing goals for ensured success.

Summary

How you make decisions for your needs will be guided by each unique situation with which you're confronted—the marketing needs of one site may be very different from that of another. Being well informed will save you a lot of frustration. And no matter the difficulties, if your site is well-designed, well-structured, and if you follow the guidelines for meta tagging and text enhancement, you are well on your way to better visibility. Add to that some well thought-out strategies, and you're sure to improve your site's visibility and potential revenue.

Next up is a look at dealing with two common Web design issues: growth and redesigns.

Dealing with Growth and Redesigns

Chapter
15

◆ ◆

Secrets in This Chapter

◆ ◆

Anyone dealing with Web sites in the past few years has had to make serious decisions about what to do regarding old content, how to bring sites up to contemporary design and standards-based functionality, and ask the toughest question of all: When is a redesign necessary?

This chapter will help you determine when a redesign is in order, provide ideas to help keep the costs of redesign low, and maintain a consistent relationship with the audience.

Secret #243: The Importance of Server Logs

In my experience, and the experience of many Web developers, the ability to access server logs and process them using some kind of analysis software has been the single most important tool in my toolbox to address browser and other site management issues with ease.

Server logs and analysis software (which can be run on your server or purchased as an external service) allow you to analyze numerous issues. Table 15-1 shows some of the features of analysis software, and the relevance to managing ongoing growth and redesigns.

Table 15-1: Benefits of Server Analysis

Feature	Benefit
Hit statistics	By analyzing how many hits, page views, page visits, and transferred KBs occur to your web site over a period of time, you can make better decisions about how to effectively purchase and manage storage, bandwidth, and scalability. You can also gain feedback as to the popularity of a newly introduced feature by watching the statistics for the document containing the feature. This helps you refine your feature choices, basing what you do real audience interest
Top URLs	By tracking which pages on your site are getting the most hits, you can better determine where to place important information and site features for your readership. You can also use this information to consider what to move up higher in your site architecture to keep visitors able to easily access the most used features on your site
Top entry pages	While similar in benefit to Top URLs, knowing exactly where the majority of your site visitors enter your site facilitates ensuring that any important update information is delivered via those documents along with the home page. This way, important information pertaining to the site and its features is seen by the majority of users possible
Top referrers	This feature lets you know the top sites that are referring to you. Using this feature can help you better target co-marketing opportunities via reciprocal linking, as well as help you determine keyword topic search information that will be best for your site based on the type of referrers you have. For example, if a large number of people are coming

Feature	Benefit
	to me from a link in an article about color, I know that making it easy to find color information on my site is going to enhance the experience for my users, making it easier to get to the information that brings them to me in the first place
Top search strings	This phenomenally helpful feature lets you see what keywords people are using to get to your site. This way, you can regularly update your keywords to what people are actually searching for. Look for misspellings too—I find this with my last name, Holzschlag, a lot (as you can imagine), and incorporating those misspellings into meta keywords can help people find me faster
Top user agents	Perhaps the holiest grail in all of server analysis, knowing which browsers are being used to access your site is knowledge you simply cannot be without. This information will help you make decisions as to how you do just about everything design-wise. A good tip is to look at current numbers, but also to watch trends very carefully. The moment you see a specific browser begin to diminish or increase in number, you know you can modify your support as needed
Color and resolution information	Knowing the color support and resolution used by site visitors can help you determine how to effectively use color for your audience and provide insight into the best layout type for your audience: fluid or static, depending upon the range of resolutions you have to support
Platform information	This information is helpful in making sure that you know how platform and operating systems might be influencing the way in which your users work and use your site
Country information	Knowing the countries that are visiting your site can be very helpful in adjusting your content to ensure that you are using appropriate color schemes, clear language, and any internationalization features necessary (such as using global time and date) to accommodate site visitors from other nations

Figure 15-1 shows the browser information from my Web site. This information is very helpful to me, because it reflects which browsers my audience is using. One interesting change in recent months is the newsfeed agents (see item 7 in the list for an example). This is a result of content aggregation via RSS feeds (discussed in Chapter 14). With 1,051 feed requests in only five days of use that month, it's pretty apparent that my RSS feeds are playing a significant role in the way people use my site.

> **note** Many Web analysis tools are available, many of them offering increasingly rich, useful features. I found a helpful, regularly updated list of vendors providing analysis for Web sites via standalone software or services at `www.terrylund.com/vendorListing.shtml`.

	Top 15 of 720 Total User Agents	
#	**Hits**	**User Agent**
1	4106	11.52%	Mozilla/4.0 (compatible; MSIE 6.0; Windows NT 5.1)
2	3616	10.15%	Mozilla/4.0 (compatible; MSIE 6.0; Windows NT 5.1; .NET CLR 1
3	1629	4.57%	Mozilla/5.0 (Windows; U; Windows NT 5.1; en-US; rv:1.6) Gecko
4	1608	4.51%	Googlebot/2.1 (+http://www.googlebot.com/bot.html)
5	1520	4.26%	Mozilla/4.0 (compatible; MSIE 6.0; Windows NT 5.0)
6	1293	3.63%	Mozilla/4.0 (compatible; MSIE 6.0; Windows 98)
7	1051	2.95%	FeedDemon/1.10 RC 1 (http://www.bradsoft.com/; Microsoft Wind
8	948	2.66%	Mozilla/4.0 (compatible; MSIE 6.0; Windows NT 5.0; .NET CLR 1
9	780	2.19%	Mozilla/4.0 (compatible; MSIE 5.0; Windows 98; DigExt)
10	731	2.05%	Mozilla/5.0 (Macintosh; U; PPC Mac OS X; en-us) AppleWebKit/1
11	628	1.76%	Mozilla/5.0 (Windows; U; Windows NT 5.0; en-US; rv:1.4) Gecko
12	616	1.73%	Mozilla/5.0 (Macintosh; U; PPC Mac OS X; en) AppleWebKit/124
13	556	1.56%	Mozilla/4.0 (compatible; MSIE 6.0; Windows NT 5.1; FunWebProd
14	485	1.36%	Mozilla/5.0 (Windows; U; Windows NT 5.0; en-US; rv:1.6) Gecko
15	368	1.03%	NetNewsWire/1.0.8 (Mac OS X; http://ranchero.com/netnewswire/

Figure 15-1: Top browser stats for Molly.Com, first few days of April 2004.

Secret #244:   Develop a Regular Assessment Cycle

Just taking a quick glance at statistical analysis programs will make you see how important it is to use this information as a regular part of assessing your site and figuring out whether you are reaching your audience effectively, as well as making adjustments to better serve your site visitors over time.

Of course, reviewing statistics is only one small part of a regular assessment. Many of the techniques you learned to do at the start of site building (discussed at the beginning of this book) are the things you get to do all over again in assessment, such as the following:

- **Reassess your audience.** In each scheduled assessment cycle, you should be using analysis tools and any other user tracking techniques you've implemented to constantly reassess your audience. What are they using, technically speaking? Where are they spending the most time on your site? The most money?

- **Redetermine your site's intent.** Is your site staying true to the original intent? If not, why not? Perhaps you fell off the path and need to tighten up your goals, or perhaps in the process of launching and following your site, the intent has to be modified because you're finding you're reaching an unexpected demographic. Either way, reassessing this information will enable you to bring your site back on track or redetermine the site's purpose, as necessary.

♦ **Re-audit your assets.** One way to avoid "organic growth syndrome" is to constantly be watching what *stuff* you've got on your site and your servers. Anything that is no longer of use should be removed. Any area that's started to grow more quickly than another will require your attention in terms of how to better organize it within the overall architecture of your site. Make sure you provide effective redirects or information pages in place of any removed documents to ensure visitors end up somewhere useful on your site.

♦ **Re-evaluate existing technology.** Are the technology choices you made early on still addressing the needs you predicted? If they are, terrific, but if not, consider researching alternatives based on your assessment so that your site technology is kept as relevant and up-to-date as possible at all times.

Ideally, implementing a regular assessment cycle will help you avoid major re-design problems related to information architecture, site technology, and other site features, because you will be making updates and changes to those aspects as you grow, rather than waiting a year or more and then suddenly having to redo everything.

tip | Most Web developers implementing regular assessment cycles aim for assessments at least once a quarter. With larger sites and more resources, more frequent assessments may be advisable, whereas smaller sites can be assessed less frequently.

Secret #245:   Ensure Scalability

One of the most difficult things to gauge is how fast a site will grow and, therefore, what kind of load stress it will place on servers and related technology used to deliver your site.

A case in point is Friendster, which took off so quickly no one could have anticipated the technical needs the site would demand. As a result, Friendster is suffering from scalability-related problems: slow response times, unavailability of service, and so on. Users who get too frustrated with these problems may well turn to other services instead.

Planning for this kind of growth is difficult, because assuming that kind of growth from the get-go means higher costs going in it may never be recuperated down the road.

So how do you manage scalability? Some suggestions include the following:

♦ Have someone within your organization stay on top of technical solutions for scalability. Typically, this person will have experience in networking and security so as to address best practices for scaling networks and bandwidth efficiently.

♦ Be wary of adding features and applications unless they are truly necessary. By avoiding the addition of unnecessary applications, less strain is placed on servers and other technical resources.

◆ Perform load-testing prior to launching new features to see how they perform under intense conditions.

> **tip** Numerous tools for load-testing are available, depending upon your server type. You can learn more about load-testing tools at `www.softwareqatest.com/qatweb1.html#LOAD`.

Secret #246:   Manage Content Growth

Content growth is also a major challenge because the more content on a site, the more important it is to have an architecture that makes sense, an interface that makes sense, and a way to manage archives.

While you looked at all of these issues during the planning stages for your site, it is highly likely that after some months online, the planning you did—even where you specifically incorporated some techniques to allow for growth—may no longer apply to the realities of your site.

As a result, it becomes imperative to perform a full reassessment of content, and look for ways to best manage it. If you haven't had a prior need, but content is becoming difficult to manage, it may be time to implement a content management system (CMS). Or, it may be time to simply clean up your site architecture a bit, rearrange a few things, and modify navigation to make sure your user interface allows your site to perform at its optimum.

> **cross ref** See Chapter 5, "Creating and Managing Fantastic Content" to learn more about CMSs.

Secret #247:   When to Redesign

When is a redesign really necessary?

This is a challenging question. Redesigns are quite problematic historically speaking, largely because the Web hasn't matured enough for all of us to get assessment cycles and adequate analysis about our sites to strategize over the care they require.

Generally, redesigns should be left for those times when a new look and feel or new technical approach requiring a major change become necessary. There are two primary instances when something like this should occur:

◆ **The visual style of your site is no longer appropriate.** The reasons for this could be manifold, such as a change in your logo or brand, or simply that enough time has passed so your site looks less than fresh visually. It's important to keep as much of a contemporary look for your site as possible, because users will judge your site based on what they see. If they see a site that looks like it was designed in 1996, they might not feel very confident in what you have to offer, so keeping things visually fresh is very important.

♦ **Technology has changed so much that a redesign is simply the most effective way to address site-wide concerns.** A good example of this is the move away from table-based layouts to pure CSS layouts. Certainly, changes of this nature—that will ultimately make your sites more effective and forward compatible, as well as easier to update both content-wise and visually—are important, and require a lot of resources. However, the improvements such a change can bring about in terms of workflow and bottom-dollar savings may be so valuable as to necessitate the redesign.

To undertake a redesign, begin by examining all the issues covered in this chapter so far: analysis, assets, and audience. That information is going to give you a great deal of insight as to whether it's the right time for a redesign, and what specifically must be addressed in terms of technical, visionary, and audience-related needs.

Secret #248:   Map Redesign Projects and Timelines Carefully

Because redesigns can be so demanding on resources, it's very important to map your projects with extreme care.

Some tips for working with redesigns follow:

♦ **If a complete redesign will place too much hardship on you, team members, and budget, consider incremental redesigns.** This means starting at your top tier with your new design, and building it out over time. Should you choose to go this route, it's especially good to actually map the timeline, and plan for the following:

♦ Show very clearly which portions of the site will be redesigned first.
♦ Set goal dates for starting and ending each incremental phase of the project.
♦ Know your budget for each increment.

♦ **Pad timelines for redesigns generously.** I have never worked on a redesign project that came in on time—ever. I've heard many other design firms—some of them absolutely top-tier firms—that have suffered the same problem time and again. Redesigns are often more difficult to gauge than new site designs because problems due to organic growth and architecture, as well as changing audience needs, throw wrenches into the process. An example of this is the current redesign we're undergoing at the Web Standards Project (WaSP). So much has changed in the past year in relation to how Web standards are being implemented, the knowledge base of our audience, and the goals within our organization, that a lot of evaluation, including audience surveys, has had to be organized and implemented to gain a deeper understanding of how to best serve our audience and site goals.

♦ **Know your competitors.** At this point in the game, you'll have a much better idea of who your competitors are and what they're doing with their Web sites. Look at their sites with care, try to get a feel for which features might be appropriate on your own site—and even better—look for features that they don't offer that you can implement to improve your user interest and increase your visitor base.

Figure 15-2 shows a prototype of the current WaSP design. At the point this was created, we knew we needed some specific changes to the WaSP site. First, we wanted to be sure that we upgraded our look and feel to match the trend in standards-based design—a necessity for our audience and goals. Also, we wanted to ensure quick access to news from inside the organization, as well as access to information related to WaSP but not available on the WaSP site.

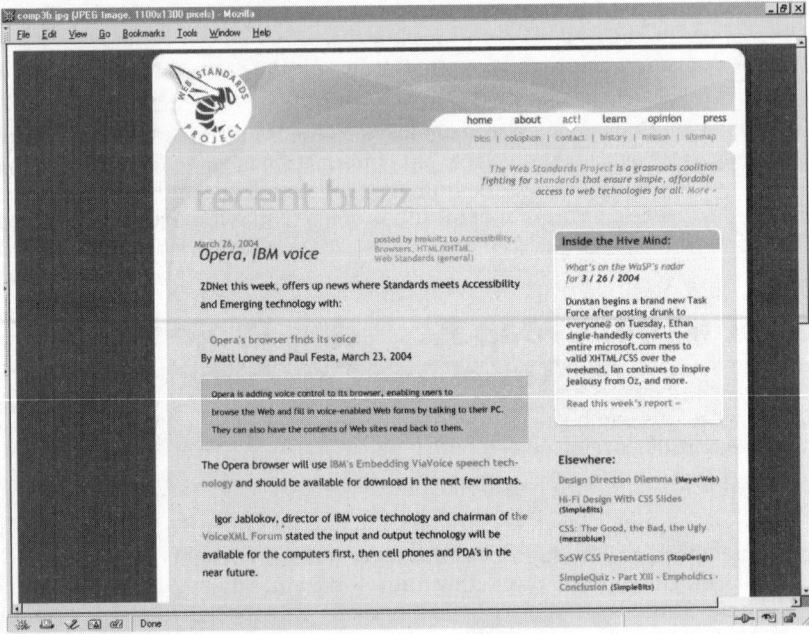

Figure 15-2: An early prototype of the WaSP redesign.

By the time you're reading this book, the WaSP site has most likely been redesigned, so check it out at www.webstandards.org/, and see how we ultimately implemented the changes.

Secret #249:   Express Upcoming Changes to Audience Members

One of the most frustrating things for audiences is to have a site changed on them with no communication.

I learned this lesson the hard way. I worked as a contractor for the Microsoft Network (MSN) for the first four and a half years of its life. MSN has come a long way in terms of figuring out what its intent is, and who it's serving, but at that time both the vision for the company and the technologies available were in a constant state of flux.

At first, we built MSN on a proprietary, non-Web platform. At that time, the main thrust of the network was community. So, as managers of individual communities, we were responsible for the technical implementation, content, and moderation of a given community. This model can work very well when the community leader can communicate freely with members, but because of MSNs unsure direction, we were limited contractually in what we could say.

MSN then made a decision to move the entire site from the proprietary format to a Web-based format. It was still a closed system, however, supporting only the Internet Explorer Web browser and available only to paying, registered members. This was certainly the hurdle where I began to get an inkling of what it means to completely change an interface on an audience without being able to tell them of the change. One morning, our audiences logged on to find a completely different site, which required a long download for installation of the correct software. Suffice it to say that about half our membership disappeared at that point, so frustrated were they with that unexpected change of scenery.

Later reorganizations and redesigns caused the same problems, with users becoming increasingly more frustrated. And, without much recourse to complaint, you can bet they came after the community managers for an explanation. After going through this six times in 4 years, I began to realize that the fact that MSN wasn't allowing us a free and open dialog with our members was far more hurtful to the membership than MSN might have been aware, thinking instead of all the cool new stuff people were going to get.

Nowadays, MSN is a free, Web-based system that has come far from its strong community-based, members-only roots. But getting it to that point was an extremely challenging learning experience for all involved, and the lesson of having a free exchange with audience members is one that will stick with me for the whole of my career.

note   To see MSN in its current, stable phase, visit `www.msn.com/`.

When getting ready to redesign, consider the following:

+ Involve your audience in the process. This gives users the opportunity to not only get excited about new enhancements, but also lets them have a role in shaping a site that they like to use—a surefire way to help forge long-term relationships.

+ Be sure that any newsletters, newsfeeds, and blogs you keep do announce in a timely fashion that a redesign will be underway and when audiences can expect it. Again, highlight the new features to come, and provide a form or e-mail address where feedback can be given.

+ When your site relaunches with its new design, consider thanking your audiences via newsletter, blog, or home page for their participation and patience during the redesign process.

Secret #250:   Re-Evaluate Long-Term Goals

As simple as this might seem, by the time you've gone through one full design and are beginning to evaluate a redesign, you will have encountered so many challenges and changes within your site and your audience that taking out the long-term goals you set down early on in the planning phase and viewing them in a new light is an extremely important step.

By working through a deep assessment of your site after it has had a chance to exist for a while, you will no doubt find that your goals have changed in some way. Maybe they've strengthened, or maybe they've become irrelevant. Most likely, the truth will be somewhere in between—you'll have reached some of your original goals, while others will no longer make sense in terms of your current site.

Re-evaluating your long-term goals will help you with a number of issues:

- **Bring your business plan up-to-date.** A re-evaluation of your site goals will allow you to bring your business plan up-to-date and introduce new goals based on site and audience analysis.

- **Prepare for new investors or related opportunities.** If you're looking for money or opportunities to move your site ahead, having a clear summary of where you've been and where you're going will give investors the kind of detail they look for in today's tougher market.

- **Knowing where you've been means avoiding past mistakes.** One of the beauties of Web development is that it's pretty easy to fix mistakes. Even if you have to wait for a redesign to fix numerous site problems, once you've got a record of what did *not* work, you know how to effectively avoid those mistakes in the future.

- **Conversely, you have an idea now of what really works!** You can be sure to keep features you know are working, and plan for more as time goes on.

At this point, be sure to document any changes your reassessment, redesign, and site analysis have brought about in relation to long-term goals.

Summary

The bottom line when it comes to redesigns is that they are difficult. The reasons for this are many, and redesigns should actually be done only when truly necessary. By following other techniques in this chapter, such as implementing regular assessment cycles into your process, you may be able to avoid redesigning for a long time.

What's more, by following the best practices offered throughout this book, you'll have a much easier time managing your sites, no matter how large or small. And, when the time comes for redesign, the fact is that you are now aware of CSS-based layouts, structured markup, accessibility, and just plain good sense when it comes to planning a project and seeing it to fruition. That in turn means a lot more efficiency in workflow as time goes on, helping you to drive your site to an exciting, successful future.

Part IV

Appendixes

Demystifying Service Provision

Appendix
A

This appendix explains different types of Internet and Web service provision for Web designers, pros and cons of various servers and server situations, and resources for finding the best Internet Service Providers (ISP) for your needs.

Service Provision Overview

Service provision is the way in which you get your sites hosted. This comes in a variety of forms, as you'll see in the *Available Services* section of this appendix.

Two primary types of services offer commercial hosting for Web sites. Almost all ISPs offer some hosting options for customers. However, the space that they offer on standard commercial ISP connectivity accounts tends to be appropriate for personal use, but not for commercial use. So, some ISPs provide business packages, too.

Because the main job of an ISP is to provide you with a means of connecting to the Internet rather than Web hosting, many independent Web hosts have entered the game. Web hosts are differentiated from ISPs because they offer no connectivity, but instead focus on often very richly featured packages geared toward a wide range of Web site hosting needs. Web hosts can provide solutions from the smallest personal Weblog to the largest e-commerce site, as well as offer related Internet services such as FTP, e-mail addresses, and Listserv software.

Web hosts solve a number of cost issues that you might encounter with an ISP because they can specialize only in the hosting and miss the high costs associated with cable, DSL, and other forms of connectivity. Typically, Web hosts can provide better customer service for their hosting products too, because their expertise is in running Web servers, not in managing connectivity.

Table A-1 shows three client scenarios, the solutions they had at the point their sites were redesigned, and the real cost associated with those solutions.

While these situations are representative of the emerging differences between ISP and Web hosting services, there are exceptions. But for the professional Web designer and developer, many are choosing to purchase their connectivity services and Web server services separately.

Table A-1: Comparison of ISP versus Web Host Costs

Client and Needs Met	Service Type Chosen	Cost
Consultant Web site, regularly updated Weblog and content management, e-mail, list, and FTP. Broadband connectivity	ISP	$25.00 USD per month
Real estate agent site, flat HTML pages, FTP access, limited e-mail needs. Broadband connectivity	ISP	$39.00 USD per month
Celebrity Web site, regularly updated content, 25 e-mail accounts, FTP, Telnet and SSH access, e-commerce enabled with shopping cart and dynamic database technology, Perl, CGI, MySQL, Listserv, and high use options	Web host	$5.00 USD per month

warning   You should be aware of the issue of reselling when choosing between ISPs and Web hosts. Sometimes, ISPs look to resellers (outside hosts) to provide the Web hosting services to the ISPs' customers.

Similarly, some Web hosts themselves resell. While reseller programs can be reasonable, there are some problems associated with them. First, if an ISP is using a reseller, your costs are bound to be higher than if you deal with the reseller directly.

But the greatest difficulty encountered has to do with technical support. If you contact the ISP or Web host who is reselling the service, quite often they have no direct means of addressing your problem. They can only provide basic technical support and have to interact with their reseller to get the information to you—a process that can take time and cause great frustration.

Preparing to Choose a Provider

Whether you're looking to host a small Web site or implement a network of your own, the choices available are vast.

Consider the following before researching the type of service that might be best for you:

◆ Needs vary from site to site. So, for each project, you must analyze your technology needs (see Chapter 2, "Managing Your Web Project"for more information on this process) and determine what kind of host situation will be required in each instance.

◆ Do you have a person or team that can manage on-site servers? If your needs require it and you have the resources, keep this in mind as you research your choices.

◆ Do you require expert help in managing servers, but cannot provide the resources in-house?

- How much technology do you really require? For example, do you need e-mail, or Perl and CGI access? Or perhaps you need to support databases, e-commerce, or other advanced backend options (see Appendix B for a rundown on server-side application technologies).
- Do you require 24-hour support but don't have the resources in-house? For many people, this is a critical concern that will influence the ultimate hosting choice.

Sit down on your own, or with your planning team, and run through the situation, asking these questions and coming up with real needs. Here's an example of what I came up with for my own site:

- Do not want to run my own Web server in-house
- Technologies required include:
    - Perl
    - Custom CGI access
    - PHP
    - SSH and Telnet access
    - FTP
    - E-mail
    - MySQL
    - Listserv
    - Statistical analysis software
    - Administrative interface
- Require some but not 24-hour customer service.

As you can see, by knowing precisely what my needs are prior to researching hosts, I am able to far more quickly match my needs to a reasonable plan.

Web Hosting Services in Detail

There are numerous types of services of which to be aware. Table A-2 shows the primary types of services you can purchase via Web hosts today.

Table A-2: Web Hosting Types

Service Type	Description
Shared (virtual) hosting	In this scenario, your Web site sits on a server where other Web sites also sit. This can be a very affordable and reasonable option for those sites that aren't enormous in size. You're almost always allowed your own domain name and allocated a number of resources. If the host is a reputable one, speed and security for your Web site should not be a problem
Co-location hosting	In this scenario, you own the Web server and have it placed with an ISP or Web host who offers co-location services. This way, you have control over the entire server and can use it any way you choose—run a large site, add features according to your needs, and so on. Co-located

continued

Table A-2: *(continued)*

Service Type	*Description*
	servers are maintained in a secure environment that has quality connectivity to the Internet. Typically, you will pay rack rental fees for the space your server takes up and connectivity charges, which are usually based on the amount of bandwidth you use. Make sure you research the company with whom you decide to co-locate, as it will be responsible for the welfare of your server. Select this option carefully
Dedicated hosting	Dedicated hosting is a good choice when you want a lot of power, want to run a very large site, or want to run multiple Web sites and have a great deal of access and control. Dedicated hosting is very much like co-location, with the primary difference that the Web host, not you, owns the server. The server belongs to them and resides with them. Typically, there are two types of dedicated service: Managed and Unmanaged. *Managed* means that you will have technical support services that keep your server up-to-date in terms of software, security, and performance. *Unmanaged* requires that you do all of this work yourself, so you must have server-savvy folks on your team. Managed dedicated hosting is typically more costly than unmanaged because you are paying for administrative services
Specialty hosting	Specialty hosting may incorporate a combination of hosting options, but for very specific purposes. An example would be hosts that accept adult Web sites, gambling sites, and other sites that require a legal location in which to operate or allow materials that are legal (such as adult sites) but are not allowed by most Web hosts
On-site hosting	With on-site hosting, all of your server administration is hosted at your site. This can be very costly because you have to pay for the connectivity, the hardware, the upkeep, the administration, and security concerns on your own. But, in many situations, it's the best option, as total control of the servers belongs to you. You have complete access to all aspects of running your site

note The type of servers and operating systems in use make an enormous difference in cost and performance. Most Web hosts offer both Windows and Linux hosting. Of the two, Linux is in greater use for Web servers. This isn't a fluke: Well-run Linux servers tend to be far more secure than Microsoft servers when properly configured, are more reliable, more flexible and configurable, and less expensive because of the many open-source software options available. On the other hand, many people using .NET and related Microsoft technologies will want to choose accordingly.

Service References

Normally, I shy away from offering information on specific services. However, I recently conducted a survey of fellow Web developers and came up with a list of low-cost, stable provider recommendations that I feel pretty confident in sharing with you.

This list is by no means comprehensive, nor do I personally take responsibility for these providers. However, I did feel that offering them to you would be useful (Table A-3).

Table A-3: Web Hosting Companies

Web Host	Contact
100 Megs Web Hosting	www.100megswebhosting.com/
Contrast Host	http://contrasthost.com sales@contrasthost.com
Data Pipe Managed Hosting Services	www.datapipe.com/ Toll-free U.S. 877-773-3306 sales@datapipe.com
Dixie Systems	http://dixiesys.com/ Toll-free U.S. 888-300-9090 sales@dixiesys.com
DreamHost	www.dreamhost.com/
Fat Cow	www.fatcow.com/ Toll-free U.S. 888.278.9780
Go Daddy	www.godaddy.com/
Hostway	www.hostway.com Toll-free U.S. 866-467-8929
Market Trends	www.marketrends.net/ Toll-free U.S. 888 203-9941 sales@marketrends.net
Media Temple	http://mediatemple.net/ Toll-free U.S. 877-578-4000
National Net	www.natnet.com/ Toll-free U.S. 877 471-9075 sales@natnet.com
Pair Networks	www.pair.com/ sales@pair.com
SiteWorks	http://site-works.com/ Toll-free U.S. 800-529-2560 mailroom@siteworks.com
Sausage Hosting	http://sausagehosting.com/
United Hosting	www.unitedhosting.co.uk/ sales@unitedhosting.co.uk
Verve Hosting	http://vervehosting.com/
Web Intellects	www.webintellects.com/ Toll-free U.S. 800-994-6364 info@webintellects.com
PHP Web Hosting	PHPwebhosting.com

warning

Please choose with caution, and I encourage you to research the issue more deeply prior to committing yourself to a Web host.

note

I've included phone numbers and e-mail addresses where possible. Please note that many of these services have international presence and contact info, so see their sites for more details. And, of course, the location of your Web server is irrelevant—it's the matching of your needs to a quality service that really matters.

Overview of Application and Database Technology

A great deal of Web design these days has to do with integration of the techniques discussed in this book with server-side applications and databases.

This appendix provides an overview of currently used application and database technologies, the pros and cons of each, and additional resources.

Front End, Back End

Client-side, front-end Web development is all about what happens in the browser. Server-side, back-end development is all about dynamically managing content on the server and sending it to the client.

The majority of the techniques in this book have to do with a Web site's front end: its face to the world. Even the planning and information architecture sections are positioned to help you create sites that look good and perform well within the browser.

All that is well and good, but without some idea of how the back end integrates with the front end, you're limited in your ability to make optimal choices. And even if you never touch application or program code, knowing a little bit about what things are, what they do, and why you might want to work with them can make you more effective and capable in your Web tasks.

Application and Programming Technologies

Application technologies are those technologies that negotiate the relationship between information on the server and how it will be sent to the client. Numerous technologies and programming languages are used in concert to do this. Table B-1 describes some of the most common, what they're used for, and some of the pros and cons of using them.

Database Technologies

Databases are of course an area of great depth and complexity see Table B-2. The goal in this appendix is to give you a rundown of the most commonly used databases in Web technologies and provide you with the basic pros and cons to better equip you to make choices for data management and discuss details with clients and/or co-workers.

Table B-1: Web Application and Programming Technologies

Technology	Description	Pros and Cons
ASP, ASP.NET www.microsoft .com/net/	Active Server Pages (ASP) and ASP.NET are Microsoft's proprietary application language. Combining .NET technologies with programming languages such as Visual Basic (VB), database technologies, and XML, dynamic Web services can be created	Pros: Very powerful, very flexible, very good support. .NET offers a very sophisticated development environment Cons: Limitations include the fact that ASP.NET development can be costly, requires proprietary servers, and basically does not play well with other technologies, especially in terms of creating sites in XHTML, or using standards effectively
CGI www.cgi-resources.com/	Common Gateway Interface is the longest-running application show on the road. CGI scripts integrate with a language, such as Perl, to negotiate actions between the server and client	Pros: In extremely widespread use, very easy to find a wide range of scripts cheaply or for free, avid community support Cons: As with most scripting, knowledge of the language and how to use it in the context of Web servers, how to modify it, and how to properly install it can be difficult to acquire
ColdFusion www.macromedia .com/software/ coldfusion/	ColdFusion is a proprietary platform that Macromedia purchased from Allaire, and under Macromedia's auspices has continued to be developed as a useful application technology	Pros: Fans of ColdFusion point to its ease of use, approachable learning curve, excellent development tools, and technical support. It is an excellent choice for small-to-medium scale applications Cons: Critics feel that ColdFusion fails to scale properly in high-demand situations. What's more, because ColdFusion is limited in terms of OS compatibility, its widespread use in a variety of operating environments is limited
Java www.java.com/	Developed by Sun Microsystems, the point of Java was to create a cross-platform programming	Pros: Java's interoperability is its finest feature, and it also has a lot of appeal for application developers in general because

Technology	Description	Pros and Cons
	language that was portable and flexible. Java is in use for a range of applications beyond the Web as well. It is used server-side for the Web in a number of forms, as a programming language along with database and XML technologies. Other variants for Web use include Java Server Pages (JSP), which is Java's answer to ASP.NET, and Java Applets, used on the Web for numerous applications from embedded animations to games	of its flexibility, development tools, and support Cons: The learning curve for Java is quite steep unless you have some programming experience. Because of its complexity, Java has become a specialty area and Java programmers are among the most highly paid in the world. As a result, implementing Java as a major part of your Web site application tools may be very costly
Perl www.perl.com/	Developed by Larry Wall and a cast of thousands, Perl is an interpreted language used for numerous applications. It's become very popular on the Web, largely due to its modularization, flexibility, power, and portability	Pros: Perl is abundantly available—you can find scripts for just about everything imaginable. It has a tremendous user base, with a very enthusiastic community that provides ongoing support. Perl is open-source, so it is free or very low cost and doesn't require expensive development environments Cons: Perl runs best in open-source environments, which is where it was originally intended to be used. Although it can be used on servers using proprietary operating systems, it can, as a result, be more difficult for inexperienced people to configure
PHP www.php.net/	PHP was developed as a scripting language especially suited for the Web. Its uses on the Web can be as simple as managing server-side includes or as complicated as shopping carts and e-commerce applications	Pros: As with Perl, PHP is open-source and has great support via community. PHP scripts are widely available and are either free or very low cost. PHP is easy to write, too, not requiring extensive programming skills. PHP is so approachable that it rapidly acquired an important place on the Web Cons: PHPs limitations are mostly related to scalability. In many cases, what PHP can't accomplish, Perl can, so they are often

continued

Table B-1: *(continued)*

Technology	Description	Pros and Cons
		used within the same site to accomplish a range of tasks
Python `www.python.org/`	Python is an interpreted object-oriented programming language that is known for its portability—it can run on just about any imaginable platform	Pros: Python is fairly easy to learn for the programmatically inclined (it's been said you can learn it in an afternoon), boasting clearer syntax than Java or Perl. It has a very good community base for support, as well
		Cons: Limitations include lack of widespread existing scripts such as is found in the Perl and PHP communities. It has limited tools, and despite its power, remains somewhat obscure due most likely to a lack of adequate promotion and documentation via books
XML `www.w3.org/XML/`	XML is used on both the front and back end in Web design and development. In its role as an application language, XML is used as a means to warehouse content that is then modified using other languages such as Java or ASP.NET along with database technology to create and manage dynamic content delivery	Pros: XML in application development is very flexible and can be used with numerous technologies. It is an open standard, so it is free, easy to author, and doesn't require expensive development environments
		Cons: Because of its simplicity and portability, there are very few cons with the exception that related tools, such as Schema, are still being developed. As such, the full promise of XML is yet to be reached
XSL/T `www.w3.org/ TR/xslt`	XSL/T is the extensible style language with transformation. It is used to transform XML into other file formats. Often, this is done on a Web server, which will in turn transform content marked up with XML into XHTML or HTML, as well as other formats such as PDF and SVG. XSL/T can be used in conjunction with database technology too, allowing multiple transformations of the same content	Pros: XSL/T is XML-based, so as an open standard, it's free. It's also extremely powerful and applicable for solving numerous problems
		Cons: Critics of XSL/T say it's semantically problematic and believe that other transformation technologies will eventually take its place

Table B-2: Common Database Technologies in Use on the Web

Technology	Description	Pros and Cons
Access http://office .microsoft.com/ home/office.aspx	Microsoft software that allows users to create data, index it, and retrieve it using custom forms and reports. As a Microsoft product, Access integrates with related products and programming languages, such as VB	Pros: Access is very easy to use and is available with the Microsoft Office suite of tools Cons: Access is not considered a robust database and is best used in lightweight situations along with other technologies
Filemaker Pro www.filemaker. com/	Filemaker Pro is a workgroup database for business applications. It includes templates and collaborative abilities far beyond a focused database application	Pros: Filemaker Pro is considered easy to use, and its templating system helps users manage complex data with relative ease. A number of developer packages are available, and the development environment is considered one of Filemaker's most attractive features Cons: Filemaker is expensive. While it delivers content to the Web, it's considered problematic in its output of markup, and requires additional attention to ensure its output is in accordance with your requirements
Microsoft SQL Server www.microsoft .com/sql/	Microsoft's proprietary server technologies based on Simple Query Language (SQL)	Pros: SQL Server is an easy-to-use development environment, and integrates well with other technologies and programming languages Cons: It is expensive both to implement and support
MySQL www.mysql.com/	This open-source database based on SQL is considered the most widely used on the Web. It can be integrated with numerous programming languages and can be used under both GNU and commercial licensing, depending upon your requirements	Pros: MySQL is widely available, free or inexpensive, and runs on everything. It's relatively easy to configure, secure, and support is abundant Lack of limitations and a constantly growing feature base have resulted in MySQL's widespread implementation Cons: Very few, except in terms of learning curve. People working with MySQL do need a certain amount of programming experience

continued

Table B-2: (continued)

Technology	Description	Pros and Cons
Oracle www.oracle.com/ database/	This proprietary database technology is known for high-end performance and security	Pros: Oracle has an excellent range of development tools, add-in packages for specific Web applications, and is capable of very complex and very demanding data needs
		Cons: Oracle is expensive and has a relatively steep learning curve
PostgreSQL www.postgresql .org/	As with MySQL, PostgreSQL is an open-source, powerful database that has broad implementation and integration features	Pros: PostgreSQL is freely available, runs on just about every conceivable platform, and shares many similarities with MySQL
		Cons: PostgreSQL has a smaller implementation base, so it's not as commonly used as MySQL

Helpful Reading, Web Sites, and Resources

The resources in this appendix are geared toward helping you keep up with changing trends in Web design, as well as learn some specialty tricks and tips, find out what's going on in the contemporary professional world, have support via lists, discussions, and those organizations related to Web professionals.

Web Sites of Interest

Table C-1 lists Web sites that provide a wide range of helpful resources and continuing education.

Table C-1: Helpful Web Sites

Resource	Description	URL
Agitprop	While not currently being updated, this is a fantastic resource for interesting articles, CSS tests, and other Web-related fun from Todd Fahrner	`http://style .cleverchimp.com/`
A List Apart	Founded by Jeffrey Zeldman, A List Apart is a cutting-edge magazine filled with tutorials and information for the standards-oriented designer and developer	`www.alistapart.com/`
Builder.com	C|NETs entry for Web developers targets information on just about every aspect of Web design, and includes vast resources, links, and great articles	`www.builder.com/`
css/edge	Eric A. Meyer provides excellent examples and explanations of cutting-edge CSS design	`www.meyerweb.com/ eric/css/edge/`
DevEdge	This site lists Netscape's developer resources. See the CSS Central area, in particular	`http://devedge .netscape.com/ central /css/`

continued

Table C-1: (continued)

Resource	Description	URL
Glish.Com	Eric Costello provides very valuable CSS layout templates, complete with explanations, insights, and articles	`www.glish.com`
IBMs developerWorks Web Architecture Zone	developerWorks offers extensive articles that delve into great detail. While there are tips and insights available, the real focus here is coverage on timely development topics with extensive examples for interested developers	`www.ibm.com/developerworks/`
Hot Source HTML Help	This is a good source for all HTML help with a good section on DHTML	`www.sbrady.com/hotsource/`
House of Style	House of Style is a very comprehensive study of CSS, along with tools and resources	`www.westciv.com/style_master/house/`
The HTML Bad Style Page	I rather like this site because it shows you what *not* to do with HTML. Sometimes it is nice to see a sample of poor workmanship so you can avoid it	`www.earth.com/bad-style/`
Lynda.Com	Here you'll find books, color references, and plenty of wisdom from Web graphics expert Lynda Weinman	`www.lynda.com/`
Mark Radcliffe's Advanced HTML	Radcliffe's site covers a variety of topics, including helpful HTML hints	`www.neiljohan.com/html/advancedhtml.htm`
MAXDESIGN	This is home to the famous *Listmatic* series of list-based navigation wizards, as well as tutorials on a wide range of all things CSS	`http://css.maxdesign.com.au/`
Microsoft Developer Network	Here you'll find an unbelievable variety of information covering Web building and publishing, including lots of community, and heavy on Internet Explorer-specific information	`http://msdn.microsoft.com/`
Real World Style	Mark Newhouse provides and regularly updates this site dedicated to CSS layouts, tips, tricks, and techniques	`www.realworldstyle.com/`
The Sevloid Guide to Web Design	This is a collection of over 100 tips, tricks, and techniques on every aspect of Web design. The tips are sorted into the categories of page layout, navigation, content, graphics, and more	`www.sev.com.au/webzone/design.asp`
Generally Markup	This site offers tutorials in XML and XSL authoring	`www.msxml.com`

Resource	Description	URL
Web Designers Virtual Library (WDVL)	For years Alan Richmond put together one of the most accessible comprehensive resources for designers and developers. Now it's available via Internet.com	`www.wdvl.com/`
Webmonkey's How To Guide For Web Developers	This well-done, eye-pleasing site has lots of tutorials and a great sense of humor	`www.webmonkey.com/`
Web Page Design for Designers	Explore the possibilities of Web design from the standpoint of a designer	`www.wpdfd.com/`
Webreference	Look here for vast references, tutorials, and hints about Web design	`/www.webreference.com/`
World Wide Web Consortium (W3C)	The W3C is the mother lode of Web standards: markup, CSS, DOM, XML, accessibility, and more	`www.w3.org/`
Yale C/AIM Web Style Guide	This guide is an excellent, straightforward overview of interface, site design, graphics, multimedia, and HTML. It's now available as a paper book as well	`http://info.med.yale.edu/caim/manual/contents.html`

Recommended Articles

Please enjoy the following articles, which cover a range of markup, CSS, and general design-related resources:

- ◆ "Web Page Construction with CSS" by Christopher Schmitt. In this article, Schmitt deconstructs the table-based design of *Digital Web Magazine*, and then redesigns it using CSS. Find the article at `www.digital-web.com/tutorials/tutorial_2002-06.shtml`.

- ◆ "A Designer's Journey" by Jeffrey Zeldman. Zeldman describes transitioning from Web hacks to Web standard. Find the article at `www.alistapart.com/stories/journey/`.

- ◆ "Roll Over, Rollovers" by Eric Meyer. Meyer teaches how to do rollovers with CSS. Find the article at `www.oreillynet.com/pub/a/javascript/2001/03/23/rollovers.html`.

- ◆ "Mo' Betta Rollovers" by Tim Murtaugh. Solving common rollover problems with CSS and JavaScript. Find the article at `www.alistapart.com/stories/rollovers/`.

- ◆ "To Use or Not to Use: An XHTML Roadmap for Designers" by Molly E. Holzschlag. Good overview of XHTML, geared toward designers. Find the article at `www.digital-web.com/tutorials/tutorial_2001-3.shtml`.

+ "Using Background-image to Replace Text" by Doug Bowman. Gain more typographic control while keeping sites structured and accessible. Find this at www.stopdesign.com/also/articles/replace_text/.
+ "Bare Bones, No Crap, CSS Text Control Primer." A down-and-dirty CSS 101 tutorial. Find it at http://wendypeck.com/css101.html.

Lists and Discussion Groups

If you're looking for help solving a problem, hoping for feedback on a design, or looking for professional networking opportunities, you may well find them on any number of popular lists and discussion groups that are available online. Table C-2 provides a hand-picked selection.

Table C-2: Popular Lists and Discussion Groups

Resource	Description	URL
Babble	Babble is geared toward advanced Web design issues, and includes a lively exchange of information, resources, theories, and practices of designers and developers	www.babblelist.com/
WebDesign-L	WebDesign-L is a mailing list community created in early 1997. The list is intended as a forum for those involved in creating the Web—whether for business, self-expression, or exploring the possibilities of a new medium	www.webdesign-l.com/
XHTML-L	This forum is here for Web developers, Web designers, Webmasters, document managers, tool builders, integrators, and anyone else with an interest in XHTML to discuss strategies and tactics for making XHTML work. Discussion of all versions of XHTML (1.0, 1.1, and the upcoming 2.0) and their integration with other technologies (HTTP, CSS, MIME, XSLT, CC/PP, and more) is appropriate, as is discussion of XHTMLs potential advantages and disadvantages relative to competing formats	http://groups.yahoo.com/group/XHTML-L/
CSS-Discuss	This very active list has approximately 2,000 subscribers. Discussion ranges in complexity, but the focus is practicality—how CSS is actually used in real-world application	http://three.pairlist.net/mailman/listinfo/css-discuss

Helpful Organizations

The following organizations, listed in Table C-3, are geared toward helping designers inform themselves, organize, and work toward Web design excellence.

Table C-3: Organizations for Web Designers

Organization	Description	URL
The Web Standards Project: WaSP	WaSP is dedicated to providing information and a voice in promoting Web recommendations	www.webstandards.org/
World Wide Web Consortium	The W3C is the first stop for all serious HTML and related technologies students when it comes to standards	www.w3.org/
The World Organization of Webmasters	This site provides educational and peer-support resources for Webmasters	www.joinwow.org/
The HTML Writers Guild	The world's largest international organization of Web designers offers community, classes, events, and an online bookstore	www.hwg.org/
Association for Women in Computing	This is a general organization for women in the computer field	www.awc-hq.org/
Webgrrls	This international networking group for women interested in the Internet provides multiple sites by country and city. Start at the home page	www.webgrrls.com/

Index

Symbols & Numbers

.NET technologies, 388

:hover pseudo class, 202

@import for graceful degradation, 227

@import rule, 227

@import workaround, 227

<em> and <strong> versus <i> and <b>, 130

<head> and <body> appropriately, use, 124

<html> tags, 123

<title>, using, 125

A

abbr element, 251, 252

abbr element for abbreviations, using, 251

about XHTML, 144

absolute positioning, 211

abstract. *See* iconography and language use

accessibility, 3

accessibility and law, 246

accessibility features, adding, 243

accessibility validators and common features

    A-Prompt, 267

    Bobby, 267

    Cynthia Says, 267

    LIFT, 267

accessibility validators, testing, 266

accesskey attribute, 254

accesskey attribute, understanding, 254

Acrobat plug-in, 30

acronym element, 251, 252

acronym element for acronyms, using, 252

Active Server Pages (ASP), 388

adding search, strategies for

    Custom search programming, 350

    Homegrown scripting, 350

    Professional Search Application Software, 350

    Professional Web Search Service Provision, 350

additive synthesis, 284

Adobe ImageReady, 23

advent of accessibility challenges, 244

affiliate programs

    considering, 361

    pros and cons of, 362

aggregate content, 349

alt attribute, 157, 249

alt attribute required, 157

alternate content, providing, 247

alternate style sheet for print, 235

alternate style sheet for small-screen media, 236

analysis software, 370

anchor element, 323

animations, designing, 4

AOL Instant messenger (AIM), 32

applet element, 320

applet, object, and embed, trouble with, 320

application and database technology, overview of, 387

application and programming technologies, 387

application language, 390

archive systems

    creating, 63

    relevance of, 63

ASCII text, 196

ASCII text editors, 8

ASCII-based languages, 8

ASP.NET scripts, 343

attribute names, 153

attribute values, 153

attributes, 133

audio, adding, 323

author documents structurally, 127

author markup and CSS, 4

automatic aggregation, 337

avoid additional spaces in hyperlinks, 106

B

back end, 387

back-end development, 387

background graphics, 207

background graphics in CSS, using, 195

binary graphic file, 292

bitmap formats

    GIF, 21

    JPEG, 21

bitmap graphics, 17

bitmap image programs, 17

bitmap imaging, 19

bitmap imaging program, 19